INSIGHT GUIDE

POLAND

Discovery CHANNEL

APA PUBLICATIONS

Part of the Langenscheidt Publishing Group

ABOUT THIS BOOK

Editorial

Editor
Clare Griffiths
Editorial Director
Brian Bell

Distribution

UK & Ireland
GeoCenter International Ltd
The Viables Centre , Harrow Way
Basingstoke, Hants RG22 4BJ
Fax: (44) 1256-817988

United States
Langenscheidt Publishers, Inc.
46–35 54th Road, Maspeth, NY 11378
Fax: (718) 784-0640

Worldwide
Apa Publications GmbH & Co.
Verlag KG (Singapore branch)
38 Joo Koon Road, Singapore 628990
Tel: (65) 865-1600. Fax: (65) 861-6438

Printing

Insight Print Services (Pte) Ltd
38 Joo Koon Road, Singapore 628990
Tel: (65) 865-1600. Fax: (65) 861-6438

©2000 **Apa Publications GmbH & Co.**
Verlag KG (Singapore branch)
All Rights Reserved
First Edition 1991
Second Edition 2000
Reprinted 2000

CONTACTING THE EDITORS
Although every effort is made to
provide accurate information, we
live in a fast-changing world and
would appreciate it if readers
would call our attention to any
errors or outdated information
that may occur by writing to:
Insight Guides, P.O. Box 7910,
London SE1 1WE, England.
Fax: (44 20) 7403-0290.
e-mail:
insight@apaguide.demon.co.uk

www.insightguides.com

This guidebook combines the
interests and enthusiasms of
two of the world's best known information providers: Insight Guides,
whose titles have set the standard
for visual travel guides since 1970,
and Discovery Channel, the world's
premier source of nonfiction television programming.

The editors of Insight Guides
provide both practical advice and
general understanding about a
destination's history, culture and
people. Discovery Channel and its
Web site, www.discovery.com, help
millions of viewers explore their
world from the comfort of
their own home and
also encourage them to
explore it first hand.

This fully updated
edition of *Insight
Guide: Poland* is
carefully structured to convey an
understanding of Poland and its culture as well as to guide readers
through its sights and activities:

◆ The **Features** section, indicated
by a yellow bar at the top of each
page, covers the history and culture
of the country in a series of informative essays.

◆ The main **Places** section, indicated by a blue bar, is a complete
guide to all the sights and areas
worth visiting. Places of special
interest are coordinated by number
with the maps.

◆ The **Travel Tips** listings section,
with an orange bar, provides
a handy point of refer-
ence for information on
travel, hotels, shops,
restaurants and more.
The listings index is on
the back cover flap.

Map Legend

—— - -	International Boundary
— — —	Regional Boundary
⊖	Border Crossing
—•—	National Park/Reserve
— — —	Ferry Route
✈ ✈	Airport: International/ Regional
🚌	Bus Station
■	Parking
●	Tourist Information
✉	Post Office
🏳 † ⛪	Church/Ruins
†	Monastery
☾	Mosque
✡	Synagogue
🏰 🏚	Castle/Ruins
∴	Archaeological Site
∩	Cave
⚑	Statue/Monument
★	Place of Interest

The main places of interest in the Places section are coordinated by number with a full-colour map (e.g. ❶), and a symbol at the top of every right-hand page tells you where to find the map.

The contributors

This new edition of *Insight Guide: Poland* was edited by **Clare Griffiths** in Insight Guides' London office and builds on the work of the original editor **Alfred Horn**, who also contributed the original story one-page story on concentration camps.

The history section, written originally by **Waldemar Paclawski**, was updated and revised by **Lieutenant Colonel P.A. Szudek**, retired. Szudek was born in Poland in 1921 and served in the Polish forces between 1939 and 1947.He is a member of the Military Commentators' Circle in London and Honourary secretary of the Polish Forces Historical Commission.

The combined chapters on the arts was significantly revised by **Michal Gieleta** who has translated several plays and musicals into Polish and contributed work to a variety of Polish magazines. His work is based on the original features on Polish literature, by **Ewa Malicka-Kingston**, and Polish art by **Dr Thomas Strauss**.

The majority of the remaining feature essays were brought up-to-date and revised by **Kristina Rees** of the Polish Tourist Board in London. Original contributors to the features section of the book include **Waldemar Paclawski; Tomasz Parteka; Jacek Ziarno** and **Mariusz Urbanek**.

The in-depth places section of the book was thoroughly revised by London-based freelance food, drink and travel writer, **Ian Wisniewski**, who is a frequent visitor to Poland and Eastern Europe. Wisniewski also found time to extended and revise the essay on food and drink and wrote the text for the *Insight On...* picture stories on spa resorts; open-air museums; Chopin and Łazienki Palace.

Original contributors to the places section include **Professor Jachowitz; Jacek Ziarno; Maria and Przemyslaw Pilicki; Stanislaw Klos; Lidia Dlugolecka; Maciej Pinkwart; Lech Szaranieç; Wlobziemierz Lekki; Janusz Umiński; Jan Baldowski** and **Thomas Urban**.

Agnieszka Wlaszczuk, who lives in Warsaw, updated the *Travel Tips* section at the back of the book. Research for the new photographs used in this book was done by **Hilary Genin** and **Britta Jaschinski** in Insight Guides' London office. **Jerry Dennis; Michael Jenner** and **Kaplan Productions** contributed the bulk of the new photographic material for this edition. Proofreading and indexing was done by **Penny Phenix**, and **Zoe Ross** copyedited the new material.

INSIGHT GUIDE
POLanD

CONTENTS

The 17th century sundial featuring Choronos the God of Time, at Wilanów Palace, Warsaw

Travel Tips

Insight on ...

Information panels

Places

THE APPEAL OF POLAND

Often caught between the geopolitical forces of east and west,

Poland has mastered the subtle arts of survival

For more than a millennium, Poland has played a vital role in European history. The country's position in the heart of Europe has always made it a bridge between the two great cultures on its eastern and western flanks. The resulting diversity of influences has helped to shape the mentality of the people, who are tolerant of differing opinions and ways of life, yet open-minded about new ideas and hospitable towards strangers.

Neither oppression nor the centuries of brutal violence perpetrated by neighbouring countries have succeeded in stifling Poland's liberal spirit. Even during times of upheaval, when the country was obliterated from the map of Europe, the safeguarding of national culture, the recollection of a glorious past, Christian-humanistic traditions and solidarity remained at the forefront of the collective memory. These values still abound, and in such a climate there has never been room for any one "truth" or a monopoly of any one doctrine. The Poles have never allowed their liberty to be curtailed.

Poland has so much to offer – seaside resorts by the Baltic, hillwalking in the High Tatra Mountains, canoeing on the rivers and lakes of Mazuria, strolling through the Old Town in the historic city of Gdańsk, touring the monuments in Kraków or enjoying a beer in Old Market Square in Warsaw, the nation's capital. In recent years, Poland's appeal as a holiday destination has grown, as the range of accommodation has improved. Now the choice runs from luxury hotel with swimming pool and fitness suite to rooms in a private house, living with a Polish family, to camping by a lake.

If you are looking for some adventurous outdoor activities, then Poland is just the place. You can explore the countryside on foot, by bike, on horseback or by boat. Hunters and anglers have also discovered the special attractions that Poland can offer. If wildlife is one of your passions, then there is a good chance that you will catch a glimpse of some unusual species. Storks, for example, are very much in evidence in Mazuria, while bison, elk and tarpan, a kind of wild horse once thought to be extinct, are much rarer.

As well as these natural treasures, Poland possesses some imposing buildings: the Teutonic Knights' castle at Malbork or the magnificent complex on the Wawel in Kraków. The Old Town in Warsaw and the heart of ancient Gdańsk have been rebuilt to their former splendour. ❑

PRECEDING PAGES: traditional wood carvings from Karpacz; murals in Kraków; farmer and his wife in Mazuria; four coachmen in national dress.
LEFT: flute-player in youth orchestra.

Decisive Dates

375 The invasion of the Huns triggers the great migration of nations, during the course of which Slav tribes settle in the territory that is now Poland.

966 The Polish court adopts Christianity. Count Mieszko and his followers are baptised. He succeeds in unifying Polanie and neighbouring tribes.

1000 In Gniezno the first Polish church province is established.

1024 Bolesław I Chrobry receives the Pope's blessing and is crowned King of Poland.

1138 Duke Bolesław Krzywousty divides the coun-

try into provinces, which are then ruled by his sons.

1226 Duke Konrad Mazowiecki summons the Teutonic Order of Knights to Poland to support him in his struggle against the Prussians. The knights then establish their own state and rule over large areas of the eastern Baltic.

1241 A Polish army under Henryk Pobozny stops the Mongol advance at Legnica. Kraków is razed to the ground.

1333–70 Władysław I Łokielek, the last of the Piasts, reunifies the country. Later, under Kazimierz III Wielki, Poland becomes an important regional power broker and begins its expansion eastwards.

1386 Poland and Lithuania become a larger realm with the marriage of Jadwiga, the heiress to the

throne, to Grand Duke Jagiełło. Poland gains access to the Baltic ports.

1410 The defeat of the Teutonic Order of Knights at the battle of Grunwald paves the way for a greater expansion of power in the unified realm.

1466 In the second Peace of Toruń, the Teutonic Knights recognise the sovereignty of the Polish kings and cede territory at the mouth of the river Vistula, including the city of Gdańsk, to Poland. The Jagiellons now rule from the Baltic Sea to the Black Sea.

1505 At the Imperial Diet of Radom the king grants unprecedented and extensive rights to the nobility. The "rule of the nobility" is established as a distinctly Polish form of government.

1525 The "Knights' State", which has been secularised in the wake of the Reformation, becomes the Duchy of Prussia, a fiefdom of the Polish crown, under Duke Albrecht of Hohenzollern.

1543 Copernicus publishes his book *De revolutionibus orbium Coelestium* on planetary motion.

1552 An Imperial Council grants the right to religious freedom. Poland is a centre of tranquillity in the turmoil of the European religious wars.

1564 Bishop Hosius of Ermland invites the Jesuits into the country, marking the start of the Counter-Reformation.

1569 Under the Union of Lublin, Poland and Lithuania are officially united to form an "inseparable whole".

1572 The death of Zygmund August brings an end to the Jagiellon dynasty.

1621 East Prussia falls to the Elector Georg Wilhelm of Brandenburg. From now on, the fate of this region is determined in Berlin.

1655–60 The First Nordic War between Sweden and Poland sees the end of Polish domination in northeast Europe.

1683 King John III of Poland (Jan Sobieski) is given the credit for expelling the Turks from Vienna.

1772 The First Partition of Poland.

1791 The Polish reform movement, headed by King Stanisław II August Poniatowski, proclaims a liberal constitution.

1795 Under the Third Partition of Poland, Austria, Prussia and Russia jointly occupy the country despite fierce resistance.

1830–32 The November uprising against Russia is the most important event in the struggle for independence, but defeat sees the beginning of the first wave of emigration. Many Poles move to Paris.

1918 After the military defeat of the three occupying forces, an independent Polish state is proclaimed on 7 October.

1920 Under President Piłsudski, Poland stops the advance of the Red Army at the Vistula and occupies part of the Ukraine and Lithuania. Under the Treaty of Versailles, Gdańsk becomes a "Free City".

1921 After fighting between Poles and Germans, Upper Silesia is divided at a conference of ambassadors.

1926 Piłsudski regains power in coup; his method of government becomes ever-more authoritarian.

1939 On 1 September World War II starts with the German assault on the Polish garrison on the Westerplatte off Gdańsk. On 17 September, the Soviet Union attacks eastern areas of Poland. Hitler and Stalin then divide the country.

1944 The Warsaw rebellion – the culmination of an embittered and protracted resistance to Nazi rule – is led by partisans and the Polish *Armia Krajowa*, backed by the government-in-exile in London.

1945 The "Lublin Committee" proclaims itself the provisional government. Supported by the Soviet army, the communists suppress all opposition. The Soviet economic system is introduced. At the Yalta and Potsdam conferences Poland's territory is extended westwards. In the east large territories fall to the Soviet Union and their republics. In the west the Oder/Neisse line is agreed as the provisional border with Germany.

1955 Founding of the "Warsaw Pact" and "Treaty of Friendship, Co-operation and Mutual Assistance" with the Soviet Union and other Eastern bloc states in reply to the founding of NATO.

1956 After strikes and unrest in Poznań, the National Communist Gomulka takes over the leadership of the country.

1970 In the wake of the new *Ostpolitik*, Willy Brandt, Chancellor of West Germany, signs a treaty restoring normal relations between Poland and the Federal Republic of Germany.

1980 Strikes in Gdańsk spread country-wide. Formation of an independent trade union known as "Solidarność" or Solidarity.

1981 General Jaruzelski declares martial law on 13 December to pre-empt an invasion by the Warsaw Pact. The opposition goes underground.

1989 At a Round Table meeting, the communist leadership agrees to share power with the opposi-

tion headed by Lech Wałęsa. After a devastating electoral defeat for the Communists, Solidarity candidate Tadeusz Mazowiecki, a Roman Catholic intellectual, becomes leader of the new government.

1990 After unification, Germany formally recognises the western border of Poland at the Oder/Neisse line. In the November presidential elections, Lech Wałęsa wins by a small majority.

1993 The body of war-time leader General Sikorski is returned. Poland's first woman prime minister, Hanna Suchocka, resigns. Soviet troops leave Poland. After four Solidarity governments, the left-wing government of Waldemar Pawlak takes over. Lech Wałęsa stays on as president until 1995.

1995 Democratic Left Alliance wins election and former communist minister Aleksander Kwasniewski, Youth Minister under General Jaruzelski, becomes president.

1997 Poland applies for membership of NATO and the EU. Parliamentary elections give the Solidarity Electoral Action alliance more seats in the Sejm than their former Communist rivals. Jerzy Buzek becomes prime minister in October. New constitution is adopted.

1998 Bill allowing individuals access to their secret service files is vetoed by President Kwasniewski.

1999 Poland joins the NATO alliance. The tenth anniversary of the country's first post-communist democratic government. ❑

PRECEDING PAGES: Warsaw as it looked at the beginning of the 20th century.
LEFT: Traditional religious wood carving.
RIGHT: Solidarity leader Lech Wałęsa.

A GLORIOUS PAST

During this period of history the newly-formed Polish nation consolidated
its power and took on much of its present-day territorial form

The vast plain between the Odra and Vistula rivers, which flow from the Carpathian and the Sudeten mountains as far the Baltic Sea, has been at the interface between two great cultures ever since the Stone Age. After a period of Celtic influences, west Slavic tribes settled here. They had already mastered the skills of iron-making and had nurtured good relations with the countries of southern Europe.

The Ślężanie, the Mazowszanie, the Pomorzanie and the Wiślanie – the tribes who inhabited the area we now know as Silesia (in the southwest), Pomerania (in the north) and Mazovia (the region around Warsaw) – combined to form a defensive pact. To protect their settlements, which quickly developed into centres of craftsmanship and trade, they surrounded them with strong defensive walls.

The early state

The semi-legendary ruler, Mieszko I, a member of the Piast dynasty and a contemporary of Charlemagne, united the Polanie tribe of the Warta Valley with other groups that were linguistically and culturally related. The land occupied by these tribes was bordered to the south and west by Christian states that were closely tied to Rome. In order to project his state onto the European stage, Mieszko was subsequently baptised, together with his subjects. He then married the Czech princess Dobrava, thereby securing the southern borders of his territory. Mieszko's son, Bolesław I Chrobry (the Brave), established an independent, ecclesiastical administration which – enlightened yet rigidly centralised – set about integrating the component parts of the state.

In AD 1000, the Holy Roman Emperor Otto III was received with great pomp at Gniezno, the then capital of Poland. However, his successor Heinrich II did not continue Otto's policy of friendship and sought to expand his empire eastwards by force. His invasions failed and as a counter-measure Bolesław attacked Prague, staking finally his western frontier along the Odra and the Saale rivers. History repeated itself just under 1,000 years later, when a German invasion of Poland culminated in a similar conclusion.

The proud victor was not content with stopping there. He wanted to expand eastwards too – in the name of Christianity. Bolesław annexed Ruthenia (present-day Ukraine) with its capital of Kiev to Poland. In 1025 he was rewarded by the Pope, who presented him with the royal insignia. Poland had become a fully-fledged member of the Christian community of states.

The Piast dynasty

Throughout his lifetime Bolesław III Krzywousty (the wry-mouthed) tightened the bonds between Pomerania and the Polish state, but in his will he divided the country among his four sons. Soon the brothers and their successors

---

LEFT: *The Black Madonna of Częcstochwa,*
a Byzantine icon of unknown age.
RIGHT: Madonna figure on the clock of
St Mary's church, Gdańsk.

were engaged in unseemly disputes over royal titles, leadership claims and commercial advantages. The centre of political life moved from Wielkopolska (Great Poland) to Małopolska (Lesser Poland) in the southwest. Its capital, Kraków, lay in a favourable position on the trade route from Ravensburg and Vienna to Kiev and Byzantium.

NATIONAL TRIBE

The Polanie tribe, who lived in the Warta valley not far from Poznań, were the peoples who gave Poland its name.

Immigrants soon arrived in great numbers from northern Germany and the Netherlands. Thousands of Jews, persecuted elsewhere in Europe, sought refuge in a part of the continent

dangerous to Mazovia. In 1226, Duke Konrad of Mazovia who bore the brunt of their constant raids, invited the German Order of Teutonic Knights to assist him (see page 263). The Order had just been expelled from the Holy Land after the failure of the last crusade and was ready to take any employment. The Order carried out the task by wiping out the Prussians and establishing a state of their own in the conquered land, but this soon began to threaten Poland. In 1308 it took over Gdańsk and massacred its popula-

that had by then become renowned for religious tolerance. They did not arrive empty-handed, but brought new tools and new ways of doing business. Before long, Kraków was enjoying a period of unrivalled commercial prosperity and cultural richness. Nor was the development of the Polish state seriously impeded by the Mongol invasions of the 13th century. It was during this time that Wrocław, Kraków and Poznań decided to adopt the Magdeburg municipal law, which afforded good conditions for economic development.

In the north, Poland bordered with Prussian pagan tribes. They resisted all previous Polish missionary attempts and were particularly

tion. In the wars between 1327 and 1333 it laid waste large parts of Wielkopolska.

Nevertheless, the old Piast dynasty managed to uphold the idea of a united Polish state during two centuries of feudal dismemberment. By the end of the 12th century, the kingdom consolidated itself again. The difficult task was successfully concluded when in 1320 Władysław Łokietek was crowned in Kraków as an undisputed king of the united kingdom.

The restored *Corona Regni Poloniae* received a modern constitution and a stable currency during the reign of his son Kazimierz III Wielki (Casimir the Great). It was said that he had found Poland built in wood, and left it built in stone. During Kazimierz's reign (1333–70) the full "polonisation" of Malopolska was finally completed.

The most important development, however, was that of establishing the Polish identity as firmly belonging to the western European civilisation. As the last Piast king, Kazimierz may have achieved much on the domestic front, but was less successful from a military point of view. He had a dense network of fortified castles built throughout the country, but the expansion to the eastern territories left other areas of the kingdom vulnerable and resulted in the loss of the whole of Silesia.

Teutonic Knights. Despite the spectacular victory of the union's army at Grunwald in 1410, the military power of the Order was not broken until the 1454–66 war. From then on Gdańsk was to have the special status of a free city state ruled by the kings of Poland.

The new king, Kazimierz Jagiełłończyk (1447–92) became known as the "Father of Europe". Of his nine children, one son became a cardinal, four became kings, one was canonised and the three daughters were married off to become the mothers of the heirs of some of the greatest dynasties in western Europe. Nevertheless, Jagiełłończyk and his successors did

The Jagiellons

After the death of the last Piast king, the Polish throne fell to the Hungarian line of the royal family of d'Anjou. Soon afterwards, however, the kingdom was united with the Grand Duchy of Lithuania. The new ruler, the Grand Duke of Lithuania, Władysław Jagiełło and his subjects converted to Christianity and Jagiełło married the Polish queen Jadwiga d'Anjou. The immediate reason for this union was the continuing threat posed by the German Order of

NICHOLAS COPERNICUS

Mikołaj Kopernik (Nicholas Copernicus) was born in Toruń in 1473. In 1491 he enrolled at the Jagiellonian University in Kraków, and studied in Italy before becoming a priest.

However, in true Renaissance fashion, his interests far exceeded the narrow confines of the church and he became particularly interested in astronomy. While canon of Frombork he constructed an observatory and from here discovered that it was the sun at the centre of the universe, not the Earth as previously thought. He published his findings as *De Revolutionibus Orbium Celestium* in 1543 but died later that year. The treatise was later banned by the Pope.

FAR LEFT: trade flourished during the Middle Ages.
LEFT: portrait of Nicholas Copernicus.
ABOVE: defeat of the Teutonic Order at Grunwald, 1410.

not manage to convert these exceedingly favourable family connections into real political power. This was primarily due to the very strong economic position of the nobility, which, as a reward for its participation in wars, was granted numerous and far-reaching privileges.

Around 1500, the population of the multinational, multi-faith Polish-Lithuanian Commonwealth stood at around 7.5 million in an area of about 1.1 million sq km (420,000 sq miles). Ethnic Poles made up only about 50 percent of

> ### RENAISSANCE ERA
>
> The Renaissance period was influential in Poland, largely because of its connections with Italy. Many Italianate buildings survive in Polish towns and cities.

administration of the Hohenzollern emperors of Germany, who were supporters of the Lutheran doctrines, and closely aligned with the house of Brandenburg.

Even though religious wars were raging in the west, the traditional and reformed religious denominations continued to live amicably in the territory ruled by the Polish crown. Religious tolerance was a central element of the "golden period of liberty", as the Polish state ideology was known at the time, In 1569 the union of the Polish crown

the total population. However, during the reign of the last Jagiellons – Zygmunt Stary (1506–48) and Zygmunt August (1548–72) – the country once more enjoyed a cultural and political boom, known in history as the "Golden Age of Poland". Polish language became the *lingua franca* of the eastern European nobility. The Polish, Lithuanian and Ruthenian gentry, which was quite used to the cohabitation of people of different denominations, readily accepted the revolutionary teachings of Luther and Calvin.

At the time of the Reformation, the Teutonic Order of Knights was also secularised. In effect, this meant it was subjugated to the secular

with Lithuania was renewed and a "Republic of Two Nations" was proclaimed.

An elective monarchy

In the mid-14th century, political and economic life had been characterised by the growing power of the Lithuanian and Ruthenian aristocratic families. Their huge estates in the east afforded them economic independence and enabled them to rise to the highest official posts. There they pursued solely their own interests, without any consideration of matters of state. At the same time powerful and aggressive forces developed within the adjoining states: in the west the Habsburgs, in the southeast Turkey, with its ambitions to conquer the continent, Moscow under the rule of Ivan the Terrible in the east, and Sweden in the north.

When the Jagiellon dynasty came to an end, the *Sejm,* the Polish parliament, introduced an elective monarchy. However, Henri de Valois, the first king to be elected (in 1573) decided to return to France to rule there as King Henry III. The next king, Stefan Batory, Duke of Transylvania (1576–86) was a superb military strategist, but constantly had to struggle to find sufficient funds to wage war: the powerful nobility evaded all state taxes and the war treasury was bankrupt. In spite of all this, he

elected for life. Although the electorate was limited to the gentry, they formed more than 20 percent of the population, comprising not only large landowners and numerous owners of one to three villages, but also (by far the largest group) those possessing a homestead with a few acres of arable land, which they tilled themselves. Their financial status may have been as low as that of an average peasant, but their social standing was as high as any magnate with thousands of peasants working his estate.

In effect, the size of the electorate in Poland in the 17th century was not equalled by the rest of Europe until the second half of the 19th

won the war with Russia and consolidated Poland's position in the east of Europe by annexing Livland.

In 1587 a member of the Swedish Wasa dynasty was elected King of Poland. Zygmunt III Wasa and his successors Władysław IV and Jan Kazimierz ruled Poland until 1668, but the country's economy continued to decline.

In the 17th century, the Polish political system became fully established. Kings of Poland were

LEFT: Prince Albrecht of Prussia, Grand Master of the Teutonic Order, swears allegiance to King Zygmunt II.
ABOVE: King Stefan Batory receives the surrender of Pskov.

century. In the absence of modern communications, new members of parliament were elected by local county assemblies. Their number varied from 65 to 75 and they elected new members of parliament at special sessions, which were, in fact, congresses of the county gentry. The assemblies' role was not limited to the election of members of parliament. Their main political task was to discuss, approve or veto any new government measures and legislation. The elected members were then issued with instructions on how to vote in parliament. In this way members of parliament truly represented the general electorate. The powers of local assemblies were considerable: they could impose their own local taxes or even raise their own county troops. The system was not only well established, but worked as efficiently as only parliamentary systems can. It was a supreme exponent of the "golden liberty of Poland", the pride of every Pole and, without doubt, the only system of its kind in Europe.

The system, based on the representation of local interests which strongly resembled a federation, more than any other demanded the universal acceptance of laws by all component parties. Consequently, it was argued that only total unanimity of all members could be just to all. This ideal was often reached after many

rest of Europe. The political systems of the west were steadily moving towards strengthening the power of central authorities, until what became known as "absolutist monarchies" were established. Whether they called themselves "enlightened" or not, any form of absolute power in the hands of central government was totally alien to the spirit of Poland. In this respect, the gap between Poland and the rest of Europe was growing.

Terror of the Turks

The Polish parliament was parsimonious in their expenditure on armed forces and each

long debates, but unfortunately it became a parliamentary tradition which, in turn, developed into a principle. Worse consequences followed. In 1652 a member of parliament protested against some matters under discussion and left the House. A baffled speaker suspended the session, and such was the enormous power of the parliamentary precedent that henceforward, one member vetoing the proceedings could cause suspension of the session, thus nullifying all laws proposed for that session by the government. The principle of *liberum veto* (veto of the free) was born, with disastrous consequences.

Whatever merits or demerits of the system, its direction was diametrically opposite to the

Commander-in-Chief, or Grand Hetman of the Republic had to fight hard to defend his army estimates and was lucky to get half of the money he needed. Consequently, the aim was to command a small but extremely efficient force. The peace establishment of the armed forces never exceeded 20,000, grouped exclusively in the Ukraine (Ukraina meaning "borderland") under the name of a Mobile Defence Force. Mobile they had to be to meet the annual raids of Tartars, Cossacks and later Ottoman Turks. The war establishment also comprised foreign mercenary troops or, in the last resort, a General Levy of all the gentry, raised under the banners of their own counties.

The army compensated its numerical weakness by its high combat effectiveness, which allowed Poland to emerge victorious from numerous wars of the 17th century. It scored resounding victories over the Russians, Turks, Cossacks, Tartars and even over the large and efficient armies of Sweden. It also produced outstanding commanders. One of them, Grand Hetman Jan Sobieski, was rewarded for his victories with the royal crown of Poland.

During the 17th century, the Ottoman Empire was steadily enlarging its Balkan possessions, aiming at the conquest of Europe. After suffering serious reverses in wars against Poland, the tember 1683, was fought one of the most decisive battles of the world – had the Turks been victorious, it is possible that Islam would have become the ruling religion of Europe. After preliminary artillery fire and infantry skirmishes, Sobieski unleashed the charge of his dreaded, winged hussars. The charge broke through the Turkish lines and in a matter of two hours, the Turkish army was annihilated. Its commander fled the field and the green standard of the Prophet fell into Polish hands. As a trophy, it was sent to Rome. The Turkish might was broken and it ceased to present a threat to European civilisation. ❑

Turks changed their strategic direction and aimed at the very heart of Europe. After defeating the field army of the German Empire, they laid siege to Vienna. With a force of some 140,000 men, they were masters of the situation and in the summer of 1683 Vienna was in dire straits. Envoys sent by the Austrian emperor to Sobieski begged him to rescue the city and the empire. Sobieski, already known throughout Europe as the "Terror of the Turks", sent 29,000 men to Vienna. There, on 12 Sep-

LEFT: an ambassador from Vienna begs for Polish help against the Turks.

ABOVE: Jan Sobieski at the siege of Vienna, 1683.

A CONGENIAL RACE

The *Description of Poland,* Oxford 1733, has this to say about the "Disposition of the Inhabitants": "The Polandres are generally of good complexion. Flaxen-hair'd, and tall of stature. The men… corpulent and personable. The women slender and beautiful, disdaining the help of art… They are naturally open-hearted and candid, more apt to be deceived then to deceive; not so easily provoked as appea'd; neither arrogant, nor obstinate; but very tractable if they be gently managed. They are chiefly led by example; are dutiful to their Princes and magistrates; inclined to civility and hospitality, especially to strangers; whose customs and manners they are forward to imitate…"

DEPENDENCY AND DIVISION

Poland's decline during the 18th century lead to its third partition in 1795.
An independent Polish state didn't exist again until 1918

Poland emerged victorious from the 17th century wars but was economically ruined. Large tracts of land were laid waste. The treasury was empty; the people were exhausted, both materially and spiritually. Polish links with Saxony had always been very close and it seemed propitious to elect a Saxon king on the death of the great Jan Sobieski. Augustus II the Strong, of the House of Wettins, was duly elected King of Poland in 1697.

Russia's dominance

Unfortunately, Augustus II was an adherent of absolutist ideas and his main endeavour was directed towards strengthening his personal power in Poland. He also sought to use the military power of the Republic primarily in promoting the interests of Saxony. To this end, he embroiled Poland in the disastrous Northern War, which lasted for 20 years and turned the country into a battleground for the armies of Saxony, Russia, Prussia and Sweden. In 1704, the exasperated gentry revolted and dethroned Augustus II, electing in his place a Pole, Stanisław Leszczyński. This gave rise to further disturbances and gave an opportunity for neighbouring powers to intervene in support of either king. This war, in which the Poles were most unwilling participants, brought about devastation on a vast scale and reduced the country to total penury. Army discipline, which only played a marginal role in the war, disintegrated.

As a result of war, Russia emerged as the dominant power. The parliamentary session which was held in Warsaw in 1717 bore the full imprint of its new might. Called the "silent" session because no member was allowed to speak, it marked the beginning of Russian rule over Poland, under the guise of protecting the old liberties of the Republic. Under Russian pressure, all gentry privileges were confirmed and even extended. It was Russia which officially became the guarantor of the "golden

LEFT: Canaletto's view of Warsaw.
RIGHT: Mural on shop wall, Wolin.

liberty" of the Poles and any true or imaginary infringement would give it a pretext for military intervention. The total strength of the army was permanently fixed at 24,000, a ridiculous figure in comparison to standing armies of more than 200,000 each of Russia, Austria and Prussia.

Under these prevailing conditions, effective

governing of the state was impossible for the king or any other body. With the rapid disintegration of its domestic market and lack of organised foreign trade relations, the state had been heading for bankruptcy since the beginning of the century. Like the sword of Damocles, the threatening coalition of neighbouring states was hanging over Poland.

In 1764, Stanisław August of the Poniatowski family was elected king. He has been brought up in the spirit of French enlightenment and he did his best to revitalise the state. His endeavours at reform and in inspiring a cultural movement that had a decidedly national character received much support from the intellectuals and the gentry. First successes were soon apparent: some form of discipline returned to parliament and the tax system was reformed. But the new custom offices, which were to provide the treasury with additional income, were prevented from functioning through intervention from Berlin. In 1768, in the town of Bar (in present-day Ukraine) a patriotic confederation was formed chiefly by conservative elements, directed against Russian dominance. It formed its own army, which

km (35,908sq miles). This annexation by the coalition of three powers became known as the First Partition of Poland. The Republic had no means of defending itself against the onslaught, but it was immediately realised that in order to survive, comprehensive reforms were imperative and the king became the leading spirit of far-reaching changes in political and social fields. A strong government was set up comprising, among other bodies, the Ministry of Education, the first ministry of its

attacked Russian garrisons in Poland. The confederation's struggle lasted for four years and effectively put a stop to economic revival and turned the country once more into a battlefield. Eventually, Russian military might prevailed and confederates were crushed.

The partition of Poland

The events served as a pretext for a Russian diplomatic initiative to partition Poland between the three powers: Russia, Austria and Prussia. In 1772 these powers annexed large parts of the state of Poland: Prussia gained 36,300 sq km (14,016 sq miles) Austria 81,900 sq km (31,623 sq miles) and Russia 93,000 sq

kind in the world, preceding other European states by almost a century.

The session of parliament which began in 1788 lasted for four years and reformed the political system of Poland. When the session ended, the country had acquired the most modern framework of political law in Europe, including that of revolutionary France.

This was embodied in the new constitution of 3 May 1791 which granted more power to all citizens, allowed greater autonomy to towns and gave full legal protection to the peasant class. "The Great *Sejm*", as the session was called, fixed the number of the standing army at 100,000 men. Again, it was

Stanisław August who led the reform. The influence of his intellect was felt in all spheres of social and cultural life.

Kościuszko and the peasants

Russia took these manifestations of Poland's revival as a serious threat. Tsarina Catherine II decided to take immediate action. First she mobilised her own adherents who belonged to the most conservative elements in Poland. On her orders, they formed a Confederation in Targowica and declared the Constitution null and void. Following this they requested Russian military intervention, which the Tsarina was

was Prince Józef Poniatowski, nephew of the king: when in the king's view the war became hopeless, he ordered capitulation and submitted to humiliating conditions by the victors.

There followed the Second Partition of Poland. But even the small part of the country nominally left free was occupied by Russia, with strong garrisons in all towns. They were there primarily to supervise the total disbandment of the Polish army, but the army, though beaten in the field, retained its high morale. Its officers, supported by large numbers of citizens, requested General Kościuszko to lead them in a new, full-scale war. He promptly

only too eager to grant. The Russian army invaded Poland. The invasion was staunchly resisted by the army which was still far from the numerical strength as fixed by the Great *Sejm*. The war lasted several months, during which two generals became known throughout Europe. One was Tadeusz Kościuszko, who had already distinguished himself during the United States' War of Independence. The other general

agreed, and in March 1794 he stood in the old marketplace in Kraków and proclaimed a national insurrection against the invaders. This scene, immortalised in contemporary prints and subsequent paintings, is known to every child in Poland – it is a part of national consciousness.

Being short of arms and ammunition, Kościuszko called upon volunteers from villages in the Kraków district; they eagerly answered his call. Their weapons were scythes, fixed vertically to shafts. With a few battalions of regular troops, squadrons of cavalry and a battalion of Kraków scythemen, Kościuszko marched to meet the Russian Army Corps. They met head on near the village of Racła-

---

FAR LEFT: Stanasław Poniatowski, the last king of Poland. **LEFT:** detail from Jan Matejko's painting portraying the 1773 partition of Poland.
ABOVE: a cartoon depicting the occupation of Wrocław by hostile forces (1741).

wice. The battle took the usual shape of the times, opening with the artillery bombardment and infantry on both sides trying to seize commanding positions. At midday, Kościuszko personally led the attack with his scythemen against a strong battery of Russian guns. The attack was delivered in the only way known to this improvised infantry: at the double and in loose column. The gunners had time for one salvo only, after which they met their deaths from terrible weapons in the hands of the scythemen. The Russian line broke and soon the whole corps was in full flight.

News of victory, the first since the relief of Vienna, was greeted throughout the country with enthusiasm. However soon afterwards, the uprising was crushed by the Russians which led to the Third Partition of the country, finally blotting out Poland from the map of Europe.

The Napoleonic era

When the last shots of the war were fired in Poland, the name of General Bonaparte was beginning to be well-known in Europe. This young general of the French revolutionary army, was fighting one of the enemies of Poland in Italy. Indeed, he had already had several astonishing successes against the Austrians.

1794 UPRISING AND MASSACRE

While Kościuszko and his men were fighting in the field, the citizens of Warsaw rose against the Russian garrison and expelled it after murderous street battles. The same happened in Vilno. Prussia sent its army to assist the hard-pressed Russians and both armies laid siege to Warsaw. After a few unsuccessful attempts at storming the city, they had to abandon the siege.

So far the uprising was victorious, but in October 1794, Kościuszko personally took command of a division with the intention of intercepting the Russians at the crossing of the Vistula at Maciejowice. Faulty intelligence caused him to meet an enemy double in numbers to his own army.

Wounded, Kościuszko fell into Russian hands and, now leaderless, the Polish army suffered reverses. A new Russian army, commanded by General Suvoroff, approached Warsaw. The right bank suburb of Praga was hastily fortified and defended by General Jasinski, the liberator of Vilno. The Russians overwhelmed the defenders by sheer numbers and butchered the civilian population. They murdered every man, woman and child in an orgy of killing which lasted throughout the day and following night.

The massacre of Warsaw's civilian population, unheard of in Europe since the Tartar invasions, shook the entire civilised world.

One of the first Poles to arrive in Italy was a general who had distinguished himself during the Insurrection. His name was Jan Dąbrowski. His plan, speedily agreed by Bonaparte and the French government, was to form a Polish Army as a force allied to the French Republic. Polish Legions in Italy – as they were called – relied on the Austrians to supply them with men. Sure enough, thousands of Poles who had been pressed into the Austrian army soon filled the ranks of the Legions, in addition to thousands of other volunteers escaping from occupied Poland. The Legions fought with distinction not only against the Austrians, but also against the Russians who invaded Italy to assist the hard-pressed Imperial Austrian Army. The Russians were led by the man known as the "butcher of Warsaw", Field-Marshall Suvoroff.

For the rest of the Napoleonic period, Poles fought alongside the French army in all its campaigns. Their hopes were dashed though when after the defeat of Prussia and Russia, Poland was not allowed to be rebuilt but only to form a small state called the Duchy of Warsaw.

Nevertheless it was a good foundation for the state which was to arise after the defeat of Russia in the "Second Polish War" which began in 1812. The Polish army, commanded by Prince Józef Poniatowski, marched to the campaign full of enthusiasm and hope. Unfortunately, the campaign ended in a disastrous retreat of the Grand Army and with this ended all hopes of the resurrection of the Polish Republic. But the army remained true to its allies. During the "Battle of Nations", at Leipzig in October 1813, Prince Józef, by then Marshall of France, fell commanding the rear guard of the army.

Unsettled century

The Congress of Vienna which ended the Napoleonic wars, reconstituted a small Polish state, more or less within the frontiers of the former Duchy of Warsaw. It was a constitutional monarchy, with the Tsar of Russia as its

---

LEFT: the Cossack massacre during the January Uprising of 1863.
RIGHT: statue of Prince Józef Poniatowski outside Radziwill Palace in Warsaw.

> ### NATIONAL ANTHEM
>
> The "Song of the Legions of Italy", in the rhythm of the mazurka, declared "Poland shall not die as long as we live". The song was sung in occupied Poland and was soon elevated to national anthem.

king. The Poles used a few liberties that were afforded them by the Congress of Vienna to help carry out the variety of tasks specified in the Constitution of 3 May 1791.

In 1816, a university was founded in Warsaw, which soon became a decisive factor in the promotion of scientific and cultural contacts with other academic centres in Europe. Russia did not yet have a single university. The idea of a national revival was also evident in the establishment of an independent, domestic industry and the

administration structures of a modern state.

However, there were frequent conflicts with Russia's stifling bureaucracy. The sharpest conflicts were those in the army whose Commander-in-Chief, Prince Constantine, was brother of the tsar. The prince attempted to introduce Russian forms of discipline into the Polish army, built on principles of military honour and patriotic duty. He had failed to introduce corporal punishment, but he interfered personally with the minutiae of army routine, driving both officers and men to distraction. This resulted in several cases of suicide among the officers each year. Secret, patriotic associations sprang up everywhere, particularly in the army. The conflicts were growing and finally they erupted in a national uprising in November 1830. The Russians replied with a general offensive which was broken at the gates of Warsaw and for almost a year the Poles were victorious in every engagement. However, Russia's overwhelming superiority in numbers began to be felt and this, coupled with strategic errors by the Polish High Command, brought them back to Warsaw.

In October 1831, Warsaw fell after a short siege and Poland, once again, disappeared from the map of Europe. One of the positive effects of the resultant new wave of emigrants was admiration in western Europe for the freedom

fight in Poland. In the European revolution year of 1848, Poles sought to re-establish their national sovereignty, but were unsuccessful, as were all other revolutionary movements.

Thirty years later, new generations of Poles again took up the armed struggle for freedom. In 1863, circumstances were far less favourable than those in 1830. The armed uprising was prepared after years of secretly gathering arms and of secret training in their use. Secondly, the Russian terror and the vigilance of the secret police made the preparations risky and difficult. The date of the uprising, in January 1863, was necessitated by the Russian plan to draft most of the young men into the Russian army

for 20 years' service from which very few returned alive. In spite of adverse circumstances, the January 1863 uprising lasted longer than the preceding ones. The insurgents continued fighting, even when members of the national government in Warsaw, were captured and executed. Without central direction, the guerrilla type of operations lasted well into 1865, with Lithuanian groups being the most effective. A wave of terror followed the end of the uprising. The Russian governor of Vitno, Muravief, gained for himself special distinction by being known as "Muravief the Hangman".

World War I

It was in the Austrian-occupied part of Poland, with centres in Lwów and Kraków, that the first Polish military organisation since the 1863 uprising was born. It was allowed by the authorities under the guise of a voluntary rifle association. It was a paramilitary organisation, but its secret work aimed at the training of officers and men for the future army of the independent Poland. The man who organised and subsequently commanded all "Riflemen" was Józef Piłsudski, born in Lithuania and an ex-convict in Siberia, where he had served a sentence for anti-Russian activities (*see page 38*).

When war, which everyone in Poland expected, broke out in the summer 1914, he led his riflemen across the line of partition to fight the Russians. When, as a result of German victories in 1916, most of Poland was cleared of Russian armies, Piłsudski launched a new, secret Polish Military Organisation, to which he transferred his best officers. They were to command the forces designated to liberate Poland when Germany and Austria were next beaten by the western Allies. For his refusal to co-operate with the Austro-German authorities, Piłsudski was arrested and imprisoned in the fortress of Magdeburg for the rest of the war.

Meanwhile, in 1917, the US president Woodrow Wilson included independent Poland in one of the US war aims. With the disintegration of Austria first, members of the Polish Military Organisation took to arms. Sharp fighting started first in Lwów which the Ukrainians, armed by the Austrians, tried to seize. ❑

LEFT: picture postcard details of Kraków before 1918.
RIGHT: a patriotic portrayal of the historic ties between Gdańsk and Poland.

REBIRTH: THE SECOND REPUBLIC

The inter-war years were marked by the re-establishment and expansion of the Polish state under the authoritarian leadership of Józef Piłsudski

In 1918 the banners of rebellion fluttered over the debris of the dynastic empires throughout Europe. Liberty was writ large – larger than it had ever been after 1848 and before 1989.

Now regionally organised, in October 1918 the Poles disarmed the Germans and Austrians, whose leadership had been overthrown and who were too exhausted even to consider a continuation of hostilities. In Poznań weapons for a Polish rebellion were collected. A national government, free from all Bolshevik ambition, was established in Lublin and in Lwów fervently patriotic high school pupils fought street battles with the Ukrainians, who had also started an uprising.

On 7 October 1918, the Regency Council met in Warsaw and proclaimed the Independence of Poland. On 10 November, released from prison, Piłsudski arrived in Warsaw. The Regency Council relinquished its power into his hands, with the title of "Naczelnik", first given to Kościuszko. This made him a virtual dictator. On 11 November 1918 Independence was officially proclaimed and world governments were accordingly notified. The reborn Republic of Poland had no frontiers, no army and no treasury, but universal enthusiasm and the well-known organisational abilities of the Poles remedied many shortcomings. Time was short, with a new danger looming across the temporary demarcation lines in the east.

The Red threat

Hard on the heels of the retreating German army came a new enemy: the Red Army. It represented a new force in world politics – that of the Communist revolution – with its aim to spread its preaching throughout Europe and to create one universal "State of Workers and Peasants". Piłsudski, by then Head of State and Commander-in Chief with the rank of Marshal of Poland, realised the imminent danger.

LEFT: Józef Piłsudski led the Second Republic to independence.
RIGHT: J. Malczewski, *Bowing before Polonia*.

Piłsudski was a patriot through and through, but neither in the Polish nor the Lithuanian tradition. His lodestar was the Jagiellonian idea of creating a strong political and military structure, capable of forming a strong barrier against any aggression from the east. In modern terms, he was a federalist on the old Polish principle of

the "Free Union of the Free People".

The first political step to turn this idea into reality came in 1919, with the establishment of a Polish-Ukrainian Confederation. For centuries, the vast lands of the Ukraine, originally populated by nomads from the east, had been the grain store for Poland, and later for the ever more powerful Russian empire. Piłsudski supported the Ukrainian nationalists and, together with allied Ukrainian forces commanded by Ataman Petlura, the Polish army marched into the capital city of Kiev. Unfortunately, the bulk of the Ukrainian population did not support their new government with sufficient strength. While Polish lines were extended, the Red

Army launched a major offensive in the north. Under the command of Marshal Tuhatchevski, the Red Army broke through the thinly held Polish front and marched west. The aim of the offensive was to turn Leon Trotsky's command into reality. "Over the corpse of bourgeois Poland" they were to march into Berlin – in socialist hands at the time – to add impetus to the expected Red world revolution.

Under this concentrated offensive, the Polish army retreated. Slowly, one after another, the intended lines of defence were broken. In the south, the dreaded cavalry army, led by Budyonny, spread havoc and panic; in the

north, the relentless pressure of the main Russian force, led by Tuhatchevski, turned an organised retreat into headlong flight. This group of armies had outflanked Warsaw defences from the north, cutting off the lines of supply from Gdańsk and crossing the Vistula at Płock. Seemingly, there was nothing to stop the Red Army from its conquest of Europe, over the dead body of Poland.

But Marshal Piłsudski was not idle. To the southeast of Warsaw he created a group of manoeuvres which he decided to command in person. On 15 August 1920 Piłsudski struck due northeast. His attack drove a wedge

PIŁSUDSKI – POLAND'S MILITARY HERO

Józef Piłsudski (1867–1935) was a poor Lithuanian who started his career as a revolutionary. But as far as his political inclination was concerned, he was a pragmatist. Throughout the last 10 years of his life he had a formative influence on the power structure of the state. In theory the structure of the democratic order remained untouched. In practice, however, all the key positions in the army and the administration were held by fervent Piłsudski supporters. A loyal élite was forged from the group of erstwhile soldiers who had fought for independence under his command. A substantial portion of the intelligentsia were employed in the state administration. Also, the influence of the

aristocracy, who for centuries had owned the landed estates, increased. The socialists in turn – initially supporters of Piłsudski – soon lost any illusions they may have had and joined the opposition.

The undoubted charisma of the Marshal was cleverly marketed and his political premises were popularised. The equality of all religious denominations – specified in the constitution – was retained due to his political dexterity. His *savoir-vivre*, his adherence to the traditions of the Polish multinational state, his preference for horses, sabres and swords; all this fused in the eyes of his countrymen to make him the embodiment of a popular hero.

between the Russian forces and cut Tuhatch-evski's lines of communications and their centre gave way. With Polish offensive pressing on, the whole right wing of the Russian army was annihilated.

A general rout of the Red Army followed. In the words of Marshal Tuhatchevski: "There is not the slightest doubt that, had we been victorious on the Vistula, the revolution would have set light to the entire continent of Europe." The British ambassador in Warsaw, Lord D'Abernon, set down his judgement, as fol-

MUSICAL POWER

In 1918 the acclaimed concert pianist, Ignacy Jan Paderewski, became Poland's first prime minister. He later lived in exile in the United States.

Poland is the barrier to the everlasting peril of an Asiatic invasion... by shielding Central Europe from the full blast of Marxist contagion, the Battle of Warsaw set back the Bolshevik clock."

A new democracy

In 1921 a general political consensus resulted in the acceptance of a democratic constitution, based on the French model. After the election victory of the National Democrats in 1922, Gabriel Narutowicz became the first president of the new republic.

lows: "The history of contemporary civilisation knows no event of greater importance than the Battle of Warsaw."

Major General J.F.C. Fuller, in his work *The Battle of Warsaw* (1920), concurred with this opinion: "It should be the task of political writers to explain to European opinion that Poland saved Europe in 1920, and that it is necessary to keep Poland powerful and in harmonious relations with western European civilisation, for

LEFT: Lwów was a centre for politics and the arts towards the end of the 19th century.
ABOVE: the modern port of Gdynia – the gateway to world trade.

Piłsudski was compelled to tender his resignation. Narutowicz did not last long: he was assassinated some days later. When Sikorski became prime minister, a new president, Stanisław Wojchiechowski, was elected and eventually a degree of stability was once more restored to the political scene.

Although the parliamentary constitution protected the fledgling democracy from the monopolistic claims of the central executive, it had insufficient control to afford total political freedom. The coalition governments of the 1920s worked in an atmosphere of mutual distrust and disunity. Their attempt to turn high-flying modernisation plans into reality did not really get off the ground – not surprising, considering the vast number of problems the country faced.

Currency reform ultimately proved advantageous, but it entailed an unpopular limitation of social rights. As was the case in other European states, this in turn encouraged radical political groupings to start to question the legitimacy and leadership mandate of parliament.

Only within the army did a strong, supra-regional link to the new, united state emerge. In May 1926 the long-awaited boom in the economy began to materialise. Piłsudski, who had long been the *éminence grise*, immediately

mediating role between the so-called "wild east" and the "civilised west". With the creation of a Non-Party Bloc for Cooperation with the Government, parliament was left with only a very few legislative functions.

Using an impending coup as a pretext, legal proceedings were instigated against the socialist deputies. The judiciary managed to save face by remaining independent and passing purely symbolic sentences, but nevertheless the young democracy lost much of its credibility.

Piłsudski not only sanctioned this development, he even consented to the new, restrictive constitution during his final hours on his death-

seized this opportunity to lead his loyal military units into Warsaw. After several days of street battles the coup succeeded and Piłsudski once again managed to gain total control. A new political strategy of restructuring, that went under the name of "*Sanacja*" ("Recovery"), was introduced.

Piłsudski's paternalistic leadership ideal was underscored by a cult of strict bureaucracy and the reliance on the obedient and loyal citizen. The encouragement of such characteristics in the national consciousness was not only designed to guarantee survival for a nation wedged between "traditional enemies", but also to enable Poland in the long run to play a

bed. On his death in 1935, he left a vacuum that was filled by the somewhat weaker General Edward Rydz-Śmigly took over from him.

Racial tensions

The only significant opposition against the Piłsudski clan came from the national democracy camp. Particularly in rural areas, this movement was inseparably linked with the Roman Catholic hierarchy. It propagated the concept that people had a natural right to their land, language and traditions. Roman Dmowski, the chief ideologist and strategist of this movement at that time, deemed the search for an ultimate solution to the nationality conflicts the most important task of any political agenda. The various peoples were to be settled on their own respective territories and a system of peaceful co-existence established. The movement also called for racial purity.

The Jewish community, who made up more than eight percent of the population, were the prime target of attack. But in addition, loyal, often non-denominational citizens whose families may have been "polonised" for centuries, became the victims of these persecutions. The main pretext for the attacks were the utopian-socialist ideas propagated by prominent members of the Jewish intellectual scene.

Economic struggles

In the period between the two world wars, Poland had become a relatively homogeneous economic unit. But radical change was needed to enable this to happen.

Provinces that for centuries had been characterised by totally diverse influences had to be economically integrated, plus a combination of radically different cultural elements within Polish society had to be assimilated: the efficient "Prussian-style" industrial machine, an easy-going "Austrian" Bohemian way of life and "Russian" dynamism, which all had to be brought under one roof. This process of assim-

When in the late 1930s the feeling of external threat increased, it soon became clear that Poland lacked anyone of the calibre of Piłsudski; the kind of figure required to maintain the integrity of the state. Nationalism grew apace and the government became ever more aligned with the national democracy movement. On the extreme right of these groups, fascist tendencies became evident. Violence against minority groups was no longer an isolated occurrence.

LEFT: the Polish parliament in session on the eve of war in 1939.
ABOVE: a 100 mark note, post World War I Polish currency replaced by the złoty in 1923.

THE IDEA OF A STATE

In 1921 the idea of a state was a very modern concept for Poles. The aim was to create a democratic political system, which withstood the efforts of the church to raise Catholicism to a state religion. Liberation from patriotic obligations was endemic in intellectual circles and there appeared to be a cultural renaissance. Through contact with the west, the belief that Poland was, once again, a member of the European family was strengthened. The cinema became the main attraction in large cities; small theatres in Warsaw flourished. The nightlife in large cities was on a par with any that may have been offered in Paris or London.

ilation – particularly with regard to legislation and infrastructure – took a long time to achieve. A port was built in Gdynia and linked to industrialised Silesia by miles of railway track. Nevertheless, even during the years of economic growth there was a dearth of funds to enable independent Polish investment. Heavy industry, for example, remained controlled by France and Germany.

At this time, the annual capital transfer to foreign banks was five times higher than any investments made at home. Moreover, the primitive banking system levied the highest interest rates in Europe; the prime lending rate

was three times higher than in the United Kingdom or in Switzerland. Even in 1939 it was still not possible to regain pre-World War I levels of industrial production.

Almost 65 percent of the population lived tied to the land in rural areas. With the exception of Greater Poland and Pomerania, the agricultural structure remained backward without modern machinery or outside investment. Seven-tenths of the rural population was only marginally involved in the circulation of goods and currency. As well as this sluggish pace of industrialisation, a catastrophically high birth rate caused a drastic decline in the overall standard of living and triggered a fresh wave of

emigration. During the time leading up to the Great Depression (1926–30) approximately 200,000 people left Poland annually to start a new life somewhere else, with the Untied States being a popular destination. In subsequent years, over-population led to further subdivision of rural estates and thus to lower revenues for those who made their living from the soil. The rural population, which was largely illiterate and highly indebted to provincial usurers, remained in a suffering, seemingly divinely ordained state of lethargy.

Controlling eastern Europe

In the 1930s Poland's foreign policy situation deteriorated rapidly. Stuck in the doldrums of the world economic crisis of 1929, the country's plans for rapid modernisation and social improvements collapsed. After 1935, the government, which was having to rely even more strongly than before on the traditional forces of the army and the landed gentry, passed a new, far more authoritarian, constitution.

In Warsaw the popular slogan of a "superpower Poland" found favour among the masses. Despite all endeavours to achieve a national consensus, in this tense situation there was far too little freedom of movement for such a conflict to be resolved. As far as the propagandists were concerned, the Polish "superpower" should, with the assistance of its culture, influence the whole of central and eastern Europe and, at the same time, form a military protection wall to the east.

An alliance with Berlin or Moscow was out of the question, but when Hitler occupied Bohemia and Moravia after the Munich agreement, Marshal Edward Rydz-Śmigly, in turn, gave orders to reclaim part of the territory of Polish Silesia which Czechoslovakia had annexed in 1920.

In this optimistic atmosphere, a young generation of Poles waited for a solution to the mystery of independence. On 11 November 1939, it intended to celebrate its 21st birthday, together with the republic. But, as it happened, matters were to turn out very differently. Another power sought to find its *lebensraum* (living space) in the east. ❏

LEFT: The Pilot monument, originally designed by E. Wittig and reconstructed after World War II, can be seen at Warsaw airport.

Lwów and Vilnius

The reunification of Germany brought about an unequivocal renunciation of the former East German territories. At the same time Poland has gained a secure western border and millions of new Polish citizens in Wrocław, Malbork and Szczecin are guaranteed a right to their homeland. Many of these people had had to leave their homes either as part of the resettlement policies within the Polish state or when they were expelled from the former Polish eastern territories, now part of Lithuania, Russia and the Ukraine. Luckily, nobody in Poland today has any intention of reclaiming these territories and triggering yet another tragic migration of the region's peoples. Instead, it is becoming apparent that only through intercultural exchange and overcoming isolationist tactics will there will be common access to regions characterised by centuries of shared cultural history.

This point is clearly demonstrated by the former Polish cities Vilnius/Wilno and Lwów/Lwiw, with their rich multi-cultural traditions. In free Poland during the inter-war years both cities developed into centres of intellectual life. Regaining them had been a considerable task for the young Poland. Vilnius, although largely inhabited by Poles, was regarded by the Lithuanian republic as their true capital and Lwów, also with a Polish majority, had to be defended against claims from the Ukraine.

Lwów was founded in the mid-13th century by the son of Prince Daniil of Galicia, who built a fort on the site of the present-day town. In the years of Polish partition, Lwów became an important city: it was located at the junction of major trade routes and its population was made up of a variety of cultures and nationalities.

In the 19th century, trade, transport and industry developed rapidly and in 1894 an electric tram system was in operation. Science and literature were allowed to flourish and the university, renamed in 1919 after King Jan Kazimierz, produced great humanists. The town also became a meeting place for Ukranians, Poles and Jews and prominent cultural and political leaders lived here towards the end of the 19th century, including Ivan Franko and Mykhailo Hrushevsky. The mathematics department of Lwów University, founded by Stefan Banach and Hugo Steinhaus, was once the leading institute of its kind in the world. It was in Lwów

that Rudolf Weigl developed the vaccine against typhoid. The theatre was deemed one of the best in the country and two legendary Polish actors, Leon Schiller and Wilam Horzyca, were members of its company.

Vilnius, now capital of Lithuania, is one of the country's oldest cities, founded in 1323 by Gediminas, a Lithuanian duke. After protracted disputes the former capital of the Grand Duchy of Lithuania was returned to Poland in 1922. Interaction between these two cultures determined the stature of this city. Pilsudski was a descendant of Lithuanian dukes; Adam Mickiewicz, the Polish national poet, began his epic poem *Pan Tadeusz*

with the exclamation: "Lithuania, my fatherland!" The literary tradition was further developed by Czeslaw Miłosz, who was awarded the Nobel Prize for Literature in 1980. Antoni Golubiew and Pawl Jasienica were also active in Vilnius during the inter-war years. Stanisław Mackiewicz, prime minister of the government-in-exile after World War I period, began his political career in the city.

Both Lwów and Vilnius retain evidence of this multicultural diversity. In Vilnius the Gorny Zamek Giedymina, the Church of St Casimir and St Anne's Church characterise the landscape. In Lwów there are Armenian, Greek Orthodox and Roman Catholic cathedrals and it is the only city in Poland to be the seat of three archbishops. ❏

RIGHT: the Church of St Michael in Vilnius.

WORLD WAR II AND ITS AFTERMATH

When Germany invaded Poland in 1939 it set off a catastrophic chain of events
that were to change the world – and totally transform Poland

In autumn 1938, the German Reich under Adolf Hitler summarily confronted Poland with a number of political demands, including the return of the "free city" of Gdańsk, access via a motorway to East Prussia across the so-called Polish corridor and a realignment of Polish foreign policy towards the Third Reich, namely signing up to the Anti-Comintern Pact.

Neither Great Britain nor France made any attempt to halt the growing expansion of the Third Reich to the east. The only obstruction to Hitler's plans was uncertainty about how the Soviet Union would react to these claims.

In fact, after Hitler's troops invaded Czechoslovakia in March 1939, the Soviet Union agreed to collaborate with the "Greater German Reich". In response, Great Britain and France concluded a treaty with Poland, assuring each other of mutual military assistance in case of a German attack on any one of the countries. It entailed a huge risk of world war.

Defeat and partition

On 23 August 1939, Germany and the Soviet Union concluded a "non-aggression pact". In an additional, secret protocol both countries specified their territorial claims against Poland: Eastern Poland was assigned to the Soviet Union, while the remainder – the whole of the western and central territories – was to come under Hitler's control.

In the late evening of 31 August 1939, the Soviet parliament ratified the Hitler-Stalin pact; only a few hours later, without making any declaration of war, the German Wehrmacht marched into Poland, the first country to offer military resistance to Nazi aggression.

Polish troops were mobilised in a matter of hours, but the unprepared soldiers faced a German army that was both numerically and technically superior. Attempts to resist the

German advance in the north, west and south, over a front some 1,600 km (990 miles) in length, were in vain. A popular myth has grown up that the Polish cavalry charged German tanks. What really happened was that detachments of mounted infantry and cavalry met German panzer divisions. The cavalry, whose

duty it was to charge the infantry following behind the tanks, naturally had to gallop towards oncoming armour in order to attempt this objective.

By the terms of their mutual defence pacts with Poland, Britain and France were duty-bound to immediately declare war on Germany, but they were procrastinating. Only on the third day of the invasion, 3 September 1939, did they make their declarations official. According to additional military clauses of the pact, Britain was to start a bombing offensive on Germany without delay, while France was to attack Germany "with the bulk of her forces" by 15 September. Neither obligation was kept.

LEFT: the free city of Gdańsk – a calamitous bone of contention between Germany and Poland.
RIGHT: Hitler crosses the Czech border in 1939.

Cut off from the rest of the country by the Russian invasion, the Polish government crossed the frontier of allied Romania to carry on the war from abroad. However, instead of being given opportunity to travel to France, the Romanians interned the allied government of Poland. Nevertheless, the armed forces continued to fight. Warsaw capitulated only after the last rounds of ammunition were fired and the city itself was turned to rubble under air and artillery bombardment. The last group, surrounded by Germans and

FLYING SKILLS

The Polish soldiers who trained with the British Royal Air Force were later to win great fame at the Battle of Britain.

these began almost immediately. Their target was France, where in October 1939 a new government of Poland was formed, headed by General Nladysław Sikorski. A new army was also being organised there. Part of the Polish Air Force personnel was directed to England, where they began training on the British aircraft. Another strong group of Polish Forces formed in Syria, then a French protectorate. By the spring of 1940, Polish Forces gathered in France had already reached the 100,000 mark.

Russians, gave up the unequal contest on 5 October. As the post-war testimonies of German generals make plain, the war could have ended in 1939 because almost the entire German army and practically the entire air force were thrown against Poland, leaving only an insignificant screen in the west. Had the Western allies intervened, as they were obliged to do by their treaties with Poland, Germany would certainly have been crushed.

Polish Army in exile

The remnants of the Polish army which crossed the Romanian and Hungarian frontiers, were put in internment camps, but mass escapes from

The first Polish group to go into action against Germany was the so-called "Podhale Brigade" which formed part of the allied expeditionary force in Norway. Some units of the Polish Navy had been in constant action already under the tactical command of the Royal Navy. It was the submarine *Orzel*, which, after her epic escape from the Baltic, torpedoed a German troop transport, thus first signalling their invasion of Norway.

Two Polish infantry divisions and one armoured brigade also fought side by side with the allies to the bitter end during the French campaign of 1940. The remnants of the army were then evacuated to Great Britain.

The Home Army

While Warsaw was still under siege in 1939, the first steps were taken to create an underground army. It was to this end that General Tokarzewski-Karaszewicz was appointed its Commander-in-Chief and given appropriate staff, with such funds as were available. This Organisation formed the basis of the future Home Army (*Armia Krajowa* or AK), which incorporated a great many clandestine groups, formed spontaneously all over Poland. The Home Army formed an integral part of the Polish Forces, subordinate to the government, first in France, later in Great Britain.

and the most effective underground army in Europe. They were armed with what they had taken from Germans and also by a continuous stream of supplies delivered by air from Britain, mostly by the Polish air-crews. Towards the end of 1943, the blowing up of bridges and rail tracks disrupted German supply lines with the Russian front to such an extent that it had begun to play a substantial part in their defeat, Finally, the Home Army power revealed itself in full force in its attempt to liberate the capital city of Poland, Warsaw.

During the last week of September, a treaty was concluded between the Soviet Union and

As part of the Armed Forces of Poland, the Home Army carried out the war against Germany, as distinct from what is called "the resistance", in which almost every Polish man and woman took part. The primary targets of the Home Army were the German forces and German police, which were kept on constant alert by the activities of partisan detachments.

By 1944, the Home Army numbered 350,000 men in active formations – by far the largest

LEFT: Home Army detachment during the 1944 Warsaw Uprising.
ABOVE: schoolgirls delivering mail at a Home Army fieldpost.

UNDERGROUND RESISTANCE

Among civilians there was a great deal of activity under German Occupation. The Poles were not allowed to receive higher education but were to remain on a barely literate level to provide labour. The vast Organisation of the "Underground State" clandestinely arranged for young Poles to obtain diplomas and university education. An underground administration and press continued; there was even a police force and law courts. It was to the nameless authorities of this State that Poles owed their allegiance, at the risk of death or concentration camps. It may be said that at no other time was national cohesion stronger than under the German occupation.

the German Reich and German and Soviet soldiers fraternised on Polish soil. In the subsequent months, the German Wehrmacht occupied Denmark and Norway and conquered France. The Soviet Union occupied the Baltic states and eventually large areas of Finland and Romania too.

Once the Polish campaign had come to an end, West Prussia, Greater Poland and Upper Silesia were swallowed up by the German Reich. After various unsuccessful attempts to

CULTURAL DEATH

Craftsmen and labourers were deported to do forced labour in the Reich. Artists, scientists and priests were taken into "protective custody", often a synonym for concentration camps.

establish a puppet state, Germany declared the rest of occupied Poland a "General Government" with its administrative seat located in Kraków. Its powers were limitless, its subjects stateless.

Hitler's reign of terror

Hitler exploited for his own ends the anti-Semitism that had long been latent throughout Europe. With the help of chauvinistic propaganda, the party apparatus and its organisations – above all the Waffen SS and the Gestapo – he ruthlessly applied his theories concerning racial purity. The final victory would give the German "master race" *leben-*

sraum in territory that stretched as far as the Urals. This aim was to be achieved in accordance with a "legal punishment system", which could be interpreted so broadly that in the occupied areas the decisions of an SS commander could never be challenged.

In accordance with the guidelines of the propaganda ministry, Poles were regarded as *untermenschen* – a sub-human species. The final aim of national socialist policy was the destruction of the Polish people, their expulsion or "germanisation", the extermination of Jews and gypsies as well as the settlement of Germans in the newly "liberated" areas. Any racial group that was deported from the provinces within the German Reich in the course of the ethnic cleansing process was to be concentrated in the General Government. The racially pure were to be resettled in the new provinces, and the "inferior races" dispatched to Kraków, where they would face an uncertain fate.

Anyone who attempted to resist had to reckon with brutal retaliation. Mass executions were the order of the day. In 1940 the Germans established a number of camps on Polish territory (*see page 54*), which, in January 1942, were semi-officially refashioned and enlarged to function as extermination camps. People deported to these camps were officially described as "vermin". Before being killed, they were abused as slave workers and used for medical experiments. From 1942 onwards the prisoners of these camps were killed by poison gas and the corpses incinerated. Of more than five million Polish concentration camp inmates, more than 3.5 million were killed – three million of those as a consequence of the *endlösung* (Final Solution) policy that had been planned for the Jews.

In conjunction with the executions in the camps, there was also the *Action Reinhand,* which simply meant that those who had been condemned to death were first relieved of any valuables they may have had. In the fiscal year 1943–44 this brought the Deutsche Reichsbank an incredible net profit totalling over 100 million Reichsmarks.

The military and political collapse of Poland was a severe shock for the Polish people and it forced them into a painful reappraisal of their situation. Terror, torture, death and starvation, and the suppression of any independence movements, further intensified the general feeling of hopelessness. Corruption and human rights abuses were rife.

Soviet control

In tandem with the German terrorising campaign, the Soviet Union set about the annexation of occupied East Poland and began with the "russification" of its newly won territory. This was personally undertaken by the head of the Communist Party in the Ukraine at the time, Nikita Khrushchev, who later, on

In February 1940 the deportation of Polish citizens to Kazakhstan, to the Russian Arctic and to Siberia commenced. Stalin was of the opinion that it was possible to expel anyone or anything: the nation from its identity and its land, the family from home and hearth. His aim was that ultimately people would lose their self-esteem and all sense of personal identity.

Stalin's method of control was based on rather different premises from Hitler's reign of terror. He believed that in the end his victims would surrender to a system in which they were forced to do slave labour and were pressured day and night by functionaries or police.

Stalin's death, became the first Secretary of the Soviet Communist Party. In Moscow, Stalin propagated the occupation of Poland as an "act of liberation from the capitalist system by a fraternal nation". A precise census was carried out, and subsequently the Soviet administration foisted Soviet passports on every east Polish citizen. The occupied regions were designated as "western Ukraine" and "western Belorussia". After a manipulated "referendum" on 1 and 2 November both were incorporated into the two Soviet republics.

LEFT: Home Army patrol.
ABOVE: the German menace in World War II.

MASS DEPORTATIONS

One Stalin method that was especially successful was the expulsion of whole sections of the Polish population from their traditional homelands. State officials, judges, foresters and small farmers were the first to be deported. Eventually whole families, merchants, members of the self-employed classes, professors and teachers followed. In one year almost 1.65 million Polish citizens were deported in cattle wagons, many of them refugees who had recently arrived from central and eastern Poland. A large percentage were taken to concentration camps for "re-education". By 1942 more than half of the people who had been deported were dead.

Sikorski versus the Communists

The Polish government-in-exile under General Sikorski was not just involved in military matters, but was also active politically. As early as 20 December 1939 and despite the harsh realities of the situation, it was calling for the liberation of Poland from enemy occupation, pleading for boundaries that would guarantee Polish security. When Hitler attacked the Soviet Union in June 1941, Sikorski, met with Stalin and was granted the concession that a number of Poles who had been deported to Soviet camps should be released in order to set up a Polish army. Stalin was even prepared to annul the earlier pact with

Meanwhile in Russia, the Germans discovered the mass graves of Polish officers, murdered on Stalin's orders. They were the bodies of officers unaccounted for in Katyń during the formation of the army in the USSR. Understandably, German propaganda was making the best possible use of the discovery. To put an end to it, the Polish Government proposed that a neutral Red Cross commission should investigate the matter. This proposal was met with a furious Russian reaction. They accused the Polish Government of siding with the Germans and, using it as a pretext, Russia broke off diplomatic relations with Poland.

Hitler concerning the partition of Poland, but he peremptorily rejected the Polish demand to be allowed to re-establish its pre-World War I border (*see page 42*).

Eventually, about 100,000 soldiers, women and children were safely evacuated to the Middle East via Iran. Men, armed and equipped by the British, formed the Second Army Corps of the Polish Forces, which subsequently landed in Italy. The Corps, commanded by General Władysław Anders, played a prominent part in the Italian campaign. Its successes included breaking through "Hitler's Line", with its key position at Monte Cassino, one of the great battles of World War II.

At the time Stalin was totally convinced of his victory over Germany and he believed that the Soviet expansion to the west would obliterate any memory of Katyń. He even had the temerity to invite Polish Communists to Moscow. Just a few years previously many of them had barely escaped the execution that Stalin had ordered for all members of the Polish Communist Party. (In 1938 the Polish Communist Party, at the time illegal, had been disbanded because of a "betrayal of the world revolution"; the party had collaborated with the Socialist Party and the Peasant Party in Poland. Some 5,000 comrades invited to the Soviet Union were murdered on Stalin's orders).

Those members of the Polish Communist Party who had formed a pro-Soviet wing in the years before 1939 – Bierut, Minc, Ochab, Gomułka and others – now made it clear that they were ready to co-operate with Moscow. In March 1943, they combined to establish the Union of Polish Patriots and, as far as Stalin was concerned, were the "true representatives of the Polish people". In autumn 1943, the newly organised Polish divisions fought side by side with the Soviet army at the Eastern

LAYING BOUNDARIES

At the Tehran Conference in November 1943 Stalin made it clear to Britain and the US that most of post-war Poland would become part of the Soviet Union.

mainly the eastern border. The government-in-exile was looking towards the restitution of the 1921 borders and the return of the areas annexed by the Soviet Union; while the pro-Soviet Poles, on the other hand, now preferred the so-called Stalin Compensation Plan. Within the guideline of this plan, in return for shifting the western border to the Oder-Neisse line, the Poles would give up claims to the eastern regions and Polish territory would, in addition, include Gdańsk and southern East Prussia.

front. As a sign of their identity, these soldiers wore the Piast eagle – without the crown – on their helmets.

Government-in-exile isolated

While fighting was continuing on various fronts around Poland, tough negotiations on the borders for the future of the Polish state were continuing at a diplomatic level. Various differing views existed at that time regarding

LEFT: Polish Prime Minister Stanisław Mikołajczyk (1901–66) in London, 1944.
ABOVE: a cabinet meeting of the Polish government-in-exile.

The Allied forces found these ongoing disputes increasingly embarrassing, as the demands of the Polish government-in-exile conflicted with those of their military alliance with the Soviet Union. By the autumn of 1943, the government-in-exile found itself dangerously out on a limb.

The Warsaw Uprising

In January 1944, the Soviet army had reached the pre-war frontiers of Poland. After the death of General Sikorski in an air crash in Gibraltar on 4 July 1943, Stanisław Mikołajczyk became the Prime Minister. He instructed the Home Army command to liberate parts of Poland from the Germans before the Red Army arrived and to co-operate with the Russians afterwards.

The plan worked well in the Vilno district, which was liberated by the Home Army division. However, when according to government instructions, the division made contact with the Russians to plan future co-operation, the officers were immediately imprisoned and their units disarmed. So ended another attempt to establish friendly relations with the Russians. But there still remained the slight chance to liberate

BITTER RETALIATION

Enraged by the activities of the Warsaw Uprising, Hitler demanded that the city be razed to the ground, hoping to leave the rubble to the awaiting Red Army.

their territory. So, in spite of the sacrifice of many a brave air-crew, mainly Polish and South African, the uprising slowly died.

When the Home Army capitulated on 3 October 1944, the casualties among the civilian population amounted to around 166,000 and 85 per cent of the city was totally destroyed.

However tragic the fate of the city, the uprising had succeeded in halting the Red Army's progress into Europe for at least two months, while it waited for the Germans to eliminate the Poles. Given these

the capital city of Poland, Warsaw, before the arrival of the Red Army and thus make it the true seat of government of Poland.

With this in view, on 1 August 1944, the Home Army attacked the German garrison in Warsaw. Eventually, considerable forces of the German 9th Army had to be diverted into the battle for Warsaw. It lasted for 63 days, with the Russian Army impassively observing it from across the River Vistula. The Home Army needed ammunition most of all, but the air supplies from Italy and England were difficult over such long distances, in the face of alerted German anti-aircraft defences. The Russians flatly refused to allow allied aircraft to refuel on

two months, it is reasonable to suppose that the Red Army would have met the Western Allies on the Rhine and Germany as a whole, not only its eastern part, would then have become a People's Republic.

Yalta and Potsdam conferences

In mid-December 1944, the Russians decided to fix the western Polish border along the line of the rivers Doer and Ness. Soon afterwards they elevated the committee of the Polish Communists to the government of Poland, with its seat at Lublin. By the time of the conference in Yalta, in February 1945, Russian troops had already reached this line, thus cleverly presenting Roosevelt and Churchill with a *fait accompli*. According to Russian plans, this shift of Polish frontiers to the west would have been a compensation for the lands of Eastern Poland, invaded in 1939 as a result of Ribbentropp–Molotov agreement. This plan received a tacit approval from Roosevelt and Churchill, although the final decisions were postponed until the end of the war. It is certainly notable, however, that the Government of Poland, still residing in exile in London, was not once consulted on matters concerning the frontiers of its country at this time.

As was expected, the Potsdam conference, which began on 17 July 1945, ended in complete political victory for Soviet Russia. It approved the Soviet solution for the post-war frontiers of Europe and consigned half of its countries into Soviet overlordship.

The Western allies, surprisingly, also agreed to the Russian method of settling nationality problems, first used in Poland, where about two million people were forcibly removed from their homes and sent to labour camps in Russia. In the same way, Germans east of the Oder-Neisse line, were to be resettled in the new People's Republic of Germany. In Churchill's opinion, this was the only way to bring lasting peace to the region.

Polish Forces disbanded

In 1945, Polish forces numbered 250,000 men, spread between the army, navy and air force. They had fought on all major fronts of the war, in the air over Great Britain and Germany and on the seas and oceans. The Second Army Corps took part in the African and Italian campaigns, ending the last named in liberating the city of Bologna.

The First Corps, with its rear echelons in Great Britain, took part in the invasion of the Continent. Its famous armoured division covered itself in glory at Falaise, while the Parachute Brigade fought with distinction at Arnhem. Ever since the conferences in Tehran and Yalta, every soldier knew that he would have had no country to return to. In spite of that, the soldiers remained loyal to their allies and fought to the last day of the war with their customary bravery.

LEFT: Monument to the Warsaw Uprising, Warsaw.
RIGHT: World War II propaganda.

In 1947, all units of the Polish forces were concentrated in Great Britain, where they were disbanded on the orders of the British Government. A small percentage of men returned to Poland, but the great majority remained in Great Britain to seek civilian employment and start a new life.

No nation throughout the world was to suffer more than Poland in the machinations of World War II. Although Hitler was clearly defeated, he had decimated the population through his racist policies and ethnic cleansing by almost 25 percent, many of the victims being among Poland's brightest and most creative pre-war

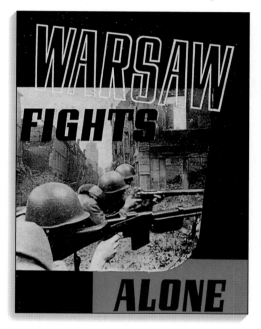

citizens. The cities and landscape were ravaged by war and the evil testaments to Hitler's "Final Solution" still haunt the country dotted with barren and eerie land that once supported his death camps. Stalin, however, far from being defeated, had gained his original aims, shifting the borders of eastern Europe and infiltrating greater areas with his politics.

Poland lost great cities, rural communities and a strong pre-war sense of national identity, despite participating bravely in a war that had begun in its defence by its Allies. It would take many decades of hardship and political struggle before the Polish nation would regain its former strength. ❏

The Concentration Camps

The Russo-German alliance of August 1939, known as the Ribbentrop Molotov pact, had a double purpose. Its most immediate aim was a joint invasion of Poland, whereas its long term purpose was the annihilation of the Polish nation. It was put in operation after the end of the September 1939 campaign on Poland, when the security organisations of both aggressors (Gestapo for

Germany and NKVD for the Soviet Union) had established friendly co-operation. In the autumn of 1939, the Gestapo carried out the first of its mass arrests comprising of people prominent in politics and the arts who were subsequently murdered or sent to concentration camps to await a slower form of death.

To provide for the fast growing number of prisoners, a new concentration camp was established in Poland, near the town of Oświęcim. It became know under its German name of Auschwitz, as the most dreaded "*vernichtungs lager*", or extermination camp in Europe. It was built to provide a killing ground for Poles, but it grew steadily between 1940

and 1945, to accommodate and destroy people of many nationalities. It is calculated that 2 million people perished there, mostly Poles and Jews from all over Europe.

It was the only German concentration camp, which tattooed identity numbers on prisoner's forearms. However, the number of prisoners thus marked did not exceed 200,000. The rest ended up in gas chambers straight from their trains, without being registered. The first test killing by the gas Cyclon B, was carried out in September 1941. After that date, additional gas chambers were constantly constructed. The camp was greatly enlarged by adding new areas near the village of Brzezinka (German Birkenau). The gas chambers of Bitkenau became the central extermination camp, established for the Jews.

On 18th January 1945, the camp was evacuated and 60,000 prisoners were marched on foot, in scanty clothing without food and in the depths of the winter to concentration camps in Germany. Most perished before they reached their destination. Another major concentration camp was built in Poland, near Lublin. At least 1 million people (almost all Poles) died in Majdanek – but it was the name Auschwitz that became a symbol of martyrdom, not only for Poles, but for the mass extermination of countless European Jews.

In the Russian occupied part of Poland, the NKVD began arrests of the "enemies of the people". As in German-occupied Poland, the term embraced people prominent in their professional capacity, with the addition of property owners. In fact, it meant anyone suspicious in the eyes of local NKVD agents, without any reference to their past, social or economic standing. Those arrested were sent to the Russian equivalents of German concentration camps, the so-called "labour camps" in Siberia, where their chances of survival were minimal. Polish prisoners of war were also sent to these camps or *gulags*, with the exception of officers. At the beginning of 1940, the mass deportations of entire families began. It is estimated that 1.5 million adults and children were deported to remote parts of Russia, in what is now known as "ethnic cleansing".

The army officers, taken prisoners of war during the defence of Poland, were imprisoned in three camps: Kozielsk and Ostaszkow near Smolensk and Starobielsk near Kharkov. Their total number in these camps amounted to 15,570. As might be expected, the majority were reserve officers, representing many professions, including 800 medical doctors. All but 448 were all murdered during April 1940, on orders from the Soviet Government.

Two years later, the bodies of officers from Kozielsk camp, were accidentally discovered by German army personnel, in a wood near the village of Katyń. All had been killed with a single pistol shot to the base of the skull. Goebels enthusiastically embraced this golden opportunity for German propaganda.

At the time, it was assumed that all 15,000 were killed there, and Katyń Forest became known as a scene of the greatest single war crime committed in modern history. German forensic authorities established the date of the crime as spring 1940. The Soviet government, however, denied any complicity and, in turn, accused the Germans. It was Germans who were subsequently accused during the Nuremberg war crime trails in 1945 and since adequate proof was lacking, the case against Germany was dropped. This didn't prevent the allied governments from supporting the Soviet version of events, right down to the end of the Soviet State.

It was only after the collapse of the Soviet Union, that the Russian authorities admitted responsibility for the crime and published the relevant orders which originated from the "Politburo", the supreme organ of the Soviet Government, presided over by Stalin himself. Only then it was possible to seek the graves of thousands of missing officers who were not buried at Katyń Forest. Those from Ostaszkow and Starobielsk were found at various sites and in all, 15,000 murdered prisoners of war were finally accounted for. Like Auschwitz in German-occupied Poland, so Katyń Forest became a symbol of the martyrdom suffered by the Poles at the hands of the Russians.

The concentration camp at Treblinka provides one of the most chilling reminders of the Nazi atrocities: the site was strategically

well chosen, about 100 km (60 miles) to the northeast of Warsaw, with its rail terminal linked with the international rail network to Russia. At the junction there was a large supply depot for the German advance to the east. It is almost certain that the two extermination camps, Treblinka I and II, were built along the demarcation line that the German Reich and Russia had drawn through Poland when they divided the country between them. In 1943 when the mass graves of Katyń were accidentally discovered, where Stalin had interred 4,000 Polish officers, the Germans made use of the massacre to their own end.

By then, the military situation had changed.

The Nazis closed the Treblinka camps in November 1943 and obliterated their bloody traces. Before the closure they had committed 2,400 murders per day. Documents were rapidly burned, all possible eye-witnesses were liquidated: the SS literally tried to let grass grow over the horrors they had committed. But their attempts at a cover-up failed – a few dozen eye-witnesses escaped and conveyed the cruel truths about the camps to the rest of the world. In 1964 a commemorative site was inaugurated that tried to do some justice to the human tragedy that this place represents. ❏

LEFT: concentration camp victims.
RIGHT: The site of the crematorium at Treblinka is covered with basalt rocks, melted and fused at 2,000°C (3632°F) to form a memorial to indescribable suffering.

THE COMMUNIST STATE

*The rise of Stalin at the end of World War II saw the whole of Eastern Europe
ruled by the restrictive and often terrifying Communist regime*

When in the summer of 1944 the Soviet army liberated parts of Poland from the German occupying forces, the generals immediately set about installing a Polish Communist administration. That same year the "Manifesto for Progress" appeared with proposals for a new social and economic order. Slogans urged Poles to welcome plans for agrarian reform, the state ownership of industry and a transformation in society, accompanied by justice and democracy. With the strong support of the Soviet army, Polish Communists began establishing a totalitarian dictatorship along Russian lines.

Communists seize power

This "revolution from outside" was not accepted passively by the Poles. Units of the Home Army were still active and considerable forces were needed to put them out of action, As Stalin had no faith in the Polish Communists, he wasted no time in putting Russian secret police in the front line. Their job was to insure the loyalty of the Polish population to Russia and to the Communist party. Those who dissented were either executed or imprisoned. In an atmosphere of terror, the Provisional Government of National Unity was set up. Bolesław Beirut became president and Osóbka-Morawski became prime minister.

Open political opposition to the Communists came mainly from the Polish Populist Party (PSL) with Mikołajczyk, the former prime minister of the government-in-exile, as its head. He garnered support mainly from rural communities and intellectuals. Other independent politicians were systematically isolated. Many were put to death.

For official purposes, the Communists gave the impression that a democratisation process was taking place. Soviet advisers urged their Polish counterparts to promise the end of

LEFT: *Manifest,* a depiction of the issuing of the Polish communist manifesto, by Wojciech Weiss.
RIGHT: an example of Socialist Realist art.

poverty and fear, the prospect of a bright future and a new beginning after the harrowing years of German Occupation.

On 19 January 1947, the long-promised general elections were held. While foreign observers recorded a 60 percent vote in favour of the PSL, the Communist-led "Democratic

Block" were awarded 394 of the 444 parliamentary seats. There followed a wave of mass arrests among the PSL members and Mikołajczyk fled abroad.

Rebuilding the economy

In 1945, the Polish economy lay in ruins. Although the people found themselves living in a new state with geographically favourable and historically acceptable borders, some six million Poles had lost their lives since 1939. A third of the national wealth had gone and two-thirds of its industrial potential had been destroyed. Those areas in the north and west that had seen the expulsion of some 3.5 million

Germans were optimistic about the future, as new arrivals from eastern Polish provinces moved in to take the Germans' places. But here, too, the war had left a bitter legacy: the Russians had dismantled any surviving industrial plants and transported them back to the motherland.

In 1946 all companies were nationalised. As compensation for Poland's properties abroad, the state received some 200 million dollars. But under pressure from Moscow, Poland was not allowed to take advantage of the Marshal Plan

JOINING FORCES

In 1955 Poland became a member of the Warsaw Pact, intended to be the reply to NATO. In 1949 it became a member of COMECON, the Union of Mutual Economic Aid.

tions from Moscow to establish a governing unity party. This was to include the remnants of the Polish Socialist Party (PPS) and the Polish Workers Party (PPR). The pre-Communist Peasant Faction, the United Peoples' Party (ZSL) and the Democratic Faction (SD) were allowed to remain independent but under the auspices of the Communists.

In June 1948, the head of the Polish Communists, Władysław Gomułka, was accused of right-wing nationalist tendencies and spent from 1951 to 1954 in prison. He was

money; the Communists imposed a centralised economy on the country. Private industry and services were abolished in 1947 but, as the new bureaucracy was unable to replace the private sector, the black market flourished. By dint of hard work, the targets set in the 1947 Three Year Plan were met and Poland quickly reached its pre-war per capita income.

The Stalinist era (1948–56)

In 1948 Europe entered the long dark tunnel in its history known as the Cold War. With the blockade of Berlin, the era of Stalinism also began for Poland. In March 1948 the prime minister, Józef Cyrankiewicz, received instruc-

in favour of a "Polish route" to socialism and advocated the maintenance of private property. Some months later, the PPS was incorporated into the Polish United Workers' Party (PZPR). With the approval of Stalin, power passed to the loyal, but incompetent figure of Bolesław Bierut, formerly a member of Comintern.

In the December of 1948 the congress of the PZPR was formed and Beirut was appointed as first secretary. With the embodiment of the pre-eminent role of the PZPR in the new constitution of 22 July 1952, the last chance to establish a democratic society in Poland passed.

Along with the tyranny of PZPR and its front organisation, the hallmarks of Stalinism in

Poland were: the adoption of Marxism-Leninism as an infallible ideology; the amassing of armed forces on a huge scale; centralised economic planning; and concentration on heavy industry. This model was transferred directly from the Soviet Union to all countries of the Eastern bloc and was retained, virtually unchanged, until the end of the 1980s.

Officially the constitution was quite democratic: it guaranteed civil rights and a so-called democratic government elected by parliament with a president and a states council. The parliament itself, the *Sejm*, was voted in by general election. In reality, however, it was little more than a front. The "working people in the city and in rural areas", according to the letter of the constitution nothing less than the true rulers of the country, were only helpless victims of the state. The party alone, the Politburo, the first secretary and the privileged élite of the nomenclature, really wielded all the power. In effect, it was a dictatorship of the party over the people.

The conviction of Stalin and his minions that the Soviet bloc was constantly threatened by an invasion from the "powers of American imperialism" led to the recruitment of an enormous Polish army (400,000 troops). The officers were trained in a Political Military Academy (WAP, founded in 1951).

Top priority was accorded to building up the steel, coal, iron and armaments industries. In order to accommodate the flood of migrant workers from rural areas who were now required to take their places on the production lines, whole new cities and suburbs were built virtually overnight. On the outskirts of Warsaw and in Nowa Huta near Kraków these municipal, architectural monstrosities can still be seen in all their ghastliness. The supply of foodstuffs was largely handed over to the newly established PGRS (national farmsteads – the Polish version of the Russian collective farms), whose gross inefficiency resulted in disastrous consequences for both productivity and quality.

The system's intention was to fashion new, socialist man: in effect that meant the abolition of humanitarian ideals. Political terror and repression reached a climax in 1951. Everyday life became a nightmare. All contacts with the outside world were immediately denounced; in bogus trials innocent people were arbitrarily accused of being spies and sentenced to internment or death. There were also executions without trial (in 1990 mass graves were found dating from this time). Many people were deported to the Soviet Union and simply vanished without trace. A dense network of informers infiltrated factories and offices, the schools and the universities.

The propaganda, of course, told a different story. The news was full of stories about the construction of gigantic collective combines, factories and other buildings, and tales of rising

LEFT: workers' May Day demonstrations in the1940's.
RIGHT: Soviet badges and medals for sale.

CATHOLIC RESISTANCE

The Roman Catholic church was one of the few "organisations" that retained a level of independence against the new Communist regime. It was generally regarded as a reactionary relic of the pre-war system. However, priests and laymen alike were openly attacked and constantly threatened with arrest by the governing forces and by 1950 the financial assets of the church had been confiscated. In 1952, one of the heroes of this frightening era, was Cardinal Stefan Wyszyński, the primate of Poland, who was arrested for his "anti-state" attitudes and was exiled to a monastery where he was kept prisoner for three years.

work quotas. The ever-increasing number of success stories perpetuated the course that Stalinism had planned for the country. Monumental sculptures in the style of socialist realism provided visible proof of the superiority of the new system and its ideology to all who saw them.

And yet in Poland the omnipotence of Stalinism never quite reached the level that it did in other Eastern bloc states. The political trials never developed into a series of propaganda trials. It proved impossible to eradicate the bourgeois and intellectual milieu. The collectivisation of agriculture was carried out slowly and incompletely. Nevertheless, the memory of the Stalinist years was engraved upon the mind of the nation.

Josef Stalin died in March 1953. Within two years the liberalising effect of his death was felt in Poland. In December 1954 the despised Ministry of Public Security was disbanded and the censorship laws relaxed. Władysław Gomułka was released from prison. There was no further talk of collectivisation. The political thaw commenced. In June 1956 worker protests in Poznań, which started with the slogan "bread and liberty", showed that the country needed a new pragmatic party leader whom the people

SOCREALISM

Social Realism – socrealism for short – was the form of visual art allowed by the Communist regime. The object was the veneration of the working class and of its self-appointed leaders. In its pure form, it was characterised by an almost photographic realism, a style which was at odds with the idealism of its message. Typical subjects were workers, happy in their work and communist leaders in Heroic poses heralding the utopia to come – aspirations which were far removed from the brutal realities of the day. The most imposing manifestation of socrealism was in architecture, much of which remains to this day – the Palace of Culture in Warsaw being the supreme example.

This gift of the Soviet Union to Communist Poland is an incongruous mix of concrete tower block and Baroque decoration. Because of its size and the strength of its construction, it is extremely difficult and costly to demolish. It will therefore spoil Warsaw's skyline for some time to come. Houses along the central Marzalkowska street are decorated with large concrete figures of workers. They lead to one of the ugliest modern squares, Plac Konstytucji (Constitution Square), with its pretentious "candelabra" for street lamps. Fortunately, apart from the monstrosity of the Palace of Culture, these excesses of bad taste are too few to spoil the overall beauty of Warsaw.

could trust. This man turned out to be Władysław Gomułka. After Khrushchev had assured himself of his loyalty, the Stalinist era came to an end in Poland.

National Communism (1956–80)

In October 1956 Gomułka managed to free Poland from total control of the Soviet Union, which determined the political life of the nation for the next 25 years. Gomułka was of the opinion that there were "various ways to socialism" and he managed to prove that Polish Communists could look after the affairs of their country on their own account, without having to take

run its priest seminars, its own social and intellectual societies and its own university. It thus became the only really independent church in the whole of the Eastern bloc.

Sociologists who adhered to the party doctrine had prophesied that industrialisation and urbanisation would change the cultural patterns of traditional society and would sever the ties between the people and church. They couldn't have been more wrong. The Polish church did not lose its adherents – on the contrary it turned out to be a place of refuge and the driving force behind the Polish opposition. The same kind of fate befell the collectivisation plans of the agri-

constant instructions from Moscow (Imre Nagy in Hungary was not so lucky).

Gomułka managed to achieve three vital concessions: an independent church, free agriculture and an open political forum. These concessions were designed to be transitional only, until the party had found a firm footing, but matters turned out differently. The church was stronger than ever before. Within the framework of its self-administration, it continued to

LEFT: Khrushchev being greeted at Warsaw Airport by Władysław Gomułka.
ABOVE: Edward Gierek (in centre) removed from power in 1980.

cultural programme. Gomułka had no intention of committing the same errors that had led to the death by starvation of millions of people in the Ukraine 30 years previously. More than 70 percent of the arable land thus remained in private hands, while collective farming was only retained in the areas where it had already been introduced (for example on the huge, former German estates in the west of Poland). The experts did not regard that as a problem. In time, the small, private farms would disappear of their own accord, as the state had other means of making it plain to the farmers that private industry was not worthwhile. In practice that meant granting privileges to the collective sector and neglecting the private sector, measures that ultimately ended in unmitigated disaster for the whole nation.

Within 40 years the government managed to lead the country to the very brink of starvation. Poland, traditionally an agricultural country, was ruined, despite its fertile soil. The population was plagued with food rationing and queuing outside grocers' shops. Nevertheless, private agriculture survived.

As for demands for pluralism, the leadership accommodated those by licensing several political organisations. However, the fact that these were all united under the one roof of the National Union Front – under the patronage of the party – meant that any ideas of pluralism were pure illusion. It soon became clear that neither Gomułka nor his successor, Edward Gierek, backed as they were by a total lack of any constitutionality, were prepared to adhere to the promised concessions. Civil liberties were severely curtailed. Again and again (1968, 1970, 1976 and 1980) dissent broke out. The slogan of the protestors was "bread and liberty". The protests were organised either by labourers or students and intellectuals. They had to be put down forcibly by the government and there were frequent casualties. By this time

BREAKING DOWN THE BARRIER OF FEAR

The protests of March 1968 not only mobilised the students, but also the whole intelligentsia. For the first time the names of several dissidents became well known, including Adam Michnik, Jacek Kuroń and Karol Modzelewski.

Unrest in December 1970 in Gdańsk and Szczecin succeeded in moulding a generation of intransigent and embittered workers. Between 1975 and 1976 the changes in the constitution, which resulted in even greater dependency on the Soviet Union, contributed to the organisation of a national dissident group (Committee of Independent Poland) within the KPN.

In June 1976, when workers in the tractor plant in Ursus and the armaments factory in Radom were punished for their participation in a protest action, intellectuals founded the KOR (Committee to Defend the Workers). For the first time intellectuals and workers were unanimous in pursuing a common goal and from this moment on one could talk of an organised, supranational opposition. The committee worked quite openly (although not legally) as an information and co-ordination centre for the whole country. With the investiture of the cardinal of Kraków, Karol Wojtyla, as Pope in 1978 and his visit to Poland in 1979, the psychological barrier of fear was also destroyed.

there could no longer be any doubt that the government had lost the confidence of the Polish people.

August 1980–December 1981

The organised opposition that emerged in 1980 had a long history that had begun with the student protests of 1968.

In summer 1980 government attempts to implement drastic price increases for foodstuffs and consumer goods caused a wave of public strikes. The epicentre of the protest was in Gdańsk, in the Lenin Shipyard (*see page 335*), whose tradition of resistance went back to

The founding of *Solidarność*

An agreement between the workers and the government was eventually signed on 31 August 1980. As an immediate consequence of this event, representatives of the strike committee from all the provinces of the country formed the national co-ordination committee of the independent, self-administered trade union *Solidarność* known in the west as Solidarity. The 37-year-old Lech Wałęsa was elected chairman. Just a few months later the Farmers' Solidarity (*Solidarność Wiejska*) was permitted as an official organisation.

In the 15 months of its activity Solidarity

December 1970, when workers had been killed during protest action. The KOR members were involved right from the start of the political agitation. Included on the list of 21 demands posed by the strike committee were the right to strike, the right to form independent trade unions and the permission to erect a monument for colleagues who had died in the 1970 uprising. In return the workers declared themselves willing to accept the leading role of the party.

LEFT: with Tadeusz Mazowiecki at his side, Lech Wałęsa holds the first Solidarity press conference in October 1980.
ABOVE: Solidarity in the streets of Warsaw.

proved to be a peaceful reform movement which, with its 10 million members, represented a broad section of the whole nation. It could only defend itself with its own ideals.

Martial law

The rise of Solidarity was viewed with great misgivings in the Soviet Union. However, the leaders of the Kremlin rejected the idea of military intervention. Unlike in the case of Czechoslovakia, it was feared that part of the Polish army, supported by the majority of the population, would actively resist the invasion, embroiling the Soviet Union in a war in Europe, while the Afghan war was still in progress.

In addition, also unlike the Soviet invasion of Czechoslovakia, NATO powers did not declare their total indifference. Taking into account the well proven fighting qualities of the Poles, the risk was too great. Instead, the Head of the Communist Party and the Commander-in-Chief, General Jaruzelski, was ordered to crush Solidarity. On 13 December 1981, he proclaimed martial law and ordered the army to virtually occupy the country. Solidarity was officially abolished and all its leaders, including Lech Wałęsa, were

PAPAL INFLUENCE

Martial law was only lifted in 1983, triggered by the second visit to his homeland by Pope John Paul II.

imprisoned. A wave of repression was put in motion and all remnants of constitutional rights disappeared. The success of martial law in suppressing Solidarity was, however, very short-lived. Its organisation simply went underground.

The entire population now clearly understood that the time for compromises had come and gone. From then on, the only true political division among Poles became between that of "us" (which meant every Pole) and "them" (the Communists in power).

The next few years were characterised by an ever more acute economic crisis. With Solidarity banned, the opposition centred around the Church. It became the only truly independent institution that could afford protection to anyone requiring it. The Church was at the same time a forum for political discussion, meetings, lectures, tuition and the dissemination of illegal literature, publicity and magazines. For all this, its members often paid a heavy price. Fearless Father Popiełuszko was tortured and murdered by members of the security police.

Life was, for the majority of the population, now divided into two spheres: the official, legal, everyday routine and the clandestine, illegal underground. The government proved entirely incapable of coping with the political and economic crisis.

Signs of a deep political crisis were also to be seen in Russia. The new leader in power, Mikhail Gorbachev, who came to the Kremlin during 1985, was only too aware of a progressive weakening of the Soviet grip on Poland but

THE FACE OF SOLIDARITY

Like the TV images of the fall of the Berlin Wall in November 1989, Lech Wałęsa's personality and the Solidarity movement has come to symbolise popular demands for the end of East European communism in the late 1980s.

Awarded the Noble Peace Prize in 1983 for his work on human rights, Wałęsa's political career had humble beginnings. Born in 1943 in Popow, Poland, in the mid-1960s he worked as an electrician in the Lenin Shipyard in Gdańsk. In 1976 he was sacked for anti-government activities but he returned to the shipyard in 1980 to lead a workers' strike demanding better working conditions, the

right to form a trades' union and the right to strike. After most of the 21 demands were met, Solidarity began to represent the national consciousness. New members were drawn from across Polish society and more than 10 million people joined the movement over a year and a half.

When Solidarity won a landslide election victory in 1989 it declared "History has taught us that there is no bread without freedom." When Wałęsa was elected prime minister in 1990, Solidarity stated "What we had in mind was not only bread, butter and sausage but also justice, democracy, truth, legality, human dignity, freedom of convictions, and the repair of the republic."

was no longer able to strengthen it. The Soviet Union for the first time no longer showed any imperialistic tendencies. An invasion, such as had been feared in December 1981, was therefore no longer a realistic possibility by the latter half of the decade.

The collapse of Communism

After a wave of strikes in the spring of 1988, the Communist Party agreed to share political power. After "round table" talks were held to discuss basic political, social and economic reforms and an agreement was signed on 5 April 1989, in which party and representa-

Solidarity movement won almost every seat it contested. Ultimately, Tadeusz Mazowiecki was entrusted with the task of forming the new government. A journalist by profession, he had already acquired authority as the editor-in-chief of the *Tygodnik Solidarność* in 1980–81 and, later, during his imprisonment, he had enjoyed popular esteem. The PZPR dissolved in January 1990 and Polish Communism was dead.

The events in Poland led to the collapse of Communism in Europe as a whole. What had begun with a wave of strikes in the spring of 1988 had resulted in general unrest; the Communist party had lost its power and was soon to

tives from the Solidarity movement specified their conditions. These included legalisation of Solidarity, the right to a free press and elected seats in parliament. The path towards democracy had finally been laid.

For the elections, Solidarity founded citizen committees to represent the opposition. Even during the "round table" talks, the Communist Party had reserved the right to form the government. But in the election of June 1989 the Communists were so soundly thrashed that any attempt to do so would have failed. The

LEFT TO RIGHT: key players: Father Jerzy Popiełusko; Lech Wałęsa and General W. Jaruzelski.

disappear altogether. Other Eastern bloc countries were quick to follow the example set by Solidarity and the process became unstoppable. It eventually led to the fall of Communism in the Soviet Union.

Twenty years later, in 1999, Poland became a member of NATO. By this act, Poland returned to its 1,000-year-old historical role. In this role, the country provided a shield to Europe, defending it from Tartars, Turks, Cossacks and from invasions of the semi-barbaric Grand Duchy of Muscovy. The shield was broken in the 18th century, with calamitous consequences, not only to Poland, but to many other nations. ❏

POST-COMMUNIST POLAND

Adapting to a free society and economy has not been as smooth as some Poles might have hoped, but, 10 years on, the country is emerging from the mire

In July 1997, the NATO (North Atlantic Treaty Organization) summit in Madrid offered Poland, Hungary and the Czech Republic membership of the western military alliance. After the conference, the US president Bill Clinton paid a state visit to Warsaw, where he urged tens of thousands of Poles to continue with the programme of reforms. Of the countries on the list of possible new European Union members, Poland is right at the top. Investment managers in the west see the country as an attractive proposition with good potential for growth.

The road to a market economy

At the beginning of the 1990s, visitors to Poland were greeted by a bizarre sight: between the city's three largest department stores (built in the 1970s as symbols of a new attitude towards consumerism) and outside the vast Palace of Culture, thousands of people were out on the streets buying and selling consumer articles of every conceivable kind. People wanted not the goods on the shelves in the shops, but those laid out on the pavements. The atmosphere amid the drab landscape of central Warsaw was more akin to that of an Oriental bazaar.

From cassettes and bananas to ladies' underwear and Lacoste tops, the booty from weekends in Berlin or trips to Turkey – anything that would sell – was spread out on blankets, if not on the ground then on the bonnet of the ubiquitous Polski Fiat 126P. The Poles were doing what they have often had to do at times of crisis: putting into practice the skills of survival, essential during this difficult period of transition to a market economy.

Prices of basic goods were rising faster than wages. In August 1989, the government lifted price restrictions and the price of a kilo of butter rose within a year from 1,000 to an astonishing 10,000 złoty. Unprofitable companies were

LEFT: the communist reforms created a new class of dispossessed.
RIGHT: first steps towards a market economy.

closed down, putting thousands of people out of work almost overnight and presenting families with severe financial difficulties. For many, street trading of almost any goods they had access to was the only way of obtaining income to continue to feed their families and pay the rent on their homes.

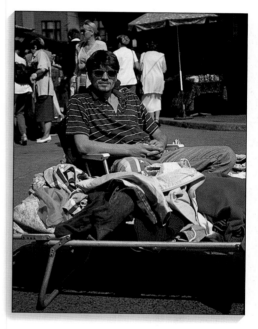

Root and branch reform

The country has undergone a dramatic transformation within only a few years, as a quick look back at history will reveal. The new government, the first freely elected non-Communist leadership in a Warsaw Pact state, took office on 12 September 1989.

The cabinet, consisting of both Communists and democrats, had to face up to some extremely serious problems: the political reorganisation of the state, a revival of democracy and political and social pluralism, armed defences, not to mention the avoidance of an impending economic collapse. Their solution was not helped by the absence of people used to high office of government. Those who governed the Peoples' Republic had simply been carrying out orders from Moscow. Since they also took part in the government of Free Poland, the attitude of the population remained highly suspicious and reserved, which manifested itself in low turnouts for elections. The first elected prime minister, Tadeusz Mazowiecki, took great pride in the fact that the revolution in Poland had been bloodless, unlike in other countries of the Soviet block. Whatever the merits or demerits of this kind of revolution, the retention of former Communists in government bodies did not add to public confidence in the new ruling party.

However, the first coalition government was quite clear in its goals and plans for reform. It also saw its principal foreign policy goal as making approaches towards integration with the west. It wanted Poland to withdraw from the Soviet-oriented group of Communist nations known as COMECON (Council for Mutual Economic Aid) and the Warsaw Pact and to become an associate member of the EU.

Domestic politics

Other far-reaching plans proposed by the Polish reform government have not yet been implemented. The new constitution, for example, has

THE POST-COMMUNIST REFORMS

The most important parts of the reform programme were:
- reform of the legal system, including a new constitution
- establishment of local administrations
- separation of the police force from the security services and the army
- abolition of censorship
- independent trade unions, freedom of opinion and religious denomination, equal rights for minority groups
- restructuring the education and health systems
- measures to protect the environment
- new regulations regarding property ownership (privatisation of state-run companies).

The minister of finance, Balcerowicz, began implementing a drastic economic reform programme which proposed:
- limiting subsidies to producers
- tightening up tax administration
- drastically raising the prices of important supplies
- making major cuts in public expenditure
- limiting pay rises to nationally-imposed percentages and enforcing these limits with penalties
- widening goods with no price controls by 90 percent. These measures proved successful in bringing down the inflation rate to below 10 percent and the złoty became the first freely convertible currency within COMECON.

still to be passed by parliament. A "minor constitution", passed in 1992, remains valid, but it is based on the old Communist constitution. The long-overdue proposals for decentralisation are still eagerly awaited.

For many, the victory of the old cadres in the elections of 1993 was an unexpected and worrying development. As in other former Eastern Bloc states, after four Solidarity-led governments – all of which had difficulty implementing their policies when there were as many as 29 different parties represented in the *Sejm* – the voters chose to elect the reformed Communists (SLD), the successors to the reviled

The coalition government of 1995

The third government to be formed after the restoration of true democratic control was an alliance between the Democratic Left Alliance (SLD) and the Polish Peasants' Party (PSL). On 1 March 1995, Jósef Oleksy, a former senior Communist party official, was elected prime minister. The dominance of the Communist old guard was further reinforced by the narrow victory in the 1995 presidential elections of Aleksander Kwaśniewski, a former Communist minister (but now no longer affiliated to any party), after a hard-fought battle with the previous president, Lech Wałęsa.

Communist Party. They increased their number of parliamentary seats from 60 (in 1991) to 171.

There are many reasons why this party became the strongest faction within the *Sejm*. Given the great economic changes, many Poles simply forgot about the political patronage and economic misery that the Polish Communist Party had presided over. Many looked back wistfully to the days of state-guaranteed employment and the harmonious interpersonal relations that they as workers once enjoyed.

LEFT: the traditional form of the market economy.
ABOVE: the *Sejm*, Polish Parliament, in session.

PRIVATISATION

On 1 December 1994, the long-delayed process of privatising 444 large- and medium-sized state-run companies began. Some 60 percent of these companies' capital was to be administered by 15 national investment funds, 15 percent to be distributed to employees. The first major wave of privatisations took place in November 1995. Every adult Pole was able to purchase a share certificate for 36 złoty from more than 500 companies involved in the mass privatisation programme. The development of the private sector has proved fast and successful. Resilience and hard work have paid off in economic near-miracles.

The Polish Peasants' Party, the SLD's coalition partner, a satellite of the ruling Communist party in the pre-1989 era, draws its strength from the fact that 30 percent of the Polish population still live from the land. The new government was able to benefit from the achievements of the previous administration, which between 1989 and 1993 had pointed the country firmly in the direction of democracy and market economics. The economy, which by now had virtually freed itself from political

NEIGHBOURLY RELATIONS

With the recognition of the Oder-Neisse line – awaited for 45 years – a new chapter has opened in the history of German-Polish relations. It is hoped that this will lead to an amicable co-existence.

interference, had been boosted by a six percent growth in Gross Domestic Product.

Critical voices can still be heard. Reforms to pensions and the bureaucracy are still awaited. Business people are also complaining that privatisation plans are too slow. Other parties are horrified by the return of the old political cadres especially in small towns. For decades these functionaries wielded unchallenged power; the comrades are taking their time to learn the new democratic rules. Parliamentary elections held in September 1997 gave the Solidarity Electoral Action alliance (AWS) more seats than their former Communist rivals and in October Jerzy Buzek was appointed prime minister.

Looking to the future

Unquestionably, however, the first 10 years of independence have resulted in enormous progress in all areas of political, social and economic life. Inflation has been reduced to figures comparable with Western Europe and stands at the end of the century at slightly above five percent. Privatisation reforms are on the whole successful (as one English woman living in Warsaw claimed: "where else would you find new shops of all kinds opening every week? Where else would you see new buildings of great architectural merit springing up in the centre of town almost overnight?").

Heavy industry, which was developed to gigantic proportions to satisfy the needs of the Soviet Union, is gradually being reduced and restructured. Craftsmanship, systematically destroyed under Communism, is being given the opportunity to develop again. The process of recovery in all areas is, of necessity, slower than people anticipated, but most of the early expectations – full employment, agricultural wealth, equal wages with the west – proved unattainable in their utopian ideals.

Of all the institutions existing under the Communist regime, the armed forces were subjected to the strictest political control. As their commanders repeated with pride, the armed forces were "the military fist of the Party". At the threshold of independence, Poland's armed forces were, strictly speaking, not her own. Ten years on, they reverted to their true role as defenders of the Republic. However, their equipment remains out of date and of Russian origin. To re-equip them will be a long and costly process.

As far as full economic integration with Europe is concerned, it is expected that Poland will become a member of the European Union in 2002. This event will finally put an end to the political and economic isolation of the country, caused by her subjugation to the Soviet conquest in 1945. ❑

LEFT: badge showing Aleksander Kwásniewski (Communist President of Poland) with the caption "I didn't vote for him".
RIGHT: a reflection of old and new in Warsaw.

THE POLISH PEOPLE

Despite the centuries of foreign rule, the Polish people have maintained a strong identity and welcome visitors with lavish hospitality

*How long, O God, shall men be ridden down,
And trampled under by the last and least
Of men? The heart of Poland hath not ceased
To quiver, tho' her sacred blood doth drown
The fields, and out of every smouldering town
Cries to Thee, lest brute Power be increased
Till that o'ergrown Barbarian in the East
Transgress his ample bound to some new
crown: –
Cries to Thee, "Lord, how long shall these
things be?
How long this icy-hearted Muscovite
Oppress the region? Us, O Just and Good,
Forgive, who smiled when she was torn in
three;
Us, who stand now, when we should aid the
right –
A matter to be wept with tears of blood!"*

These lines by Alfred Lord Tennyson, written in 1833 after the Russians had invaded Poland, eloquently express a theme that runs through Polish history. In 1774 the English statesman Edmund Burke referred to Russia's aggressive designs by saying: "Poland was but a breakfast." And in 1794 the poet Samuel Taylor Coleridge wrote: "Poor Poland! They go on sadly there."

Although few people would doubt that Poland's geography is the main reason for its historical problems, a close analysis of the location of Polish land would indicate that the open plain from the east to the west was a perfect platform for the migrations of different groups of people. This resulted in an exchange of cultures, rapid progress and an equal amount of trouble.

On the other hand, rivers flowing to the Baltic Sea would become, in the history of the country, the main factor speeding the cultural, economical and political development of this first democracy in modern Europe.

PRECEDING PAGES: under Zygmunt Column in Warsaw.
LEFT: sitting for a portrait in Gdańsk.
RIGHT: feeding the pigeons in Gdańsk.

The history of the people

The first written information about Poland survives from AD 965, from letters of a Moorish Jew from Spain, Ibrahim–Ibn-Jakub. They talk of very fertile land ruled by Prince Mieszko I. Ethnographers and archaeologists have since found on this land signs of the presence of

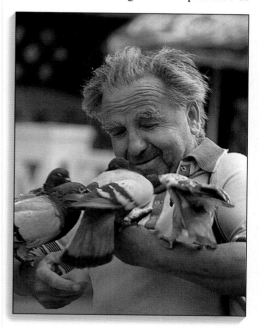

Laplanders and Celtic tribes, which established the foundations for the city of Kraków. One of the first of the major aggressors to Polish territory came from the southeast, from Huns, who in the 5th century BC plundered the land.

Mieszko I baptised the country in AD 996, more as a political than a religious act, which brought Poland to the Christendom of western Europe. His son Bolesław I went further in this incorporation and became the first king of Poland in 1025, to the great irritation of his German neighbours (*see page 21*). Polish land was fertile and rich, with its rivers flowing into the Baltic full of yellow "gold of the north" – amber – and, even more important in the years to come, wheat. Consequently, the country was the object of occasional attacks from its western neighbours, the Germans. The first capital city, Gniezno, was established in the western province of the country, Greater Poland, but as of the 11th century, Kraków's role as a capital city began to grow (*see page 22*).

Tragic in its consequences had been the act of inviting the Order of the Teutonic Knights to establish themselves in Poland, issued by the Duke Konrad of Mazowsze (*see page 22*). The militant order brought for two centuries destruction and misery to the whole country. The Piast family, who ruled the country for the whole of the early period of its formation, never managed to combat the German Order. Nor did Casmir the Great, the first to build solid foundations to the Polish legislation and give freedom and privileges to minorities. "He found Poland made of wood," the saying goes, "and left it made of stone".

Especially prosperous was the period of the Jagiellonian dynasty, beginning with Władsław Jagiełło, a Lithuanian Prince who became Polish King in 1386. He refounded Jagiellonian University in 1400 and won the battle of Grundwald in 1410 that eventually led to the end of Teutonic era in Poland (*see page 22*).

LAND OF RELIGIOUS TOLERANCE

Poland in the Middle Ages has a far less brutal history than many other European countries. When Polish Jews were obtaining their Statute of Jewish Liberties at Kalish, the rest of Europe in 1265 was engulfed in religious wars and later in the Holy Inquisition. Monks from all over Europe came here to practise their religion; the Convent of Cistercian Brothers had a tremendous input into the growth of Poland's wealth. From countries torn by religious wars and reformation, waves of Huguenots, Protestants, Jews, Hussites, and members of the Orthodox church all came to Poland, where they lived in unison under the watchful eye of the Polish rulers.

Fertile land, the economic wealth of its citizens, especially from the 14th–17th centuries and religious tolerance appealed to the greedy neighbours as much as to the oppressed religious and ethnic minorities from all over Europe. The thriving economy and liberal attitudes, unique in Europe, also made Poland and its 16th-century democracy very attractive to the royal courts of Europe. They longed to have their sons elected as kings and to have them on the Polish throne.

However, the power and untamed prosperity of the Polish nobility and aristocrats, and the abuse of democracy through "Liberum Veto", severely undermined the strength of the country. The 18th century saw the decline of Poland's political strength and in 1772, the first partition took place when the Austro-Hungarian Empire, Prussia and Russia divided the country among themselves (*see page 30*). They did so in 1793 and again in 1795. For 125 years, Poland was deprived of full sovereignty.

Patriotic nation

But the indefatigable spirit of Polish national feeling has been ever present and has led to exceptional accomplishments in arts, music, science, culture, the civilisation of Europe and indeed the world. These many achievements

leaders and heroes over the past two centuries.

Tadeusz Kościuszko, who fought against the English as a general of George Washington and later led the uprising of his people against the Russians, used these words (*see page 31*). They turn up again in the speeches of Józef Piłsudski, who commanded the forces of the young country at the "Miracle of the Vistula".

This so-called "miracle" occurred when the Soviet army was defeated and forced to abandon its attempt to advance into central European territory through the open Polish plains, which for centuries had been the route of Western expansion of Russian regimes (*see*

prevailed for the 125 years of political and formal nonexistence of the country. Names such as Frédéric Chopin (composer), Adam Mickiewicz (poet), Maria Sklodowska (Curie scientist), Henryk Sienkiewicz and Joseph Conrad (writers) and many others are connected with this period of Polish history. Patriotism was always very present in their lives.

The Poles, when attacked, have always stood up to their aggressors. The sentence "*Nie damy sie!*" ("We will not give in!") has been repeated in countless great speeches by the country's

page 29). The battle and the whole war of 1921 is now generally considered as one of the most historically significant of all European wars, for it stopped the Soviet expansion in its tracks and changed the course of history.

Finally, these same words are inseparably linked with the figure of Lech Wałęsa, the workers' leader from Gdańsk who played a crucial part in the defeat of the Communist regime in the Solidarity Movement of the 1980s (*see page 63*). "We will not give in!" The Poles have always had plenty of reason to express their defiance with this rousing declaration. It has lost none of its significance today, nor is it likely to do so in the future.

LEFT: horse and carriage Warsaw Old Town Square.
ABOVE: violin player in traditional costume.

Troublesome neighbours

The geographical position of Poland has often caused political problems: to the west they have the Germans as neighbours, to the east the Russians. In their relationship to both countries, military conflict has historically played a much more prominent part than peaceful coexistence. And, as a result, the three countries have seldom a good word to say about one another. The Russians generally find their neighbours unreliable and much too happy-go-lucky for their liking. In

MILITARY DISDAIN

Bismarck's opinion of Poland was as uncompromising at its other neighbours: "The Pole has to be beaten until he loses heart" he is said to have remarked.

the Polish Legion under the leadership of Józef Piłsudski who was the spiritual and military leader of Poland of that period, and from 1926 the political leader as well (*see page 38*).

Poland in the early 20th century cultivated an intellectual class of society unique for Europe at the time, which was given the task of rebuilding the country after more than 120 years of oppression. This intellectual force was used by Allied forces in World War II, when Polish mathematicians cracked the German

German "Polish economy" is an expression denoting a shambles. To the Prussians in particular, with their authoritarian state, their dynamism and their moral code which frowned on every kind of instinctive behaviour, Poland was not merely a mystery, but a positive horror. In 1814, a Prussian field marshal wrote to Baron Von Stein: "Disorder and a life of chaos is the Pole's element. No – these people deserve to be trodden underfoot!"

The Treaty of Versailles in 1918 included Polish delegation in peace talks as a representation of a sovereign state. The 11th November became and still is Polish Independence Day, commemorating the re-entering into Warsaw of

encoder Enigma. However, the internal stability of the state was constantly under threat from Greater Poland's nationalism on one hand and separatist resistance on the other.

Caught in the middle

The liberal attitude of past governments of Poland was tarnished during this era of nationalistic movements in Europe by the Polish National Democratic party, who believed in the Jews' collaboration with the Soviet Union against the interest of Poland. Weak Poland was again a target to the expansion policy, this time of Hitler's Germany and Stalin's Russia. After a secret agreement with Soviets in August

1939, Hitler attacked Poland on 1st September. Left to her own devices, abandoned by France and England, the Polish Army fought the war until 2 October when the last of the Polish strongpoints succumbed to German power.

The long five years of war still evoke very strong emotions and opinions in Poland today. The Nazis applied without mercy their propaganda and philosophy of prejudices and racism to Poland. When they occupied the country, they established a reign of brutality and cruelty that cannot be forgotten.

The nation was fighting. Several thousand Polish soldiers and officers through Hungary and Romania, under General Sikorski, re-created the Polish Forces, which fought throughout the war together with the British Army, the Royal Air Force and the Royal Navy. Polish pilots fought in the Battle for Britain and their courage became legendary. In Poland itself, the Home Army (*Armia Krajowa*) fought an underground war with the occupants. The Polish government-in-exile in London was the co-ordinator and the organiser of the Polish Resistance. Crucial information such as facts of existence of Holocaust, V-1 and V-2 missiles and information about the German defence of Atlantic, were obtained and passed on to London by the AK.

One cannot forget that Poland at the beginning of the war was also occupied by Russians. Massive deportations to Siberia of Polish soldiers and civilians took place, especially in 1940 – about 300,000 people were sent to camps and 10,000 imprisoned Polish officers were among the many Poles murdered, each with a single gunshot. When Stalin changed Allies, he permitted the creation of a Polish army in the Soviet Union and allowed her to leave Soviet territory. Through the Middle East this army, under the command of General Anders, fought in the battle of Tobrouque. In 1944 in Italy they conquered the monastery of Monte Cassino, converted by the Germans into a fortress.

Warsaw particularly remembers the two uprisings that took place during the years of the German Occupation. One in 1943 in Warsaw's ghetto, where the Germans had barricaded within just a few streets hundreds of thousands of Jews, condemning them to death if not from brutal killing then from hunger and disease (*see page 40*). From here and from all over Europe, Jews were transported to concentration camps. The most horrific of them all was Auschwitz–Birkenau, in which Poles, gypsies, but mostly Jews were murdered in specially designed gas chambers (*see page 54*). Reparations against

> ### STRANGER THAN FICTION
>
> The Polish underground informed the Americans and British about the Holocaust, but the report of Jan Karski was thought to be too horrific to be believable.

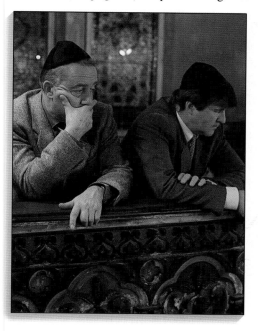

the Poles for helping the Jews were the worst in Europe, with whole families being wiped out. In Yad Vashem memorial park in Jerusalem, many trees planted have been planted by Polish heroes who helped save Polish Jews, in memory of those who did not survive.

In 1944, as the Soviet Army approached Warsaw and the end of war was inevitable, the Polish resistance began the Warsaw uprising. It lasted 63 days, and the Soviets watched the flower of Polish youth and the whole of Warsaw bleed in order to state Polish will and their right of self-determination and sovereignty (*see page 51*). During the 50 years of Soviet Occupation after the war, the fear of this same

LEFT: World War II veterans in Gdańsk.
RIGHT: synagogue in Kraków.

attitude prevented the occupying force from implementing military interventions in 1956 and 1981, when Poland again stood up against the foreign presence on its soil.

The final Soviet offensive against the German army started from Wisla valley in January 1945. The new partitioning of Poland began, this time with only Russian participation. What the Germans and war did not destroy, Soviets did, by robbing and burning.

Western regions and Upper Silisia were

> **PROPAGANDA TACTICS**
>
> Propaganda directed by the NKWD, the Soviet secret service, began its reign in Poland after World War II. Using methods of the KGB, the regime imposed Soviet ideals.

numbered 3.3 million, the Belorussians, of whom there were 1½ million, and a total of 500,000 Lithuanians and Germans. With such a mixed ethnic structure, potential conflicts could have arisen, but the government never took advantage of the Constitution of 3 May. Demographic boom, agricultural reform, idealism of popular democracy carried Poland through the post-war years.

The new Poland within the borders established at the conferences of Yalta and Potsdam

returned to Poland due of the agreements with Stalin and western governments. The Soviets spared this territory, counting on it being a future supply centre for steel and coal. As Polish borders shifted, Poland lost important centres of culture such as Wilno in Lithuania and Lwów in Ukraine (*see page 43*).

Multinational state

The Second Republic of Poland (1918–39) was a multinational state: out of 35 million inhabitants, only 24 million were of Polish origin. After the Poles came the Ukrainians, of whom there were an estimated five to seven million. They were followed by the Jews, who

was to be an ethnically homogeneous state free from conflict between different nationalities. Its borders were pushed westwards and the non-Polish inhabitants inside these new boundaries were to be resettled. It soon became apparent, however, that the alteration of the borders and the mass resettlements under the pompous name of repatriation did not heal old wounds, but inflicted newer, more painful ones.

Added to this was an atmosphere of hostility between the individual nationalities that were all reproaching each other for their behaviour during the war. The Ukrainians were accused of having collaborated with the Gestapo, the Belorussians of having sympathised with

Stalin's secret service, and the Poles of having blackmailed the Jews and denounced them to the Germans. There was no mention of the fact that it was often only individuals who had been guilty of such behaviour and the prejudices were merely fuelled by the propaganda of the nationalists from each group.

Ukrainians

Although the Polish eastern border had been moved westwards, some 700,000 Ukrainians remained in Poland. Some of them moved to

ANNUAL REUNION

In Bieszczady the Ukrainians hold hikes and integration meetings lasting several days to keep national consciousness alive.

doxical result is that the administrative regions of Wrocław, Szczecin, Koszalin and Olsztyn are now the main centres of the Ukrainian population in Poland.

Today there are around 300,000 Ukrainians living in Poland. They have only one primary school (in Biały Bór/ Koszalin), where the children are taught in Ukrainian, and two high schools (in Legnica and Goróv Ilawecki), where, although the children are taught in Polish, Ukrainian is also incorporated into the timetable. The Department of Ukrain-

the Ukrainian Socialist Soviet Republic, but many refused to leave their homeland. In southeast Poland, a war broke out between the Polish militia and the pro-German UPA (Ukrainian Army of the Uprising). In 1947, the Polish authorities decided to distribute the remaining 200,000 Ukrainians over the whole country.

What this meant in practice, however, was resettlement in that part of the country that had formerly been eastern Germany, since it was the only area where there were still unoccupied farms, abandoned by the Germans. The para-

LEFT: players in a traditional music festival.
ABOVE: colourful folk costumes.

ian Studies at Warsaw University enrols only a few students each year. The only museum dedicated to Ukrainian culture, in a wooden hut in the small village of Zyndranowa near Dukla (Krosna wojewodztwa), was founded by a private individual, Teodor Gocz, although it was officially prohibited. The Ukrainian churches around Przemyśl and Krosno were either handed over to the Catholic Church, and in the process stripped of all signs of their past, or they were allowed to fall into disrepair.

There is one Ukrainian language newspaper, *Nasze Slowo*. One established event is the Festival of Ukrainian Culture which takes place in alternate years in Sopot and brings together

Ukrainian choirs, music ensembles and dance groups. The most famous of these are Zurawie, composed of Ukrainians from all over Poland, Poloniny from Legnica and Lemkowie from Bielanka near Gorlice.

Lithuanians and Belorussians

Fate was kinder to the Lithuanians and the Belorussians. The several thousand Lithuanians who lived around Suwałki on the Lithuanian border were left more or less alone after World War II. In Puńsk there is a primary school and a high school, several folk ensembles and an ethnographical museum, and the Lithuanian

political party to represent an ethnic minority, is now attempting to counteract this development. The Orthodox Church assists it in this aim. The Holy Mount of Grabarka near Siemiatycze has again become very important as a shrine for Belorussians and other Orthodox believers. At the festival of Corpus Christi the Belorussians make a pilgrimage to the summit of the mountain with penitential crosses on their backs. These are later set in the ground next to the church; there are already tens of thousand of crosses there. In June 1990, however, the church was plundered and set on fire, but the perpetrators were never identified.

Social and Cultural Society has its national headquarters in Sejny. Of the over 200,000 Belorussians who were still in Poland after the war, 36,000 had resettlement forced on them. Those who remained in the country lived in concentrated groups in their home villages and towns in the area of Białystok, Bielsk Podlaski and Hajnówka. In spite of this, the Belorussians are one of the best integrated of Polish minorities. As they have a relatively good social position, participate in local government, and the number of Belorussian schools is on the decrease, their national consciousness is weakening. The Belorussian Democratic Union, which was founded in 1990 and is the first

Germans

The situation on the western border of Poland has always been quite different from that in the east. At the Potsdam Conference it was decided that the Germans should be resettled. Some had already fled from the advancing Red Army and a Polish army eager for vengeance, but about 4.4 million remained. They were systematically driven out of their houses and marched in columns to the border.

On 13 November 1945, a Ministry for Regained Territory was established by the Polish government and this set up a citizens army which had the power to carry out arrests, transported Germans to labour camps, confiscated property and handed over German homes to Polish people. In 1970, the signing of the Warsaw Treaty heralded a return to normal relations between Poland and the Federal Republic, and five years later an emigration agreement came into force. In return for the payment of DM2.3 billion, at least 125,000 Germans were officially allowed to leave Poland. In fact, between 1976 and 1989 some 770,000 Germans were granted visas to leave.

In 1989 after the fall of the Communist

BURYING DIFFERENCES

Sympathy from the Germans towards the Poles emerged after the imposition of military rule at the end of 1981, when the West Germans sent millions of aid packages to the crippled country.

ment officially recognised the Oder-Neisse line, which helped to dissipate the Polish sense of insecurity. The German-Polish Co-operation Treaty, signed in 1991, consolidated the rights of the German minority in Poland.

On St Annaberg, a mountain that is considered holy by both Poles and Germans, mass is now also read in German; it is now perfectly legal to attend German classes and new music ensembles and choirs have been founded. The Social and Cultural Association of the German

regime, nationalistic prejudices flourished, mainly on the part of the Poles, who had undergone years of indoctrination and been presented with countless distorted versions of history, but also on the part of the German minority. The government of Tadeusz Mazowiecki sought to strike a balance. Soon after coming to office, he introduced legislation that abolished any discriminatory rules and regulations and sought to educate the population.

In 1990, the new, unified German govern-

minority has established its headquarters in Gogolin and in Katowice the regional television programmes are broadcast in German. In Kemielnica/Himmelwitz the first sign in German has appeared in a bar, and the letterbox also bears a German sign. The German minority is concentrated around Strzelce Opolskie/Gross-Strehlitz, Głogówek/Oberglogau, Gogolin and Krapkowice/Krappitz. Krapkowice is the home of Henryk Król, the leader of the German minority party which now has five deputies in the Warsaw parliament. His party is guaranteed seats in the *Sejm*, even if it does not achieve the five percent share of the vote that the other smaller, countrywide parties must obtain.

LEFT: pilgrims at the Jasna Góra shrine in Częstochowa, Małopolska for the Feast of the Assumption.
ABOVE: sharing a beer together.

A question of identity

When the Soviet Union fell apart in the early 1990s, the old argument was resumed about whether Poland belonged culturally and politically to the east or the west. What the Poles have in common with the east – the Russians, the Belorussians and Ukrainians – is that they are also a Slavic people. What has bound them to the west throughout their history and still keeps them firmly linked to this half of Europe is western culture – the Renaissance and the Enlightenment, and religious faith, which they share with many western European countries.

The Lithuanians demanded a guarantee that their capital city Vilnius would not be annexed again as it had been in 1920 under Marshal Piłsudski, who had pushed the border of Poland further east to absorb chunks of Belorussian and Ukrainian territory. And the Ukrainians asked what justification Piłsudski, a figure who is incidentally greatly admired by the workers' leader Lech Wałęsa, had had when he led a Polish army of invasion into their capital, Kiev, in 1920.

In Czechoslovakia the people had not forgotten that after the Munich Dictate that gave Hitler Sudetenland, the Poles took advantage

When the debris of the Communist system had been cleared away, however, the old hostilities between the Poles and their neighbours were shown to be still very much alive. It was not only the relationship between the Poles and the Germans that was troubled again by the emotions of the past: Lithuania, Belorussia, the Ukraine and Czechoslovakia also brought up old grudges they had against the country.

Some of the issues are not that old. At last, it was possible to talk not only about past German dealings with Silesia, Pomerania, West and East Prussia, but also the expulsion of the Germans from Poland after the war and the fate of the German minority.

of the situation to get a share of the land themselves and invaded a part of Bohemia.

The Poles were confronted with the fact that they still had to come to terms with much of their past, and were eventually forced into acknowledging that in their conflicts with their neighbours, even those that had taken place this century, they had not always been the victims.

Looking forward

With respect to minorities, the Polish government has adopted camouflage tactics right from the beginning in the post-war period. It was as if, failing to grasp the true facts of the situation, the government was taken in by its own propaganda that glorified a "homogeneous Poland". The annual statistics contained no information about minorities, since the powers-that-be proceeded according to the assumption that if something is not mentioned then it does not exist.

The minorities themselves, whose insecurity was compounded by the ambivalent attitude of the Catholic Church, could only take this as a declaration of war and thus refused to co-operate with a state that was highly suspicious of independent cultural activities of any kind. The constitution of 1952 – on paper perfectly democratic – guaranteed the minorities equal

forced for decades was one of the reasons why, after the change of government in 1989, only the German minority showed any interest in putting forward candidates for election and the minorities in general did not take the opportunity to secure representation in local government. There are already signs that this was a big mistake, since, as has often happened during crises in the past, strong nationalistic tendencies are again making their appearance in parts of Poland.

This time, however, they are not the result of encouragement from above, but are being generated by the discontent of the middle classes.

rights in every respect. In practice, however, the aim of this totalitarian state was "polonisation" and the uprooting of the other nationalities. The state executive bodies interpreted the constitution to suit themselves. In the face of such despotism every attempt on the part of a minority group to preserve and develop its culture naturally came up against numerous bureaucratic obstacles.

The mutual mistrust that had been thus rein-

LEFT: freedom of choice: choosing rings in the market at Kazimierz Dolny.
ABOVE: young people in Poland, as in the rest of Europe, catch on to trends quickly.

In his inaugural speech in September 1989 the first Prime Minister of a democratic Poland, Tadeusz Mazowiecki, said: "Poland is our homeland, but it does not belong only to Poles. We share this country with people of other nationalities. It is our wish that they should feel at home here, keep their own languages alive and enrich our community with their culture."

However, like people of their age everywhere else in the world, Poland's younger generation is not interested in carrying on the conflicts and arguments of yesterday. For years, both the culture and political values of the west have become increasingly familiar to Poles, and increasingly attractive. ❏

LIFE IN RURAL POLAND

More than a quarter of the population works on the land and many people
maintain their traditional customs and way of life

The airline stewardess announces: "We have just flown over the Polish border," and all heads turn to look out of the window. Far below, the landscape is gradually turning into a colourful mosaic and the first impression is of a country totally different in appearance from its western neighbours.

The fantastic, brightly coloured carpet of small fields and meadows is what the new visitor to Poland notices first. If a weaver had taken all the colours available and put them together at random to make a rug, the effect would not be very different: there is the yellow of the rape crop, the ochre-coloured fields of wheat and rye, and dark green squares of bushy-topped potatoes. Narrow strips of land are separated from one another, and hardly any of the farmers have more than one diminutive field to till.

A further surprise is the number of trees lining the roads. Such avenues are all too rare elsewhere in Europe, where "efficient" agriculture has had them felled; here they have been preserved, providing a bright green border along the way.

The rural landscape

Poland's landscape is one of almost endless greenery, with many shades of forests, woods, fields and meadows. There are six different determined types of landscapes in Poland which fall into six parallel belts: the Baltic lowlands, the lake district, the central lowlands, uplands, the sub-Carpathian depression and mountain regions. The central Polish plains are the most agricultural area of the country, with a specific charm of their own. The landscape here is enlivened by isolated hills, dune embankments and the wide valleys of the largest Polish rivers, the Vistula, Oder, Warta and Bug.

Rural Poland, however, now has a modern appearance in some places, with large, mech-

anised farms, yet in other areas it still recalls the 19th century. The west and northwest regions (Wielkopolska, Pomerania, Kashubia) in particular bear the imprint of the German and Prussian presence (*see page 30*).

The villages vary in appearance as well. In the west the houses are large, wide and built

from stone. In Mazuria they are smaller and sometimes thatched. The eastern provinces still sport thatched wooden cottages. In the mountains they are built of wood with stone foundations and a pointed roof to deal with heavy snowfalls. Zakopane is famous for its particular wooden architecture and interior decoration (*see page 243*).

The economy of Poland's agricultural regions has also altered since the Communist days. The houses are better built and the surrounding areas are far cleaner and well tended by the farmers. Today, large private farms have developed, financed by credit from banks and better equipped with modern machinery.

LEFT: a village harvest festival procession
RIGHT: storks are common in the Mazurian region and nest in available chimneys and roofs.

Folk traditions

Polish village life and old traditions have successfully survived down the years. Catholic traditions and family ties have remained intact and the church is still present at every important occasion: christenings, weddings and funerals. The local church, shop, restaurant and administrative office are the focal points of village life.

Polish country villages, are still home to talented embroiderers who continue to copy the designs passed down from their great-grandmothers. Folk artists specialising in paper cut-out decorations (particularly in the Kurpie region), self-taught craftsmen capable of turning out the most wondrous shapes at the potter's wheel or using the most primitive penknife to carve mournful religious figures out of wood from pear or linden trees are also strong in numbers.

Christmas has its own set of very specific traditions. Hay is placed under the white tablecloth when families eat their Christmas meal (*see page 125*). Afterwards they predict their health and fortune based on the length and quality of the stalks. On Christmas Eve many country people still share their food and homes with their animals, because it is believed on this

night all creatures should share each other's fate; the animals are said to understand what the people say.

Christmas is also associated with the preparation of nativity crèches – miniature models of the kind of small stable once found on every Polish farm and considered to be the birthplace of Christ in Polish folk tradition. Each crèche has models of the infant Jesus and Joseph beside each other, together with a group of animals who, according to legend, are capable of speaking in human voice once a year on Christmas Eve.

The feast of Christmas has for centuries been the most important in the Polish calendar. One

TRADITIONAL COSTUMES

In regions such as Kashubia, mountain people still wear traditional coloured aprons and headscarves, particularly when going to mass or a church fair. Picturesque peasant dress, dances and customs are also still very much alive in Lowicz, the biggest feast of Corpus Christi.

In the Tatras villages, men wear low rounded black hats, embroidered cloth jackets, white cloth trousers and mocassins made from one piece of leather, holding a "*ciupaga*" (walking stick) in one hand with an axe-shaped handle, the shaft decorated with brass studs. The women sport flowery kerchiefs, colourful jackets and aprons, beads round their necks and leather mocassins.

of the old customs is "*Jaselka*". A group of youngsters, called "herods", go from door to door asking for money and in each group there is always one youngster dressed up as a winged angel, one as the Grim Reaper, complete with scythe, and one as the wicked King Herod. Buying off the young actors is said to bring good luck in the New Year.

MIDSUMMER TRIBUTE

To celebrate Midsummer's Night wreaths of flowers are cast into the Vistula with burning candles on St John's Night (24 June).

At Easter, brightly painted eggs are knocked against each other as in the English game of conkers. The person whose egg proves most resistant wins the next Easter egg. The tradi-

for emotional demonstrations and patriotic and religious ceremonies, performed in smoky cemeteries among burning candles, resembling pagan rituals.

Town meets country

Social changes in the 20th century have brought the rural population into the towns. This migration has greatly benefited the country as a whole. For individual rural families it brought an improvement in living standards and opened up new opportunities. But this migration was selective – it was the

tion of sprinkling people with water is on Easter Monday (*see page 89*).

An equally ancient custom is the drowning of the "Marzanna", an ugly scarecrow figure symbolic of winter, on the first day of spring.

For the Catholic feast of Palm Sunday, commemorating the Biblical account of Christ's entry into Jerusalem on a donkey, symbolic palms are prepared, often several metres high, from dried flowers and coloured paper, to be carried in the procession to church. All Saint's Day has never ceased to be an occasion

LEFT: farm workers enjoying lunch.
ABOVE: ploughman at work in an orchard.

more enterprising individuals, better educated and with greater aspirations, who moved.

Once in the towns, children from the country often cease to identify with their own village, especially after having made a considerable effort to shed the rural elements of their language, traditions and everyday culture.

However, not all the ties are broken: some rustic traditions and rituals are still common in the big cities. In Katowice, in the mining region of Silesia, for example, the most visible elements are probably the grand costumes worn by the miners on such ceremonial occasions as the veneration of St Barbara, patron saint of all miners, which is universally evident all over the region on her feast day, 4 December. An interesting urban folklore is also maintained in Kraków to commemorate the Tartar invasions in the 13th century by the bugle call at midday from the tower of the Church of St Mary. During Kraków festivals, the "*Lajkonik*", an Orientally-clad rider on a hobbyhorse cavorts round the Market Square.

PURITAN ATTITUDES

Modern attitudes to sex meet with conflict in rural Poland, where puritanism and intolerance on the part of parents and the priest conflict with risqué images seen in the cinema and on television.

Country people

Country people in Poland have a highly developed sense of honour. Business agree-

blooded temperament. When they take to someone they will do anything for them, but if someone falls foul of them, he would be better to keep his distance. On summer evenings, farmers often still sit on the benches in front of their homes and tell stories about the mysteries of nearby forests and marshlands.

Poles like a big family occasion, when several dozen members of the family can get together and eat and drink for two or three days. This includes the imbibing of large quantities of

ments in the marketplace are often sealed with a handshake. The code of honour also includes completing military service and appearing at celebrations in uniform.

Poles, be it in the cities or in the remote countryside, generally have a friendly disposition towards their fellow human beings – they raise their hats to greet them and gladly show them the way. Polish men also follow the code of chivalry – they still kiss a lady's hand and let her pass through a doorway first. They are friendly and hospitable towards foreigners. They laugh and chat naturally, and speak their mind openly without hesitation. Highlanders in particular, combine this friendliness with a hot-

hard vodka. A celebration without vodka would be interpreted as an act of inhospitality, or even a sign of poverty on the part of the host. When weddings take place, tradition dictates that the festivities must last at least three days.

Agrotourism

Whereas for so many years it was the country people who sought out urban life, now some people suffering from the pressures of big city life wish to own a second home in rural villages, called a "*dacza*". Weekends in a rural setting have become increasingly popular, but people generally crave a high standard of luxury despite wanting to rest on an actual farm in a typically rural environment. Polish agro-tourism is becoming increasingly fashionable. A lot of tourists from the west and from urban Poland prefer rural holidays with unspoiled countryside, a beautiful landscape and interesting flora and fauna. It also allows long-standing city dwellers to learn about the traditional country lifestyle.

Host families serve as tour guides for visitors, using their knowledge of the neighbourhood, parks and nature reserves, local history, culture and historic monuments. All attractions and recreation can be tailored to the wishes of individual guests. Possibilities

associations and the 180 farms nationwide which offer accommodation (*see page 381*).

Open-air museums

Every historic region of Poland today has an open-air folk museum, called a "*skansen*", in which the tourist can often view within a few acres of land traditional buildings such as a wealthy country manor house made of valuable larch wood, prosperous farm buildings, a poor peasant's hut thatched with straw and a small country chapel. In addition, there may well also be a village inn, watermill and windmill. Inside these buildings are usually authentic wooden,

include hiking, cycling, horse riding, cooking over open fires and camping out and walks in the forest. Some farmers also offer fresh milk, home-made cottage cheese and genuine country broth made from the cockerel that was strutting around the farmyard the day before.

The Federation of Country Tourism now publishes a catalogue in several languages entitled "Host Farms", which includes detailed descriptions, photographs and addresses of all

LEFT: relaxing after a day's work with a glass of beer.
ABOVE: *skansen* (open-air museums) preserve traditional rural architecture and crafts and can be found all over Poland.

metal or clay implements and utensils and sometimes demonstrations of traditional crafts and skills such as thatching and weaving.

Moreover, every region, no matter how small, also has presentations in its folklore museums – permanent ethnographic exhibitions exist in more than 120 Polish museums.

But despite the popularity of *skansens*, nothing competes with the real thing. Many villages in Poland may resemble outdoor museums but are in fact genuine communities, where the wells still creak, pots and jugs are hung on the fences to dry, and on the roofs of many houses storks in their nests prepare their off-springs for a long flight over the oceans. ❑

THE JEWS

The history of Polish Jewry is one of the most tragic of the last century. Today, the Jewish community is slowly coming to terms with the past and building a future

According to the earliest reliable records, Jewish exiles arrived from Prague towards the end of the 11th century. For centuries, Jews then converged on Poland from all over Europe, fleeing political or economic persecution in their home countries. However, there were also many who came, not because of any external threats, but because they were drawn by the opportunities in the most tolerant country of the continent. It was not without justification that Poland was known as "a paradise for the aristocracy, heaven for the Jews and hell for the peasants".

A safe nation

The Jews called Poland "Polin" ("po" means "here" and "lin" means "rest") because they felt safe there. Poland's masters needed Jewish traders and craftsmen and their knowledge of commerce. Jews were subject only to the king's own courts or those of his representatives; the murder of a Jew was punishable by death, and even failure to help a Jew who was attacked was punished with a fine. Towns that did not step in quickly enough to quell anti-Jewish riots were also fined, ritual murders could be brought to court, the distribution of anti-Jewish literature was forbidden, and so on.

In 1265, by the decree of the Statute of Jewish Liberties issued in Kalish, the Polish King established a Jewish social class, an unprecedented attitude at that time in Europe which was engulfed by the Holy Inquisition.

The Jewish Council of Four Lands, founded in 1581, was another political institution unique in Europe. It was responsible for Great Poland, Little Poland, Lithuania and Russia, the four main territories within the Polish-Lithuanian kingdom. It was concerned mainly with internal Jewish affairs and kept in close contact with the authorities. The Jews' main occupation was banking, money-lending and financial activity, often leading to conflicts with nobility deprived of the rights of financial operations. But these disagreements were acted on the individual not on an ethnic or religious level.

During the First Republic (1569–1795) there were relatively few anti-Jewish excesses in comparison with the rest of Europe. This is partly explained by the financial status of the

state and the pragmatism of the Polish aristocracy: in Poland, there was simply no general hatred of the Jews, and the aristocracy was not inclined to harass the Jewish communities.

In contrast, in the violent uprising of Bohdan Chmielnicki in the Ukraine (1648–54), which was actually directed against the Polish rulers, the Jews were massacred in their thousands as suspected allies of the Poles. The tragedy was repeated during the popular uprising in the Ukraine and Podolia in 1768, when thousands of Polish aristocrats as well as Jews suffered terrible deaths.

The Catholic Church in Poland was ambivalent towards the Jews. While on the one hand

LEFT: remembering the victims of the Warsaw ghetto.
RIGHT: the Zionist Dov Ber Borochov and friends in Płońsk.

they were regarded as "the chosen people", on the other they were also "the murderers of Jesus". The church accordingly announced that they should not therefore be persecuted, but that they should live together in a separate community. This attitude fell upon fertile ground with Polish peasant communities, where Jews ran inns and mills. Peasants, oppressed by the nobility found themselves often indebted to the landowners and their rich Jewish advisors alike. Their animosity towards both grew with the level of oppression.

POLAND'S FIRST VOICE

Notably, it was a Jew who made the first mention of Poland in print – Ibrahim-Ibn Jacob, a Moor from Spain, visited Poland in AD 965.

dom as farmers. They were often wealthy. The basic unit of Jewish autonomy was the community, governed by the *kahal*, a body responsible for the judicial system, administration, religion and welfare, where all were responsible for one towards the outside world.

During the 17th century, however, the Jews were badly affected by the weakening of Poland because of wars and internal anarchy. Gradually their economic and political situation deteriorated. In 1764 the Polish parliament, the *Sejm*, dissolved the Council of Four Lands

The unique position of the Jews in Poland is illustrated by the fact that a Jew who had been converted to Catholicism could even be elevated to the nobility.

Wealth and poverty

Because most Jews remained true to their faith, for centuries Polish culture was enriched by specific Jewish characteristics. They made major contributions to scientific development and frequently occupied leading positions in medicine, mathematics and astronomy as well as in architecture, painting and goldsmithing.

Jews were industrious and usually worked as craftsmen, merchants, doctors and bankers, sel-

for economic reasons, but it did not touch the communities. Although the government was aware that the status of the Jews in Poland was in need of fundamental reform, no changes were made before Poland finally lost its independence. In 1795 some 900,000 Polish Jews automatically became citizens of the three occupying countries.

In the 19th century the occupying powers abolished many of the laws that protected the Jews, but patriotic feelings towards Poland prevailed and they supported the struggle for independence, fighting alongside them in the Kosciuszko uprising (1794), the November uprising (1831) and the People's Spring (1848–49).

But as nationalism swept Europe at the turn of the 20th century, the Jewish community turned increasingly to Zionism. The worsening economy, the politics of the occupying powers and growing signs of anti-Semitism led many Jews to emigrate, many to the United States.

The growth of anti-Semitism

During the Second Republic (1918–39), the National Democracy Party, which had strong right-wing leanings, became increasingly radical in its attitudes towards the Jews. The party had placed a high value on the "national cultural community". From this perspective,

Jews responsible for every social evil. They were accused of Communism, association with the Freemasons, economic parasitism and of an inability to assimilate themselves into Polish society. There were pogroms, harassment at the universities and an economic boycott.

The sections of society that supported Marshal Piłsudski (in power from 1926) did not share these attitudes. Many Jews had fought for the independence of Poland under his leadership and their loyalty to the state was more important to the political realist Piłsudski than their forced assimilation. After his death in 1935, however, his followers' programme grad-

the fact that the Jews used a language similar to that used by Poland's enemies, Germany and Austria was perceived as a threat and an attempt to maintain an separate cultural identity. Also, in a country devastated by wars and partitioning the financial strength of the Jewish community and the unwillingness of some of its members to invest in the country, could be interpreted as deliberate alienation from Poland.

Again, it became fashionable to make the

LEFT: the standard of living was high for most Jewish families before the growth of anti-Semitism.
ABOVE: the age of many Jewish graveyards indicate the strong roots of the community.

JEWISH SECTS

The Jewish way of life in Poland remained by no means unaffected by the religious and social trends of the times. As well as Sabbatarianism with its strict observance of the Sabbath, there was Frankism, a mystical cabbalistic sect that emerged in Podolia in 1755, and the haskalah of the Enlightenment, Hasidism, a popular movement of both a religious and mystic nature based on the cabbala and Judaism, also had its origins in Podolia in the 18th century; its founder, Baal Schev Tov, was born in Poland, and the movement, within the Jewish population till today is regarded as Polish with its characteristic philosophy, traditional dress, music, dance and warm joy of life.

ually grew closer to that of the nationalistic right. Although the state condemned the use of force, various politicians seemed to support an economic boycott of the Jews.

The Zionists had a good relationship with the government of Poland. The left wing of the Zionist movement, under the leadership of Wlodzimierz Zabotyňski, was even supplied with weapons and money, and offered military training. The first "Kibbutz" communities were established in Poland.

The Orthodox Jews, represented by the party Agudas Israel, were also on perfectly normal terms with the state administration. The Jew-ish socialists, on the other hand, acknowledged only one homeland: Poland. Understandably, however, the right-wing rulers did not approve of some of their political programmes, which sympathised with the Soviet programme of Communist ideologies.

Poles and the Holocaust

Of the 3.5 million Polish Jews, only 250,000 survived the war, mostly because they were able to escape from the Nazis. Opinions differ greatly when it comes to evaluating the attitude of the Poles to the Jews and the concentration camps during the Occupation. Nevertheless,

many Poles took the risk of helping Jews. Often, in this changing climate, people even overcame their own pronounced anti-Semitic prejudices.

It is known that Jews were hidden and saved from the Nazis by National Democrats. The Christian community was also very much involved in rescue operations, above all the clergy themselves; nunneries were particularly active and saved many Jewish children. An important part was played by the Council for Jewish Assistance, ZEGOTA, an organisation which the government-in-exile helped finance.

The risks cannot be overstated – helping Jews was punishable by death of not only the "guilty" but also his family. There were, of course, many cases of denunciation and some Poles enriched themselves unscrupulously by appropriating Jewish possessions. In what were desperate times, many are known to have handed Jews over to the Nazis in exchange for a kilo of sugar. It is, however, known that Jews themselves were not always loyal to their fellow men. War and fear of death evoked all sorts of emotions and behaviour.

One of the most tragic moments in the history of the Jewish nation is connected with the Polish capital Warsaw. During the occupation of the city by Germans, they locked part of the city and brought into it Jews from all over Poland.

IN MEMORIAM

In the memorial park Yad Vashem in Jerusalem, many trees have been planted by Polish heroes who helped save Jews, in memory of those who did not survive.

took their own lives. A very few of them escaped through the sewer canals network to bear witness to the terrible crimes committed on their race in the Warsaw Ghetto (*see page 169*).

Of all the concentration camps in the whole of Poland Auschwitz-Birkenau is the most horrific. Built in 1940 it became one of the most sinister creations of humanity. According to their "final solution", the Nazis in this camp exterminated Jews in gas chambers and in death blocks. It is estimated that

Cramped and oppressed, hungered and persecuted, in desperation the Jews took to using guns in April 1943. For about one month a desperate fight took place. To combat the uprising, the Germans used tanks and soldiers. The Jewish fighters either died of bullet wounds or

LEFT: child victims of the Holocaust are remembered in a simple memorial.
ABOVE: visitors to the Warsaw ghetto.

four million people died in Auschwitz-Birkenau, 1.5 million of them Jews. Others were gypsies, and Poles, Czechs, Austrians, Danes, French, Dutch and Germans who opposed the Nazi regime. It remains a place of great sorrow for people from all over the world, regardless of their faith (*see page 54*).

However, Auschwitz was not simply a place where human values disappeared under the bullying heel of the Nazis. It was also a place of great sacrifices and the noblest of human behaviour, as people risked their lives to help others. One such prisoner, Gertruda Stein, a nun of Jewish origin who helped and tended other prisoners, was recently beatified.

Great hopes for Israel

In the first half of 1946, some 137,000 Jews who had either fled or been deported returned from the Soviet Union to Poland. The new government was anything but charitable towards the survivors of the Holocaust and often actively prevented the Jews from reconstructing their communities. There were even isolated cases of anti-Semitic riots, culminating in the Kielce pogrom of 1946, when Poles killed 46 Jews. Because of this climate, many Jews finally decided to emigrate to Palestine to make a new life.

Immediately after the war the Communist

leadership of Poland was still hoping that the new state of Israel that was just coming into being would be socialist-orientated, or would at least sympathise with the countries within Moscow's sphere of influence. For this reason, a military camp offered training to volunteers who belonged to the Zionist Haganah movement. However, these friendly feelings soon evaporated when it became evident that Israel was developing along the lines of a bourgeois society.

The Jewish exodus reached record levels during the political crises of 1956–57 and 1968–69, which were often accompanied by anti-Semitic propaganda. Soviets now needed good relations with the Arabs and enticed this attitude which was not always in tune with the general feeling of the people. This all took place against the background of the Arab-Israeli war, when the whole of the Eastern Bloc was vociferous in its condemnation of the Israelis. Many artists, scientists and students were of Jewish origin, and the Polish rulers found that the simplest thing to do was to make the Jews the scapegoat, since they were likely to offer the least resistance. To the country, however, it was a tremendous loss of much of its intellectual capital.

In order to stir up the population against them, the Polish rulers drew attention to the inglorious part some of the Jews had played during Stalin's reign of terror. The campaign forced at least 20,000 Poles of Jewish origin to turn their backs on the country of their birth and which they considered to be their homeland to seek a new life in Israel or the USA.

Jewish renaissance

The reduction of the Jewish population from 3.5 million to 5,000 was an irreplaceable loss to Polish society. As a result of a shortage of pupils, the three Jewish high schools had to be closed and rabbis brought over from the USA. It is even more startling that, at election time, old demagogic formulas have been revived and the "Polishness" of Jewish candidates is often questioned.

In recent years, however, this is changing again. Today the Jewish minority has its own cultural, religious and scientific institutions, folklore, magazines, a theatre, and a Jewish Historical Museum with a library and a museum in Warsaw. Poland also now has a Chief Rabbi and Kosher restaurants are in great demand. There appears to be a strong revival of interest in Jewish tradition and folklore among the young generation of Poles who want to grow up without the label of prejudice their parents had. Many liberal forces still remember the tolerance for which, hundreds of years ago, the Poles were renowned.

Moreover, Poland is now a destination favoured by Jews from all over the world who come in search of their roots and traditions. ❏

LEFT: Jewish cemetery in Kazimerz, Warsaw.
RIGHT: the Monument to the Heroes of the Ghetto Uprising, Warsaw.

THE CATHOLICS

Until recently the Catholic church played a hugely significant role in the country's politics. Today its cultural and social role is dominant

If on a Sunday you are anywhere near a church it is as well not to be in a hurry. The roads and squares are full of families dressed in their Sunday best making their way to mass. And on special religious holidays the procession of brightly coloured flags extends for miles as the miraculous picture of the Madonna Częstochowa is carried for several hours from house to house. In the home of every family a picture of the Virgin Mary or a portrait of Pope John Paul II occupies pride of place.

Religious origins

Christianity was introduced to Poland in the 10th century. It was primarily for political reasons that the first ruler of the land Mieszko I, the Polish Duke, had himself baptised and took the country from the Pope as a fiefdom. He did not consult all of his subjects and followers, members of the Slavic tribes and adherents of a very different religion based on ancestor and nature worship, and resistance to Christianity continued for two centuries.

In spite of this, at around the turn of the first millennium the archdiocese of Gniezno proceeded to expand its influence. In AD 1000 it became the Archdiocese of Poland with subordinate dioceses of Kraków, Wrocław, Kołobrzeg and Poznań. Missionary-style groups left from here with the purpose of converting neighbouring tribes. The first Christian missionaries did not have it easy and many, like Bishop Wojciech of Prague, who sought to convert the Prussians, met a martyr's death: he became the first Polish saint, St Adalbert. His brother Gaudenty became first Archbishop of Poland.

Gradually the rulers imposed their will. Polygamy and working on religious holidays were prohibited, times of fasting and contributions to the church were made compulsory. The Cistercians established the new religion in the towns as well as the new economy system in the country. Religion brought with it a rich cul-

tural tradition and skilled craftsmen from all over Europe worked on the construction of places of worship. By the middle of the 12th century all babies were christened and the old faith merged with the new without conflict.

The church in Poland, as it has in most of Europe, made concessions to tradition by

allowing memorials to be built to ancestors, tolerating ancient customs and introducing festivals involving intercessions for good weather and rich harvests. But with the breakdown of central secular power in the 13th century the church was able to escape secular domination. From then on it followed the doctrine of St Thomas of Aquinas, according to which it was the duty of the church to admonish tyrants and protect the rights of the faithful.

As early as the 11th century, the Kraków bishop Stanisław had publicly opposed a prince. The conflict resulted in the fall of the ruler, which strengthened the authority of the clergy as defenders of justice, and the Polish

---

LEFT: postcard portraits of Pope John Paul II.
RIGHT: a roadside shrine.

church has taken this role seriously ever since.

At the beginning of the Reformation the Catholics lived in the western half of the enormous Polish-Lithuanian state and the adherents of the Orthodox church in the eastern half. In order to establish a counterweight to an increasingly powerful Moscow and to the Orthodox church, the national Roman Catholic church, based on the Greek Catholic tradition, was founded in 1596 after the Union of Brześć.

In later years, with misfortunes falling upon the country from Protestant Germany and Orthodox Russia, the maxim "to be a Pole is to be a Catholic" overruled all else.

The church and the people

The church in Poland was always tuned to the worship of saints. In the 17th century the Mother of God, the mother and queen of Poland, was the chief object of veneration, especially after the attack by the Swedish army on Jasna Góra monastery in Częstochowa (*see page 256*). Success in the uneven defence was accredited to her divine protection.

While the state fell apart, religion flourished. Superstitious beliefs were also popular. There were over 400 local cults based on miraculous manifestations and pictures that were supposed to save people from having unpure thoughts. It

LAND OF RELIGIOUS TOLERANCE

Although Poland is a Roman Catholic country, religious tolerance has always gone hand in hand with national belief. There has never been any religious persecution in Poland. Protestant Scots, fleeing the Counter-Reformation in Scotland, Huguenots and followers of Jan Hus, and Jews fleeing the Inquisition all found in Poland a safe haven.

Calvinism and Lutheranism had their followers, especially in Pomerania, Gdańsk, and a radical group the Aryans or Polish Brothers, separated from the Calvinists. But activity by the Jesuits halted these movements and the Counter-Reformation in Poland did not develop.

was at this time that the idea of "Catholicism under siege" became part of the church's ideology, the idea of the one true faith in a heretical world.

Historic events such as the wars against Swedish and Turkish infidels, whom the Poles resisted at Częstochowa and Vienna respectively, reinforced their belief that they and their nation were a bulwark of true Christianity. Some members of the high-ranking clergy – who were, after all, principally aristocrats from the ruling Polish families then fighting for power and influence – were not entirely blameless when Poland was split up in 1772, and frequently made deals with the occupying powers. But the bond between the church and the people was never destroyed. Aided by the uprising against Russia and the Vatican's defence of Polish independence, the church was able to win back the trust of the nation. It became a stronghold of what the nation stood for; it educated, often in conspiracy conditions; it taught patriotism and, above all, it gave hope to the majority of people.

Numerous monastic orders also settled in Poland and established the image of the church through their ministering work. At the dawn of Polish Christianity monks taught the art of writing and copied books.

The Cistercian Order, established in the 12th century was noted for its role in the development of education, culture and economy. The Dominican Friars opened schools. The Franciscans taught how to construct brick buildings. The Bernardine Order built monasteries and churches. The monks of the Pauline Order built the most famous of Polish sanctuaries, Jasna Góra, with its icon of the Black Madonna. The Piarists and Jesuits opened colleges. Ursuline Nuns opened orphanages and worked as nurses in hospitals.

A momentum developed of its own and became something for the people to hold on to; the idea that the cultural identity of Poland, including its freedom and religious tolerance, was guaranteed as long as the Catholic church continued to exist – even if state sovereignty was a long way off. The church went along with this, at first tentatively then more actively. Throughout the occupation by Nazi Germany and the terrors of the Stalinist regime, as well as the persistent endeavours of the Communist leaders, the church held firm.

Two men stand out among the countless heroes who confronted these troubled times. The Franciscan friar Maximilian Raimund Kolbe went voluntarily in 1941 to the hunger block to be killed with a phenol injection through the heart to save the life of an unknown man. He was later canonised.

In October 1984, Father Jerzy Popieluszko, a young Warsaw priest, was abducted by the secret police and brutally murdered for his defence of his community and the political goals of Solidarity which he supported.

LEFT: finding solace in the church.
RIGHT: a Catholic nun.

Spokesman of the nation

When in 1976 the Polish conference of bishops published a pastoral in which the Catholic church was portrayed as the legitimate representative of the people and the nation, it received the people's unanimous approval. The election of Cardinal Karol Wojtyła as Pope in 1978 strengthened this claim still further. In 1979, on his first journey home, the Pope encouraged millions of his countrymen with the words "Do not be afraid!" John Paul II visited his homeland on seven occasions: in 1979 just after his elevation to the St Peter's Throne and then again in 1983 after the marshal

law was lifted, in 1987 to help Poles to cope with the realities of the Communist stronghold, and most happily in 1991 to enjoy with them a free Poland. He has returned again for short visits in 1997 and again in 1999.

Even today Poland is universally synonymous with Catholicism, but whether the people's faith will suffer as political liberalisation advances is debatable. Democracy has forced the church to reconsider its role in Polish society. In the end it will have to withdraw from politics, and as a consequence the process of secularisation that is inevitable in a democratic society. Yet the Catholic "Radio Maryja" still has more than its fair share of listeners. ❑

„MAŁA KOMEDIA"
(II scena Państwowego Teatru Komedia)

Krakowskie Przedmieście 21|23

Felicien Marceau

JAJKO

PRAPREMIERA STYCZEŃ 1958 R.

THE ARTS

Poland has always had a high profile in the international arts scene because of the deep cultural awareness of its population and its artistic traditions

Although Poland's historical presence in Christian Europe dates from the 10th century, Polish literature was late in emerging. Medieval Poland was frequently attacked by foreign invaders and weakened by division into small principalities. Additionally, as in other European countries, Latin was the only literary language. Early medieval writings are confined to the lives of the saints and historical annals and chronicles.

Poetry and drama

Even though the Renaissance reached Poland late and lasted for a comparatively short period, the country flourished during that time and the name "golden age" was attributed to it. The leading personality of the period is Jan Kochanowski (1505–68) whose influence on future generations of poets gained him the title "Father of Polish poetry". His masterpiece *Treny* (*Laments*, 1580) speaks of the death of his infant daughter and of his subsequent recovery of spiritual harmony. The poems put him among the great European poets of that era.

In contrast with the Renaissance, the Baroque period appeared in Poland very early, almost at the same time as in Italy. The 17th century was dominated by constant military conflict with Russia, Sweden and Turkey and by internal unrest and disputes over constitutional reforms. The masterpiece of Baroque lyrics is the poetry of Jan Andrzej Morsztyn (1613–93) who supplied the royal theatre with superb translations of Corneille's tragedies.

After the decadent period of the Saxon reign in Poland, the Enlightenment literature was genuinely preoccupied with building political awareness and recreating Polish national culture in order to save the weakened country from its inevitable collapse. The notable event was

PRECEDING PAGES: examples of poster art, a well-respected art form in Poland.
LEFT: a painting by Polish artist Leon Tarasewicz.
RIGHT: the late theatre director Tadeusz Kantor at rehearsals.

the inauguration in 1765, on the king's initiative, of the first public theatre. The comedies by Franciszek Zablocki (1750–1821) and Aleksander Fredro (1793–1876) successfully combine the foreign plots borrowed from Molière and Goldoni with typical Polish archetypes and their anxieties. The period was mainly didactic

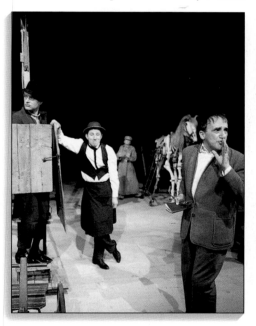

in character yet it saw the emergence of the first professional periodicals, the first *Dictionary of the Polish Language* (1807–14), the introduction of the sentimental novel and, in poetry, of western genres, all of which were practiced with high artistic standards.

Romanticism coincided with the most tragic moments in Polish history. The juxtaposition of the loss of national independence with the up-lifted Romantic ideology led to the emergence of some extraordinary poetic output which makes Polish Romanticism one of the most distinctive literary periods in Europe. On the one hand there was the poet's duty to keep the spirit of Polishness alive, on the other there was the fascination with Byron and Shelley's Promethean myth. According to the formula, the evil Gods were either the oppressors or the Christian God who let them reduce the nation's position to mere martyrdom. The human being was the poet who "suffers for millions". The rebellion was of course the fight against the tyrants often in a truly Promethean situation, as the genius trio of Polish Romantic poets all fled the country to live in exile. Had they stayed they would have been deported to Siberia along with the

> ## EARLIEST TEXT
>
> The oldest Polish literary text is a song in honour of the Virgin Mary, the *Bogurodzica*. The first copy dates from the 14th century but it was probably written earlier.

Practicality and realism
The Romantic vein continued until 1863 when another unsuccessful uprising began. After the nation was severely punished for rebelling against the Russian oppressors, all hopes were abandoned and the period that followed is now called Positivism. It was a mood of practical thinking which expressed a rationalist reaction against Romanticism and the domination of literature over life. "Work from the foundations" was the new realistic slogan, implying the renunciation

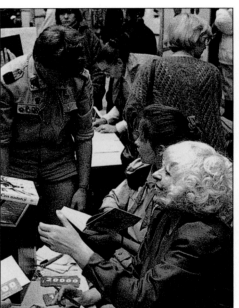

most luminous people of their generation.

The star trio are Adam Mickiewicz (1798–1855), Juliusz Słowacki (1809–49) and Zygmunt Krasiński (1812–59). Mickiewicz is the most popular and accessible of them all. His works have been translated into many foreign languages and among the highlights are *Dziady* (*The Forefathers' Eve*, 1832) a Messianic drama presenting Poland suppressed by foreign powers as the Christ among the peoples destined to rise in glory. His poetic tour de force is *Pan Taduesz* (1843) presenting the Polish landed gentry in the context of Napoleon's expedition to Moscow in 1812 which, it was thought, would bring Poland its independence.

of armed resistance and the concentration on the preservation of the ideological and cultural assets of the nation. The period produced two extraordinary novelists Bolesław Prus (1847–1912) and Henryk Sienkiewicz (1846–1912). The latter was the first Polish winner of the literary Nobel Prize in 1905. Recently published in England, Prus's *Lalka* (*The Doll*, 1890) is an accomplished and vivid picture of contemporary Warsaw with an intricate plot and a collection of unforgettable characters. *Trilogy* (1884–88) by Sienkiewicz is a picture of Poland's struggles against its enemies in the 17th century and the Nobel Prize winning *Quo Vadis* (1896) is a historical novel of Rome under Nero. Historians argue over their factual value but their literary qualities are undeniable.

While positivism flourished in Warsaw, Kraków saw an emergence of the Young Poland movement which proclaimed the return to the expression of feelings and to imaginative writing. The most outstanding figure of the movement was Stanisław Wyspiański (1869–1907) (*see page 112*). In his play *Wesele* (*The Wedding*, 1901), based on the foundations of the primitive folk theatre, he created a visionary drama which

> ### RURAL SUCCESS
>
> The epic *Chlopi* (*The Peasants*, 1909) by Władysław Reymont (1868–1925) was translated into every European language and was awarded the Nobel Prize in 1924.

prose has influenced the birth of the Theatre of the Absurd on an international scale. Other playwrights who exercised the genre were Stanisław Ignacy Witkiewicz (1885–1939), known as Witkacy (*see page 247*) and later Sławomir Mrožek (born 1930), both translated into many languages and given numerous international performances.

The reconstruction of an independent Polish state was harshly interrupted by the invasion of the Germans and the Soviet Russians in 1939. The rich literary har-

he used as a vehicle for scathing criticism of the problems of his age.

The newly found freedom in 1918 turned the artists' attention to subject matters other than independence, which had dominated Polish literature for over 120 years. Between the two World Wars Polish writers produced a wide range of distinguished literary works. One of the most interesting writers of that time was Witold Gombrowicz (1905–1969) whose satiric

vest of these years was only fully revealed after the end of the war. One of the most devastating works of this period is Tadeusz Borowski's *Prosze Panstwa do Gazu* (*Would You Please Proceed to the Gas Chamber*, 1949) based on the author's personal experiences in the concentration camp at Auschwitz-Birkenau (*see page 54*).

From 1945 until the political "thaw" after Stalin's death, literary life in Poland was dominated by Socialist Realism. The factory worker or collective farmer was now to become a literary hero. After 1956 Polish literature concentrated on the nuances and contradiction of everyday life in a Communist country. The

FAR LEFT: writer Barbara Wachowiz. **LEFT:** Wisława Szymborska won the Nobel Prize for Literature in 1996. **ABOVE:** film director Andrzej Wajda (right), a leading light of the Polish Film School (1955–63).

most important authors of this epoch are Taduesz Konwicki, Slawomir Mrožek, Zbigniew Herbert, Tadeusz Rózewicz, Andrzej Szczypiorski and the two Nobel Prize winners Czesław Miłosz and Wisława Szymborska.

Since the collapse of Communism, the Polish literary scene is enjoying all the privileges of democracy. Along with the discovery of the writers whose works were banned under the Communist regime, the young generation of writers is preoccupied with such phenomena

MUSIC FESTIVALS

Many musical festivals are held in Poland: the annual Warsaw Autumn Festival of modern music and every four years the Chopin Competition in Warsaw and the Wieniawski in Poznań.

It became fashionable in the 18th century onwards and features in the works of Bach, Mozart, Beethoven, Schubert and Liszt, and of course the famous piano polonaises by Chopin. The most famous Polish polonaise is Oginski's *Pozegnanie ojczyzny* (*Farewell to the Homeland*) written soon after the country disappeared from the map of Europe in 1795. For the following 120 years Polish music, like its literature and fine arts, was an expression of national spirit full of allusiveness and

as feminism, sexual revolution and the discovery of the national identity under the new political system. There remains a literary bequest; a moral issue of a dichotomised nation, split over the last 50 years into oppressors and oppressed. The contemporary literary climate looks set to resolve this.

A national rhythm

Frederick Chopin (*see page 196*) is not the only Polish contribution to world music, although he is undoubtedly the most important composer to represent Polish music abroad. The first international success was probably the polonaise, a lofty court dance in simple triple time.

political message. Chopin (1810–1849) and his contemporaries were putting elements of folk music into their works – elements that achieved the status of a national Polish musical style in the words and music of the "father of Polish national opera", Stanisław Moniuszko (1819–1872). They allude to the heroic era of Polish nobility in works such as *Straszny Dwor* (*The Haunted House*, 1864) and introduce common people as victims (*Halka*, 1857). The patriotic plots along with a great use of Polish dance rhythms such as the mazurka and polonaise were to foster deep patriotic feelings.

Henryk Wieniawski (1835–1880) was both a patriotic composer and one of the most important violinists of the generation after Paganini. He combined the technical advances of the great Italian virtuoso with Romantic imagination and Slavonic spirit, showing Polish nationalism in his mazurkas and polonaises.

After the country regained its independence in 1918 folk tradition was still present in music. The most distinguished composer of the entreguerre period was Karol Szymanowski (1882–1947) who took the challenge of translating folk music into the symphonic spirit of Modernism. He spent half of his life in the Tatra Mountains resort of Zakopane (*see page 244*), where he studied the songs and dances of the

the horrors of World War II and on the other were dependent on the political situation in Communist Poland. Lutosławski's early works were composed under official restraints insisting on a style grounded in folk-song. When the political situation in Poland became less repressive, he became internationally active as a teacher and conductor of his own music. Baird also started out toeing the party line but the cultural thaw of 1956 enabled him to pursue his own artistic vision. Penderecki gained international acclaim with *Threnody for the Victims of Hiroshima* (1960), *St Luke Passion* (1965) and his dynamic operas.

mountaineers which led to the composition of an exotic ballet *Harnasie* (1935). His other major works are the opera *King Roger* (1913) and the choral orchestral *Stabat Mater* (1926), both outstanding examples of modern Romanticism. Szymanowski's villa in Zakopane is now a museum and a popular tourist attraction.

Post-war music is represented by Witold Lutosławski (1913–1994), Tadeusz Baird (1928–1981) and Krzysztof Penderecki (born 1933). Their works are closely linked with history. On the one hand they were influenced by

LEFT: dancing the polonaise in the late 18th century.
ABOVE: Krysztof Penderecki conducts.

MUSIC AND POLITICS

The combination of music and patriotism found its best expression in the life of Ignacy Paderewski (1860–1941) who was not only an outstanding composer and a world-class pianist but also an important politician. His works are deeply rooted in the Romantic Polish national school among which the opera *Manru* and the *Fantasie polonaise* are most noteworthy. During World War I Paderewski represented the Polish nation abroad, making speeches and assisting victims of oppression, and eventually becoming Prime Minister in 1919. Paderewski lived much of his life in exile, but in 1992 his remains were returned for burial in Warsaw and a "free Poland".

Fine Arts

As with literature and music, it is impossible to appreciate Polish art without an understanding of their references to the historical situation. Polish artists worked either in exile or in the partitioned country trying to convey some implicit political message.

One of the most outstanding figures of the first half of the 19th century was Piotr Michałowski (1800–58) who settled in Paris and produced works that were on a level with those of Géricault and Delacroix. His patriotic scenes of horsemen from the Kościuszko Uprising and the Napoleonic wars (now in the

Kraków Museum) demonstrate a more lively and explosive temperament than the Paris artists trained in the tame classical tradition.

Michalowski's successors in allegorical and historical art were Juliusz Kossak (1824–99), Artur Grottger (1837–67) and Jan Matejko (1838–93). Their works portray the nation's grand historic events with patriotic emotiveness. The depiction of the nation's fate and the fight for independence fulfilled the criteria of the patriotic mission being enthusiastically received by large sections of the population.

Matejko's pupil, Stanisław Wyspiański (1869–1907) was a versatile painter, poet, playwright, architect and man of letters who translated historic Romanticism into eerie visions of Symbolism. His paintings revealed a genius for dramatic construction, but the loss of the use of his hand forced him to turn to designing and writing.

Most of Wyspiański's architectural designs still exist on paper. Notably, he turned the attention of his generation to the wooden homesteads and churches built by the Polish peasants, wishing to apply the rural forms to monumental buildings in order to create a national style. Wyspiański was one of the first artists to choose Zakopane as his home, which was to later become an artistic centre.

Another outstanding artist of early 20th-century Polish Symbolism was Jacek Malczewski (1855–1926), who combined the dreamlike visions of the past with a psychoanalytical perception of humanity.

After Poland achieved independence, Leon Wyczolkowski (1852–1937) and Julian Falat (1853–1929) were the major creators of Polish Impressionism. In Poland the younger generation was no longer prepared to convey patriotic duty and new artistic groups emerged. The Futurists and late Expressionists made a break from all that had gone before.

After the war artists had to conform for over a decade to painting in the style of Socialist Realism in order to gain any recognition. One of the most interesting alternative movements was the group Blok, which introduced its own interpretation of constructivism. Its reference points were architecture, sociology and the new technical civilisation. Władysław Strzemiżski (1893–1952) and Henryk Stażewski (1894–1988) gave their particular approach to arts the name "unism". The movement had a charismatic influence on the constructivist avant garde. Recently Stażewski has become the central figure of the younger generation of art analysts and representatives of concrete art.

Contemporary aesthetics embrace installment art: instead of pictures there are now "environments". The showing of slides and films is being used to supplement the traditional media. The opening up of the Eastern Bloc and the consequent free-flow of ideas across Europe means that Polish art now participates within a universal framework as opposed to the isolated national movements of before. ❏

LEFT: *Self-portrait* by Jacek Malczewski.

Film School of Łódź

In his autobiography, Roman Polański writes: "It was through a mere whim of history that Łódź became the film capital of Poland... after the war the capital, Warsaw, lay in ruins and... the government chose the nearest suitable town when looking for a place to establish a centre of cinematography. It was common sense to site it where there was already a film institute: the choice was Łódź and so it has also remained."

Two years after World War II the Kraków film course was also transferred to Łódź and from then on it was here that film-makers received their training. The Communist authorities appropriated a small palace belonging to an industrialist, and by 1948 they had already promoted the school to the status of a college. From the beginning the school was orientated towards the production of an élite. Despite the war devastation, the school was well equipped and had excellent teachers, no expense spared. The reason why they went to so much trouble is summed up in the quote by Lenin carved in marble in the main hall: "Of all the forms of art we have, film is the most important."

In the 1950s Polish film-makers were bound by the Socialist style and there was no room for originality. Only after Stalin's death did it become possible to make films that did not reflect the propaganda clichés of the Communists. There emerged what came to be known as the Polish Film School and its founders portrayed the war and the heroism of that period in a new light. For the first time they were able to concentrate on the problem of human loneliness. *Kanal* by Sewel (Silver Palm winner in Cannes, 1957) and *Ashes and Diamonds* by Andrzej Wajda (FIPRESCI in Venice, 1959) and *Eroica* by Andrzej Munk – the best-known postwar productions – all date from this period. A few years later Jerzy Kawalerowicz made *Mother Jeanne of the Angels* (Silver Palm in Cannes, 1961) and Roman Polański made the Academy Award nominated *Knife in the Water* (FIPRESCI, 1962).

Almost all contemporary Polish directors are graduates of the Łódź film school, among them Andrzej Wajda and Roman Polański, both now world-famous. Wajda (born 1926) has been heaped with prizes: for *The Promised Land* (Moscow 1975; Valladolid 1976; Cartagena 1978; Academy Award

RIGHT: Roman Polański, one of the leading Polish film makers.

nomination), *The Iron Man* (Grand Prix Cannes 1981), and *Danton* (Prix Delluc 1983; Cezar 1983) to name but a few. Today Wajda is the undisputed authority among young directors. In 1989, in the first free elections in Poland, he also became a member of the Senate. Polański, in contrast, left Poland at an earlier stage and made films abroad that enjoyed huge international success, including *Rosemary's Baby, Repulsion, Cul-de-Sac, Chinatown, The Tenant* and *Dance of the Vampires*.

Towards the end of the 1980s the films being produced by young directors dwelt with painful precision on the social realities of the decade while attempting to establish a new manifestation of

solidarity. Krzysztof Kieslowski's 10-part television series *Dekalog* about the Ten Commandments is a good example of this development. While his works, such as *Film about Love* and *The Double Life of Veronique,* received more acclaim abroad than at home, his trilogy *Three Colours: Blue, White, Red* did bring greater recognition among his compatriots. He died in 1996 at the age of 55.

Today, the school continues to train directors and cameramen. Its curriculum includes humanities and practical training, combining the qualities of a university, polytechnic and academy of fine arts. It has its own studios where students make short films, and full-length feature films are made in conjunction with professional film institutes. ❏

MAINTAINING TRADITIONAL CULTURE

Numerous ethnographic museums showcase regional folk arts, crafts and architectural styles and illustrate the life of rural communities

Skansens (open air museums) comprise different types of buildings, brought together within a park to recreate a village community. The range of buildings show how peasants as well as owners of small-holdings lived and worked, with these houses decorated in period style, while other buildings such as a windmill or blacksmith's forge show how these rural crafts were operated. One of the earliest *skansens* was established in 1906 at Wdydze Kiszewskie. A vast park features cottages, farmhouses and barns dating from the 18th and 19th centuries, together with a Kashubian school house, a wooden church and a centre of folk arts and crafts. *Skansens* can also be found in city centres, with Toruń for instance having a *skansen* occupying a central park containing farmsteads, a windmill, forge, and even a fisherman's barge moored on the river Vistula. There are also museums with collections of folk arts and crafts in many major cities, such as the Museum of Mankind in Warsaw, and in Kazimierz, the historic Jewish district of Kraków, where an extensive collection is housed in the former town hall.

▷ **OLSZTYNEK**
The *skansen* at Olsztynek includes a 19th-century inn and this half-timbered, arcaded building.

▷ **BEE KEEPING**
Bee keeping is an ancient rural occupation, with honey also made into alcoholic mead. *Skansens* such as Biskupin display historic bee hives.

△ **WIND POWER**
Windmills were essential to every rural community. This one is from the Olsztynek *skansen* near the town of Olsztyn in the Mazurian lake district.

▷ **SACRAL BUILDINGS**
S*kansens* contain a wide range of wooden Russian orthodox churches, mosques and Roman Catholic churches.

▽ **CHOCHOŁÓW SKANSEN**
This *skansen* includes 18th- and 19th-century houses with their characteristic small front gardens collected from the Tatra mountains.

GÓRAL CULTURAL STYLE

One thriving ethnic community culture is the Górals, who live in the Podhale and Pieniny regions of southern Poland. Traditionally they are shepherds and farmers, have their own dialect and maintain traditional customs and regional costumes. Góral style can be seen in the local architecture with ornately carved wooden houses and churches still remaining in Tatra villages, as well as in Zakopane. There is also an important collection of Góral folk art in Zakopane's Tatra Museum. In addition to architecture, music and folk dancing are essential elements of the culture. Among a varied programme of cultural events, Zakopane hosts the annual international Festival of Highland Folklore in September.

◁ **TRADITIONAL SKILLS**
Skansen buildings are maintained in using traditional skills. This scene shows thatchers at work repairing the roof at the Olsztynek *skansen*.

▽ **FOLK COSTUMES**
Krakowiacy, wearing the traditional folk costumes of the Kraków region can be seen singing folk songs in Kraków's Main Market Square on a daily basis.

FOOD AND DRINK

Polish food is a delicious mixture of influences drawn from Russia to Ukraine,
served in up in hearty portions and accompanied by freely flowing drinks

Poland has always been better known for politics rather than cuisine, and when the cuisine is thought of it is usually in terms of clichés, such as herrings, stuffed cabbage leaves and various other rich, stodgy dishes. These elements do of course exist, as they do in virtually every national cuisine, but Polish food also offers a wealth of light, elegant dishes. Specialities include Baltic salmon, ceps and truffles, a wide range of game led by venison and wild boar – typically flavoured with juniper berries, while various dishes are garnished with dill (the national herb). Terminology also shows how powerful associations can be: if you translated soured cream into crème fraiche, which is the same thing, then it automatically receives approbation simply for being French.

Polish cuisine was constantly evolving as new ingredients and techniques became known to cooks. From the 12th century Poland was already on the spice route from the East to Europe and Scandinavia, with the salt mines at Wieliczka just outside Kraków also mined from the 12th century.

In the 16th century the Italian Princess Bona Sforza married King Zygmunt Stary and introduced Italian favourites such as tomatoes, chicory, asparagus, artichokes and, of course, pasta. King Jan III Sobieski, who reigned in the 17th century, had a French wife who brought the omelette and various French specialities with her, while Jan Sobieski's defeat of the Turks at Vienna in 1683 resulted in him bringing back coffee, which was booty taken from pavilions which the Turks had abandoned. The Austrian emperor also gave the king some potato plants, which were initially planted at Wilanów, the royal summer residence outside Warsaw, and were considered an "exotic" novelty. In the 17th century the Polish and Lithuanian commonwealth was Europe's largest country reaching from the Baltic to the Black Sea, with Lithuanian dishes like boiled meat dumplings being integrated. A large Jewish community also contributed various dishes.

Soup and dumplings

Polish hospitality is warm and generous, summed up by a popular saying: "a guest in the house, God in the house." Breakfast is typically

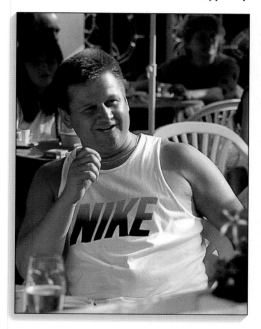

a selection of sliced charcuterie, tomatoes and cheese, rye bread and plenty of strong coffee. A late lunch is usually the day's main three-course meal, with a light buffet-style supper typically comprising cold cuts, vegetables such as tomatoes and pickled cucumbers, with rye bread.

Soup is a popular starter. Poland's more than 30 types of mushrooms are put to good use in numerous versions of mushroom soup, while *kapuśniak* is a hearty winter warmer of boiled cabbage. The most popular soup is *barszcz* (beetroot soup), served either "clear" or with chopped beetroot and boiled potatoes added. Ukranian *barszcz* means extra chopped vegetables including cabbage. *Chłodnik* is the sum-

LEFT: food from the sea.
RIGHT: Poles take their food seriously.

mer version, served cold garnished with a freshly boiled egg, chopped dill and soured cream, which turns the soup a shade of lilac.

Pierogi are variously translated as dumplings or ravioli, but this makes them sound like a derivative rather than a speciality in their own right. Where they originated is unclear – they may have arrived during the 12th century from Russia or they may already have been an original Slavic folk dish. *Pierogi* are prepared by placing a small amount of stuffing in a circle of dough, which is then folded over the stuffing and sealed with a scalloped edge, making them look rather like large ears. The most

with curd cheese mixed with candied zest and raisins, or various fruits such as blueberries, diced apples or thick preserves, which are served with caster sugar and soured cream.

Meat and vegetables

Bigos ("hunter's stew") is a classic example of a one-pot dish, originally prepared with whatever game a hunter (or poacher) could get. The line-up of extras is also variable, though the usual basis of *bigos* is chopped white cabbage, sauerkraut and dried mushrooms, cooked with pork, bacon and *zywiecka* (Polish sausage). Adding a little lard is traditional and gives a

popular filling "*z seren*" ("with cheese"), also known as "*ruski*" ("Russian"), means a combination of curd cheese, mashed potato and chopped fried onion.

Another popular style "*z kapsutą*" ("with cabbage") means either cabbage or sauerkraut (or a combination of both) mixed with chopped sautéed mushrooms; while "*z mięsem*" ("with meat") is ground beef mixed with breadcrumbs and onion. Buckwheat, a staple of the Slav diet, is the most historic style. Once boiled, the typical garnish is breadcrumbs fried in butter. Alternatively, the *pierogi* can be lightly sautéed to give a crispy texture, and served with soured cream. Sweet *pierogi* are also served, stuffed

wonderful depth of flavour, whereas the question of whether or not to add a few tablespoons of tomato purée is a great talking point among serious cooks.

Meat essentially means pork in Poland, whether a fried breaded cutlet, roasted with prunes or served with stewed cabbage. Chicken (not usually considered to be "real meat") is typically served as *de volaille* (stuffed with butter and garlic). Beef is also less popular, unless it is served as the ultra-popular *zrazy*, established in the 14th century by King Władisław himself. Pieces of beaten, seasoned sirloin of beef are rolled around a filling of chopped fried bacon, breadcrumbs, dill cucumber and mushrooms, and then fried or grilled.

The usual accompaniment of *zrazy* – and indeed other meat dishes (but never fish) – is buckwheat. This is also the most traditional stuffing for favourites such as *gołąbki*, literally "little pigeons", which are stuffed cabbage leaves and roast suckling pig. Another favourite side dish with various roast meats is a cucumber salad named *mizeria* (literally "misery"). The name is no indication of the wonderfully refreshing flavours, with wafer thin slices of cucumber dressed in a combination of soured cream, lemon juice, a dash of caster sugar and salt, garnished with minced dill or spring onion,

most historic, made with baked or cooked beetroots, sliced and layered with a dressing of vinegar, caraway seeds, horseradish and lemon juice. Beetroot is also popular puréed, sliced and fried in batter, or grated and combined with a little soured cream or minced onion.

Modern Polish cuisine

Under Communism Polish cuisine virtually disappeared, with rationing and frequent shortages a daily reality. Even having a ration book entitling you to a certain amount of butter, meat, and so on was no guarantee, as it still meant having to find a shop that actually had those

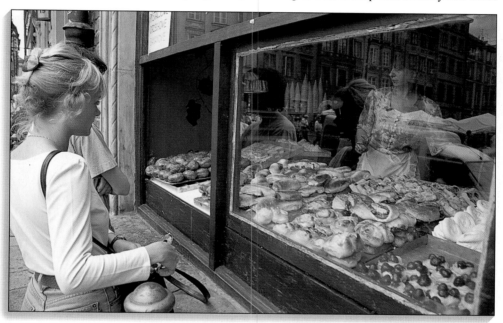

and chilled before serving. The origins of *mizeria* are attributed to Queen Bona Sforza, but the reasons vary. The name may have stemmed from her weeping nostalgically for Italy whenever she ate it (before settling in and living happily in Poland). Alternatively, she may have eaten *mizeria* in such quantities that the consequent pain of indigestion made her ask for a misericord (a dagger for committing suicide).

Meat dishes are also frequently accompanied by various beetroot dishes. *Cwikla* is one of the

LEFT: a butcher's shop in Wrocław.
ABOVE: choosing a pastry treat at the *cukiernia* (cake shop).

POLISH SWEETS

Beetroot grated with caster sugar and lemon juice served hot is a favourite dessert, and all-day partner to coffee. Many Polish cakes and patisseries originally arrived from France, such as *napoleonki* (millefeuille) and *eklerka* (eclair). Among the classic Polish cakes are *sernik* (cheesecake) prepared with either curd or cream cheese (or a combination of both) and always baked. Variations include adding cream to the cheese (for greater moistness), raisins (Viennese-style), and with a surface layer of either icing sugar or dark chocolate and crushed nuts. *Makowiec* is prepared like a sponge cake and rolled around a filling of poppyseeds or a "poppyseed cream".

items in stock. Consequently, Poles refer to the cooking of this era as "Communist food".

Not surprisingly, restaurants offered a very erratic menu, while chefs also had to endure various other restrictions. The government issued every restaurant with a compulsory menu (the ultimate "set menu"), which never changed, seasonally or even annually, and no deviation was allowed. Chefs also had to follow government cookery manuals which not only stipulated the cooking method, but also the exact amount (in grams) and number of ingredients in each dish. Vigilant controllers would subsequently cross-reference the num-

ber of dishes served with the remaining amount of stock in the kitchen.

It is only since privatisation that chefs have become liberated and able to use their own ideas, and of course have the advantage of regular supplies. Not only was real Polish food back on the menu, but Polish chefs also began returning from having worked abroad, bringing with them a modern European perspective. As chefs began to re-interpret their national dishes, so Modern Polish cuisine began to emerge in a few key Warsaw restaurants during the mid-1990s. The Malinowa within the Hotel Bristol, Fukier, and the Hotel Jan III Sobieski were among the key pioneers.

Modern Polish is, fortunately, retaining the authentic character of classic dishes, but producing lighter, more subtle and interesting versions. A new style *barszcz*, for instance, comprises delicate jellied consommé with soured cream and a beetroot julienne; herring appears as a tartare, *pierogi* may feature brains or Baltic seaweed, while *bigos* benefits from a wider repertoire of choice cuts such as smoked duck and venison.

Communism also sought to wipe out regionalism, which is now beginning to return. Poznań, for instance, is known for *pyzzy* (steamed yeast dumplings), Warsaw thrives on tripe soup, while *polewka Gdańska*, is a goulash soup flavoured with pickled cucumbers, olives and capers.

Vodka

"Vodka doesn't taste of anything", and the subsequent conclusion that "all vodkas taste the same", are two popular clichés – but they are very far from the whole story. The traditional style of vodka in the UK and USA doesn't, in fact, taste of anything, being entirely neutral and only intended as a means of adding alcohol to a mixer such as tonic water, or a cocktail, without adding any flavour. Polish vodka, however, offers "character", drawn from the raw material, which is either rye or potatoes.

Wyborowa vodka, for instance, provides distinct rye aromas, while the flavour combines wonderfully mellow rye and nutty notes with a natural, elegant sweetness.

Potato vodka may seem as though it's produced from a "second class" source, but not only are some of the most popular brands produced from potatoes, but potatoes have in fact been elevated into a speciality, being more expensive to cultivate and distil than rye. A special variety of potatoes is used, cultivated in specific microclimates by the River Vistula and on the Baltic Coast. Vodkas such as Luksusowa and Cracovia yield fresh potato aromas, while the palate thrives on a subtle sweetness, with hints of creamy mashed potatoes.

There has been a long-standing dispute between the Poles and Russians about the origins of vodka. After all, who wouldn't want to take the credit for inventing such a drink. While there is no definitive evidence, circumstantial evidence points to Poland. Knowledge of distillation spread from France across Europe around the 14th century, and is likely to have reached Poland before going on to Russia via Lithuania and the Ukraine. Moreover, the earliest recorded use of the word "vodka" in Eastern Europe is on a Polish document, dated 1405. The Russians, however, claim vodka was first distilled in a monastery outside Moscow in the 14th century.

NATIONAL TIPPLE

As early as the end of the 16th century vodka was established as the Polish national drink.

At least the Poles and Russians agreed on the name for this drink, with vodka being the diminutive of *woda*, meaning water (so vodka literally means "little water".) When this term

flavours and aromas. The answer was to disguise these imperfections by adding aromatic oils, fruit, herbs and spices, and to sweeten it with honey. When rectification was developed during the 19th century, flavourings were added for their own sake, as there was nothing left to hide.

During the 19th century around 100 flavoured styles were available, and Poland continues to produce the world's largest range of flavoured vodka. Flavourings can be used in a "minimalist" way, solely to enhance the flavour of the grain, with a hint of aromatic

was coined using the diminutive it indicated that it was an improved version of the original. The earliest centres of commercial distillation, during the 16th century, were Kraków, Poznań and Gdańsk. By then vodka had developed from being purely medicinal into a social drink.

Commercial distillation was originally limited to the aristocracy (providing plenty of tax revenue), though early distillation methods were inevitably rudimentary, as it was impossible to rectify (purify) the spirit. This meant that the resulting vodka was marred by unpleasant

LEFT: perusing the menu in Warsaw.
ABOVE: café-bars are part of the new drinking culture.

fruit and apple spirit maximising the rye flavours of Extra Zytnia. At the other extreme is Gnesnania Boonekamp, flavoured with 23 herbs and spices, which originated from Gniezno, briefly the capital of Poland during the 11th century.

A classic style dating from the 16th century, and still going strong is Zubrowka, which includes the simpler reference of "Bison Vodka" on the label. The flavour is derived entirely from bison grass, and not from any part of a bison, with this wild herb growing only in the Bialowieza Forest, a national park in eastern Poland (*see page 186*). A blade of grass features in each bottle of Zubrowka, but that is merely a decorative accessory, as it takes far more bison grass to create this complex, aromatic vodka with herbaceous, fresh grass/hay aromas, and beautifully balanced herbaceous flavours of thyme and lavender, together with lemon, tobacco and chocolatey hints. The most popular way of serving Zubrowka today is known as "Tatanka", which means a measure of vodka topped up with apple juice, creating a refreshing but dry combination.

The name Tatanka was coined after the release of the 1995 film *Dances With Wolves* in Poland, because this was how the Native Americans referred to bison.

After enjoying vodka with *zakąski* there's no need to stop there, and indeed vodka is often served with a meal in Poland, after which a choice of digestif-style vodkas take over. Goldwasser ("Gold Water"), which originated in Gdańsk during the 16th century, is based on an aniseed-flavoured vodka infused with various flavourings such as gypsy rose, valerian root, sandalwood and rosewood, before adding the final touch: 23-carat gold leaf.

This twinkles beautifully within the vodka, and is of course an automatic talking point, though the original rationale was the alleged medicinal benefits of gold leaf. Whether gold

VODKA PARTIES

A great benefit of having a vodka session in true Polish style is that it's an instant party, because Poles always serve food with vodka. There is actually a specific range of specialities called "*zakaski*" (literally "a nibble") all of which have a genuine rapport with vodka. This is typically salted herring fillets and *blinis* with soured cream, pickled cucumbers, pickled mushrooms, sausage, ham, rye bread and curd cheese. These flavours are substantial enough to stand up to the vodka, while vodka tames the saltiness of herring fillets, and melting soured cream. Moreover, rich, salty, spicy flavours naturally encourage another glass of vodka, so it's a perfect relationship.

leaf actually contributes to the flavour is debatable, and actually irrelevant, because there's already plenty to enjoy with rich flavours spanning aniseed, liquorice, cooked fruit (particularly rhubarb and oranges), culminating in an elegant, dry finish.

Another rarity is Starka (meaning "old"), a style that dates from the late 14th century. Aristocrats traditionally celebrated the birth of a daughter by filling empty wine casks with vodka, which were aged in a cellar until the daughter's wedding day and served at the wedding banquet. The intervening years saw the vodka gently mature into an elegant, aromatic style. Starka is still produced, and aged for ten years in oak barrels, yielding an indulgent rye flavour.

High strength vodkas extend the range of choice, with Polish Pure Spirit at either 57 per cent or 79 per-cent abv, while Rectified Spirit (*Spirytus Rektyfikowany*) at 95 percent abv, the world's strongest spirit, is distillation strength vodka. These styles are usually a base for home-flavour-ing, with a favourite com-bination being Rectified Spirit and cherry cordial, resulting in *wisniowka*, while *karmel-*

WORDS OF WISDOM

Numerous "vodka sayings" have evolved in Poland, such as "*wodka grzeje, wodka chlodzi, wodka nigdy nie zaskodzi*", meaning "vodka cools and vodka warms, but vodka never harms."

Beer and wine

Beer and mead were the earliest alcoholic drinks prepared by the Slavs, with major cities such as Warsaw and Wrocław still featuring mead bars. Mead is kept hot by serving it in ceramic beakers that stand on a tray heated by a small candle.

Additionally, a range of fruit wines are very popular and make the most of readily avail-able favourites such as cherries, strawberries, redcurrants, blackcurrants, goose-berries, apples and blackberries.

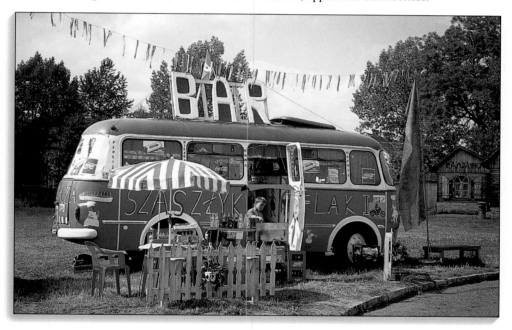

owka means adding a sugar syrup to Rectified Spirit for an instant caramel vodka.

The Polish toast "*na zdrowie*" (meaning "to your health") is not simply a polite line. Vodka is renowned for purity, and actually contains a lower level of congeners (impurities res-ponsible for hangovers) than other spirits. While devotees claim that drinking vodka is a guarantee against hangovers, this also depends on the quantity of vodka consumed, particu-larly as an enthusiastic refrain in Poland is "*do dna*", meaning "to the bottom" (of the glass).

Polish beer is generally larger, though porter, stout and other dark beers are also brewed in some parts of the country. Some of the most famous brands come from the south, including Żywiec and Okocim, both produced at the brewery and town of the same name.

Coincidentally, the north of Poland is also the source of some excellent beers, with Gdańsk the source of Hevelius (originally brewed by the family of Jan Heweliusz, the renowned 17th-century astronomer, who boosted his income from brewing).

One of the leading brands, EB is produced in nearby Elbląg, where beer has been brewed since 1309, when the Teutonic Knights who

LEFT: relaxing at a cafe-bar in Zakopane.
ABOVE: an imaginative place to stop for refreshment.

then controlled the region (*see page 263*) granted the first brewing licence to Siegfried von Feuchtwanger. By 1336 the town had a brewers' guild with more than 160 members. Moreover, there is a fascinating link between Elbląg and Great Britain, as from 1580 English merchants who were then trading with Baltic ports purchased land around the area, which includes the site of the current Elbląg brewery. The land provided a recreational area from which the English merchants could watch

HAIR OF THE DOG

If, after all this vodka and alcohol, you have a hangover, you can try a classic Polish remedy – drinking the juice drained from a glass of sauerkraut. Failing that it's back to the drink that caused the problem.

Soft drinks

Poland's vast amount of spas also means a comprehensive selection of mineral waters, all with varying taste profiles, as spas across the country increasingly commercialise their finest liquid assets. Krystynka, for instance, is bottled at the Ciechocinek spa, while Perła Bałtyku ("Pearl of the Baltic") hails from the spa in Kołobrzeg on the coast (*see page 330*).

Among a wide range of fresh juices produced from indigenous fruits, the clear leader in pop-

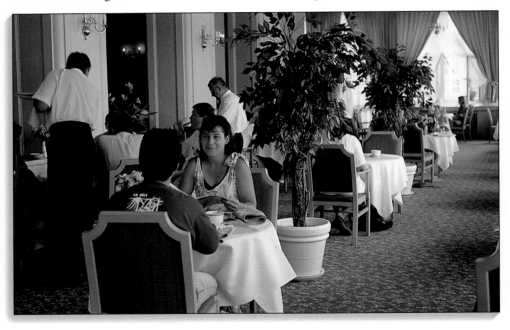

their ships and simply relax and gossip. The locals referred to the area as "*Angielski Zdroj*" ("The English Springs"), after the springs of pure water which flowed there at a very low temperature.

Not surprisingly, these springs now provide the water used in the production of EB beer. As one of the world's few beers that is actually triple filtered, with an alcoholic strength of 5.4 percent abv, it has an unusually clean, crisp taste. Polish brewers and fans of EB will try to convince you that however much EB you drink, you won't get a hangover. If only. Draft beer is not common in Poland although it can be found in small villages in the south.

ularity must be *sok z czarnek porzeczki* (blackcurrant juice), deliciously ripe and rich, but with a dry finish. Bottled fruit juices mixed with mineral water are refreshing, with strawberry and apple being the most popular flavours.

Coffee (*kawa*) is typically served *cappuccino* style, strong and full-bodied with a dash of milk, while tea (*herbata*) is served without milk but with a slice of lemon and in tall glasses. In a café or restaurant this usually means a glass of boiling water and a tea bag on the saucer will arrive at the table for customers to brew the tea according to their own preference. ❏

ABOVE: the restaurant at the Grand Hotel Sopot.

Festive Food

The religious and gastronomic focus of Christmas is Christmas Eve rather than Christmas Day. However, until the Christmas Eve dinner (traditionally comprising 12 dishes, one for each apostle) a semi-fast is observed, involving a small helping of rye bread and salted herring fillets.

There is no set time to assemble for Christmas Eve dinner, known as Wigilia – it depends on when the first star appears, symbolising the star that guided the Three Kings to Bethlehem. The table is laid with a white tablecloth, under which a small amount of hay is placed, recalling the hay of the crib. Traditionally an extra place is set, so that no unexpected visitor will be turned away and experience the same treatment that inns in Bethlehem extended to the Holy family. Christmas greetings are then exchanged and food is served.

Everyone has a small wafer, blessed by a priest, and small pieces of wafer are exchanged. As this is a Holy day, the entire meal excludes meat products of any kind, even animal fat. Consequently, the Christmas Eve *barszcz* (soup) is based on vegetable stock. The soup can be garnished with "*uszka*" (literally "little ears") which are scaled-down *pierogi* filled with sliced mushrooms. Several types of fish, prepared in various ways, provide the subsequent dishes. Salted herring fillets, for example, are served with a garnish of chopped onion and soured cream or apple. Baltic salmon and pike are popular, though the archetypal choice is carp, either fried or served with "*szary sos*" ("grey sauce") prepared from ground honeycake, raisins and almonds. An old superstition states that saving a scale from the carp and keeping it in your wallet ensures prosperity in the new year. Fish is followed by a selection of *pierogi* including curd cheese and potato, and mushroom with sauerkraut or cabbage. Fruit compote is the classic dessert, prepared by stewing dried fruits flavoured with a vanilla pod, followed by *makowiec* and various other cakes with lemon tea. Then it's off to church for midnight mass.

Roast goose is the main event on Christmas Day, with the festive period known as Carnival lasting until Shrove Tuesday. This is the season when people go from house to house celebrating. Hot honey vodka is the usual tipple, accompanied by

doughnuts filled with rose petal jam and *chrusty* (literally "brushwood"), also known as *faworki* ("little favours"). These light, deep-fried pastry twists are served with a sprinkling of icing sugar.

Easter celebrations begin with a semi-fast on Good Friday, usually herrings and rye bread, prior to the Easter Sunday breakfast served after an early morning mass. A basket of hardboiled eggs decorated with rustic motifs forms the centrepiece of the table, with the host and hostess exchanging an Easter greeting by passing everyone a small piece of egg. The breakfast fare represents daily staples, which are taken to church to be blessed on Easter Saturday in baskets decorated with

colourful napkins and greenery. These foodstuffs, known as *święcone* ("blessed") include various types of Polish sausage, hardboiled eggs, rye bread, salt and horseradish. There are also cakes, including Easter Babka, a yeast cake flavoured with chocolate and vanilla, baked in a tall fluted tin. Egg shells and sausage skins are burned, as anything that has been blessed must be eaten or burned.

Easter Monday sees a ritual known as " *śmygus dyngus*". Until noon everyone has the "right" to splash people with water. The victim is not supposed to retaliate. Traditionally young boys sought out unsuspecting girls. A sprinkling of cologne water is more gentlemanly, though jugs of cold water are not uncommon. ❏

RIGHT: traditional *brindza* (smoked cheeses) are a speciality of the southern highlands.

POLAND'S NATIONAL PARKS

*The country's national parks have excellent hiking, cycling and horse riding trails
and exceptional opportunities for anglers, climbers and skiers*

Nature lovers will find few other countries in Europe that can offer such a diverse range of natural landscapes and rare fauna and flora as Poland. The woods, marshland and valleys are not the only places where walkers will find plants and animals that are now extremely rare elsewhere in Europe. Even areas of land that are used for agricultural purposes, fields, meadows and forests, remain that are still farmed and managed using the traditional methods, preserving the natural habitat.

The most valuable areas are now designated as national parks and are generally open to the public. There are currently 23 national parks in Poland, covering a total area of approximately 312,000 hectares (770,000 acres). Six of them, the Babiogórski, Białowieski, Bieszczadzki, Karkonoski, Słowiński and Tatrzański National Parks have been registered on the UNESCO list of World Biosphere Reserves; additionally, the Białowieski National Park has been included in UNESCO's list of Humanity's World Heritage, and two – Biebrzański and Słowiński – have been made a part of the International Ramsar Convention of protection of waterways.

All aspects of the Polish natural world are preserved here: from the rocky, almost alpine Tatra Mountains to the wooded Pieniny and Bieszczady, from the shifting dunes in the mini-desert beside the Baltic to the lakes and rivers hidden among the forests of the Suwalskie region and the Roztocze Heights.

Although standards are modest in comparison with western Europe, accommodation and restaurants can be found in or near to all the 23 national parks. Tourist trails and educational paths leading through the parks also make getting acquainted with nature much easier. Way-marked footpaths and nature trails help visitors to explore deep into the parks and the nearby natural history museums invariably

have interesting collections. Services offered by professional guides and specialist travel agencies are available to those who wish practise different forms of nature tourism.

The most productive region for nature-loving tourists is the Nizina Polnocnopodlaska lowland plain (Bialystok and Lomza provinces)

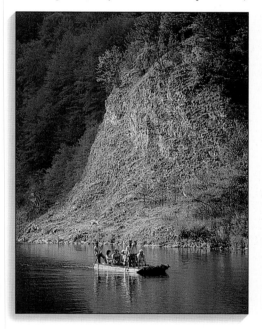

with the Puszcza Białowieska primeval forest and the marshes of the Biebrza and Narew river valleys. This area, together with a section of the Suwalki-Augustów Lakes and the Great Mazurian Lakes, is often described as Poland's "Green Lung".

Białowieski National Park

The preservation of this area as a park goes back to 1921, when the forestry " Reservation" was created. In 1932 it was transformed into the "National Park in Białowieza" and restored in 1947 as Białowieza National Park; the area was enlarged again in 1996. It is the oldest national park in Poland and one of the most

---

PRECEDING PAGES: a European bison.
LEFT: nesting storks in Pomerania.
RIGHT: the Dunajec Gorge in the Pieninski National Park.

precious natural legacies to be found in this part of Europe. The Białowieza park is located in the central part of Białowieza Forest, in the eastern part of the Podlasie-Belorus Uplands, on Mazurian-Podlasie Land, in the natural forest region of the Białowieza Primeval Forest. According to biogeographical division, it lies in the boreonemoral province.

At first sight it seems an untidy place, with trees growing in strange ways and places. But this is the key to Białowieza – this is how nature intended and

of Eastern Europe. Altogether the park is host to 600 types of flora – including many 300-year-old trees – and some 11,000 types of fauna, including 62 species of mammals and 2,000 bird species. Here one can come across, elk, fawn deer, wild lynx and wolves. But the park is probably most famous for its wild bison, now restored to their natural habitat.

There are many outstanding attractions in the park, but particularly recommended are the grounds surrounding the palace

is much how forest would have looked in pre-historic times. The untidiness of the forest also allows an amazing range of flora and fauna to flourish freely. The most protected part of the forest is its central-northern region, where all types of human activity are strictly banned – even gathering berries or collecting dead leaves. Nature alone is king here.

The most common trees are oak, hornbeam, lime, maple and spruce. Much of the forest is covered with a mixture of trees and vegetation and there are two very distinct areas: one with leafy deciduous trees, with a distinctive Central European flavour; and another part which is full of spruce trees and much more reminiscent

built by the Czar of Russia in the latter half of the 19th century (*see page 186*). In fact, all who know the park agree that it is almost impossible to capture its essence in words.

From water to desert

The Biebrzański National Park, which covers an area of 59,223 hectares (146,280 acres) is an eldorado for ornithologists. This, the largest and probably the most popular of Poland's national parks, extends along the River Biebrza and contains some marshland and peat bogs unique to Europe. The wide range of bird wildlife includes golden eagles, white-tail eagles, owls and ruff.

The main attraction of Słowiński National Park (*see page 331*), stretching for 33 kilometres (21 miles) along the Baltic coast, are probably the shifting dunes, some of which can reach 42 metres (140 ft) high. The most spectacular of these are found on the sandbar between the sea and the river Łeba. They can move at a speed of 10 metres (35 ft) per year, burying everything in their way. Nearby are attractive lakes, rich in birdlife, beaches and a mini-desert.

Tourism is rapidly gaining ground in the Pieniński National Park in the Pieniny Mountains in the southeast of Poland. The peaks of the Karkonosze Mountains in the western Sudetens with Mount Sniezka (1,602 metres/5,254 ft) the highest point (*see page 282*). Characteristic of the Karkonosze are the *kotly* (cirques) – huge hollows carved by glaciers during the Ice Age. Kociol Malego Stawu and Kociol Wielkiego Stawu near Mount Snieżka are the most spectacular. The climate in this region is notoriously unpredictable and yet it is popular with hikers. Warm, waterproof clothes are essential whatever the time of year.

The natural beauty of the East Carpathians is preserved by Bieszczady National Park, created in 1973 (*see page 237*). It is located in the

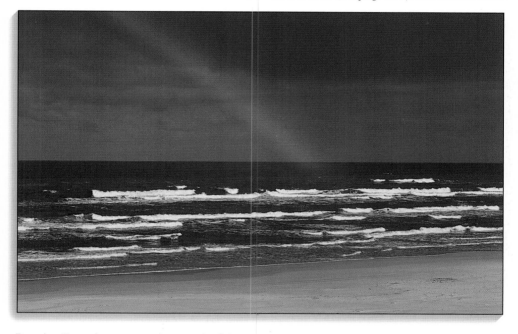

Dunajec Gorge is a spectacular stretch of river, which snakes for about 8 kilometres (5 miles) between steep cliffs, often over 300 metres (1,000 ft) high. Although raft rides have been an attraction since the 19th century, the modern versions, consisting of coffin-like canoes tied together with rope and navigated by local guides, attract 200,000 passengers every year.

Mountain country

A narrow belt running along the Czech frontier, the Karkonoski National Park includes the

LEFT: tarpan in the Białowieza National Park.
ABOVE: Słowinski National Park.

SAVING THE BISON

One of the species that may be encountered in Białowieza is the bison, Europe's largest animal. Once these were plentiful, numbering almost 2,000 in the mid-19th century, but by 1914 their numbers were reduced to around 700, and during the war the Germans killed them for food. By 1919 the last wild one died. The national park was set up to protect what was left and in 1929 wild bison were reintroduced into a closed area.

The bison population reached 211 by 1997 but bison remain an endangered species. The world population is around 3,000, of which almost 2,000 live in the wild in special reserves like Białowieza.

southeast of the country, at the frontier with Ukraine and Slovakia, and covers 27.834 hectares (68,780 acres).

In the highest part of Polish upper West Bieszczady are "*poloniny*" (mountain pastures) – peaks which are free from forests and over the forest limit, such as Carynska and Wetlinska. These mountain meadows host a great number of rare, East Carpathian plant species. The forests, mostly beech with some fir and sycamore stands, cover 87 percent of the park. About 50 species of mammals are native to the area, including typical forest species: European bison, brown bears, wolves, red deer, the lynx

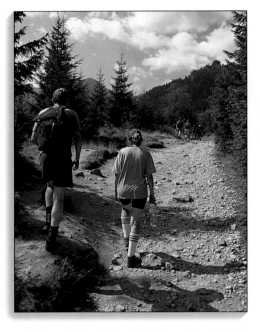

and the wild cat. About 150 species of birds have found a haven here. If visitors wish to spot the wild inhabitants of the park, they should walk quietly along the trails in small groups. The best time for wildlife watchers is the early morning – grazing red deers may be seen even from the roads in the valleys.

At Ustrzyki Dolne is the park's natural science museum and educational centre.

Tatrzański National Park surrounds and protects the whole Tatra mountain range on the Polish side. It is the only region of alpine character in Poland, with the highest peak being Mount Rysy, 2,499 metres (8,198 ft) above sea level. The 21,164-hectare (52,297-acre) park

covers the whole area of the Polish Tatra mountains, the youngest and highest mountains in the country. There are post-glacial pot-holes (Czarny Staw), Sniezna cave which is 780 metres (2,560 ft) deep and an abundance of lakes – Morskie Oko, with an area 34 hectares (84 acres) and Wielki Staw Polski, 79 metres (260 ft) deep. The foothill zone is dominated by spruce forests mixed with fir, larch, beech and sycamore. The highland zone is covered with spruce with a few stone pine stands. The dwarf pine layer gives way to alpine meadows and pastures, while over 2.300 metres (7,546 ft) above sea level stretch crags and peaks.

The flora and fauna of the Tatra range abounds in indigenous and alpine plant species as well as and marmot, chamois and a small population of bears. The Tatra range is also one of Poland's last refuges of the golden eagle.

The park has a natural history museum with many interesting objects and a scientific laboratory. The main tourist base is Zakopane, the winter capital of Poland (*see page 243*).

The Babiogorski National Park encompasses Mount Babia Góra, at 1,725 metres (5,660 ft) the highest peak of the Western Beskid Range. The woods here are very much like a primeval forest. The lower plant zone is dominated by fir and beech forest mixed with spruce and sycamore. Spruce, mountain-ash and dwarf mountain pine predominate in the upper zones. Next comes the alpine zone with its rare mountain plant species. Gullies filled with rubble can be found in the top rocky zone. The forests shelter a multitude of animals including bear, red deer, wolf and lynx; they are also a habitat for the rare wood grouse.

The Gorczanski National Park comprises the central part of the Gorce Range, with the exception of its highest peak, Turbacz. This is a typical mountain forest park with storied layers of tree stands. The Carpathian beech and fir woods make up the lower layer, while the upper layer is dominated by spruce forest. Both alpine and endemic plants cover the numerous mountain glades. The park's fauna includes such typical forest animals and red deer, roe deer, wild boar, lynx, wildcat and wolf. Worth special note is the population of wood grouse and the spotted salamander.

The Góry Stołowe National Park envelops the Góry Stołowe (Table Mountain) massif. The main attraction is the original landscape of rocky plateaux with sheer ledges, which has developed due to the specific tabular geological structure of these mountains. Nature has formed labyrinthine passages among the rocks. The most interesting clusters of rock formations may be seen in the " Błędne Skały" reserve and on Mount Szczeliniec Wielki (919 metres/3,015 ft). The slopes and foothills of the plateaux are covered with spruce and beech forests, while the high moors with marsh plants developed in places on the flat table-like tops.

MOUNTAIN STROLLS

One of the pleasures of Poland's mountain areas is its accessibility. Hiking trails are aimed more at leisurely walks than strenuous hard climbing.

and larch. The park's rich plant population includes many rare species of mountain and lowland plants. The king of the wildlife here is the red deer.

Forested landscapes

The Bory Tucholskie National Park protects the most valuable area of the Bory Tucholskie Forest. The sandy flat land is overgrown with pine woods, cut across with river valleys and dotted with lakes, nestling in deep ravines. In depressions and at the edges of some lakes are bogs which

The territory of Świętokrzyskie National Park includes the Łysogóry Mountains, with Mount Łysica reaching 612 metres (2,007 ft) above sea level, the highest range of the Swietokrzyskie Mountains and fragments of the adjoining valleys. The Świętokrzyskie Mountains, the oldest in Poland, were formed of paleozoic rocks. Worth particular attention are the small deforested areas (*goloborza*), covered with quartzite boulders and stripped of green vegetation. The Łysogóry Range is covered with fir forests mixed with pine, beech

are the home of rare species of post-glacial plants. The wildlife includes trout found in the crystal-clear rivers, as well as water fowl, birds of prey, beaver and elk.

The Drawienski National Park, located in the Dravska Forest, contains parts of the Drava river valley (one of the most beautiful rivers in Polish Pomerania), the Plocizna river, its tributary and 13 lakes.

Pine forests cover 78 percent of the park's total area, but there are also forests where pine is mixed with oak, beech, and alder. Of particular interest are the high moorlands in the Plocizna river basin, which abound in rare species of marsh plants and post-glacial remains. Var-

LEFT: on the mountain trail in the Tatras.
ABOVE: undisturbed lake and surroundings.

ious species of fish inhabit the crystal-clear waters of the park. The park is also home to beaver, otter and osprey, a rare bird of prey.

The Kampinoski National Park is located in the vicinity of Warsaw and encompasses the Kampinoski Forest, spreading over the Vistula river pro-glacial valley. Belts of inland dunes, overgrown with pine woods, add to the attractiveness of the park's landscape. In the depressions between the dunes there are peat bogs, meadows and marshes covered with a growth of

CASTLE TRAIL

The Ojcowski National Park is popular with history lovers as well as nature lovers, located near the Eagles' Nest Trail of ancient castles and fortresses.

tain species and protected plants. The park fauna is represented by bear, wolf, lynx, wildcat, golden eagle and eagle owl.

Valleys and plateaux

The greatest natural asset of the Narwianski National Park is its well-preserved and unspoilt swampy River Narew valley which features a unique system of flood waters, meanders, old river beds, bulrushes and low-bogs, all of which are called "Polish Amazonia". It has particularly rich birdlife with over 200 species, out of

alder. The park's flora abounds in rare protected species. Its wildlife includes such animals as elk, beaver, and lynx.

The Magurski National Park occupies the central part of the Lower Beskid Range, dominated by Mount Magura Watkowska (846 metres/2,775 ft). It covers areas typical for the Beskid Range landscape with forested dome-like hills separated from each other by rivers and brooks.

The river Wisloka is born in the park and runs across its territory, forming numerous scenic gorges and meanders. The hills are overgrown with beech, fir and spruce forests. The flora of the park boasts many rare moun-

which 154 species have their nesting grounds in the park. Some species of the local waterbirds are difficult to spot elsewhere in Europe.

The Ojcówski National Park (19 sq km/7 sq miles) is situated near Kraków and occupies the southern part of the Krakówsko-Czestochowska Plateau and the valleys of the Pradnik and Saspowka rivers. Numerous caves, scenic ravines, rocky passes and spectacular rock formations, including the famous "Hercules Club", have been created by nature. Forest covers the majority of the park area.

The most characteristic species of the park's flora are those of stenothermal lichens. The insect population is extremely diversified (over

3,000 species) including 1,142 species of beetles and 520 species of butterflies. The caves are a shelter for a multitude of species of bats.

The Poleski National Park is located in the Leczynsko-Wlodawskie Lake District (Lublin Polesie) and includes a unique flatland of extensive peat bogs and swamps, which in places is reminiscent of the tundra or the transitional zone between tundra and taiga. The peat bogs shelter many species of rare plants. The park is also a refuge to such animals as elk, wolves and the rare marsh turtle.

The Roztoczański National Park encompasses the central part of the Roztocze region. The eminences are divided by deep ravines; the Wieprz and Tanew rivers gently wind their way across the park. Forests, mainly beech and fir, cover 93 percent of the park's territory. The rich flora includes both lowland and highland species, as well as stenothermal species originating from southeastern Europe. There are also some 190 species of birds.

Lakes and islands

The Wielkopolski National Park near Poznan, in the Wielkopolskie Lake District, has all the characteristic elements of post-glacial landscape. Thus, there are hills 130 metres (426 ft) above sea level, subglacial channels and plenty of lakes. Pine and mixed forests cover the majority part of the park. The park's flora includes many rare and protected species and the forests are home to such animals as red deer, roe deer, wild boar, marten, badger, hare and numerous bird species.

Lake Wigry, one of the largest lakes in northeastern Poland, is an important element of Wigierski National Park. In addition, there are 25 lakes in the park interconnected by a network of rivers, the biggest being the Czarna Hańcza river. Small, marshy mid-forest lakes, surrounded by peat bogs are one of the special features of this park. The vegetation is dominated by pine and spruce forests, but there are also large colonies of moor, aquatic and meadow plants.

Mammals living in the forest include elk, red deer, roe deer, wolf and beaver. There is a profusion of various species of water birds, and the park waterways teem with such rare fish

species as lavaret, European whitefish, bulltrout and European smelt.

The Woliński National Park occupies the western part of Wolin Island. It includes the morainic heights which end with a picturesque, steep 95-metre (312-ft) high cliff at the shore of the Baltic Sea and the Bay of Szczecin. Here the shore continuously retreats because of the destructive action of the waves. Almost the entire area of the park is covered with dense forests, the most valuable of which are the beech stands.

A group of lakes and sandy beaches is found in the southern part of the park. The diversified

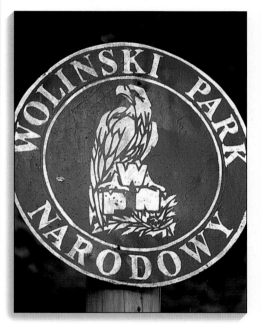

plant cover is made up of many rare species of undergrowth, stenothermal and sand plants. Among the wildlife are such rare species as the white-tailed eagle, Aquila pomarina and numerous species of water birds. In the heart of the park there is a bison exhibition reserve (*see page 402*).

For visitors to Poland who wish to take full advantage of the many national parks, as well as learn about much of its unique flora and fauna, the addresses of the national park headquarters and the Polish tour operators specialising in tourism for naturalists can be found in the *Travel Tips* section (*see page 375*) at the end of this book. ❏

LEFT: lakes are the perfect environment for storks.
RIGHT: Woliński National Park.

THE ENVIRONMENT

During the communist era, Poland suffered years of environmental damage from heavy industry. Now regulations are in place and the clean-up has begun

Poland is a land of contrasts and that applies just as much to the country's politics and its society as it does to the culture and the different landscapes. When it comes to the demands of the environment and the conservation of the natural world, there are also some huge disparities.

Large parts of Poland have a reputation as refuges for rare fauna and flora, but many visitors are still shocked to discover how carelessly the Communist authorities treated the environment, particularly in the industrial regions. For years the damage that the natural surroundings were suffering was ignored by the people and covered up by the party; now, however, everyone is aware of the problems – and they are posing a major headache for the current government.

Nature protection

Nearly one third of Poland's surface area (29 percent) represents natural attractions and is protected by law. This includes national parks, nature reserves, landscape parks and protected natural landscapes.

National parks are the highest form of nature protection in Poland (*see page 129*). They generally encompass a protected area distinguished by its singular scientific, natural, cultural and educational values. All nature and the characteristic features of a particular landscape are protected within the boundaries of 23 national parks throughout the country. These parks can be visited freely – nearly 1,700 km (1,050 miles) of tourist trails have been marked out within the parks' territories.

Apart from offering very popular hiking routes, the park areas are also available to skiers, mountain climbers and canoeists. Some trails for cycling have also been marked out recently within some of these national parks. Nature reserves are the second most

important form of nature protection and they embrace natural or only slightly changed ecosystems, selected species of plants and animals, and elements of still nature; all these of particular value from either scientific, natural or cultural viewpoints.

So far, 1,169 nature reserves with a the total

surface area of 116 hectares (287 acres) have been established in Poland – about 0.4 percent of the country's total area.

Landscape parks and special protection zones occupy about 10 percent of the country's area. Landscape parks are created in areas which have not only natural but historical value as well. Unlike the national parks, they may be economically exploited under certain conditions, but no activities undertaken in the parks must ruin their landscape values: the beauty of the landscape should be preserved.

Certain zones are marked out and used for short-term holiday recreation, holiday stays and special interest tourism. Therefore, landscape

LEFT: the use of coal and brown coal for energy have caused many environmental problems.
RIGHT: many species of birds thrive nature reserves.

parks often contain organised campsites with good facilities, bivouac fields, and even recreation and holiday centres.

Other areas of protected landscape include individual forms of nature surviving in clusters, which have either scientific, cultural, historical or landscape value, such as large, old trees, springs, waterfalls, rock formations, ravines, boulders and caves. The most fascinating caves are found in the Pieniński, Ojcówski and Karkonoski national parks.

All legal regulations in Poland concerning environment protection conform with the international conventions and agreements.

Communist policy

For decades Polish industry used far too much water, and contaminated the air, the forests and the soil with toxins and discarded raw materials. As early as the 1950s, the government introduced laws and regulations that would, in theory, have protected the environment, but in the years that followed the pollutant emissions from manufacturing industries increased.

An Environment Ministry was established in 1972 and plans were drawn up for the closure of the worst industrial plants by 1990, but these measures were purely for the sake of propaganda and were never taken seriously by the government. If a party leader declared in a speech that the state of the environment was improving every year, it was hoped that eventually everyone would believe it, even though it was apparent that the fish "living" in the Vistula simply refused to swim in the normal way, floating instead with their bellies down, and many of the people, children in particular, who lived in areas close to the coalfields of Silesia were constantly ailing with respiratory disorders and other chronic diseases.

Nevertheless, the truly committed environmental campaigners were able to point to some small successes in their battles with the government. For example, Polish people protested long and hard against the planned nuclear power station and the project was eventually abandoned by government environment officials.

But it was only when the Communist regime collapsed in 1989 that environmental policy really changed and was finally considered to be an important part of national policy.

ENVIRONMENTAL DISASTER AREAS

Despite an apparent concern for the landscape shown in its many national parks and nature reserves, are many regions in Poland that have suffered badly at the hands of an economic system that paid only lip service to environmental concerns.

There are areas such as the Upper Silesia-Kraków agglomeration, Turoszow and Konin brown coal-basins, Belchatow Industrial District, Legnica-Głogów Copper-Basin and Tarnobrzeg Sulphur-Basin, all of whose natural resources are highly degraded as a result of the long-term influence of destructive factors. Possibly it is the province of Katowice, however, that has the worst problems. While this local authority region comprises only two percent of the country in terms of land area, it is home to 10 percent of the entire population and approximately 20 percent of the inhabitants are employed within the country's heavy industries. As well as coal, zinc ore and lead ore mining, energy and steel production are the main sources of employment in this region. As a result of its industries, Katowice suffers from serious air pollution which puts the health of its inhabitants in jeopardy.

To this day, politicians tread warily in this part of the country, any major restructuring would inevitably have devastating consequences in social costs.

Ecological optimism

The state of the natural environment has greatly improved in recent years, according to the State Inspectorate for Protecting the Environment. This was due to the decreased use of energy, water and other resources by the government. A major part was also played by the reduction in output of heavy industry and the bankruptcy of many polluting enterprises.

A major success in the past decade is the almost 50 percent decrease in the emission of sulphur dioxide and nitrogen dioxide. In addition, the amount of untreated sewage has been reduced by over 35 percent, which thousand tons, were also put into place to neutralise gas pollution.

More and more used batteries are being recycled and in this way the ecological threats they had posed will be lowered. In 1998, 70,000 tons of scrap batteries were recycled, an increase of 60 percent over 1997 figures.

Polish tax laws will soon also bring changes to provide greater tax relief for pro-ecological activities. Already relief on excise tax is in effect on lead-free petrol and petrol containing ethyl alcohol. There is also a lower tax in place to encourage the production and use of biodegradable packaging.

decreased the pollution of Polish waters flowing into the Baltic. The emission of dusts and gases into the air also considerably diminished, as did the volume of liquid waste thrown into the country's waters and the mass of industrial wastes contaminating the natural environment.

As far as the investment in air protection is concerned, some devices, with a total annual capacity of 686 thousand tons, were put into operation reducing the rate of dust pollution. Others, with the total annual capacity of 248

LEFT: visible signs of industrial pollution are just the tip of the iceberg.

RIGHT: environmental awareness is increasing.

Foreign aid

Poland has not been forgotten by the international community and is receiving financial assistance for its work in cleaning up the environment. In 1995 and 1996, some 23 million ECU were paid out from EU PHARE funds (the French acronym that originally stood for Assistance for Economic Reconstruction in Poland and Hungary).

These funds were earmarked for expenditure on the introduction of environmentally friendly technologies – including technology transfer, the construction of a waste disposal system in Szczecin harbour, bio-diversity conservation in the Biebrzański National Park (the marshlands in the northeast of Poland) and considerable improvements to the management of solid waste in various parts of the country.

The Paris Club, an organisation of creditor countries that reschedules debts amassed by developing countries, has a clause that is contributing greatly to Poland's environmental clean-up.

In return for waiving 50 percent of Poland's debt, an independent body known as ECO-FUND will pay 10 percent of Poland's pre-1991 debt to countries that invest in environmental projects. So far, the United States, Switzerland, France and Finland have waived some of their debts and the environmental technology industries in these countries are reaping the rewards. Poland is hoping that Germany, one of its main creditors, will also join in this scheme.

As an immediate neighbour, Germany would benefit directly from this financial arrangement, mainly from the fact that German companies specialising in environmental technology would almost certainly be awarded lucrative business contracts in the Polish market.

From 2000, the EU will also offer another 500 million Euros per year to candidate members for environmental projects, and Poland could

THE COSTS OF CHANGE

Environmental protection is likely to prove obstructive to Poland's plans to join the EU at the beginning of the new millennium. Some of the regulations passed by the Polish government are more stringent than those required by Brussels, but the state has not been able to force companies to abide by these standards.

It is often cheaper for a company to pay the fine imposed by the government than to make the investment necessary to bring down emission levels of pollutants. In addition, many of the major offenders are state-owned companies, usually in heavy industry. They are in receipt of state subsidies and cannot be forced to pay fines.

receive about 200 million Euros from this scheme. This funds will be granted once Poland presents a timetable for the introduction of laws adjusting Polish regulations to EU standards particularly its directives concerning the environment.

Cross-border projects

For several years now, Germany and Poland have worked together on environmental improvement schemes and there are several committees working on joint projects, for example water purification and sewage treatment plants situated near the border.

One of the spin-offs from these schemes has

been an improvement in water quality in the Baltic Sea. The Odra, the Nysa and the Vistula rivers have for many years been the main carriers of domestic and industrial waste seaward. In 1996, the Czech Republic was invited to join Poland and Germany on the International Commission for the Protection of the Odra River Against Pollution.

Environmental problems obviously do not respect man-made geographical borders and the former Communist states of East Germany and Czechoslovakia had a record on environmental pollution that was no better than that of Poland. All three nations were guilty of siting "dirty" manufacturing or processing industries on international borders which polluted the environment of neighbouring countries.

The three parties to the Commission have agreed to a programme of immediate pollutant reduction for the River Odra and its catchment area. Measures to improve this corner of Poland where the three borders meet – often referred to as the Black Triangle because of the level of pollution – will include the construction of several water treatment plants.

Bringing people together

Co-operation in the area of environmental protection has also led to agreements in other spheres which benefit all three countries and Europe as a whole. The number of points at which it is possible to cross the border has been increased; the roads to the Karkonosze Mountains, for example, have been improved to encourage tourism and regular meetings have been organised between local historians, sportsmen and women and cultural groups. It often turns out that, where problems can be sorted out in a co-operative atmosphere, the different factions can discover in the process that they have other things in common.

Returning to a local and regional level, multi-level co-ordination on environmental action is being attempted. The Green Lungs of Poland initiative is an experimental regional conservation strategy among five *voivodships* (counties) involving both local administration and international assistance.

LEFT: preserving the eco-system requires constant vigilance.
RIGHT: the future looks brighter for the environment.

The initiative includes policies on industrial development, conservation, forestry, organic farming and ecotourism. If the initiative proves to be successful, it may become the model for regional co-operation in other parts of Poland as well as across international borders.

International co-operation

The Ministry of the Environmental Protection, Natural Resources and Forestry has taken a more active role in recent years in its international co-operation with foreign partners in the field of ecology, in particular with its counterparts in Europe and the United

States and other international organisations specialising in this field. The ministry is now actively co-operating with 20 other European nations, as well as with the United States and Canada, and today Poland has concluded bilateral agreements with as many as 12 foreign ministries that are similar to the Polish ministries.

The Polish representatives participate in the work carried out by those authorities, drawing up international agreements to which Poland is a party, as well as taking part in negotiations for new multilateral agreements. Poland has now ratified approximately 20 international conventions and agreements. ❏

PLACES

A detailed guide to the entire country, with principal sites clearly cross-referenced by number to the maps

Despite the world becoming a smaller place, Poland typically remains an unknown quantity, even among seasoned travellers. Moreover, not having visited Poland doesn't prevent people from having definite views of "how it really is". The Communist era gave rise to an image of cities comprising bleak concrete blocks, inhabited by amorphous people who spent their lives either working, or queueing outside shops which only had shortages on offer. As for the countryside, the only landscapes were imagined to be industrial, dwarfed by towering chimneys belching out toxic fumes.

The reality is that the Polish landscape offers a great variety of immense natural beauty, protected by a large number of national parks throughout the country. In the east, the Białowieza National Park is a primeval forest, sheltering various rare species, including herds of European bison. In the northeast the Masurian Lake district comprises more than 1,000 lakes, many of which are linked by rivers and canals, and bordered by vast areas of natural wetlands including lakes, bogs and marshes. Meanwhile, the Carpathian mountains extend across the entire southern border of Poland, offering skiers as well as hikers some magnificent terrain to enjoy. In the north, the Baltic coast is characterised by secluded beaches fringed by pine trees and small cliffs.

Every architectural genre can be seen in Poland, with some extra-ordinary examples of Romanesque, Gothic, Renaissance, baroque, neoclassical and Seccessionist buildings. Most Polish cities have retained their medieval layouts, which means an "old town" district with a central market square featuring a town hall and burgher's houses. Having been a Roman Catholic country since the 10th century there are also numerous historic churches to see.

Joseph Conrad, the Polish-born novelist, referred to Poland as "that advanced outpost of western civilisation". Having endured various oppressors, most recently 45 years of communism, Poles have tremendous resilience and spirit. These characteristics were at the heart of the Solidarity movement which defeated the communist regime and, in turn, led to the liberation of the entire Eastern bloc. As Poland rapidly acclimatises to a "western" lifestyle, Polish culture and national identity are also stronger than ever. ❏

PRECEDING PAGES: the castle in Malbork on the Nogat; the old town, Warsaw; the gables of the town hall in Wrocław.
LEFT: one of the tall houses Gdańsk Old Town.

BALTIC SEA

GERMANY

POLAND

CZECH REPUBLIC

Berlin

Praha

Poland

0   40 km

0   40 miles

WARSAW AND MAZOVIA

Warsaw's rejuvenation as it shakes off the legacy of communism will draw more visitors both to the city and to the surrounding region of Mazovia.

Warsaw encapsulates Poland's extraordinary history, with the city subjected to a continual cycle of invasion, destruction, rebuilding and resurrection. While much of the historic centre was reconstructed, after the city was devastated by the Nazis, the ensuing regime also established monuments to communism and modernism. This helps to account for the city's diversity of architecture and atmosphere, which can take you from aesthetic highs to bleak depths.

Warsaw also encapsulates a country in transition, as Poland becomes fully integrated into Western Europe, while also nurturing a distinct national identity. As Poland's most progressive city, Warsaw is a touchstone of modernity, yet also provides a direct link to the past. The city's rapidly developing infrastructure means that visitors can now enjoy a classic Polish experience, whether its shopping for specialities such as amber, crystal and leathergoods, or dining on modern or classic Polish cuisine, while also having the pick of international restaurants, brand names and services.

The following chapter includes a comprehensive tour of Warsaw, spanning the city's historic, architectural and cultural extremes, which could be completed within a day, although several museums deserve leisurely visits.

Warsaw is also an ideal base for visiting the surrounding Mazovian region. The chapter entitled *Through Mazovia* (*see page 179*) includes suggestions for day trips, as well as more extended tours, of Mazovia's historic towns and villages. This includes Żelazowa Wola, the manor house in which Frédéric Chopin was born, the enchanting Nieboròw Palace (now a museum) and the deeply romantic landscaped park of Arkadia. Mazovia's low-lying, pastoral landscapes also lead on to the Bialowieska National Park, a vast primeval forest extending to the border with Belarus, where European bison and other rare species still roam. ❏

LEFT: postcards for sale.

Warsaw

0 — 200 m
0 — 200 yds

K.S. Polonia

Intraco

Muranowska

Konwiktorska

Kościół O.Franciszkanów Św. Franciszka Serafickiego

Kościół O.Bonifratów Św. Jana Bożego

Zakroczymska

Przyrynek

Kościelna

Rynek Nowego Miasta (New Town Market Square)

Kościół O. Redemptorystów Św. Benona

NOWE MIASTO

Wybrzeże Gdańskie

35 Kościół Św. Kazimierza (St Casimir's Church)

34

Niska

25 Pomnik Umschlagplatz (Umschlagplatz Monument)

Stawki

Gen. Władysława Andersa

Sapieżyńska

Franciszkańska

Ciasna

Freta

33 Muzeum Marii Skłodowskiej Curie (Marie Skłodowska-Curie Museum)

Kościół Św. Jacka (St Hyacinthus' Church)

St. Dubois

Mila

Zamenhofa

Nowiniarska

Świętojerska

Kamienne Schodki (Stone Steps)

Muzeum Historyczne m st Warszawy (History Museum)

2

3 Muzeum Literatury im A Mickiewicza (Literature Museum)

Pomnik Bohaterów Getta (Monument to the Heroes of the Ghetto)

24

Bonifraterska

Kościół Św. Ducha (Church of the Holy Spirit)

32

Barbakan (Barbican)

Rynek Starego Miasta (Old Town Market Square)

STARE MIASTO

Pomnik Żołnierzy 1 armii WP

Nalewki

Biblioteka Narodowa

26 Plac Krasińskich (Krasiński Square)

Długa

PWST

Pomnik Małego Powstańca

1

Katedra Św. Jana (St John's Cathedral)

4

Karmelicka

Anielewicza

Zamenhofa

Pawia

Mordechaja

OGRÓD

Kościół Św. Jana Bożego

Pomnik Kilińskiego

Podwale

Kolumna Zygmunta III Waza

Plac Zamkowy

5 Zamek Królews (Royal Castle)

Pomnik Ofiar Pawiaka

Dzielna

Nowolipki

Pałac Mostowskich

KRASIŃSKICH

Kościół O. Kapucynów Przemienienia Pańskiego

31

Ul Miodowa

6 Kościół Św. Anny (St Anna's Church)

Fermoi

Dzielna

Muzeum Archeologiczne (d. Arsenał)

Pałac Prymasowski

Kaplica Res Sacra Miser

Kościół Św. Augustyna

Nowolipie

Kościół Ewangelicko-Reformowany

Muzeum "Solidarności"

Bielańska

Pomnik Bohaterów Warszawy

Pomnik Adama Mickiewicza (Adam Mickiewicz Monument)

7

Kościół posemina

Nowolipie

Smocza

Al. Jana Pawła II

Kościół Narodzenia NMP

Intraco II

30 Plac Teatralny (Theatre Square)

Senatorska

Teatr Wielki Opery i Baletu

J.B. Molera

Trebacka

8 Kościół Wniebowzięcia NMP i Św. Jozefa Oblubienca

Urząd Dzieln. Wola

Sad Najwyzszy

Aleja Solidarności

Orla

Plac Bankowy (Bank Square)

27

Urząd m. st. Warszawa

Kolekcja im Jana Pawła II (The Pope John Paul II Collection)

Kościół Św. Antoniego z Padwy

Wierzbowa

Niecała

9 Pałac Namiestnikowski (Namiestnikowski Palace)

Karowa

Kos Św Wiz

Ogrodowa

Elektoralna

Przechodnia

Pomnik M. Konopnickiej

Grób Nieznanego Żołnierza (Tomb of the Unknown Soldier)

29

Plac Piłsudskiego (Piłsudski Square)

10 Kościół Opieki Św. Józefa (St Joseph the Guardian)

Biała

Chłodna

Ptasia

OGRÓD SASKI (SAXON GARDENS)

28

Uniwersytet Warszawski (Warsaw University)

Akademia Sztuk Pięknych

Kraków

Zelazna

pl. Mirowski

Hala Gwardii

Krolewska

R. Traugutta

Ogrodowa

Hala Mirowska

Zbór Ewangelicko-Augsburski

Mazowiecka

11

Kościół Św. Karola Boromeusza

Krochmalna

Pomnik Czynu Chłopskiego

Krolewska

Kredytowa

12 Kościół Św.Krzyża (Church of the Holy Cross)

Kościół Baptystów

MIRÓW

Al. Jana Pawła II

Walicow

Grzybowska

Ciepła

Grzybowska

Synagoga Nożycka

Prózna

Zielna

Marszałkowska

Świętokrzyska

NBP

Wareck

Zelazna

Żelazna

Ciepła

Kościół Wszystkich Świętych

Bagno

Prosta

Filharmonia

Blikle

Grzybowska

Pereca

Świętokrzyska

H. Sienkiewicza

Chmi

Łucka

Twarda

Śliska

Marszałkowska

Szpitalna

Świętokrzyska

Rondo Onz.

Śliska

Sienna

Sosnowa

Pl. Defilad

Pałac Kultury i Nauki (Palace of Science & Culture)

23

Złota

Złota

Zgoda

Domy Towarowe "Centrum"

Prosta

Panska

Twarda

Złota

Zelazna

Sienna

Złota

Warszawa Śródmieście

CDD "Smyk"

Al. Jerozolimskie

Sienna

Miedziana

Twarda

Chmielna

Warszawa Centralna

Rondo im R. Dimowskiego

Nowogrodzka

Srebrna

Warszawa Śródmieście WKD

Emilii Plater

Urząd Dzieln. Śródmieście

Poznanska

Marszałkowska

Pankiewicza

Żurawia

Nowogrodzka

Wspólna

WARSAW

Warsaw's post-war reconstruction produced an eclectic mix of contrasting architectural styles, from the monolithic Palace of Culture and Science to the quaint streets of the Old Town

Map on page 154–5

Warsaw is a city full of extreme contrasts. "Depressing" is the verdict of some visitors, who are overexposed to the city's most brutal post-war redevelopment, and underexposed to the immense beauty which is also present throughout the city. As it is possible to go for long walks which can yield either unrelieved ugliness (in the mid-town area, for example), or spectacular architecture that exemplifies various genres (along the "Royal Route"), you need to know exactly where you're going and what the real options are. In fact, some of these contrasting "zones" are so rigidly defined that you can leave one and enter another simply by crossing the road.

Enormous changes since the 1989 democratic elections have turned Warsaw into a thoroughly European, metropolitan capital. Cafés are full of people enjoying a leisurely break of coffee and cakes, bars and restaurants are full of business people in power-suits brandishing mobile phones, and a growing number of shops stock everything from Cartier, Versace and exotic foodstuffs, to local specialities such as folk crafts. Of course the fact that everything is available doesn't mean it's accessible to all. Moreover, the "victims" of privatisation, left unemployed and homeless, beg on the streets – just as in any other major 20th-century European city.

LEFT: typical street in the old town.
BELOW: memorial to the heros of the Warsaw rebellion.

Warszawa (Warsaw) lies in the heart of Mazowsze (the Mazovia region) in central Poland, on the banks of the River Wisła (Vistula). As the capital and commercial centre of Poland, with a population of around 1.8 million, Warsaw is also a major cultural centre. Various institutions such as the Academy of Science, the National Library, National Museum and National Philharmonic are based here, while the city also hosts various international events such as the International Chopin Competition and the International Book Fair. Nevertheless, anyone from Kraków will tell you that their city is, and always has been, Poland's cultural centre. Throughout Poland, Varsovians are caricatured as being fast-talking, fast-driving, corporate climbers who consider themselves superior to the rest of the country.

Warsaw's history

While the exact origins of Warsaw have eluded historians, one legend states that an amalgamation of the names of two historic lovers, Wars and Sawa, who lived by the Vistula river, provided a name for the city. Another legend states that a mermaid swimming in the Vistula told Mazovian fishermen of an indestructible city which would be founded there. Warsaw has certainly fulfiled the mermaid's prophecy, with the city's history being a continual cycle of invasion, destruction, rebuilding and resurrection.

Using one of the 30 tram routes in Warsaw is a great way to get about the city. Tram stops and routes are marked in red on city maps.

BELOW: the roofs of the Old Town.

The Old Town evolved around the residence of the Mazovian dukes, established on the site of the present Royal Castle in 1281. The city's evolution continued on the basis of its key position on trade routes through Poland. Moreover, Mazovia was also growing in importance as the central point between the two capitals of the Polish-Lithuanian Commonwealth, Kraków and Vilnius.

Parliament first met in Warsaw in 1529, and from 1573 royal elections were held here (the king being elected rather than hereditary). However, the king continued to reside in Kraków, the capital of Poland since 1040, until King Zygmunt III Waza proclaimed Warsaw the capital city in 1596.

Between 1655–60 the Swedish invasion, known as *"Potop"* ("The Flood") devastated Poland, and seriously depleted Warsaw's buildings and population. Under King Jan III Sobieski, elected in 1674, the city enjoyed great prosperity, with numerous buildings, palaces and principal thoroughfares dating from this time, including the king's summer residence Wilanów on the outskirts of the city.

During the period of the Enlightenment, during the second half of the 18th century, commerce and culture evolved rapidly, which included the founding of the National Theatre and several periodicals, while the first constitution in Europe was ratified in Warsaw on 3 May 1791.

However, three successive partitions of Poland, beginning in 1772, saw the country progressively divided between Prussia, Austro-Hungary and Russia. Initially under Prussian rule, Napoleon established the city as the capital of the Grand Duchy of Warsaw. Following the Congress of Vienna in 1815, Warsaw was capital of the Congress Kingdom of Poland, ruled by the Tsar of Russia. Warsaw was also the centre of numerous insurrections during this time, with the uprisings of 1830 and 1863 the most significant.

One of the most tragic periods in the city's turbulent history was World War II, with more than 700,000 citizens killed during the German Occupation. After the Warsaw Uprising (*see page 51*), Hitler ordered that the Poles be punished by razing Warsaw to the ground. The city was systematically destroyed and left virtually uninhabited, with the total wartime damage resulting in almost 85 percent of the city being reduced to rubble. A massive post-war rebuilding programme recreated the Old Town and New Town districts, as well as numerous palaces, churches and important civic buildings. Ironically, the Communists demolished 19th-century mansion blocks and tenement buildings in the centre of Warsaw, which had survived the Nazi regime, and converted this area into a "showpiece" of Socialist Realism architecture. The wartime legacy means that various poignant sites are marked throughout the city. There are numerous plaques set on walls and pavements, stating when and how many Poles were executed on each site by the Nazis, with candles and flowers still placed by many of these memorials. The Old Town and adjacent New Town took around 30 years to reconstruct, which was done so authentically that both were awarded UNESCO World Heritage status. If you didn't know the history you'd never guess they were "repro". Fortunately they are not a case of "splendid isolation" either, as the surrounding areas are also historic and aesthetic.

Old Town Market Square

The centre of the Old Town is **Rynek Starego Miasta** (Old Town Market Square) ❶. It's always bustling with people visiting the square's numerous cafés, bars and restaurants, while street-traders and artists ply their wares outside the galleries and shops. During the summer the square is covered with café

Map on page 154–5

Small wartime memorials to the dead of World War II are found around the city.

BELOW: the Zygmunt Pillar at the entrance to the Old Town.

TIP

Some of the finest restaurants with authentic Polish character, are located in burghers' houses on Old Town Square. Fukier is decorated in a "folklore chic" manner. Gessler is a 19th-century Bohemian restaurant; its cellar houses a recreation of an 18th-century country inn, with a folk musicians trio adding to the atmosphere.

BELOW:
carriage driver waits for a fare in the Old Town.

tables, while horse-drawn carriages clip-clop from here to the Old Town (which is closed to traffic). Beautifully recreated burghers' houses, dating from the 15th and 16th centuries, line the square, each with individual architectural features. This includes a late Gothic portal at Number 21, while the house "*Pod Bazyliszkiem*" ("Under the Basilisk") at Number 5 features the mythical Old Town monster, whose stare apparently brought instant death.

"*Pod Murzynkiem*" ("Under the Negro"), featuring a Renaissance portal and carved head of a negro, is one of three burghers' houses which were linked behind their façades to accommodate the **Muzeum Historyczne Warszawy** (Warsaw History Museum) **2** (Rynek Starego Miasta 28; tel: 635 16 25; open Tues, Thurs 11am–5.45pm; Wed, Fri 10am–3.30pm; weekends 10am–4pm; entrance fee except Sun). Numerous exhibits detail the city's history and evolution, while a film screened daily includes footage taken by the Nazis documenting their systematic destruction of the city.

Also set within a burgher's house is the **Muzeum Literatury im A. Mickiewicza** (Literature Museum dedicated to A Mickiewicz) **3** (Rynek Starego Miasta 20; tel: 831 40 61; open Mon, Tues, Fri 10am–3pm; Wed, Thurs 11am–6pm; Sun 11am–5pm; entrance fee except Thurs). Dedicated to Adam Mickiewicz (1789–1855), Poland's greatest romantic poet (*see page 307*), the museum also provides insights into the life and work of various other Polish writers and temporary exhibitions of authors of other nationalities. Beyond this museum, in the square's northeast corner, are the **Kamienne Schodki** (Stone Steps), a picturesque thoroughfare leading from the Old Town to the Vistula.

Leaving the Old Town Square along Świętojańska leads to **Katedra Św. Jana** (St John's Cathedral) **4** (Świętojańska 8; open daily 10am–1pm and 3pm–6pm except Sun; entrance fee to crypt). Warsaw's oldest church, and the largest church in the Old Town, the cathedral was rebuilt after World War II in the original 14th-century style known as "Vistulan Gothic", defined by an austere but spiritual simplicity. The crypt contains various Mazovian dukes and some of Poland's most renowned leaders and artists, including Nobel Prize-winning novelist Henryk Sienkiewicz (1846–1916), author of *Quo Vadis*, and the first president of independent Poland, Gabriel Narutowicz. A side altar contains the sarcophagus of Poland's former primate, Cardinal Stefan Wyszyński.

Warsaw's Royal Castle

Świętojańska culminates at Plac Zamkowy (Castle Square), dominated by the **Zamek Królewski** (Royal Castle) **5** (Plac Zamkowy 4; tel: 657 21 70; open Tues–Sun; entrance fee; ticket office at Swietojańska 2). A castle was first established here in the 13th century as the residence of the Mazovian dukes. From the end of the 16th century it became the royal residence, as well as the seat of the *Sejm* (Parliament). In 1791 the 3rd of May Constitution was drawn up here, the first of its kind in Europe. Between the two World Wars, the castle was the president's official residence. The Nazis' total destruction of the castle extended to drilling thousands of holes in the foundations for sticks of dynamite (a few holes can still be seen in parts of the crypt). The decision to reconstruct the castle was taken in 1971, funded by private subscriptions raised in Poland and from émigré Poles around the world. The Communists did not contribute, considering this to be too overt a symbol of Polish sovereignty. Opened to the public in 1984, the surviving architectural fragments, including Baroque, Gothic and rococo, were incorporated into a recreation of the 17th-century façade.

Map on page 154–5

The interiors are largely 18th-century, with most of the works of art and furniture either original to the castle (some items were sent to Canada prior to the outbreak of war), or donated by museums and private collectors. All the rooms have individual characteristics. The pillared and gilded ballroom is in contrast to the mausoleum-like character of the Marble Room, or the Picture Gallery devoted to views of Warsaw painted by Bernardo Bellotto. (Known as the "Polish Canaletto", he was the nephew of the renowned Venetian painter.) In the former chapel is an urn containing the heart of the Polish hero Tadeusz Kościuszko (1746–1817). He led Polish troops against the Russians in a bid for freedom during the partitions, and was also a hero of the American War of Independence.

Adjoining the royal castle, but also offering a different experience is **Pałac Pod Blachą** (Plac Zamkowy 2; tel: 31 91 99; open Tues–Sun; entrance fee). This Baroque palace has a collection of rugs and carpets, with rare examples from Persia, Turkey, and the world's largest collection of Caucasian rugs.

The bronze Kolumna Zygmunta was erected in 1644 by the king's son. It is 22 metres (72 ft) high.

The Royal Route

Plac Zamkowy features Warsaw's oldest monument, **Kolumna Zygmunta** (Zygmunt's Column). Erected in 1644, the king is depicted bearing a sword and a large cross (reflecting his counter-reformatory stance). This square also

BELOW:
the Royal Castle.

marks the beginning of the so-called Trakt Królewski (Royal Route), a favourite stroll for Varsovians and a good way to see numerous historic sights with almost no visual interference from modern buildings. Extending along Krakówskie Przedmieśie, the Royal Route continues along Nowy Świat and Aleje Ujazdowskie, past Łazienki Park and ends at Wilanów Palace. Walking all the way to Wilanów is unrealistic, but a leisurely stroll with café breaks en route should get you to Łazienki Park (*see page 166–8*).

The name Krakówskie Przedmieście (literally "Kraków Suburb") originated shortly after Warsaw replaced Kraków as the capital, as this street eventually leads to Kraków. It was on this thoroughfare, and adjacent streets, that magnificent churches were established, while numerous aristocrats constructed palatial residences. At Krakówskie Przedmieście 68 is **Kościół Św. Anny** (St Anna's Church) **6** (open daily). The earliest sections are late 15th-century Gothic, though the church was refashioned several times. Its current neoclassical incarnation includes a façade modelled on a Venetian church, Il Redentore, designed by the renowned 16th-century Italian architect Andrea Palladio. Ornate interiors, predominantly cream and gilt, create a sense of restrained flamboyance.

Continuing along Krakówskie Przedmieście, decorative railings delineate a small square with lawns and flower beds featuring the **Pomnik Adama Mickiewicza** (Adam Mickiewicz Monument) **7**. This monument dates from 1889, the centenary of the poet's birth. Small cafés surround the monument. At Numbers 52–54 is the mid-17th-century **Kościół Wniebowzięcia NMP i Św. Jozefa Oblubienca** (Church of the Assumption of the Blessed Virgin Mary and St Joseph the Betrothed) **8** (open daily). A neoclassical façade belies the dazzling Baroque interiors, culminating in a beautiful altar.

BELOW: the Adam Mickiewicz Monument.

Another grand neoclassical building is **Pałac Namiestnikowski** (Namiestnikowski Palace) ❾ (not open to the public) established as the residence of the Polish president in 1994. Formerly owned by various aristocratic families, it served as the residence of the Viceroy of the Kingdom of Poland, the Russian Tsar's official representative, during the partition of Poland. In 1955 the Warsaw Pact was signed at the palace (*see page 53*), and in 1989 the historic round-table talks between the Communist government and the Solidarity trade union movement were held here. The entrance to the palace is flanked by sculptures of four lions, while the courtyard features an equestrian statue of Prince Józef Poniatowski, who led Napoleonic troops at the beginning of the 19th century. The original statue, cast by Danish artist Bertel Thorvaldsen in 1832, was destroyed during the war. The replacement was cast from a replica kept in Copenhagen and erected in front of the palace in 1965.

The neighbouring **Hotel Bristol** at Numbers 42–44, which re-opened as the city's premier de luxe hotel in 1992, is classified as a national monument, being a superb example of Seccessionist architecture and interiors. A coffee in the hotel's Viennese-style café is the least expensive way of enjoying its immense style. Opposite at Krakówskie Przedmieście 13 is the Europejski Hotel. Dating from 1855, this is Warsaw's oldest hotel, and features an impressive neo-Renaissance façade. The interiors are, unfortunately, a post-war disappointment, and are long overdue for a similar revival to its more illustrious neighbour.

One of the few churches to survive the Nazis, **Kościół Opieki Św. Józefa** (St Joseph the Guardian) ❿ (open daily) has an elaborate façade. This artistry continues within, providing some of Warsaw's finest Baroque and rococo interiors. The church is also known as Kościół Sióstr Wizytek (Church of the Nuns of the

Map
on page
154–5

Guard on patrol outside Namiestnikowski Palace.

BELOW: the façade of the Bristol Hotel.

TIP

Ironically, Sunday can be a good day for "church tourism". The city is much quieter as many Varsovians head off for the weekend to their "*dzialka*", small wooden houses set in a small plot, within about an hour's drive from Warsaw.

Visitation), as this order has a convent adjacent to the church. At Krakówskie Przedmieście 26–28 is the entrance to **Uniwersytet Warszawski** (Warsaw University) ⓫ (open daily). Several imposing buildings which serve as the university's lecture halls, set amid courtyards and greenery, have a distinguished provenance. This aesthetic enclave provides a delightful diversion, animated by the bustle of students arriving for lectures and meeting friends. The most imposing building is the Pałac Kazimierzowski (Kazimierzowski Palace), originally the summer residence of King Władysław IV Vaza and the royal family during the 17th century. The neoclassical Tyszkiewicz Palace, the Baroque Uruski Palace, and other buildings were the residences of aristocratic families.

Opposite the university is the **Kościół Św. Krzyża** (Church of the Holy Cross) ⓬ (open daily). This imposing twin-towered Baroque church, completed in 1760, also managed to survive the Nazis. By the entrance is an impressive double stairway, with a poignant figure of Christ carrying the cross. In a side pillar of the main nave are urns containing the hearts of Frédéric Chopin and the writer Władysław Reymont, who won the Nobel Prize for literature in 1924.

Nowy Świat to Ujazdowskie Avenue

A monument to the astronomer Mikołaj Kopernik (Nicholas Copernicus), also the work of Danish sculptor Bertel Thorvaldsen, stands in front of the early 19th-century neoclassical Staszic Palace, at the point where Krakówskie Przedmieście meets **Nowy Świat** ⓭ (literally "New World" Street). This has a totally different character, being much narrower and more uniform in style than Krakówskie Przedmieście. Rebuilt in its early 19th-century neoclassical style, both sides of the street feature attractive façades. As one of the city's smartest shopping venues, just as it was in the 1920s and 1930s, designer boutiques, jewellers and art galleries are neighboured by smart delicatessens, bakers and bookshops. All the street's cafés are eclipsed by **Blikle Café** at Number 35. This traditional rendezvous, with excellent patisseries, has an elegant pavement section screened by greenery, and *fin-de-siècle* Bohemian interiors. At Number 45 is an apartment in which novelist Joseph Conrad (born Józef Korzeniówski) spent his childhood, before leaving Warsaw for Marseille at the age of 17.

BELOW: standing in the bus queue on Nowy Świat.

Continuing to the Rondo Charles de Gaulle, and turning left into Jerozolimskie Avenue, leads to the **Muzeum Narodowe** (National Museum) ⓮ (Jerozolimskie 3; tel: 621 10 31; open Sun–Fri; Thurs 12am–5pm; entrance fee). The museum's "concrete block" appearance, the negation of aestheticism, belies an amazing collection, and the user-friendly layout which makes it easy to do either a grand tour or select your own highlights. The choice includes 16th- to 20th-century Polish paintings with works by Jan Matejko (1838–93), Poland's greatest historical painter, and various genres such as Romanticism, Realism and Impressionism.

Among the Polish decorative arts are china, leather, silver and gold artifacts, as well as furniture. Various Ancient Greek, Roman and Egyptian exhibits include early Christian frescos from Pharoahs in the Sudan, which were saved by Polish archaeologists from the waters of the Aswan dam.

Nowy Świat then leads to **Plac Trzech Krzyży** (Three Crosses Square) **⑮**. Despite the name, this square only features two crosses, each mounted on a column. On an island at the centre of the square is the neoclassical Kościół Św. Aleksandra (St Alexander's Church), dating from 1818.

Beyond the square extends Aleje Ujazdowskie (Ujazdowskie Avenue), which marks another change of character. This avenue is considerably wider and busier than Nowy Świat, and showcases a different architectural genre, being lined with elegant *fin-de-siècle* Seccessionist villas and mansion blocks. Many of these are embassies, diplomatic buildings or headquarters for foreign legations. Nearby at Numbers 2–6 Wiejska is the seat of the *Sejm* (Polish Parliament) and the Senate of the Republic.

The Centrum Sztuki Współczesnej (Modern Art Centre) is housed within **Zamek Ujazdowski** (Ujazdowski Castle) **⑯** (Aleje Ujazdowskie 6; tel: 628 12 71; open Tues–Thurs 11am–5pm; Fri 11am–9pm; weekend 11am–5pm; entrance fee except Thurs). The site of the castle was the first residence of the 13th century Mazovian dukes, and subsequently became the summer residence of the Vaza royal family during the 17th century. Burned down during World War II, the remains of the castle were demolished in 1954. After careful reconstruction it is totally credible in its 17th-century Baroque incarnation, with this "modern-ancient" castle holding temporary modern art exhibitions. A terrace at the rear of the castle has extensive views over the Ujazdowski Park below and the castle has a superb post-modern style restaurant, Qchnia Artystyczna.

The **Ogród Botaniczny** (Botanical Gardens) were established in 1819 (Ujazdowskie 4; tel: 628 75 14; open daily, May–Oct). They have a comprehensive

Map on page 154–5

Coffee and cake at the Blikle Café, 35 Nowy Świat, established in 1869.

BELOW: the chi chi shops and cafés of Nowy Świat.

layout including flower beds, medicinal herbs and water plants, set around a fountain and pool. The beautiful grounds are not a complete "urban escape" as this is also the site of the neoclassical **Obserwatorium Astonomiczne** (Astronomical Observatory) dating from 1824, which is part of Warsaw University.

Łazienki Park and Palace

One of Europe's most beautiful palatio-park complexes, **Łazienki Królewskie** (Łazienki Park) **⑰** (entrances along Ujazdowskie, or Agrykola; tel: 621 62 41; open daily until dusk. Guided tours to Palace on the Water; the White House, Myślewickich Palace and the Old Orangerie tel: 625 79 44) extends to 200 acres (81 hectares). Originally royal hunting grounds, the park's numerous avenues, woodlands and formal gardens were laid out by Johann Christian Schuch, who created both French- and English-style gardens during the late 18th century. He was commissioned by Stanisław August Poniatowski, Poland's last king, who was a great patron of the arts during the Polish Enlightenment. The park opened to the public in 1818, and continues to be a favourite promenade for Varsovians, particularly on a Sunday afternoon, with cafés in the park doing a roaring trade. While obviously peaking in the summer, the park is popular throughout the year for its escapism – here you can totally forget you are in the centre of a major city. Autumn is spectacular, with the densely wooded park assuming various hues.

Several palaces, pavilions and other buildings throughout the park were designed by the Italian architect Domenico Merlini, in conjunction with the king. This resulted in a combination of neoclassical and Baroque elements referred to as the "Stanislaus style", which is exemplified by **Pałac na Wyspie**

BELOW: a boat trip on the lake in Łazienki Park.

Map on page 154–5

(Palace-on-the-Isle) ⑱ (open Tues–Sun; entrance fee). Romantically located in the centre of a lake, and approached by bridges, the palace was built in stages from 1784–93, on the site of earlier bathing pavilions. The Bacchus room, decorated with Delft tiles, was part of the original bath house. The palace also features a ballroom, portrait gallery with works by the court painter Marcello Bacciarelli, and the principal reception room, Solomon's Hall. While these rooms were always intended to be showpieces, other rooms nevertheless provide a more personal insight into life at the palace. The king's bedroom, for instance, has a discreet little gallery from where he could keep an eye on proceedings in the ballroom below; in the dining room, the king held his celebrated "Thursday dinners", a salon for writers, artists and intellectuals. The bedroom of the king's valet also gives another perspective.

The neighbouring **Teatr na Wyspie** (Theatre on the Isle) dating from 1790, was modelled on an ancient amphitheatre. The stage is a "ruined temple", while a canal separates the auditorium, which can also be used as part of the stage. The park includes several other romantic neoclassical buildings within walking distance of each other: Słwiątynia Sybilli (Temple of Sibyl), Wodozbiór (Watertower) and Słwiątynia Egypska (Egyptian Temple). The compact Hermitaż (Hermitage) accommodated the king's fortune-teller, Madam Lhullier, who is said to have predicted his election to the throne.

Biały Dom (The White House) ⑲ (open Tues–Sun; entrance fee) does indeed have a white façade, and this small square villa was completed in 1774 as a residence for the king's sisters. Between 1801–5 the exiled Louis XVIII of France lived here. The dining room bears exquisite murals in the "grotesque" style (floral motifs in conjunction with human, animal and fantasy figures),

BELOW: piano recitals are held at the foot of the Chopin Monument in Łazienki Park.

TIP

If you are visiting
Warsaw in summer,
try to visit the Chopin
Monument on a
Sunday afternoon
when concerts are
held. Despite a hint of
kitsch, the
combination of the
statue, lake and
surrounding park
create an ideal setting
for the romanticism of
Chopin's music.

BELOW: the
meditative
atmosphere of
Łazienki Park.

while the drawing room and bedrooms are decorated with superior chinoiserie. **Pałac Myślewickich** (Myślewicki Palace) ⓴ (open Wed–Mon; entrance fee) is early neoclassical with two semi-circular wings. This was the residence of the king's nephew, Prince Józef Poniatowski. In addition to paintings and furniture, the palace includes elements of chinoiserie, while murals in the dining room depict views of Rome and Venice. The compact but fascinating museum creates a lasting impression; it has been so skillfully assembled that the aristocratic residence still feels as if it is occupied as it was in its heyday.

A sculpture gallery occupies one wing of the **Stara Pomarańczarnia** (Old Orangery) ㉑ (open Tues–Sun; entrance fee), while another wing houses one of Europe's few remaining 18th-century court theatres. Apart from its rarity, it is worth seeing for the extravagant Baroque interiors in what is otherwise an intimate setting. The Nowa Oranżeria (New Orangery) provides an atmospheric setting for the Belweder restaurant, one of Warsaw's finest. There are two dining rooms, one decorated in a neoclassical style, and one in the original glazed section of the orangery amid lush greenery. Nearby is the **Pomnik Chopina** (Chopin Monument) ㉒, a reconstruction of the original 1926 work by Secessionist sculptor Wacław Szymanowski (which was melted down by the Nazis).

Around the Palace of Science and Culture

Returning to the central district known as Śródmieście (mid-town) means another dramatic change of character, Socialist Realism and Modernism, exemplified by **Pałac Kultury i Nauki** (Palace of Science and Culture) ㉓ (Plac Defilad 1; tel: 620 02 11; open Tues–Sun). Built on Warsaw's largest square, Plac Defilad, between 1952–5, it was officially a "gift" to the Poles from the

Map on page 154–5

Soviet Union. Needless to say, the palace of culture was universally loathed – as both a symbol of Communist oppression and for its uncompromising architecture. A traditional Polish joke poses the question: "where's the best place to live in Warsaw?" Answer: "In the Palace of Culture, because then you can't see it when you look out of the window."

Meanwhile, the statistics make interesting reading: 3,288 rooms on 30 floors and a total height of 235 metres (770 ft), with the palace playing an important scientific and cultural role, comprising scientific institutes, cinemas, theatres and a multi-purpose Sala Kongressowa (Congressional Hall) seating 3,200. The observation terrace on the 30th floor provides a magnificent panorama of Warsaw and its suburbs. Maintaining such a colossus, however, has become such a financial burden that office space within the palace has been let to businesses. Since the mid-1990s there have also been various plans to soften the impact of the palace, such as large "screening" structures at each corner of the square.

Opposite the east side of the Palace of Culture is Marszałkowska, a principal thoroughfare on which numerous office buildings, fast food outlets and department stores are located. At best this thoroughfare is bland Modernism, at worst it seems harsh and depressing. Some of the surrounding streets only provide more of the same, with the **Warszawa Centralna** (Central Railway Station) an example of hideous 1970s Modernist architecture.

The Warsaw Ghetto

Northwest of the Palace of Culture is the area of the former **Warsaw Ghetto**, which has obviously lost some its pre-war Jewish character, though various monuments and important buildings between Stawki and Świętokrzyska convey

Statue outside the Palace of Science and Culture.

BELOW: the Palace of Science and Culture.

The Warsaw Ghetto was the largest in Nazi-occupied Europe. Jews were forced to identify themselves by wearing yellow stars.

the tragic plight of Warsaw's Jews. The sufferings of the Jews in the ghetto and their courageous uprising are commemorated in one of the most poignant areas of the city, by Trakt Pamiecłci Męczeństwa i Walki Zydów (Memorial To The Struggle and Martyrdom of the Jews) on Zamenhofa Street. Also on this street is the grass mound Pomnik Bunkra (Bunker Monument), from where the ghetto uprising was led, raised to the level of the rubble that was left behind after the ghetto was destroyed.

The bleak **Pomnik Bohaterów Getta** (Monument to the Heroes of the Ghetto) ❷ symbolises the Jews' bravery and eventual helplessness in the face of Nazi anti-Semitism; in 1970 the German Chancellor Willy Brandt knelt here as a gesture of reconciliation. Memorial stones mark the route to **Pomnik Umschlagplatz** (Umschlagplatz Monument) ❷ in the adjoining street, Stawki. It was here that Jews were assembled before being transported in cattle trucks to concentration camps. There remains talk of plans to construct a museum in honour of the Polish Jews near the former ghetto, although nothing has yet been commissioned.

Krasinski Gardens to the New Town

Continuing to another historic area, Ogród Krasińskich (Krasiński Gardens) provides a nice stretch of greenery leading to **Plac Krasińskich** (Krasiński Square) ❷ where Pałac Krasińskich (Krasiński Palace) houses the **Biblioteka Narodowa** (National Library). The elegant façade was designed by Dutch architect Tylman van Gameren in 1677. Opposite the palace are the newly built Law Courts, and a Monument to the Heroes of the Warsaw Uprising. Unveiled in 1989, this moving monument includes figures emerging from the sewers, which

BELOW:
Monument to the Heros of the Ghetto, built in 1948.

DESTRUCTION OF A RACE

Before World War II the Jewish community accounted for around one-third of Warsaw's population – the largest Jewish community in the world. In November 1940 the Nazis began rounding up and confining Jews to the ghetto, a district of about 4 sq km (1½ sq miles) – the largest of its kind in Nazi-occupied Europe. Ultimately around 500,000 Jews were enclosed within the ghetto, where they endured inhumane conditions, suffering inevitably from overcrowding, disease and starvation.

Even the Nazis realised that the situation was untenable. In April 1941 the uprising in the Warsaw Ghetto was brutally suppressed and the area razed to the ground. In 1942 the Nazis began transporting Jews to the death camps of Auschwitz and Treblinka (*see page 54*) until only 60,000 Jews remained.

An underground resistance movement led by the Jewish Combat Organisation (ZOB) culminated in the desperate month-long uprising of 1943, but the ZOB did not have the manpower or arms to defeat the Nazis. A few ZOB commanders escaped, but 7,000 were shot and the rest deported to the camps, leading Himmler to declare "the Jewish quarter in Warsaw no longer exists." At the end of World War II only about 300 Polish Jews survived.

were a vital means of communication and escape during the uprising. Długa Street takes you towards the bustling, expansive metropolitan **Plac Bankowy** (Bank Square) ⓴, with its multi-laned roaring traffic and multiple tram lines. Nevertheless, this square has a metropolitan appeal, and includes two neoclassical buildings, the monumental Ratusz (Town Hall), and the more scaled-down former Bank of Poland and Stock Exchange, which now houses the **Kolekcja im Jana Pawła II** (The Pope John Paul II Collection, plac Bankowy 1; tel: 620 27 25; open summer Tues–Sun 9.30am–5pm; winter Tues–Sun 10am–4pm; entrance fee). This collection of European painting from the 15th to 20th centuries, including still lifes, portraits and Impressionist works, was amassed by expatriate art collectors, Janina and Zbigniew Porczyński.

Plac Bankowy leads to **Ogród Saski** (Saxon Gardens) ⓱, Warsaw's first public gardens, opened in 1727, where you immediately leave behind the roar of the traffic. Originally Baroque in design, the gardens were laid out in the style of an English garden in 1827, and include a neoclassical watertower, decorative statuary and a fountain.

At the edge of the gardens, on Plac Piłsudkiego is **Grób Nieznanego Żołnierza** (Tomb of the Unknown Soldier) ⓲. Consecrated in 1925, it includes urns from battlefields in which Polish troops fought, as well as from the graves of Polish officers murdered by the Red Army in Katyń (*see page 55*). The tomb is under a small section of a colonnade, which is all that remains of the former Pałac Saski (Saxon Palace) destroyed by the Nazis. Every Sunday at noon a ceremonial changing of the guard takes place by the tomb. Ul Wierzbowa leads to **Plac Teatralny** (Theatre Square) ⓳, which is dominated by the Teatr Wielki (Grand Theatre), also known as Teatr Narodowy (National Theatre). Dating

Map on page 154–5

BELOW:
the Tomb of the Unknown Soldier.

from 1833, the monumental neoclassical façade was designed by the Italian architect Antonio Corazzi. With an auditorium of almost 2,000 seats, this is Poland's largest opera house. Opposite is the former Town Hall building, recreated in 1997–8 in its original splendour and currently a financial centre.

Senatorska leads to the tranquil street **Miodowa** ❸, which features several palaces (mainly used as government buildings and so inaccessible to the public) and historic churches.

From here Długa and Podwale streets lead to the **Barbakan** (Barbican) ❸, fortress which dates from the 16th century as part of the Old Town's defensive wall, and now a popular haunt of street artists and entertainers. Continuing along the elegant street **Freta** takes in the Baroque Kościół Św. Jacka (St Jacek's Church), opposite which stands Kościół Św. Ducha (Church of the Holy Spirit) founded in 1688 to commemorate King Jan III Sobieski's victory over the Turks at Vienna.

Muzeum Marii Skłodowskiej Curie (Marie Skłodowska-Curie Museum) ❸ is set within her former home (Freta 16; tel: 31 80 92; open Tues–Sat 10am–4pm; Sun 10am–2pm; entrance fee). Twice winning the Nobel Prize, Curie is best known for her experiments with radium, conducted with her husband Pierre Curie in Paris. The museum documents her life and work.

Freta leads to **Rynek Nowego Miasta** (New Town Market Square) ❸. Less formal than the Old Town Market Square (and not a perfect square shape either), it is also far less busy. Nevertheless, there are several cafés and restaurants from which to admire this beautifully re-created area, dominated by the domed Kościół Św. Kazimierza (St Casimir's Church) ❸ (open daily), designed by Tylman van Gameren, one of the most prominent Baroque architects in Poland.

BELOW:
the Barbican.

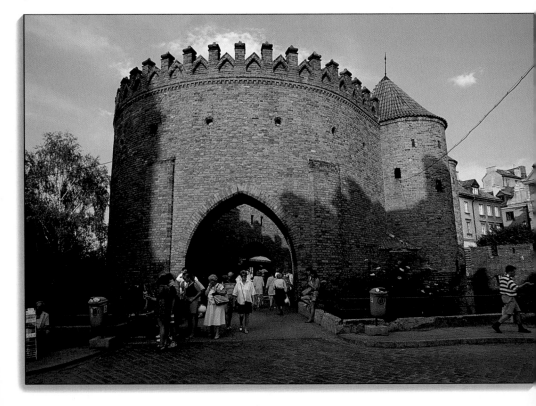

Greater Warsaw

Just to the south of Warsaw is King Jan III Sobieski's summer residence, **Wilanów** ❸❻ (Wiertnicza 1; tel: 42 81 01; open Mon, Wed–Sun 9.30am–3pm; entrance fee except on Mon). Wilanów is a popular day-out for many Varsovians, even if it's only for a stroll through the park rather than a full museum visit.

Dating from 1679, the palace was built on the site of a country manor house, with the new royal residence named "Villa Nova", literally the "New Villa". which was "translated" into Wilanów. The architect was Augustino Locci, who subsequently designed some of Poland's most renowned Baroque buildings. After the king's death (1696) the property changed hands, and in the following decades various extensions and annexes were added to accommodate galleries and towers, while pavilions were added in the grounds.

Renovation work, following the Nazis ruination of the palace, also uncovered 17th- and 18th-century paintings which had been concealed by plasterwork applied in the 19th century. The Nazis also plundered the most valuable works of art.

Nevertheless, the palace has one of the largest collections of portraits by Polish artists spanning the 16th to 19th centuries. This includes a portrait by Jacques-Louis David, of Stanisław Kostka Potocki, who acquired Wilanów in 1799. As a connoisseur of fine art, Potocki established one of the first public museums in Poland at Wilanów in 1805, exhibiting *objets d'art* from the time of King Jan III Sobieski, together with furniture, Chinese and Japanese art and ancient ceramics. A tour of the palace includes royal apartments from the 17th to the 19th centuries, decorated with period furniture and works of art.

Map on page 154–5

Wilanów Palace gardens, designed by astronomer Jan Hevelius.

LEFT: Wilanów Palace wing.
RIGHT: figure of Atlas, Wilanów Palace.

Map on page 154–5

Two sculpted horses stand at the entrance to the mid-19th-century Riding School, which now houses the **Muzeum Plakatu** (Poster Museum; open Tues–Sun 10am–4pm; entrance fee). Established in 1968, this was the first of its kind in the world, housing a collection that acts as a vivid record of Poland's post-war history. The Oranżeria (Orangery) exhibits Polish arts and crafts.

On the east side of the palace is an Italian Baroque garden, comprising several parterres, while the English-style garden was laid out between 1799–1821 and includes a Chinese pavilion with a pagoda roof, dating from 1806. Also within the grounds are the Potocki family mausoleum built in the early 19th century in a neo-Gothic style, and the late 19th-century neo-Baroque Kościół Św. Anny (St Anne's Church).

The city's oldest necropolis, **Cmentarz Powązki** (Powązki Cemetery) was founded in 1790. Many of its gravestones are works of art in their own right, and a number of celebrated writers, artists and scientists are buried here, including Nobel-prize winning novelist Władysław Reymont and author Bolesław Prus, architects such as Domenico Merlini whose work included the palaces and pavilions of Łazienki Park, various actors, the 20th-century opera singer Jan Kiepura, musicians such as Henryk Wieniawski, and Chopin's parents.

Various other cemeteries within walking distance of Powązki include Cmentarz Komunalny (Communal Cemetery), which is effectively a military cemetery, serving as the final resting place for soldiers who lost their lives in the two world wars, many of them victims of the Nazi and Stalinist regimes. This cemetery also contains the graves of scouts who lost their lives during the 1944 Warsaw Uprising, and a symbolic tomb containing earth from the graves of Polish officers murdered at Katyń.

BELOW:
remembrance of victims of the Warsaw Uprising at Powązki Cemetery.
RIGHT:
Wilanów Palace.

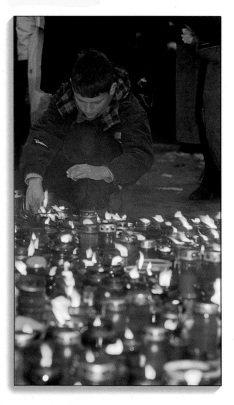

On 1 August, the anniversary of the first day of the 1944 Warsaw Uprising, many people bring flowers and light candles at the graves of relatives.

In **Zoliborz**, one of Warsaw's more exclusive residential areas and political hotbeds, is the Modernist church dedicated to St Stansiław Kostka, situated on Kraśinska Street. By the church is the grave of Father Jerzy Popiełuszko, a priest who was a prominent supporter of Solidarity, murdered by the Communist regime in 1984. His grave has now become a national memorial. A Stations of the Cross route in the church grounds pinpoints landmarks in modern Polish history.

The rightbank of the Wisła river includes the district of **Praga**, which became part of the city of Warsaw in 1916 and was relatively undamaged during the war. Although this district is also where most of the city's industrial and manufacturing plants are located, there is also plenty of *fin-de-siècle* architecture with characteristic alleys and small courtyards to see, as well as Cerkiew Św. Marii Magdaleny (Russian Orthodox Church of St Mary Magdalene, al Solidarności) with its splendid interiors. A particularly local character thrives at Bazaar Różyckiego (Różycki Market), which also offers a fine view of the Old Town across the Wisła River. Across from the Old Town is the Warsaw Zoo (open daily 9am to sunset). Established in 1928, it has animals from around the world. ❏

THE BEAUTY OF ŁAZIENKI PARK

The extensive woodland of Łazienki Park features several palaces, pavilions, orangeries, and even an amphitheatre in the very heart of Warsaw

Łazienki Park is a delightful haven, with avenues lined by chestnut trees and beautiful formal gardens leading to several palaces, pavilions, orangeries, and other historic buildings. Visitors can enter the park free of charge until sunset every day.

Apart from the big attractions of the palaces and the Theatre on the Isle, contemporary art exhibitions are held in the Old Guardhouse which is on the edge of the lake to the north. Another interesting place to visit is the Ignacy Jan Paderewski and Polish Expatriates in America Museum, housed in the Great Outbuilding next to the Old Guardhouse. It was opened in 1992 to celebrate the life of the great Polish pianist and composer and the return of his body to Warsaw from America. It contains all kinds of personal memorabilia of the exiled composer along with exhibits relating to Polish emigration to America. Other attractions in the park include a circular neoclassical watertower which was used to store and pump water to the palace, an Egyptian temple, another small pavilion called the Hermitage and the early 19th-century Astronomical Observatory. The Belweder Palace, an official residence made available to visiting foreign dignitaries, is also within the grounds of Łazienki Park. The 18th-century building was redesigned for the governor of Warsaw in the 1820s and has not been used to house the Polish head of state since 1995 when the official residence was moved to the Namiestnikowski Palace by Lech Wałęsa. (*For more information on Łazienki Park see page 166.*)

▽ **WATER FEATURES**
Water features in the park include lakes, fountains set amid formal gardens, canals and water's edge paths which heighten the sense of tranquillity.

▽ **DREAMY BOATING**
Taking a boat on the park's lake provides a different perspective of the surrounding greenery as well as the buildings which overlook the lake.

◁ **ORNAMENTATION**
A detail showing a bas-relief above the entrance on the southern elevation of the Palace on the Water.

▷ **BELWEDER PALACE**
The Belweder Palace is an elegant example of early 19th-century neoclassical architecture.

RELAXING IN THE PARK

Łazienki Park is a favourite place to relax and unwind for the people of Warsaw, and while visitor numbers obviously peak in the summer months, the park is popular all year round for its sheer beauty and escapism. Clusters of artists sell views of the park or offer their services as portrait painters while buskers provide a musical background as you leave the city far behind. Many visitors choose to sit at one of the two cafés in the park and watch the world go by. One café occupies a neo-classical pavilion neighbouring the Palace on the Water, while another is within the Theatre on The Isle. If you're looking for a more formal setting, the botanical garden of the New Orangery provides a highly atmospheric setting for the Belweder Restaurant. Specialities of the house include roast fillet of beef with fois gras and truffles and hazelnut grouse.

△ **PALACE ON THE WATER**
The southern elevation of the palace was a bathing pavilion before being turned into a summer residence for the last Polish king.

◁ **NORTHERN ELEVATION**
The northern elevation of the Palace on the Water, as seen from the bridge featuring a monument of King Jan III Sobieski.

▽ **CHOPIN CONCERTS**
The park's lake provides the perfect setting for summer Chopin concerts, held on Sunday at noon by the Chopin statue.

THROUGH MAZOVIA

Day trips from Warsaw to the region of Mazovia can be made by public transport. Places to visit include dense forests, historical towns and Chopin's birthplace

Map on page 180

Warsaw

The region that surrounds **Warsaw ❶** is known as **Mazowsze** (Mazovia). From the early Middle Ages to 1526 it was an independent branch of the Piast Dynasty, yet because of its geographical situation between the two capitals of the Polish-Lithuanian crown, Kraków and Vilnius, the region's bridging function made it inevitable that eventually the town in the middle, Warsaw, would be elevated to the capital of Poland. After the Third Partition, Mazovia was shared between Prussia and Austria, but in 1815 the Congress of Vienna set up the Congress Kingdom of Poland; effective power over the region passed to the Russian czar. Mazovia became part of independent Poland in 1918.

The landscape of Mazovia was formed by Ice-Age moraines. Its broad river valleys, sandy plains and rolling hills are particularly beautiful. Visitors will discover fascinating national parks, national costumes and folk art in the Lowicz and Kurpie regions, two mosques and a stud farm for Arab horses. Mazovia is one of Poland's poorer regions.

On the outskirts of Warsaw

Immediately adjacent to Warsaw is **Kampinoski Park Narodowy** (Kampinoski National Park) ❷ which, with an area of 350 sq. km (135 sq. miles), is the largest national park in Poland. Moors, dunes – some 20 metres (65 ft) tall – and large areas of broadleaf and conifer woodland between the Vistula and Bzura rivers are accessible via signposted footpaths. Rare black birches grow in the wetlands, while elks, boars, beavers and lynx have been reintroduced. In Truskaw the park authorities run a natural history museum which details local flora and fauna.

During World War II many Poles, including politicians, artists and scientists, were secretly brought to this wooded region and executed by Nazi firing squads. The most notorious location of such executions is **Palmiry** in the Puszcza Kampinowska at the northern edge of the park. After the war a proper cemetery was constructed, which contains the graves of 2,500 victims.

Not far from Palmiry, where the Bug and Narew rivers flow into the Vistula, stands the gigantic **Modlin Fortress**, made of earth bricks and constructed in 1806 under the orders of Napoleon. Later it was reinforced and extended by Russian troops; the barracks alone have a perimeter of 2,800 metres (8,650 ft) and it is the longest building in Europe. It accommodated the entire garrison of the fortress, with 26,000 men, and it remains in the hands of the military. East of Modlin lies the Zegrzyńskie Reservoir that was created in 1964 by high water and the water pressure of the Narew.

LEFT: bison in the Białowieża National Park.
BELOW: sunset in Mazovia.

Market towns and woodlands

Further down the Narew is **Pułtusk** ❸, an old town situated on an island. This town has twice achieved world fame: in 1806 a battle was fought here between the Napoleonic and Russian armies, and in 1868 the enormous Pułtusk meteorite landed nearby. The marketplace is the longest in Poland – a cobbled square dominated by a Gothic town hall, now home to a regional museum (open Tues–Sat 10am–4pm; Sun 10am–2pm; entrance fee). The tower affords a fine view of the surrounding area that extends as far as the Collegiate Church. This dates from 1443, with a splendid Renaissance nave added in 1554. Pułtusk also has a number of other attractive old churches that are worth visiting as well as parts of its original town wall.

The road that leads northwest out of Pułtusk passes next through **Gołymin-Ośrodek**, which is also famous for its Gothic church. A further 40 km (25 miles) from Pułtusk is **Ciechanów** ❹. Old Gothic buildings testify to the town's long history; the impressively large castle and two churches are striking

The former Bishop's Palace in Pułtusk is today the headquarters of Polonia, a non-profit-making organisation that looks after Poland's cultural heritage among émigrés.

Map
on page
180

examples of Mazovian brick Gothic architecture. The countryside north of Ciechanów was the scene of a massive battle in September 1939, when the Germans attempted to march straight through to Warsaw. The many military cemeteries in this area serve as a reminder of the conflict, in which numerous soldiers lost their lives.

Close to Ciechanów is the little village of **Opinogóra**. In the crypt of the church is the tomb of one of the greatest Polish romantic poets, Zygmunt Krasinski. The town's small castle houses a museum documenting his work, and in the splendid park there is a monument to the poet.

Further to the east is an expanse of wooded countryside known as **Kurpie Heath**. The wooden houses here are some of the most beautiful in all Poland. The best place to stay and admire them is Nowogród where the River Pisa flows into the Narew. The town has an attractive open-air museum.

Between Nowogród and Myszyniec lies the village of **Łyse**, where people congregate each Palm Sunday to see a prize presented for the most beautiful Easter Palm. The palms are kept for a long time in the wooden church, the work of carpenters from Kurpie, with an impressive interior decorated by local artists. From Łyse the road continues to the "capital" of Kurpie, **Myszyniec ❺**. Every year on the Thursday after Trinity Sunday the Corpus Christi procession sets out from the square in front of the neo-Gothic church. It is a colourful occasion, with all the participants dressed in the traditional national costumes. A similarly colourful procession can also be seen in nearby **Kadzidło**. This is the place to watch women skillfully cutting traditional silhouettes from coloured paper. In the town's church there is an exhibition devoted solely to this form of folk art.

Continuing eastwards, Łomża on the River Narwia, has an interesting permanent exhibition of amber, which was once mined in Kurpie. Also in Łomża is an attractive Gothic cathedral with a beautiful interior.

Płock Cathedral has copies of the Płock bronze doors made for the town in the 12th century in Magdeburg.

BELOW: the Narew haff (lagoon).

On the banks of the Vistula

The lower reaches of the Vistula towards Warsaw are lined by many interesting towns with long histories.

In **Czerwińsk ❻** a church displaying both Romanesque and Gothic features towers above the river valley. Romanesque frescos in the east chapel are among the art treasures within. In the adjoining monastery an ethnographical museum houses many exhibits which were brought back by monks after doing missionary work abroad (open daily; entrance fee). The late Gothic bell-tower contains some of the oldest bells in the country. During the summer it is possible to climb the bell-tower for a magnificent view of the town with its dilapidated wooden houses and its surroundings.

Further down in a picturesque setting by the Vistula lies **Płock ❼**, the "capital" of northern Mazovia. The ruins of a castle, many churches from all periods and styles and the oldest grammar school in Poland (founded in 1180) are the dominant features of this historic town. In the crypt of the impressive Romanesque cathedral are the tombs of two Polish kings, Władysław Herman (1040–1102) and Bolesław Krzywousty (1086–1138). The **Muzeum Mazowieckie**

(Museum of Mazovia; open Tues–Sun; entrance fee) is well worth a visit. It houses one of the best Art Nouveau collections in Poland, including paintings and ceramics from the Młoda Polska movement and other pieces from Germany and Austria.

North of Płock, near Sierpc, is a picturesque open-air museum with examples of the traditional architecture of northern Mazovia. Further south, on the right bank of the Vistula, lies Maciejowice where, in 1794 Kościuszko led his troops into battle against Russia: their defeat was to seal the fate of the Polish state.

Warka ❽, on the opposite bank, is a suburb of Winiary. It is best known as the birthplace of General Kazimierz Pulaski, the freedom hero of Poland and the USA, and the town contains both a museum and two monuments named after him. Continuing in the direction of Warsaw, you will come to **Góra Kalwaria**, which was modelled on the city of Jerusalem and is the destination of many Catholic pilgrims. Later in its history it also became a centre for Orthodox Jews and the home of a rabbi who was said to perform miracles.

Czersk ❾, with a medieval castle commanding a fine view over the banks of the Vistula, lies about 3 km (2 miles) from Góra Kalwaria. During the 14th and 15th centuries the town was home to the dukes of Mazovia. It lost much of its prominence due to the rise of Warsaw's importance and the reflowing of the Vistula, cutting if off from commercial trade. The Gothic castle (open Tues–Sun) is still worth a visit, including its exhibition of regional art.

The Podlasie lowlands

Below: vernacular architecture in Podlasie.

The open countryside of the region known as **Podlasie** begins east of Warsaw and extends right to the eastern border of Poland. In the Middle Ages this area

Map on page 180

was uninhabited, separating the Polish tribes from the East Slavs. The heathland was later settled from the west by Poles and from the east by Belorussians; even today there are places that contain both a Russian Orthodox and a Catholic church. Until 1939 every town in this region also had a synagogue, and in addition there were many Protestant churches and even two mosques in the area. Podlasie was always a melting pot for many different cultures and peoples, a region where the Latin traditions of western Europe met the Byzantine culture of eastern Europe.

The town of **Węgrów** ❿ is typical of the Podlasie region. Next to the market square is a Gothic parish church, which was rebuilt in Baroque style and decorated with frescos by Michael Angelo Palloni in the early 18th century. In the sacristy hangs the famous "Magic Mirror" dating from the 17th century. The Church of the Reformation was built by the Polish architect of Dutch origin, Tylman van Gameren. It also has frescos by Palloni and the splendid tomb of Jan Krasiński which dates from 1703. Among those buried in the Protestant cemetery are Scottish weavers who settled in this area. The Jewish settlement has long since vanished. The village of **Liw**, west of Węgrów and already within the borders of Mazovia proper, is dominated by a massive castle. It was built in the 15th century and after being destroyed twice by the Swedes was only partially reconstructed. A later building dating from the Baroque era, the Starostei, houses a museum of weaponry.

Siedlce, the administrative centre of the *woje wództwa* (county), is predominantly an 18th-century town. The figure of Atlas crowns the Jatusz (Town Hall). The former prison (1841–44) is now a museum, and the town has many monuments to the persecution of the community's Jews during World War II and

BELOW: rural scene in Góra Kalwaria.

the advance of the Soviet army in 1944. **Biała Podlaska** , a town which like Siedlce is situated on the railway line between Warsaw and Moscow, was founded in the 15th century and for a long time belonged to the Radziwills, one of the richest families in Poland. Radziwill Castle only partially survived the upheavals of Polish history. A pavilion with towers and a chapel, surrounded by a parapet, are all that remains. The castle's museum, however, illustrates just how impressive the original structure once was (open Tues–Sun; entrance fee).

The churches of Biała Podlaska date from the 16th and 17th centuries, although the new Greek Orthodox church was consecrated only in 1989. The monument to Józef Ignacy Kraszewski (1812–87) recalls that this was where the famous Polish writer went to school. The museum dedicated to his memory is located in **Romanów**, the picturesque village in which Kraszewski spent his childhood, approximately 50 km (30 miles) southeast of Biała Podlaska.

Beside the River Bug

A few kilometres east of Romanów run the tranquil waters of the River Bug, which forms the border between Poland, Belarus and the Ukraine. **Jabłeczna** is the centre of the Greek Orthodox faith in Poland. The most important buildings in the town are the Church of St Onufry (built in 1840) and the only Greek Orthodox monastery and seminary for priests in Poland. Each June a country fair is held here.

Still further upriver is **Kodeń**, destination of many pilgrimages because of the miraculous picture, the *Virgin of Kodeń*, in the town's church. Kodeń has a special significance for the Catholics of Podlasie and Belarus, similar to that of Częstochowa for the rest of Poland (*see page 256*). On the site of the former

BELOW: the calm waters of the River Bug.

castle is a Gothic church that was once Greek Orthodox; it contains a wooden sculpture depicting the martyrdom of the Polish people and the stations of the cross. The most interesting town on the Bug, however, is **Drohiczyn** ⑫. It was once the scene of a coronation when Prince Daniel crowned himself King of the Ukraine. The barrows in the area surrounding the town date from the 7th to the 9th centuries and the settlement itself, with a history that goes back to the 7th century, was once the customs post between the Congress Kingdom of Poland and the Ukraine.

Archaeological excavations uncovered thousands of lead seals from all over Europe, some of which are now on display in the town's museum. A dominant feature of the town is the castle hill, which towers over the river. Also of interest are the Orthodox church and the three Baroque churches, which were badly damaged in World War I.

Northwest of Drohiczyn is the little town of Ciechanowiec, with a fascinating Agricultural Museum. The museum has an open-air section (*skansen*) with a range of wooden buildings from Podlasie. On the other side of the Bug, near Malkinia Gorna is **Treblinka**. In the work camp Treblinka I (1941–44) and the extermination camp Treblinka II (1942–43) nearly 800,000 people were murdered by the Nazis (*see page 55*).

The **Puszcza Białowieska** ⑬, a vast forest that has been left untouched since the Middle Ages and the largest of its kind in Europe, runs along the eastern border of Poland. Once the hunting ground of Lithuanian princes, Polish kings and Russian czars, this national park is now a world reserve under the special protection of UNESCO. Some 300 bison roam free, and other species of animals and plants threatened with extinction are also protected. Wild horses (tarpans),

Map on page 180

TIP

Janów Podlaski, 20 km (12 miles) from Biala Podlaska, is famous as an equestrian centre and home to a stud farm that produces world-class Arab horses.

BELOW: Poland's stud farms are world famous.

bears, wolves, beavers, lynx and rare species of bird, such as the black-headed eagle, live in the wild. The park may be visited only in the company of a guide.

In the village of **Białowieża** the former palace has been converted into a hotel, next to which is an informative natural history museum with exhibits relating to species found in the forest (open Tues–Sun; entrance fee). On the way to **Hajnówka** there is a reserve for bison and wild horses. In the town itself, on the western edge of the park, stands an imposing Greek Orthodox church, the combined work of artists from Poland, Greece and Bulgaria.

Palaces and mosques

The largest town in northeast Poland is **Białystok** , the administrative town for the *województwa* of the same name. In the 18th century the town was dominated by the Branicki aristocratic family, and their massive Baroque palace is a particularly interesting piece of architecture, also called the Versailles of Podlasie. Today it houses the Medical Academy. The adjacent arsenal, built in 1755, is used for exhibitions. Extensive gardens in French and English style surround the palace.

In the Town Hall is an exhibition of Polish art with an unusual section dealing with the art of the Jadzwingers. The Orthodox cathedral dates back to the 16th century, when Białystok was part of Russia: the 1920s modernistic Church of St Roch provides an interesting contrast. The former summer palace of the Branickis in **Choroszcz**, 12 km (7 miles) away, is worth a detour for anyone with a keen interest in interior design (open Tues–Sun; entrance fee).

Some 42 km (26 miles) northeast of Białystok is Sokółka. It was in this region that Jan III Sobieski allowed Tartar prisoners-of-war to settle, and a whole section of the local museum is given over to the arrival of this ethnic Muslim group. The villages of **Bohoniki** and **Kruszyniany** have the only two remaining mosques in Poland and there is an active Tartar community here. Many of the characteristics of Polish woodcarving can be seen in the architecture of these wooden Islamic buildings, which date from the 18th and 19th centuries. The *mizars*, as the Islamic cemeteries are known, are also of interest, with gravestones inscribed in both Polish and Arabic.

Nearby, on the banks of the Biebrza river, the **Biebrzański Park Narodowy** (Biebrza National Park) is the largest marshy area in Poland, and almost certainly one of the largest unspoilt river landscapes in Europe to be preserved in its original state. Beavers, wolves and thousands of waterfowl, including sea eagles, sandpipers and herons, enjoy this protected environment of some 592 sq. km (228 sq. miles). The Biebrza is ideal for watersports, and safaris are organised on the river and in the surrounding area with guides who are expert in Biebrzandski's natural history (tel: 85-162266).

Between Warsaw and Łódz

There are two possible routes that can be taken west from Warsaw. The northern route runs along the edge of the Puszcza Kampinowska and passes through the village of **Kampinos**. Here the little wooden church

Bialystok is also notable as the birth place of Ludwik Zamenhof (1859–1917), the creator of Esperanto, the "international language" made up of common words from several European tongues. Although it never truly caught on, there are an estimated 100,000 speakers in the world today.

BELOW: the mosque in Kruszyniany.

dating from the 18th century is a good example of how the craftsmen in the villages made use of the simple building materials available to them to imitate the Baroque stone churches in the towns. If you wish to explore the Kampinoski National Park, horse-drawn carts and sleighs can be hired in the village.

Further along this route is **Żelazowa Wola** , the birthplace of Frédéric Chopin in 1810 (*see page 196*). In the inn – his childhood home – is a museum documenting his life and work (open Tues–Sun; entrance fee). The house has been restored to resemble the family's 17th-century residence and the music room has manuscripts of early works and a cast of Chopin's left hand on display. In the summer, piano recitals are held almost every day in the park by internationally renowned performers. In **Brochów**, where Chopin's parents were married, Chopin's baptismal certificate is kept in the late medieval fortified church.

The second route along the E30 from Warsaw to the west runs south through **Paprotnia** ⓰, which has a classic inn and a smithy, both of which are at least 200 years old. Napoleon is said to have once feasted in the restaurant, hence the name Kuznia Napoleonska. The Franciscan Niepo-Kalanów monastery was built in 1927 by St Maximilian Kolbe. Monk and abbot of the monastery, Kolbe died to save the life of a fellow-prisoner in Auschwitz in 1941 and was canonised in 1982. The church of Niepokalanów was built between 1948–54; it also houses a Maximilian Kolbe memorial. In the vault is an exhibition entitled "one thousand years of Polish history".

The two routes leading west out of Warsaw meet in **Sochaczew**, which contains the ruins of the palace of the princes of Mazovia and a museum devoted to the Battle of the Bzura. This was the biggest defensive battle fought by the Poles in 1939. The Narrow Gauge Railway Museum sets a happier tone. From

Map on page 180

BELOW: the grand façade of the Branicki Palace.

The ethnographic section of the regional museum (above) has a comprehensive collection of exhibits detailing the customs and traditional crafts of the region.

BELOW: the spire of Łowicz Cathedral.

Sochaczew there is a road branching off to the south to **Bolimów**. This community has no buildings of architectural interest, but is well known as the place where, on 31 December 1914, the Germans first used tear gas as a weapon.

Not far from Bolimów is **Nieborów** , one of Poland's most magnificent palaces and parks (open Tues–Sun; entrance fee). The palace, designed by Tylman van Gameren and built from 1690–96, today houses a museum with valuable exhibits, among them a Roman sculpture of Niobe, portraits of European monarchs and a huge Italian globe dating from the 17th century. These works of art were collected by the Radziwill family, who owned Nieborów until 1945. A second romantic park known as **Arkadia** is situated 5 km (3 miles) from Nieborów. It contains almost everything you would expect to find in a park laid out at the end of the 18th century: a Gothic house, Greek temple, aqueduct, lakes and a ruined castle.

The 12th century trading city of **Łowicz** forms the centre of the region and was for several centuries the seat of the archbishops of Gniezno. Here, folk arts and crafts have not yet degenerated to the level of mass-production for the tourists. The wood carvings, paper silhouettes and colourful hand-woven materials of Łowicz are famous and much in demand throughout Poland, and can be bought from shops around the main square.

Anyone who is especially interested in traditions of this kind should pay a visit to the museum housed in a Baroque palace located right on the market square (open Tues–Sun; entrance fee). The processions that take place at Corpus Christi in late May are particularly lively affairs. The nearby Collegiate Church contains the tombs of the Polish primates, the princes of the church who took over leadership of the state between rulers, until the new king was crowned.

South of Łowicz, close to the railway line, is the village of **Lipce**. The famous Polish writer and Nobel prize winner Władysław Reymont lived here from 1889–91, and set the story of his best-known novel *Chłopi (The Peasants)* in this village (*see page 164 and 174*).

Łódź

With its 850,000 inhabitants **Łódź** ⑲ is today the second-largest town in Poland, with light industry and 50 percent of the Polish textile industry located within its boundaries. Łódź was granted a town charter as long ago as 1423, but in 1820 still only had 800 inhabitants – a place of no significance whatsoever. Things began to change in 1823 with the building of Nowe Miasto, the first textile workers' estate. The removal of the customs barriers between Poland and Russia led to an enormous increase in the export of textiles to Russia, and in the second half of the 19th century Łódź became the most important textile centre in the world.

During World War II the Germans opened two large transit camps in Łódź for Polish prisoners-of-war, as well as a camp for Russian airmen, a camp for 5,000 gypsies from Germany, Austria and the Balkans and also a camp for 4,000 Polish children. Approximately 260,000 Jews were murdered in nearby Chełmno nad Nerem, and the people of Łódź itself were also affected; of its 600,000 inhabitants only around half survived the war.

After the war new estates grew up around the original districts of the town. In addition to the traditional textile industry, electrical engineering and chemical industries also came to Łódź. The first institutions of further education were founded, the most famous being the State College of Cinematic Art, Drama

TIP

The brightly coloured Mazovian national costume (*pasiaki*) hails from Łowicz and can be bought at many local souvenir shops.

LEFT: exterior of Poynański Palace in Łódź.
BELOW: the hallway and staircase.

Map on page 180

Detail of intricate house façade along Piotrkowska.

BELOW: entrance to the Jewish cemetary in Łódź.

and Television (*see page 113*). The University of Łódź now also has a Department of Polish for foreigners. Typical of Łódź are a group of buildings which date from the 19th century: an industrialist's villa, a factory and the modest little houses of the textile workers. They were built in imitation of previous architectural styles, Gothic and Baroque in particular, as were the interesting town residences in Piotrkowska and Moniuszko streets. At least 30 houses in the Art Nouveau mode, *Secesja* in Polish, have also been preserved.

There are three museums in Łódź that are particularly worth visiting. The **Art Museum**, in the palace once owned by the Poznański family, is where Polish and international art from the 19th century onwards is exhibited. The main emphasis is on modern art, including works by Chagall and Mondrian and Polish artists such as Strzeminski and Witkowski (Więkowskiego 36; open Tues–Sun; entrance fee). The **Historical Museum of Łódź** (Ogrodowa; open Tues–Sun; entrance fee) is accommodated in another of the Poznański family's palaces, which has a flamboyant interior. The museum documents the town's past, showing how it looked prior to World War II's devastation. Also on display is a collection of the memorabilia of Artur Rubinstein, the famous pianist and composer, who was born here. The excellent philharmonic hall of Łódź has been named after him.

The **Central Textile Museum** (Piotrkowska 282; open Tues–Sun; entrance fee) is set in the White Factory, in 1838 the first spinning mill in Łódź to be fitted with a steam-driven engine. There is a portrayal of the development of technology in the textile industry and its social consequences in Poland, and the museum is rounded off with a collection of 16th- to 19th-century textiles from all over the world, along with impressive displays of modern textile work.

CHAIM RUMKOWSKI

One of the most controversial figures in the whole tragic history of Polish Jewry during World War II was Chaim Rumkowski.

A former textiles manager, Rumkowski was chosen by the Nazis to lead the Łódź ghetto that they set up in the north of the city, a position that involved negotiating – some say collaborating – between the Germans and the ghetto inhabitants as their spokesman and leader. The Łódź ghetto soon became one of the most productive in Poland, but stories abound of Rumkowski's dictatorial manner and power-hungry motives, including offering children up to the camps in place of healthy adults – he believed that he would emerge as the head of a Jewish protectorate after the war. However, it cannot be denied that he reduced the numbers deported to the camps and that the ghetto was a place of culture and education, not simply slave labour.

In 1944, at the height of the Final Solution frenzy, Himmler ordered that the Łódź ghetto be liquidated despite its profitability, and Rumkowski volunteered to go to Auschwitz, where he died soon after – possibly murdered by vengeful fellow ghetto residents, although this has never been proved.

Before the war over 30 percent of the inhabitants of Łódź were Jewish. The Jewish community, both synagogues and the old Jewish cemetery were destroyed during the war. Only the new **Jewish Cemetery** survived, with around 120,000 gravestones and the Izrael Poznański Mausoleum erected between 1893–1939. Today it is the largest Jewish cemetery in Europe and one of the largest in the world.

Map on page 180

Villages around Łódź

North of Łódź is **Łęczyca** ⓴, which, in the Middle Ages, was one of the most powerful towns in Poland. It still has a number of monuments: a Gothic castle with an ethnographical museum, well-preserved town walls and a classical Town Hall. In the nearby village of Tum is a Romanesque church dating from 1141–45, and, adjacent to it, the ruins of an old castle. Not far from Kutno is **Oporów**, which has an attractive Gothic castle situated on a man-made island.

East of Łódź, in Rawa Mazowiecka, is another Gothic castle. Unfortunately, it suffered severe damage in both world wars, so that much of the present building is a reconstruction. The village of Boguszyce, near Rawa, Mazowiecka seldom attracts visitors, but is well worth a detour for its splendid wooden church. It was built in 1558, and although not much to look at from the outside its interior is magnificently decorated with paintings in Renaissance style.

To the southwest is the industrial town of **Piotrków Trybunalski**, which has a well-known glassworks. The former Royal Palace, which was built between 1511–19, now houses a museum. Other historic sights in Piotrków include the remains of the town walls, some fascinating churches and the synagogue. The municipal station dates from 1850, when the railway line was built from War-

BELOW: reliefs in one of the palaces of the Poznański family in Łódź.

saw to Vienna. Brick-built stations like this are typical of this particular area. A favourite place for weekend excursions is **Pilica**, with its romantic villages and medieval castles surrounded by water. In **Inowłódź** is a Romanesque church founded by the Polish king Władysław Herman, with a high stone tower that dominates the surrounding countryside. In the suburb of Tomaszów Mazowiecki there is the **Niebieskie Źródła**. Literally meaning "blue springs", its name is a reference to the blue sheen of the water, which is caused by the minerals it contains. Further upriver, in **Sulejów**, is an old Cistercian monastery, one of Poland's most important architectural monuments. It was founded and financed by Prince Kazimierz the Just in 1177. The well-fortified complex includes a church, the ruins of a monastery, defensive walls with bastions and farm buildings. Today it houses a hotel.

Southwest of Łódź is **Zduńska Wola**, where, in 1894, the holy abbot and saint Maximilian Kolbe was born (*see page 103*). As long ago as the 6th century a castle stood by the River Warta, not far from Sieradz, and the round church is one of the remaining buildings.

In **Wieluń** the fortified walls and the Kraków Gate have also been preserved; the classical Town Hall was built in 1842. The Pauline Church, which was originally Gothic, also has a splendid Baroque interior. There are 37 old wooden churches in the vicinity of Wieluń. One of them, the **Church of the Holy Spirit** which stands in Sieradz cemetery, was built after the victory over the Crusader knights near Grunwald in 1410.

The church in **Grębień**, near Wieluń has interiors decorated with well-preserved Gothic-Renaissance wall paintings which date from 1500–31. Also well worth seeing is the 14th-century walled manor in nearby **Trubadzin**.

BELOW: children on a horse-drawn wagon.

Between the Vistula and the Pilica

In the past this area was part of Little Poland (*see page 199*). In the north it is mainly flat, but towards the south it becomes more hilly. Between Radom and Puławy is **Czarnolas**, where Jan Kochanowski (1530–84) lived. This poet was one of the first to write in Polish rather than Latin, the usual written language in those days (*see page 108*). He is buried in the church of nearby Zwoleń.

Further to the west a monumental Gothic-Renaissance palace, now in ruins, towers above the town of **Drzewica ㉑**. This region was the scene of the fiercest partisan battles in Poland, and in the whole of Europe, during World War II. The commander of the Polish freedom fighters, Henryk Dobrzanski, generally known as "Hubal", did not capitulate in 1939 but fought on with his uniformed division for another six months. He fell not far from the village of Studzianna, which is well known for its Baroque church. In revenge for Hubal's resistance many of the surrounding villages were burned down by the Germans and all men over 15 years of age were murdered. The village that suffered the most was Skłoby, where 265 people lost their lives and 400 buildings were set on fire.

The area surrounding Drzewica and Studzianna is referred to by ethnologists as the **Opoczyński region**. Here traditional costumes are rather like those of Mazovia, with different striped patterns. Timber is still frequently used as a building material in this region and there are many folk artists dedicated to continuing the silhouette tradition.

The largest town in this region is **Radom ㉒**, an important centre with metal industry, leather and tobacco factories. The oldest monument is the Church of St Wacław. The medieval town centre has also been preserved, and there is an open-air museum with examples of the various building styles of this area.

Map on page 180

Milk is delivered straight from the churn in some places in the region.

BELOW: landscape near Radom.

There is also a display of old beehives of many shapes and sizes. A little further along road E77, in the local palace of Szydłowiec, is the **Folk Musical Instrument Museum**, the only one of its kind in Poland. Other features of Szydłowiec are a Renaissance Town Hall, a large Jewish cemetery and a well-known sandstone quarry.

An alternative route, the B9, leads from Radom to Sandomierz. Immediately after Radom you come to **Skaryszew**. The horse market held here on the sixth Monday after Easter attracts large numbers of gypsies, farmers and horse-lovers from all over Poland. It's an event well worth catching if you can.

Further along this road is **Iłża**, the scene of a major battle in 1939. The tower of the palace of the bishops of Kraków, a building that is now a ruin, was used as an observation point by the Polish army in the battle. A few kilometres from Ostrowiec Świętokrzyski in **Krzemionki Opatowskie** there is a quartz mine which is known to have been in existence in the Neolithic period, when it was one of the largest in Europe. One section of it can be visited.

Between the industrial town of Skarzysko-Kamienna and Starachowice is **Wchock**, which has a Romanesque-Gothic church and a Cistercian monastery dating from the beginning of the 13th century. The monastery contains the most beautiful examples of Romanesque art in the whole of Poland. Another famous partisan leader from World War II, Jan Piwnik "Ponury", is buried here.

The Holy Cross Mountains

Further to the south runs a line of rocky mountains known as **Góry Świętokrzyskie** (Holy Cross Mountains) ㉓. This is the oldest Polish mountain range, an area of pine forests, exposed mountain peaks, quartz rock, a type of larch

BELOW: hiking in the mountains.

Map
on page
180

peculiar to the region, the remains of coral in the pre-Cambrian rock and a multitude of rare but protected fauna and flora. Amid the wild and romantic scenery there are many places worth taking the time to visit.

In **Samsonów** are the ruins of a metalworks dating from the beginning of the 19th century and now a technological monument. Nearby is "Bartek", one of the largest and oldest oak trees in Poland. The trunk has a circumference of over 9 metres (29 ft). Nearby **Oblęgorek** is where Henryk Sienkiewicz, the author of the novel *Quo Vadis*, lived until 1914.

The capital of this region is **Kielce ㉔**. Its bishop's palace was built in the 17th century, and now houses the National Museum: this includes a gallery of Polish art and a section dealing with the interior decor of palaces. Just opposite the palace is a Baroque cathedral with an interior preserved in its original style and a beautiful sculpture of the Virgin Mary made of galena, a lead ore (open Tues–Sun; entrance fee).

To the east of Kielce rises the Łysa Góra (Bare Mountain), with its forbidding scree slopes. Situated on this mountain is the **Święty Krzyż** (Holy Cross Monastery) belonging to the Benedictine order, where a relic of the Holy Cross is kept. Before the monastery came into existence there was a pre-Christian sanctuary on this spot. Today the countryside is sadly marred by a television broadcasting tower.

South of Radom on the E77 road is the village of Oronsko, where a centre of Polish sculpture has been established at Heimstatt, the manor that once belonged to the painter Józef Brandt (1841–1915). Stone and ceramic sculptures by modern artists are visible from the road.

The whole area surrounding Łysa Góra is a **national park**, which extends over a total of 6,000 hectares (15,000 acres). The heath has splendid pine and larch woods and there are numerous clearings and deforested areas which are dotted with large boulders. At the foot of this range of mountains is the attractive village of **Nowa Słupia**. There was already an iron industry here in the second century and it is perfectly possible that iron was exported from this area to the Roman Empire. Remains of the old furnaces are on display in the local history museum.

BELOW: shrine.

All these mountains are composed of sandstone, and it is only north of Kielce that limestone begins to predominate. Here magnificent marble is also to be found, and even semi-precious stones such as malachite and azurite are relatively common. While on the way from Kielce to Chęciny along the E77 make a 10-km (6-mile) detour to see the most beautiful Polish grotto, known as **Raj** (Paradise), filled with beautiful stalactites and stalagmites (open May–Oct).

The ruins of an old castle tower above the little town of **Chęciny**, once a place of considerable wealth. For centuries the town was the centre of the lead ore mining industry.

The next place of importance on the road towards Kraków is **Jędrzejów**. Its 13th-century Cistercian monastery was rebuilt in Baroque style. However, the town is best known for its museum, which is named after the local Przypkowski family and includes their fascinating collection of sundials (open Tues–Sun; entrance fee; guided tours obligatory). In the region east of Jędrzejów lies **Szyłdów**, a sleepy little village that once had a town charter. It's a pleasant place to stop for a wander; its town walls and church have survived the upheavals of the ages undamaged. ❏

THE SPIRIT OF POLISH ROMANTICISM

Frédéric Chopin's lyricism and unparalleled melodic genius has produced some of the most beautiful and spiritual music ever written

Chopin was born in 1810 in a country manor house in the village of Żelazowa Wola, outside Warsaw. His baptismal certificate is kept in the medieval church of the nearby village of Brochów, where his parents were married and his father, an emigrant from France, was engaged as a tutor at the nearby estate of Count Skarbek. He made his professional debut as a child prodigy, appearing at charity concerts organised by Warsaw's aristocratic circles. While Chopin was studying at the Warsaw School of Music he was captivated by Polish folk music and become familiar with various songs and dances in the villages surrounding Warsaw. In the autumn of 1830 Chopin left Warsaw and never returned to his beloved Poland. After performing in Dresden, Vienna, Salzburg and Munich, he finally arrived in Paris, where he initially gave numerous recitals before concentrating on composition. Chopin's social circle included many prominent musicians including Franz Liszt, and the love of his life, George Sand, the pseudonym of the French writer Aurore Dudevant. Their intense relationship resulted in her nursing Chopin for several years after he contracted tuberculosis. She finally left him in 1847, when he was seriously ill and virtually penniless. A desperate but highly successful visit to London briefly revived his fortunes, where he gave his final public concert in 1848. Returning to Paris, Chopin died in 1849 in his home in the Place Vendome.

▷ **ŻELAZOWA WOLA**
Chopin's mother's room at the family home in Żelazowa Wola has been beautifully restored and combines elements of folk art with formal decoration.

△ **BURIED HEART**
Buried originally in the Pére-Lachaise cemetery in Paris, Chopin's heart was finally laid to rest within a central pillar of the Holy Cross Church in Warsaw.

▷ **SUNDAY RECITALS**
Summer concerts are held on the terrace at Żelazowa Wola, which is surrounded by delightful parkland containing a small lake.

▷**ŁAZIENKI PARK SCULPTURE**
This Art Nouveau sculpture of Chopin contemplating the beauty of nature was designed in 1926 by sculptor Wacław Szymanowski.

△ **POZNAŃ'S PIANO**
The Musical Instruments Museum in Poznań has a piano that Chopin played and other mementos of the composer's life.

CHOPIN'S MUSICAL LEGACY

Chopin's earliest compositions date from his childhood. He began composing seriously when he settled in Paris in the 1830s, and it was while convalescing in Majorca in 1838 that he composed the renowned Preludes, the Polonaise in A major, and the Sonata which includes the Funeral March. His music was as controversial as it was passionate, and his most vehement critics condemned its overt emotionalism as the ravings of a lunatic. Nearing the end of his life he wrote: "Where have my abilities gone, what has happened to my heart? I can hardly remember how they sing at home. The world is sinking round me in a strange fashion." At Chopin's funeral service, Mozart's Requiem was played according to his wishes and he was buried in the Pére-Lachaise Cemetery in Paris.

◁ **CHOPIN MUSEUM**
Chopin's restored 19th-century family home is now a museum, with a collection of various family possessions and early piano manuscripts.

▽ **OUTDOOR CONCERTS**
Łazienki Park's highly romantic atmosphere provides one of the best venues to listen to recitals of Chopin's music.

MAŁOPOLSKA – LITTLE POLAND

Małopolska is not small in either size or significance. From the historic city of Kraków to trekking in the Tatras, this region is packed with things to see and do

A region of immense natural beauty, which also includes some of Poland's most attractive and historic towns, Małopolska embraces the southern and southeastern corner of Poland, between the Ukraine and Slovakia.

To the south the Carpathian mountains and foothills extend along the border with Slovakia, while the centre of the region features the lowlying Koltina Sandomierska basin. To the north rises the Wyżyna Małopolska (Małopolska Upland), comprising a number of separate, low-lying ranges of hills, bordered by the Wyżyna Krakowsko Częstochowska (Kraków Częstochowa Upland). To the east the Wyżyna Lubelska (Lublin Uplands) jut out above the surrounding plains. The region is also traversed by important rivers such as the Vistula, Dunajec and San, as well as numerous picturesque streams and lakes, which continually add variety and heighten the appeal of the surrounding countryside.

The region's most important city is Kraków, the capital of Poland between the 11th and the 16th century. Although the city's political power subsequently diminished, it continues to be regarded as Poland's cultural and intellectual capital. Kraków is also one of Poland's most beautiful cities, with a wealth of museums including the Wawel Royal Castle and Cathedral, and a comprehensive range of architecture that includes definitive examples of Renaissance style.

The chapter entitled *Through Little Poland* (*see page 219*) highlights the vast number of attractions within easy reach of Kraków, including the salt mines at Wieliczka, dating from the 12th century, a network of ruined castles along the so-called Eagle's Lair on the border with Slovakia; Łancut, one of Poland's most impressive palaces (now a museum) and the town of Zamość, a remarkable example of Renaissance architecture and town planning. ❑

LEFT: Corpus Cristi Church, Kazimierz.

Kraków

Dworzec Kraków Główny
Kremerowska
Sobieskiego
Batorego
Stefana
Biskupia
Dluga
Krzywa
Św. Filipa
Pawia
Łobzowska
A. Asnyka
Seweryn Fenn'a
Krowoderska
Płac J. Matejki
T. Paderewski
Pomnik Grunwaldzki (Monument to the Battle of Grunwald)
Zacisze
Garbarska
Bąsztowa
Pomnik Lilii Wenedy
PLANTY
Pomnik B. Zalewskiego
Barbakan (Barbican)
Płac Kolejowy
Lubicz
Michałowskiego
Kościół Św. Marka (St Mark's Church)
Brama Florianska Bąsztowa (Florian's Gate)
Jama Michalikowa
Dawnych Młynów
Rajska
Szujskiego
Czysta
Muzeum Czartoryskich (Czartoryski Museum)
Pomnik Miniatura
Krupnicza
Muzeum Szołayskich (Szołayski Museum)
Dom Jana Matejki (Jan Matejko's House)
Pomnik Słowackiego
Zamenhofa
Kościół Św. Krzyza
Podwale J. Dunajewskiego
Płac Szczepański
Teatr im J. Słowackiego (Juliusz Słowacki Theatre)
Pomnik M.Bałuckiego
Loretańska
Kościół Św. Anny (St Anna's Church)
StaryTeatr (Old Theatre)
Pomnik Adama Mickiewicza (Adam Mickiewicz Monument)
PLANTY
Kopernika
Studencka
Bagatela Teatr
Szewska
Sukiennice (Cloth Hall)
Kościół Mariacki (St Mary's Church)
Kapucynska
Collegium Maius (Maius College)
Wieża Ratuszowa (Town Hall Tower)
Rynek Glówny
Mały Rynek
Garncarska
Płac Sikorskiego
Jabłonowskich
STARE MIASTO (OLD TOWN)
Kościół Św. Wojciecha (St Adalbert's Church)
Sienna
Zyblikiewicza
H. Kołłątaja
Sołtyka
Blich
Marsz. J. Piłsudskiego
Gołębia
Grodzka
Westerplatte
Mikołajska
Franciszkańska
Kościół Dominikanów (Dominican Church)
Wielopole
Starowiślna
Muzeum Narodowe (National Museum)
Smoleńsk
Kościół Franciszkanów
Płac Wszystkich Świętych
Dominikańska
Felicjanek
Zwierzyniecka
Pomnik Grożyny i Litawara
Poselska
Teatr Cricot
Kościół Św. Piotra i Pawła (St Peter & St Paul's Church)
STRADOM
Teatr Kameralny
Józefa
Sarego
Wrzesińska
Dietla
Oświęcim (Auschwitz)
A.Z Krasińskiego
Restorya
Mala
Tarłowska
Wł. Boya-Żeleńskiego
PLANTY
Kościół Św. Andrzeja (St Andrew's Church)
PLANTY
Św. Gertrudy
Powiśle
Boisko Miedzyszkolne
Podzamcze
Św. Sebastiana
Most Dębnicki
Pomnik Tadeusza Kościuszki
Muzeum Katedralne (Cathedral Museum)
Wawel (Royal Castle)
Katedra
Droga do Zamku
Bernardyńska
Św. Idziego
Stradomska
Dietla
Józefa
Brzozowa
Joselewicza
Starowiślna
WAWEL
Smocza Jama (Dragon's Cave)
Miodowa
Remu'h Synagoga
Szeroka
Dąjwór
Wieliczka
Rynek Dębnicki
Zamkowa
Barska
Różana
Konfederacka
Smocza
Koletek
Miodowa Podbrzezie
Warszauera
Kupa
Jakuba
nm. Żydowski
Ajzyck Synagoga
Stara Synagoga (Old Synagogue)
Wąska
Wisła
Most Grunwaldzki
Dietla
Józefa
KAZIMIERZ
Kościół Bożego Ciała (Corpus Christi Church)
Wawrzyńca
Monte Cassino
Dębowa
J. Bułhaka
Barska
Marii Konopnickiej
Kościół Św. Katarzyny (Church of St Catherine)
Paulińska
Św. Katarzyny
Augustiańska
Skałeczna
Św.
Krakowska
Bożego Ciała
Płac Wolnica
Muzeum Etnograficzne (Museum of Mankind)
Gazowa
Podgórska
Rondo Grunwaldzkie
(Vistula)
Kościół Paulinów
Skawińska
Trynitarska

0 300 m
0 300 yds

N

KRAKÓW

There's so much to do in Kraków that the city requires a week's stay to do it justice. It contains both low-brow and high-brow culture mixed with vitality and a sense of history

Map on page 200

Formerly the capital of Poland, Krakóvians have always continued to think of their city as Poland's cultural and intellectual capital – despite the counter-claims of Varsovians. But no one can dispute the city's immense beauty, which is readily accessible within the pedestrianised Old Town. Hailed as European City of Culture in 1992 and 2000, Kraków (Cracow) is frequently termed an "al fresco museum", with UNESCO's World Heritage Listing classifying 55 of the city's buildings and monuments as of the highest class. Meanwhile, 18 museums, containing more than two million works of art, span an amazing range of themes, including rarities such as the pharmacy museum and the insurance museum.

Alongside the sense of history, Kraków is also a vibrant, progressive city, with a full cultural programme of music (classical, jazz, alternative, whatever), film and theatre, including the country's foremost Helena Modrzejewska Theatre, as well as avant garde troupes. Numerous annual festivals include the Music of Old Kraków in August, with concerts held in atmospheric burghers' houses, churches and palaces throughout the Old Town. The International Festival of Short Feature Films at the end of May and beginning of June continues the city's heritage as the site of the first Polish film screening in 1896.

The Jagiellonian University (the "Oxbridge" of Poland) ensures a high youth quota, with the inevitable accompaniment of Bohemian and various alternative sub-cultures. Even during the summer vacations there is an "academic" influx, as the university holds summer schools with courses on Polish language, culture and history for overseas students, particularly Polish émigrés.

BELOW: the Wit Stwosz altar in the Church of St Mary.

The history of Kraków

According to legend, a duke and leader of a Slavic tribe called Krak erected a fortified settlement on a hill known as Wawel. Being on key trade routes meant the settlement developed into a town, with the earliest recorded reference dated AD 965, when a merchant from Cordoba, Ibrahim ibn Jakub, wrote that Kraków was already a major town known throughout Europe.

The diocese of Kraków was founded in 1000, following the country's conversion to Christianity in 966. In 1040 King Casimir "The Restorer" made Kraków Poland's capital. In 1241 the town was destroyed by a Tartar invasion, although it was rapidly rebuilt, and blossomed again under the Jagiellonian dynasty (1386–1572), with commerce developing alongside art and culture. The Jagiellonian University was founded in 1364. The country's first university has retained its reputation as the country's premier educational institute. During the 15th century Kraków became a town of some 30,000 inhabitants, surrounded by fortified walls and turrets. Situated at the junction of trade routes from western Europe to Byzantium, and from southern Europe to the Baltic, the city joined the Hanseatic League in 1430, which attracted many German craftsmen and merchants. The first half of the16th century saw trade and handicrafts flourish, with as many as 60 different guilds. However, the union of Poland and Lithuania in 1569 decreased Kraków's status, as Mazovia and Warsaw emerged as the new "centre" of Poland, with King Zygmunt III making Warsaw the capital in 1596. Yet, as Polish kings continued to be crowned and buried in the Kraków's Wawel Cathedral, the city retained some of its importance.

Foreign rule

Under the Third Partition of Poland in 1795, Małopolska became a part of the Austrian Habsburg empire. After the Congress of Vienna, Kraków was a free city and capital of the so-called Kraków Republic from 1815 until, in 1846, the city was incorporated into the province of Galicia. The relatively liberal attitude of the Austrian authorities enabled Polish culture and science to progress; even the activities of the independence movement were tolerated. It was during this period that the painters Jan Matejko, Jacek Malczewski and Leon Wyczółkowski emerged as maestros. Subsequently, the forerunners of Secessionism (Polish Art Nouveau), Stanisław Wyspiaski and Józef Mehofer, developed a movement called *Młda Polska* (Young Poland) centred in the city. Austrian rule also transformed Kraków into a resilient "fortress" which even managed to withstand the Russian offensive of 1914.

In November 1939 the Nazis established the headquarters of the General

The eagle of Kraków is also Poland's coat of arms.

BELOW: detail of the Renaissance-style Cloth Hall in the Main Market Square.

Map on page 200

Government in the city, with the Governor General Hans Frank taking up residence in the Wawel royal palace. Having wiped out the Jewish population, as well as the Polish intelligentsia, the Nazis mined the city for systematic destruction (which was the fate of Warsaw) in 1945. However, nothing was detonated as they retreated from a sudden advance by the Red Army, which liberated the city on 18 January 1945. In fact, this is one of the few Polish cities to have survived the war more or less intact (*see page 45*).

Kraków, the third largest city in Poland, now has a population of 745,000, with the post-war suburbs being purpose-built industrial centres, including engineering, metal processing, electronics, pharmaceuticals and foodstuffs. However, it was for political rather than economic reasons that the Lenin steelworks employed a vast proletarian labour-force. A horrific consequence was pollution from the factories, which attacked not only the inhabitants, but also the historic buildings. Fortunately, a tough policy of dealing with industrial waste has brought this under control.

The Main Market Square

The heart of the city, the **Rynek Główny** (Main Market Square) is always busy with locals and tourists, and during the summer this continues until late into the night. Measuring 200 metres (650 ft) on each side, it is one of Europe's largest medieval squares (only St Mark's Square in Venice is larger), with plenty of space for numerous restaurants and cafés, as well as flower stalls, pavement artists and street performers. Being such a cultured town, there are plenty of duos and trios playing exquisite classical refrains, with some buskers having a cheerful placard stating: "I'm healthy and happy, I'm just collecting money for beer."

BELOW: feeding the pigeons in Main Market Square.

The market square is surrounded by grand burghers' houses and palaces, with façades reflecting various architectural genres, while many of the rear courtyards serve as *al fresco* cafés and restaurants. It's essential to dine at **Wierzynek** (Rynek Główny 15), which serves some of the city's finest dishes. This restaurant occupies three Renaissance houses, one of which belonged to the patrician Wierzynek family. In 1364 King Kazimierz invited a number of European monarchs to a royal wedding in Kraków – a case of strategic political union rather than true love – with the wedding feast hosted by the Wierzynek family in one of these houses. One of the restaurant's dining rooms has a copy of a 14th-century painting depicting this wedding feast. Other options include the Clock Room (featuring a wall full of antique clocks) and the Sala Rycerska (Knight's Hall); 14th-century sandstone Gothic arches are also a feature of the restaurant. The cellar is a wine bar specialising in Hungarian Tokay wines, continuing a vogue established by Hungarian-born Queen Jadwiga Jagiełłon.

At the centre of the market square stands the **Sukiennice** (Cloth Hall) 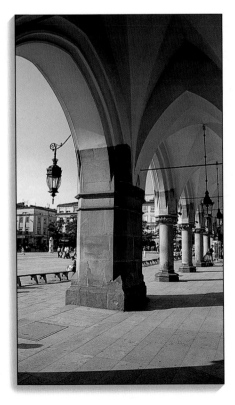 (open Tues–Sun 10am–3.30pm; Thurs 10am–6pm; entrance free on Sunday). Originally a covered market with stalls, shops and warehouses, the current Renaissance façade was designed by Giovannia Maria of Padua (known as Padovano) between 1556–60. The Italian sculptor Santi Gucci of Florence decorated the façade with mascarons, for which (apparently) Kraków's most distinguished burghers posed.

The ground floor of the Sukiennice continues its commercial role, with stalls selling folk arts and crafts, amber jewellery, leather goods and souvenirs, which are definitely a cut above the usual, while the arcades on either side house cafés. On the first floor of the Sukiennice is the **Galeria Sztuki Polskiej XIX**

BELOW: the arches of the Cloth Hall.

LIFE UNDERGROUND

The original medieval buildings of Kraków were not built with cellars because of their shallow foundations. Instead, they had three levels, the top level being used as the attic room. As the city became more wealthy and expanded, new houses were built on top of the old and the street level was raised when new roads were added. The old houses consequently "developed" basements as the original ground floors now existed below street level. Many basements were largely ignored by their owners for hundreds of years and the situation was exacerbated by Communist property laws which controlled the use of all buildings. As a result, until recently, only two buildings around Rynek Główny had cellars that were accessible to the public.

It has only been since the late 1980s and 1990s after a change in the property law that these cellars, so distinctive of the city's architecture, have been put to use and celebrated as a unique feature. Today, many of the cellars have been converted into atmospheric bars and restaurants – even art galleries. The cosy ambience, combined with unique medieval ceiling decoration in many instances, make them an experience not to be missed by any visitor to the city.

Map on page 200

Wieku (Gallery of Polish 19th-century Painting and Sculpture). The name says it all, with this small but concentrated museum enabling you to see a lot in a short time (Rynek Główny 1; tel: 422 11 66; open Tues–Sun 10am–3.30pm; Thurs 10am–6pm; entrance fee except Sun). The collection includes Polish landscapes, portraits and historic scenes by Jan Matejko and Adam Chmiełowski, together with some works by late 18th-century artists such as Marcello Bacciarelli, the court artist of Stanisław August Poniatowski, Poland's last king. The **Wieża Ratuszowa** (Town Hall Tower) **E** (Tues–Fri 10am–4.30pm; weekend 10am–3.30pm; entrance fee) provides fine views of the immediate area. The tower also includes a museum (open Wed–Sun; entrance fee) detailing the city's evolution.

The tiny Romanesque **Kościół Św. Wojciecha** (St Adalbert's Church) **C** (open daily) dates from the 11th and 12th centuries, and features ornate interiors. The vaults include Romanesque and pre-Romanesque architectural fragments.

In front of the Cloth Hall is the **Pomnik Adama Mickiewicza** (Adam Mickiewicz Monument) **D**, commemorating Poland's greatest romantic poet, and meeting "by the monument" is a favourite rendezvous for locals. The Main Market Square also hosts cultural events such as the colourful Lajkonik pageant, which takes place shortly after Corpus Christi. This procession of Tartars marching through the streets, is led by the Lajkonik, a legendary Polish hero disguised as a Tartar, "riding" a hobbyhorse which dances to the sound of drums. Being touched by the Lajkonik's wooden mace is considered to good luck.

The imposing, twin-towered **Kościół Mariacki** (St Mary's Church) **E** (open daily) was built during the 14th–16th centuries. The triple-naved design features ornate interiors including an incredible late-Gothic altar piece entitled "The

TIP

If visiting Kraków in December, head for the Adam Mickiewicz monument to see the spectacular Christ Child Crib (Nativity Manger) competition which is held here.

BELOW: the Adam Mickiewicza Monument.

lives of Our Lady and Her Son Jesus Christ". Completed between 1477–89 by the master carver of Nuremberg, Veit Stoss (known in Poland as Wit Stwosz), it entailed carving around 2,000 realistic figures and decorative elements in linden, which were given the features of contemporary Cracovians. The central panel, 13 metres (43 ft) high and 11 metres (36 ft) wide, depicts the death of the Virgin Mary, while side panels depict scenes from the life of the Virgin Mary and Jesus. Stoss subsequently remained in the city for 20 years fulfilling commissions for the king and other Polish aristocrats. The interiors, including 19th-century murals by Jan Matejko, are so rich and concentrated that it requires a leisurely visit to appreciate the various details. There are two entrances to the church, one for tourists (entrance fee) and another for those who wish to pray or attend a service. Tourists are not admitted during mass.

Every hour on the hour a trumpeter plays the "*hejnał*" from the taller of the two church towers, which originally served as a warning against attack by the Tartars. One watchman who began the *hejnał* during an attack in the 12th century was struck by an arrow after the first few notes and it took a few moments before a replacement continued: now there is always a pause after the first few notes, in the watchman's honour. The *hejnał* now acts as a greeting for visitors.

Around the Old Town

Taking Floriańska street from the market square leads to **Dom Jana Matejki** (Jan Matejko's House) **F** (Floriańska 41; tel: 422 59 26; open Tues–Sun 10am–3pm, Fri 10am–5.30pm; entrance fee except Sun). The grandeur of the neoclassical façade and first floor wrought iron balcony immediately distinguish this house, where Poland's greatest historical painter Jan Matejko (1838–93), was born and subsequently worked. Retaining the sense of a private house, the original interiors include a salon with neo-Renaissance furniture commissioned by Jan Matejko in Venice. The top floor studio, where his linen jacket and walking stick hang on coat hooks, contains easels and various accessories such as palettes and preparatory sketches.

Nearby, at Number 45, is **Jama Michalikowa G**, a famous café which was traditionally the haunt of the city's Bohemian set, including the *fin-de-siècle* "*Młoda Polska*" (Young Poland) group which pioneered Secessionism (Art Nouveau). The café is also the home of the Zielony Balonik (literally "Green Balloon") cabaret troupe, with cabaret still performed here. The interiors are a pot pourri of Secessionist decor, including a stained-glass dome, eccentric chandeliers, elaborate mirrors, drawings, and one of the Christ Child's cribs for which the city is renowned. Inevitably the clientele divides between those who admire the café's style over a drink, and those who turn it into a photographic opportunity.

The street culminates at **Brama Floriańska** (Florian's Gate) **H**. This is the Old Town's only remaining gateway, and features a section of the city wall together with four fortified turrets dating from the 14th century. The city wall is hung with pictures by local artists (spanning the usual range from kitsch to artistic).

Beyond Florian's Gate is the **Barbakan** (Barbican) ❶ (Mon–Fri 9am–5.30pm; weekend 9am–4.30pm; entrance fee), a circular Gothic bastion built in 1499, and the largest example of its kind in Europe. The rest of the city walls were pulled down in the 19th century, and this area was laid out as the **Planty**, a wooded park with fountains and numerous benches that extends for almost 3.5 km (2 miles), encircling the historic centre.

Various monuments erected in the Planty include a statue of astronomer Nicholas Copernicus who studied in the city. **Pomnik Grunwaldzki** ❶ on Plac J. Matejki is the monument to the Battle of Grunwald in 1410, when Poland defeated the Teutonic knights (*see page 263*). The monument was commissioned by the pianist and statesman Ignacy Paderewski in 1910, on the 500th anniversary of the battle.

The walls of the Barbican are three metres (10 feet) thick and it has 130 windows.

Modelled on the Paris Opera House, the flamboyant neo-Renaissance late 19th-century **Teatr im J. Słowackiego** (Juliusz Słowacki Theatre) ❸ (Plac Zwitego Ducha; tel: 423 17 00) is one of the city's leading theatrical venues, while one of the city's most important museums is the **Muzeum Czartoryskich** (Czartoryski Museum) ❶ (Św. Jana 2; tel: 422 55 66; open Tues–Sun; entrance fee except on Sun). This palace, former monastery and armoury provides a suitably historic setting for an art collection which includes German, Italian and Dutch masters, including *Landscape with a Merciful Samaritan* by Rembrandt. The renowned *Lady with an Ermine*, painted by Leonardo da Vinci around 1490, hangs in an individual room with a bench in front of it so that you can savour this enigmatic portrait. The Tent Room houses a collection of Turkish effects taken from the Battle of Vienna in 1686, including a pavilion and suits of armour. The former armoury houses Ancient Roman and Greek artifacts.

BELOW: looking at paintings at Florian's Gate.

The arcaded courtyard of Maius College restored almost to its original form.

A prime example of Gothic architecture, **Kościół Św. Marka** (St Mark's Church) **Ⓜ** (open daily) on Św. Marka has impressive interiors including a Passion scene in the apse. The nearby **Muzeum Szołayskich Ⓝ** (pl Szczepański 9; tel: 422 70 21; open Tues–Sun; entrance fee) has a collection of paintings and sculpture up to 1764, much of it taken from churches around Little Poland. The 14th-century *Madonna of Kruzlowa* is the best known exhibit. The Baroque **Kościół Św. Anny** (St Anna's Church) **Ⓞ** (open daily) on Św. Anny was designed by Tylman van Gameren between 1689–1703 as the university church. The stucco works and polychromy of the magnificent ceiling, let alone the side chapels, make this a worthwhile visit. Opposite the church is **Collegium Maius** (Maius College) **Ⓟ** (Jagiellońska 15; tel: 422 05 49; Mon–Fri 11am–2.30pm, Sat 11am–1.30pm; entrance fee except Sat). This is the oldest college of Kraków University, established by the Jagiellonian dynasty in 1364. It was also Poland's first university college, and the second in Central and Eastern Europe after Prague. The Gothic arcaded courtyard is magnificent, and you can stroll through it whenever the college is open. Admission to the museum is only as part of a guided tour. This takes in the original library with its blue skyscape ceiling, senate room, professors' dining room and chambers, including numerous *objets d'art*, and scientific instruments used by Mikołaj Kopernik (Nicholas Copernicus) who studied here from 1491–95. The Golden Globe of 1510 is one of the first to show the New World (America), with the inscription "*America, terra noviter reperta*" ("America, a newly discovered land").

A detour to the **Muzeum Narodowe** (National Museum) **Ⓠ** (3 Maja 1; tel: 634 30 82; open Tues–Sun; entrance fee) offers one the city's most important and extensive galleries. It covers 20th-century art, from Secessionism to con-

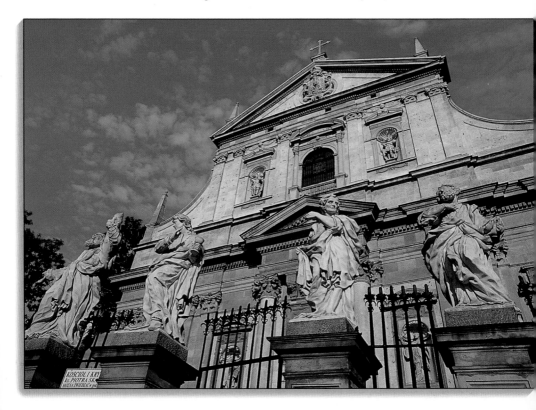

temporary art, and details Kraków's history as Poland's most important centre of fine art. Other galleries in the museum include a collection of military uniforms and weapons, and a collection of decorative arts including furniture. Despite the vast number of exhibits, you can get around the entire building in a morning or afternoon session without experiencing gallery fatigue. Grodzka leads to the Royal Castle and Cathedral, but before this it is worth exploring the numerous galleries and restaurants on this street, such as the traditionally Polish "Pod Aniołami" ("Under the Angels") at Number 35.

Among the historic buildings is the city's earliest Baroque church, **Kościół Św. Piotra i Pawła** (St Peter and St Paul's Church) **R** (open daily). In front of the church is an impressive walled courtyard with 12 late-Baroque sculptures of the apostles. The architect modelled his designs on Il Gesù, Rome's renowned Jesuit church. The austere and strikingly simple Romanesque **Kościół Św. Andrzeja** (St Andrew's Church) **S** (open daily) is one of the city's oldest, with elegant stucco work by Balthasar Fontana and a pulpit in the shape of a horse-drawn carriage. Parallel to Grodzka is one of the city's most beautiful streets, Kanonicza (literally the "street of the canons", as it once housed clergymen) with ornate Renaissance and Gothic houses. Additionally, the life of one of Poland's leading early 20th-century artists is documented in Muzeum Stanisława Wyspiańskiego (Kanonicza 1; tel: 422 83 37; open Tues–Sun; entrance fee).

The Royal Castle and Cathedral

At the end of Grodzka, which is an easy stroll from the main market square, you have an inspiring view of the **Wawel** (Royal Castle) **T** (tel: 422 16 97; open Tues–Sun 10am–4pm; last visitor 3pm; entrance fee except Thursday), built

Map on page 200

The Hen's Foot Watchtower at Wawel Castle, part of the old Gothic castle.

BELOW: Wawel Castle.

Part of King Sigismund's Flanders Tapestries (which number 136 pieces in all) and throne chair.

on a limestone hill rising above the Wisła (Vistula) River. Serving as the royal residence between 1038 and 1596, this complex of buildings includes medieval defensive walls and towers, the royal castle, royal cathedral, treasury and armoury. The earliest surviving architectural fragments date from the 10th century, and each architectural genre, from Romanesque and Gothic to Renaissance and Baroque can be seen here. The immense importance of the Wawel to Poland's heritage is summed up by the eminent artist, Stanisław Wyspiański, who wrote: "Here everything is Poland, every stone and fragment, and the person who enters here becomes a part of Poland."

The castle's perfectly proportioned, three-storey arcaded courtyard, from which the castle extends along four wings, is one of Europe's finest examples of Renaissance architecture. Built from 1502–36, it was designed by the Italian architects Francisco the Florentine and Bartolomeo Berrecci. The royal apartments include a magnificent collection of arrases depicting Biblical scenes, commissioned in the mid-16th century by King Zygmunt August. While many treasures were saved from the Nazis, having been shipped to Canada prior to the outbreak of World War II, only 142 of the original 360 arrases survived the war. The tour passes through Renaissance and Baroque apartments, and there are usually a couple of musicians in period costume performing medieval songs. The **Treasury and Armoury Museum** includes coronation regalia and royal jewels, including the 13th-century *szczerbiec* ("jagged sword") used at Polish coronations from 1320.

At the entrance to the Gothic **cathedral** is a prehistoric tusk, which has hung here for centuries; superstition states that so long as the tusk hangs by the entrance the cathedral will be safe. Built on the site of an earlier Romanesque church, the triple-naved design includes side chapels that were added later. The most spectacular are the Renaissance Kaplica Zygmunta (Sigismund's Chapel) built from 1519–33, crowned with a magnificent gilded dome, and **Kaplica Świetego krzyża** (Holy Cross Chapel) with frescos incorporating Ruthenian and Byzantian elements. From the 14th century the cathedral was used for royal coronations and funerals. Royal tombs vary in design from the highly ornate, such as the marble sarcophagus of the Jagiellonian King Kazimierz IV, completed by Veit Stoss, to the entirely modest, such as the tomb of St Stanisław Szczepanowski in the central nave.

Map on page 200

The labyrinthine **crypt** is usually much quieter than the cathedral which can be full of tour groups, and is the final resting place for members of the royal family and national figures such as Adam Mickiewicz, Tadeusz Kościuszko (who led uprisings during the partition of Poland), and the 20th-century statesman Marshal Józef Piłsudksi.

The crypt of the Royal Cathedral is where the newly ordained Fr Karol Woytyła (subsequently Pope John Paul II) celebrated his first mass.

One of the cathedral's three towers contains the Dzwon Zygmunta (Zygmunt's Bell) which was cast in 1520, and weighs 8 tons. Climbing the steep and cramped staircase is a bit of a struggle, but it's worth it, particularly as a Polish superstition states that anyone touching the bell will enjoy good fortune. Moreover, an observation terrace provides great views of the Old Town.

Opposite the main entrance to the cathedral is a separate building housing the **Cathedral Museum** established on the initiative of Pope John Paul II when he was Cardinal Karol Woytyła, Bishop of Kraków.

Beneath the Wawel is the **Smoczna Jama** (Dragon's Cave), home of the mythical Wawel dragon. The entrance to the cave is marked by an incongruously modern metalwork sculpture of a slimline, 1960s-style dragon periodically breathing gas flames. Apparently the dragon was woken from a deep thousand years' sleep by the constant noise as the castle was constructed, and ventured out in search of something to eat. As the dragon preferred virgins, he soon depleted Kraków of this valuable commodity. King Krak, by then too elderly to take up the challenge of slaying the dragon himself, said that whoever defeated the dragon would receive half the kingdom and his daughter's hand in marriage. An apprentice shoemaker used ingenuity rather than brawn. Filling a sheepskin with sulphur and salt, he sewed it up, equipped it with four wooden legs to make it appear life-like and left it outside the cave. The dragon had it for breakfast. At this point there are two versions of what happened next. Either the contents made the dragon so thirsty that he went to the river and drank so much that he burst, or the sheep blew up inside him, ignited by the fire that the dragon breathed. The shoemaker consequently married the princess and, true to fairy-tale tradition, they lived happily ever after. By the Wawel, on Bulwar Czerwińskiego (tel: 422 08 55) you can join boat trips along the River Vistula.

BELOW: the fire-breathing dragon of sculptor Bronisław Chromy.

Kazimierz, Kraków's Jewish Quarter

Kraków's Jewish quarter, Kazimierz, was originally a separate walled town established in the 14th century by King Kazimierz Wielki (Casimir the Great), with its own gateways, town hall and market place, centred around what is now **Szeroka ⓤ** (literally "Wide Street"). Kazimierz became a part of Kraków in the 18th century. In 1941 the Nazis confined Jews to the Kazimierz ghetto before sending them to the death camps. Of the 68,000 Jews who lived in Kazimierz in 1938, only a few hundred survived the war. Kazimierz itself escaped destruction by the Nazis – but only because they planned to establish a macabre museum here of what they termed "vanished races".

Jewish shop sign in Kazimierz, now a thriving Jewish quarter.

Szeroka has retained its Jewish character, though parts of this and some surrounding streets are still so run-down you would think the war had only just ended. Restoration work is on-going, and in the meantime the area receives plenty of tourists, particularly American Jews tracing their roots, or other visitors taking "Oskar Schindler tours". Making the most of this, wandering musicians play nostalgic tunes in Szeroka's Jewish cafés and restaurants. Szeroka also has two synagogues. The **Jewish Museum** (open Wed, Thurs, weekend 9am–3.30pm; Fri 11am–6pm; closed first weekend of every month) is housed in the **Stara Synagoga** (Old Synagogue). Dating from the 15th and 16th centuries, the façade has Gothic and Renaissance elements, while period interiors house an exhibition of Jewish history and culture. A monument in front of the synagogue marks the site where 30 Jews were shot by the Nazis in 1943.

The **Remu'h Synagogue**, the smallest in the city, is not only a historic monument but still has a small congregation. A courtyard opens onto one of Europe's only Renaissance Jewish cemeteries, laid out in 1533 (the other is in Prague). The renowned writer and philosopher Rabbi Moses Isserle, known as Remu'h, was laid to rest here. While overgrown, this cemetery has a very poignant atmosphere, with some highly ornate tombstones.

BELOW:
remembrance of
the struggle for life.

OSKAR SCHINDLER AND PŁASÓW

Oskar Schindler was a German industrialist living and working in Kraków during World War II, who is credited with saving hundreds of Jews by employing them in his factory. Although his motives remain controversial and were not altogether altruistic – he was a businessman at heart and the Jews were effectively slave labour – the number of lives saved cannot be disputed. Schindler has now reached hero status to many, immortalised first in the award-winning book *Schindler's Ark* by Thomas Keneally and later in the Academy Award-winning film *Schindler's List*, directed by Steven Spielberg, much of which was filmed in and around Kraków. Schindler's Emalia factory is still standing on Lipowa street and features a small Schindler exhibition near the entrance.

Also immortalised in Spielberg's film is the Płaszów concentration camp, just south of Kazimierz, which was overseen by the cold-blooded Nazi commander Amon Goeth. Many of Kraków's Jews were imprisoned and murdered here. Although the Nazis blew up much of the camp as they retreated in 1945, leaving behind little more than a deserted wilderness, parts of the gate remain and on the hill is a 1960s monument to the victims of the camp. Goeth's villa is now a private residence.

Map on page 200

One of the most recently restored buildings is the **Isaac Synagogue** (Kupa 18; open Sun–Fri; entrance fee). Dating from the 17th century, this was the city's largest and originally the most lavishly furnished synagogue. Retaining a Renaissance façade, the Baroque hall has fragments of recently uncovered 17th-century wall murals, while the women's gallery is separated from the main hall by an arcade of Tuscan columns. Having been left unfurnished as a "shell", the slightly austere appearance makes visiting this synagogue all the more moving.

The Jewish Cultural Centre, which includes an art gallery, bookshop and café, is nearby at Meiselsa 17, while the former Ratusz (Town Hall) now houses the **Muzeum Etnograficzne** (Museum of Mankind; pl Wolnica 1; tel: 656 56 01; closed Tues; entrance fee except Sun). An extensive collection of folk art and culture from villages in the Kraków, Podhale and Silesian regions, it includes paintings, sculpture and folk costumes, as well as exhibits relating to traditional folk-rites such as Christ Child's cribs and Easter eggs. Recreated rooms comprising authentic furniture and decor mean you can walk around in what still manages to feel like someone's home.

The International Biennial of Regional Dolls and the Annual Folk Art Fair in September are also held in Kraków, as part of the Museum of Mankind.

Modern Kraków

The most recent part of the city is **Nowa Huta**, a large post-war housing and industrial area featuring the uncompromising style of "concrete blocks" typical of the Communist era. This area is hardly on the tourist trail – but that only makes it more interesting.

A statue of Lenin stood in the central square until the beginning of 1990, when it was pulled down. At the heart of Nowa Huta is a vast steelworks which accounts for around 50 percent of Poland's total steel production and was a

BELOW: Jewish café-bar on Szeroka Street.

centre of the Solidarity movement in the 1980s (*see page 63*). But it is not all gloomy industrialisation: Nowa Huta also has some historic buildings, including the 11th-century Cistercian Abbey in Mogiła, which is opposite the wooden elaborate 15th-century Church of St Bartholomew. The neighbourhood of Bieńczyce features the vast Church of the Holy Mother Queen of Poland, built in the shape of a ship, which was used as a rendezvous and shelter for opposition groups during the period of martial law declared by President Jaruzelski in December 1981. Its congregation is still made up of local steelworkers and their families every Sunday.

Greater Kraków

Various national parks, historic towns, palaces and attractions are within easy reach of Kraków. The region has also preserved its *Folklor Krakówski*, the traditional folklore, which includes a dance known as the Krakówiak (similar to the polka). Many surrounding villages have also retained the architectural style typical of this region. A visit to the Benedictine Abbey in **Tyniec**, 10 km (6 miles) from Kraków, is highly recommended. Formerly a Romanesque abbey fortress, it is romantically situated on the summit of a limestone cliff overlooking the River Vistula. While the church and cloisters are a prime example of Baroque, much of the abbey is in ruins. However, during the summer the abbey hosts a series of organ recitals as part of two festivals, "Days of Organ Music" and "Tyniec Organ Recitals". A stroll along the banks of the River Vistula beneath the abbey is also very picturesque.

BELOW:
the Benedictine
Abbey in Tyniec.

Around 13 km (8 miles) outside Kraków is the **Kopalnia Soli Wieliczka** (Wieliczka Salt Mines). Listed by UNESCO on the World Cultural Heritage List,

Map on page 200

this is Poland's (and possibly the world's) oldest working salt mine, dating from the 12th or even the 10th century (Daniłowicza; tel: 78 73 02; open daily, guided tour only; entrance fee). Currently the deposits are mined at eight levels, down to a depth of 315 metres (1,030 ft), with the total length of the galleries, chambers and tunnels over 150 km (93 miles). Almost one million visitors a year now come to see the amazing features of this salt mine, including a vast underground cathedral carved from salt, including an altar, gallery and chandeliers, three further chapels also carved from salt, a gallery of salt gnomes carved by miners in the 1960s, and caverns with lakes, while the extraordinary effect of refracted light creates an magical "underworld". The mining museum exhibits local geology, tools, clothing and documents dating back 600 years. There is also a subterranean sanatorium treating patients suffering from asthma and various allergies.

The superb acoustics in the underground cathedral in the salt mines have turned it into a spectacular concert venue and state banqueting hall.

To the east of Kraków, at the confluence of the Wisła and Raba rivers, lies **Puszcza Niepołomicka**, a primeval forest which was formerly hunting grounds for the royal court, and which now includes a reserve for aurochs. At the edge of the forest in the town of Niepołomice is a castle with a delightful arcaded courtyard, modelled on the Wawel Royal Castle (*see page 209*) and now serving as a regional museum (open Tues–Sun; entrance fee). Trails from the town lead into the forest. On the other side of the Wisła, located about an hour's drive from Kraków, is the village of **Wiślica**. This was the main fortress for the Wiślanie tribe between the 9th and 10th centuries. The crypt of the town's Gothic church has Romanesque foundations and a handsome floor relief, as well as fragments of an earlier church, complete with a font – evidence that Christianity was already established in this region long before Poland's official conversion to

BELOW: the Salt Mines in Wieliczka.

Map on page 200

Christianity in AD 966. The village of **Igołomia** is the home town of Brother Albert (Adam Chmielowski). This painter and monk founded the order of St Adalbertus, which devoted itself to caring for the poor. Numerous archaeological digs have also taken place in the Igołomia region.

The beauty of the surrounding countryside is spectacularly displayed throughout the **Krakówsko-Częstochowska Jura**. This mountain range to the northwest of Kraków includes limestone hills and cliff-faces, caves, deep valleys and extraordinary rocks in the shape of clubs and needles. The region is also home to wild boar and roe deer, not to mention 12 different species of bat. Part of the Jura now comes under the auspices of the Ojcówski Park Narodowy (Ojców National Park) which covers an area of 1,890 hectares (4,650 acres). The most interesting part of this park is the 14-km (9-mile) long valley that follows the River Prądnik near Ojców, surrounded by thick forests which provide a dramatic backdrop to limestone cliff-faces. The valley's unique flora includes the so-called *ojcowska* (shrubby birch). Two caves, Ciemna (literally "dark") and the larger Łokiełek, are open to the public (daily, Mar–Oct). It is said that King Władysław Łokiełek hid here after an attack by King Wenceslas of Bohemia. Some traces of human settlement, found in the Ciemna Caves are thought to be about 120,000 years old, and are on display in the Władysław Szefer Museum in Ojców (open Tues–Sun, Apr–Nov; Tues–Fri, Dec–Mar; entrance fee). The town also has ruins of a 14th-century castle.

A few kilometres from Ojców on a dramatic elevation overlooking the Prądnik Valley is the Renaissance castle of **Pieskowa Skała** ("Dog's Rock"). Once the residence of aristocratic families, it is now a branch of the Wawel's National Art Collection (open Tues–Sun; entrance fee), with an exhibition of household and castle furnishings dating from the Middle Ages to the 19th century. On the ground floor of the palace is the historic Zamkowa restaurant, while a short walk from the castle leads to an unusual 25-metre (82-ft) rock called the Club of Hercules.

Pieskowa Skała was one of several hilltop castles built on the so-called "Trail of the Eagle's Lair", in order to secure the route from Kraków to Silesia during the Middle Ages. Most of those castles are now in ruins, with one of the most impressive being Ogrodzieniec, which lies further west.

At the plateau's western edge is **Olkusz**, once known as "silver city". This is Poland's oldest mining region. Lead and zinc ore, both with a high silver content, were found in this area. The Pustynia Błędowska (Błędow Desert) covers 30 sq km (11 sq miles) and is the only large expanse of sand in Poland. It was once much larger, but it is progressively giving way to vegetation: now only parts of it truly resemble desert.

En route to Bielsko-Biała (*see page 260*) is **Wadowice**, 50 km (35 miles) from Kraków. Set in the valley of the River Skawa at the foot of the Little Beskid Mountains, this is the town where Pope John Paul II was born and spent his youth. His childhood home is now a museum (Koscielna 7; open Tues–Sun; entrance fee) documenting his life and work, while the Market Place features a 15th-century church where the Pope was baptised. ❏

BELOW: statue at Wieliczka of miner with winding gear. **RIGHT:** festival costume with ceremonial eagle.

THROUGH LITTLE POLAND

On this route through Małopolska, places of outstanding natural beauty alternate with the Renaissance and Gothic architecture of cities such as Zamość and Łańcut

Map on page 220

I n the south and east of Małopolska (Little Poland) large tracts of land have retained the character of primeval forest – the Puszcza Niepołomicka, Puszcza Sandomierska, Puszcza Solska. Amid broadleaf and coniferous woodland live indigenous wolves, lynx, bison and brown bears. Seven national parks in total, about a dozen protected areas and several hundred nature reserves have been established in the area.

East of Kraków

If you travel from **Kraków ❶** (*see page 201*) eastwards along the E40, which leads through Tarnów, Rzeszów and Przemyśl all the way to Medyka on the Ukraine border, you will come to yet another region of Małopolska. In Bochnia, not far from Wieliczka, is a second salt mine, almost as old as that in Wieliczka (*see page 214*). It is also open to visitors.

To the south of Bochnia, in the neglected village of **Nowy Wiśnicz ❷**, stands a palace owned by the Lubomirski family. After the war, the property was confiscated by the state as part of the land reform policy, but the land registry documents were never altered, so when democracy was restored to Poland and changes were made to the constitution, the property was legally returned to its former owners. It is an impressive structure with five towers, massive walls and a pentagonal courtyard. Formerly a Gothic fortification, the castle was renovated in the 17th century by Mattia Trapole. The walls and inside of the palace are decorated with wall paintings and stucco work.

The next town along the route is **Brzesko**, justly famous for its excellent beer, known as Okocim. The brewery was founded in 1845 by the Bohemian industrialist Baron Goetz. Not far from Brzesko, in the town of **Dębno** is a small but interesting Gothic castle where a museum keeps an interesting collection of weapons, paintings and furniture.

The next important settlement along the route through Małopolska is **Tarnów ❸**, the administrative centre for the *wojewódzki* (county) with a charter dating back to 1330, was once the seat of the powerful noble Tarnówski family, ancestors of the Polish general Hetman Jan Tarnówski. Some 350 buildings in Tarnów are listed under the Polish national monument protection scheme. Tarnów is now an important industrial centre surrounded by large chemical plants, initiated by Ignacy Moscicki, president of Poland before World War II.

Medieval Tarnów is built on two levels with the upper and lower towns connected by steps. The former defensive walls were removed and replaced in the late-19th century by a road around the old town

LEFT: statue of Cupid in Łańcut Palace.
BELOW: a typical roadside shrine.

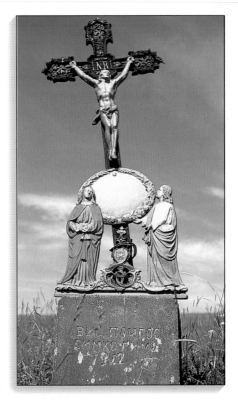

centre, thereby preserving the character of what was formerly a provincial capital during the era of the Austro-Hungarian empire. Sights of particular interest in the Old Town are the Town Hall with Renaissance attics topping the roof, its arcades, patrician houses and a vast 15th-century cathedral containing the tombs of the Tarnówski and Ostrogski families.

Not far from the Old Town is the **Plac Bohaterów Getta** (Square of the Ghetto Heroes) and, beside the square, the baths where the Jewish community performed their ritual washing ceremonies. It was from here on 14 June 1940 that the first transport left for the concentration camp at Auschwitz with 738 people on board (*see page 54*). In the **Church of St Joseph and the Holy Virgin of Fatima**, which dates from the 1950s, a chapel is dedicated to the suffering of the Polish people during the war. Equally impressive is the sculpture of St Maximilian Kolbe who sacrificed his life in Auschwitz to save a fellow prisoner. In 1997 Kolbe was canonised by the Pope.

The nearby village of **Wierzchosławice** is the birthplace of Wincenty Witos (1874–1939), leader of the radical peasant movement which gained momentum between the two world wars.

Lovers of folk art should take a detour to the village of **Zalipie** ❹, about 32 kilometres (20 miles) to the northwest of Tarnów. In this unusual village, situated in a low-lying region beside the Vistula, folk artists have covered the the interiors and exteriors of their houses, their tables, barns, fences, furniture and even their dog kennels with colourful and original paintings of plant motifs. The town is also renowned for its embroidery, hand-cut silhouettes and straw dolls. In the house where the painter Felicja Curyłowa (1904–74) lived, a museum keeps alive these unusual rural crafts. The village of **Ciężkowice**, with

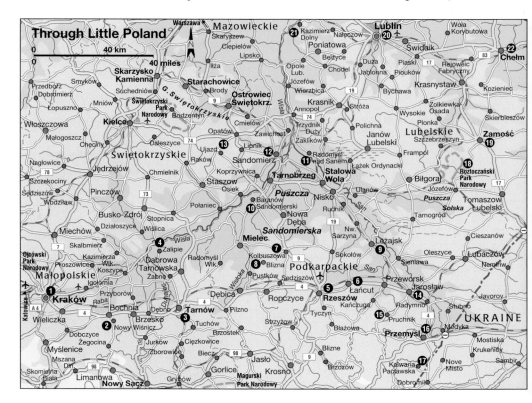

a history dating back to the 10th century, lies in the Biała valley. Wooden houses with open galleries looking out on to the town make a picturesque sight. The **Skamieniałe Miasto** (Petrified City) nature reserve is situated near Cięzkowice. An amazing rock formation here has given rise to numerous myths and legends.

The Sandomierz Basin

The central region of Małopolska is dominated by a wide depression known as the Kotlina Sandomierska (Sandomierz Basin). Fields interspersed with large wooded areas are typical of this flat, rural landscape. Most of the farms are small, about 2 hectares (5 acres) in area, and the narrow strips of cultivated land form a regular pattern. The population here has a reputation for militancy, a tradition which last manifested itself in the winter of 1981 when an uprising and strike led to the foundation of the Solidarity movement (*see page 63*).

The most important town in this region is **Rzeszów** ❺. Founded in the 14th century, Rzeszów has always been provincial in character. Up until 1939, half of its population were Jews, but during World War II almost all of them were murdered. Two synagogues, rebuilt from the rubble of the war, and a Jewish cemetery serve as memorials to the town's former Jewish community.

The townscape today is dominated by the magnificent 18th-century Lubomirski Palace, which is surrounded by bastions and moats; it is now used as a prison. The Baroque church and the Bernardine Monastery have also been preserved. A regional museum is housed in the former Piarist Monastery. As well as a collection of Polish paintings, the museum documents the history of the region and its people (3 Maja; open Tues–Sun; entrance fee).

Map
on page
220

 TIP

Every other July since 1969, Rzeszów has been the venue for the World Festival of Polish Folklore Groups Living Abroad.

BELOW:
folk art in the village of Zalipie.

Twice weekly, on Tuesdays and Fridays, a bustling market takes place in Rzeszów, but sadly this event has lost some of its traditional character and today, with many cheap products on sale, it is reminiscent of a car-boot sale.

Situated on the international E40 motorway, 17 kilometres (10 miles) east of Rzeszów, is the medieval town of **Łańcut** ❻ with its magnificent palace. This former residence of the aristocratic Lubomirski and Potocki families was built on old foundations between 1629–41 by Stanisław Lubomirski. At the beginning of the 19th century the structure was expanded into a modern residential palace with the encouragement of Princess Elzbieta Lubomirska (1736–1826). This renovation was carried out according to plans drawn up by the famous architect Piotr Aigner. Later, at the turn of the 20th century, a façade in the French neo-Baroque style was added.

Today the palace is a museum (tel: 17 225 23 38; open Feb–Nov 10am–2.30pm Tues–Sun; entrance fee, guided tours only). The centrepiece of the palace is an almost square structure with corner towers and a central inner courtyard. A bulwark in the form of a five-pointed star surrounds the complex. The main building houses a Museum of Interior Design where some well-preserved furnishings from the 18th and 19th centuries are kept. The unusual library contains over 20,000 precious tomes. The upstairs living quarters, the ballroom, large dining hall and theatre, as well as the Turkish room on the ground floor, are all remarkable. Visitors to the former stables will find a collection of old Russian icons. An international music festival has been held in the palace every May since 1961. Several outbuildings were added at a later date: the library, a greenhouse and a court building which is now a restaurant and hotel. The palace is encompassed by a park laid out on a grand scale. A smaller palace and a riding school are located within the grounds. To the south of the castle, the old coach house is now used as a museum of about 50 horse-drawn carriages.

BELOW:
Łańcut Palace.

Traditional country fairs are still held in the small towns around Rzeszów, such as Sokołów, Kolbuszowa and Strzyżów. Visitors to these fairs will find authentic arts and crafts on sale made by local craftspeople. A few of the villages in this region, in particular Medynia Głogowska, Pogwizdów, Medynia Łańcucka and Zalesie, are also centres for the traditional craft of pottery. Here almost 120 potters produce decorative ceramic dishes and sculptures, as well as traditional crockery for everyday use.

A range of hills known as the **Pogórze** lie to the south of Rzeszów. The River Wisłoka meanders peacefully through this picturesque landscape. In the many little towns and hamlets, wind-battered farmhouses recall a bygone age, but following the expulsion of the native, mainly Jewish, population, these primitive settlements have lost much of their charm.

The village buildings of Małopolska were originally built almost entirely out of wood. Although many examples of this type of construction still exist, an exceptionally good one is the small church in **Blizne**, which is situated between Rzeszów and Sanok. Built in Gothic style at the end of the 15th century from thick larchwood beams, it has remained, remarkably, unchanged to this day.

North of Rzeszów

Map
on page
220

The section of the Kotlina Sandomierska to the north of Rzeszów is covered with the rich forests of the vast **Puszcza Sandomierska**. Mushrooms, berries and wild game all flourish in this environment. The region is inhabited by the Lesowiaki, a people who pride themselves on their self-sufficiency. Old farmhouses remain unspoilt, quaint traditions and intriguing rituals survive. Some aspects of the local folk customs have been preserved in the open-air museum at **Kolbuszowa** ❼. This museum also serves as a venue for cultural events.

During World War II, the German army established two large military training grounds in Puszcza Sandomierska. Several prison and work camps also formed part of this complex. The most notorious work camp was in **Pustków**. Some 15,000 people, mainly Poles, Jews and Russians, lost their lives here.

Experiments with V-1 and V-2 rockets were carried out on a strictly guarded site close to the village of **Blizna** ❽. The underground intelligence wing of the Polish home guard (*Armia Krajowa*) recorded a major success in its struggle against the occupying forces when locals managed to retrieve a rocket which had been fired by the Germans and, after dismantling it, smuggled it to London.

The ancient town of **Leżajsk** ❾ lies about 50 kilometres (31 miles) to the northeast of Rzeszów, not far from the River San. Numerous historic buildings and other reminders of a distant past can be found here. Produce markets take place weekly. In the northern part of the town is a 17th-century Bernardine monastery, which was later converted into a fortress. The beautiful and richly decorated interior of the monastery is dominated by the organ, one of the largest in Poland. Built at the end of the 17th century, this instrument, with its 74 organ stops and 5,894 pipes, spans all three naves of the church. In recent years, organ

BELOW: the Coach Museum, Łańcut Palace.

concerts have been held here every May and their reputation has been spreading. In other months the in-house organist will perform on special request. *The Miraculous Image of the Virgin Mary with Child* has been famous since 1634 as a painting that performs miracles. On Assumption Day in August, both believers and unbelievers alike are drawn here by the festivities.

Economically, the northern portion of this region, at the confluence of the Vistula and San rivers, is the most interesting. The centre of this area is the village of **Tarnobrzeg**. Once poverty-stricken and neglected, its sulphur deposits have recently brought employment and prosperity. The seams of sulphur are exploited in open-cast mines at Machów, and the foul-smelling mineral is then exported in granular form via the harbour in Gdańsk.

Baranów Sandomierski ⑩ is located at the eastern edge of this sulphur basin, on the right-hand bank of the Vistula. The town is especially renowned for its palace, a building regarded by many as one of the brightest jewels of Polish Renaissance architecture. All that remains from the original 16th-century fortress, however, is a rectangular structure with corner towers and a gate. The courtyard with arcaded passageways, an unusual stairway and rooftop attics, which are certainly the most distinctive features of the palace, were added between 1591 and 1606. Inside, the palace is richly decorated with murals and stucco works and is today the site of a museum as well as a luxury hotel. The museum, housed in the cellar, has exhibits relating to the sulphur industry (open Tues–Sun; entrance fee). Happily, the excellent wines and food of the adjoining hotel restaurant are not affected by the proximity of this unsavoury chemical.

A short distance to the east of Tarnobrzeg is **Stalowa Wola**, one of Poland's newer towns and an important centre for the metal industry. Stalowa Wola was

BELOW: driving through typical Małopolskan landscape.

built in 1937, in conjunction with a weapons manufacturing plant. Today, the works manufacture steel and construction machinery. Nearby, on the opposite side of the San, lies the old village of **Radomyśl nad Sanem ⓫**. This is the venue for an unusual patriotic and religious play which is performed every year at Easter. A group of residents, dressed in the colourful robes of Turkish soldiers, head a military parade through the village. Afterwards they go from house to house wishing the inhabitants luck and asking for a donation to pay for their costumes. They are accompanied by a marching band and countless spectators, many of whom travel great distances to watch the spectacle.

This area is also very well known for its crafts. A little further to the east of Stalowa Wola, along the road leading from Nisko to Janów Lubelski, lie the villages of Łążek Ordynacki and Łążek Garncarski. These two woodland settlements, with craftsmen working in traditional family potteries, are renowned for the production of imaginative and beautiful ceramic designs. The small town of **Rudnik** lies half-an-hour's drive away from Stalowa Wola in the direction of Jarosław. Rudnik is famous for its basket-making. Two manufacturing workshops and several thousand helpers working in their homes produce baskets which are then exported to many different countries all over the world.

Sandomierz ⓬, one of Poland's finest towns, is situated to the north of the basin on a terrace above the banks of the Vistula. Once the capital of an independent duchy, the town was an important trading port. Founded on the site of an ancient settlement, it is one of the oldest and most picturesque towns in Poland. Thanks to its strategically important fortress, as early as the 12th century it was one of Poland's three largest commercial centres and enjoyed great prosperity during the Renaissance. The Old Town is perched on an oval-shaped hill

Map on page 220

Sandomierz town square and town hall.

LEFT: the cathedral clock tower, Sandomierz. **BELOW:** civic pride flourishes in Sandomierz.

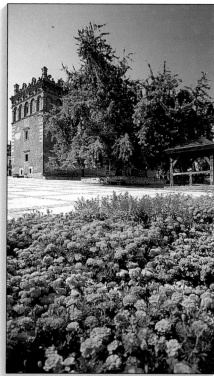

30 metres (100 ft) above the river valley and has managed to preserve much of its medieval character, including several narrow streets with nooks and crannies, although the perfect restoration still cannot conceal a certain urban shabbiness. Like so many Polish towns, these old quarters successfully convey the impression of working communities where ordinary people still lead normal lives.

The remains of a royal palace can be seen at the southern edge of the town. Adjacent to these is a triple-naved Gothic cathedral dating from the 14th century. The Russo-Byzantine frescos in the chancel merit special attention. Adjacent to the cathedral is the Gothic house of **Długosz**, a medieval historian and chronicler of Poland (1415–80). Today, the Diocesan Museum, with its collection of art and *objets d'art*, is housed here (open Tues–Sun; entrance fee).

Nearby is the **Church of St James**, which formerly belonged to the Dominicans. This is Poland's best remaining example of a Romanesque brick church and serves as a memorial to the bloody Tartar invasion of 1259. The plain Romanesque north portal is particularly impressive, while the interior is tastefully finished with glazed bricks. Glass cases contain the bones of the monks who were murdered during the 13th-century Tartar attack.

The marketplace in the centre of the town is surrounded by a number of stylish houses. One, belonging to the Olesnicki family stands out, mainly because of its ornate gallery. The Town Hall dominates the middle of the marketplace and the remains of the old fortifications, with the tall Brama Opatowska (Abbot Gate), mark the northern boundary of the Old Town.

Visitors to Sandomierz should spend some time exploring the surrounding area as there are a number of places of interest. The arable land here is well suited to the production of fruits and vegetables. An old Cistercian abbey and

BELOW: Church of St James, Sandomiez.

Map
on page
220

a late-Romanesque church dating from the early 13th century are found in **Koprzywnica** 17 kilometres (10 miles) to the southwest of Sandomierz. In the small village of **Ujazd** ⓭, the impressive ruins of the Krzyżtopór palace can still be seen. This enormous edifice was built in the 17th century by the Ossolinski family, but was partially destroyed soon afterwards by the Swedes. Before the construction of the Palais de Versailles near Paris, this was the largest official residence in Europe. It has some very unusual design features: four towers for the four seasons, 12 large halls for each of the months, 52 rooms for each week and 365 windows. There was even an additional window for leap years which was covered up for the rest of the time.

Some 16 km (10 miles) to the northeast of Ujazd lies **Opatów** with its Romanesque theological college. A far-reaching system of passageways, cellars and vaulted chambers winds its way under the streets and houses. Five centuries ago, this served as a refuge from the marauding Tartars; today part of it is open to the public.

Eastern Małopolska

The economy of the eastern section of Małopolska, which nestles in the valley of the River San, is dominated by agriculture. Those journeying eastwards from Rzeszów should make plans to stop off in **Jarosław** ⓮ close to the Ukrainian border. Sited on the banks of the river, Jarosław is one of the oldest towns in this area. During the Middle Ages its markets and fairs attracted merchants from all over Europe. The Old Town, with its abundance of interesting architecture, is still a veritable paradise for photographers.

The old houses around the marketplace, with their distinctive passageways, covered courtyards, decorated stairways and galleries, are particularly picturesque. The house that formerly belonged to the patrician Italian Orsetti family, built in Renaissance style with an open gallery and attic, is definitely worth seeking out. It now houses the Regional Museum (open Tues–Sat, morning only; entrance fee). Other interesting sights in Jarosław are the attractive Town Hall, a number of older churches, one of which is Russian-Orthodox, and several synagogues. Entering the town from Rzeszów, you will be able to see the late-Baroque **Dominican Monastery** hidden behind its surrounding walls. Outside these walls is a small well. The water in the well not only tastes good, but is also reputed to work magical powers on those who drink it. According to legend, a sculpture of the Madonna was found here in ancient times. Soon afterwards, the sculpture was found to have miracle-working powers. An exceptionally valuable work of art is the Gothic wooden sculpture of Mater Dolorosa from Zbawiec which is now located on the main altar.

Near Jarosław is **Sieniawa**, further downstream, where the recently restored palace of the Czartoryski family is well worth a visit. Equally interesting are Zarzecze with the Dzieduszycki Castle and **Węgierka** with its ruins of a medieval manor house. In the small town of **Pruchnik** ⓯, a few miles to the south of Jarosław, time seems to have stood still for several

BELOW: cathedral spire Sandomiez.

centuries. The wooden houses by the marketplace and nearby streets have open galleries and precise, extremely complex decorative woodwork. Many are very old and, as they represent rare examples of Polish architecture, are now officially listed as ancient national monuments. Long-standing traditions have also been preserved: for many years now it has been the custom to hang an effigy of Judas publicly on the Saturday before Easter.

The eastern area abounds with sacred myths. Near Jarosław is the Sanctuary of the Holy Virgin in Jodłówka, with a chapel and well. Legend has it that here, too, the Virgin Mary appeared and performed miracles.

East meets west

The border between the Catholic world and the Russian Orthodox, effectively the border between the two main elements of European culture, runs to the east of the River San. For centuries this stretch of land has been the scene of confrontations between the east and west, and the various nationalities in the regions have lived and fought both together and against each other. At the end of World War II, for example, the Ukrainian partisans fought a bitter two-year battle for their right to autonomy and to establish settlements. In the end, having suffered enormous destruction and the loss of many lives, they gave up their fight. In April 1947, regardless of whether they had supported the resistance movement, the Ukrainians were forcibly resettled, either in what was then the USSR or in the former German regions. Only evacuated and burnt-out villages remained. Even today many regions are only thinly populated and settlements can be found that are almost totally overgrown by woodland and shrubs.

Characteristic of this part of Poland is the wooden architecture of the Russian-Orthodox and Ukrainian churches, which frequently occurs in the old villages. These are real gems of folk architecture. Some of the more beautiful Orthodox churches are found in Rudka near Sieniawa and in Chołyniec (both 17th-

BELOW: a pilgrim in penitential robe.
RIGHT: celebrating first communion.

century), in Pożdziacz and Piątkowa near Przemyśl (18th-century) and in Radrużnear Lubaczów (16th-century). Some of the old churches in the Ukrainian villages, also excellent examples of folk art, are now used by the Roman Catholic church. The iconostases have been preserved in many of the churches. These traditional altar screens often show icons dating from the 17th–19th centuries and many are of great artistic value.

The National and Diocesan Museum in the town of **Przemyśl** ⓰ houses an interesting collection of painted icons (open Tues–Sun; entrance fee). The countryside surrounding the border town of Przemyśl, a melting pot of various cultures and traditions since the 7th century, is enchanting. The densely wooded and hilly Pogórze Przemyskie (Przemyśl foothills) stretches out to the south of a town that receives few tourists. In recent years, the Ukrainian minority here has started celebrating its national holiday, the **Feast of St Jordan** again. On a winter morning, the faithful, bearing flags and crosses, congregate on the banks of the San and the deeply religious, almost mystical festival then begins. After the ceremony, the people wash their faces and eyes with river water. Freshly cleansed, they then consider themselves able to face up to their daily lives with renewed vigour.

A charming Renaissance palace belonging to the Krasicki family is located in **Krasiczyn**, 10 kilometres (6 miles) west of Przemyśl. Once the seat of one of Poland's most powerful families, it is a large building with fortifications comprising four bastions and a tower over the entrance. Stylish stucco work and paintings decorate the meticulously restored palace. Not far from Krasiczyn, 16 kilometres (10 miles) south of Przemyśl is **Kalwaria Pacławska** ⓱, where a Franciscan monastery with a painting of the Virgin Mary has been revered for

Map on page 220

LEFT: the round tower of the Renaissance palace in Krasiczyn.
BELOW: old wooden church Nałęczów.

centuries because of its miracle-working powers. In the area around the monastery, the Stations of the Cross are illustrated in 42 picturesquely situated chapels. The wooden houses in the village which grew up around the monastery are also worth taking the time to see. This is an extremely quiet and almost deserted area. Only in August, when the annual fair takes place, does it show any real signs of life.

A little further to the south, in the woods around the former village of **Arłamów**, is a holiday hostel that used to belong to the Communist Party and where Lech Wałęsa was kept prisoner for a time (*see page 64*). Today it is open to the public and, among other activities, hunts are organised in which visiting foreigners can participate. Anyone who enjoys horses and riding will want to visit **Stubno** to the northeast of Przemyśl where the Polish state maintains a stud farm with English thoroughbreds and a riding club.

The Roztocze, which begins a bit further to the north, is also an extremely picturesque region. A unique mixture of flora and fauna can be found in the rolling forest-covered hills. In the most beautiful part of the Roztocze around the towns of Zwierzyniec and Krasnobrod, the **Roztoczański Park Narodowy** (Roztocze National Park) ⑱ has been established. About 10 percent of this 7,900-hectare (19,500-acre) park is under very strict protection. Geologically, the landscape is mixed and the climate changes dramatically with altitude. Consequently the vegetation is very varied: tough steppe plants, an abundance of mountain flora and other flora which require warmth. The wooded regions are also very varied: pine, oak and beech forests proliferate. Running through the centre of the park is the spectacular River Wieprz. Varieties of game, wolf, tarpan, beaver, eagle, osprey and capercaillie are all native species to this park

BELOW: town houses on Market Square, Zamość.

and thrive in great numbers. On the southern faces of the Roztocze hills the remains of the Molotov Line fortifications from World War II can still be identified. Maps of hiking routes are available but small areas of the park are restricted and require the accompaniment of a guide.

Map on page 220

Zamość

At the northeastern end of the national park in the Kotlina Zamojska (Zamość Basin) lies the attractive settlement of **Zamość** ⑲. This fascinating town, founded in the heart of the wilderness during the Renaissance (1579–1616) by the chancellor and Grand Hetman of the Crown, Jan Zamoyski, was designed by the Venetian Bernardo Morando.

Playing with the water pump. Zamość.

The Old Town of Zamość consists of a palace and residential area surrounded by fortified walls with bastions and gates. This mighty fortress was built so solidly that it was able to resist the attacks of both the Cossacks and the Swedes. The palace, renovated between 1821–31, gives a gloomy barrack-like atmosphere to the town, despite the fact that a large portion of the complex was turned into a pleasant park after a part of the fortifications were destroyed in 1866. Zamość Old Town is so greatly prized as an example of Renaissance architecture that it has been awarded UNESCO World Cultural Heritage status.

The **Rynek Główny** (Market Square) lies at the heart of the Old Town. Its famous Town Hall (designed by Morando between 1591–1600) includes later additions of a grand double staircase (1768) and the octagonal 50-metre (165-ft) high tower (1770) with a Baroque roof. Today it houses local government offices. The square is surrounded by town houses in Renaissance style, linked together with arcades. The German revolutionary and socialist-feminist theorist Rosa Luxembourg was born at Number 37.

BELOW: Town Hall on Market Square, Zamość.

The Collegiate Church (1587–98), another of Morando's works, is located to the southwest of the market square. The high altar paintings here are usually ascribed to Domenico Tintoretto. Adjoining this central marketplace are two other squares: the Rynek Solny (Salt Marketplace) and the Rynek Wodny (Water Marketplace). The western part of the Old Town is dominated by the palace formerly owned by the Zamoyski family (1585). It was converted into a military hospital in 1831.

Zamość was once a town with a multicultural population, including Poles, Russians, Jews and Armenians. During the Nazi occupation, it was renamed Himmlerstadt. The Polish population was expelled and Germans were brought in to create what Hitler hoped would become the eastern bulwark of the Third Reich. Consequently, the historic buildings, including the old Orthodox church, the synagogue and an Armenian meeting house survived the war. The Germans were unable to complete their inhumane resettlement plan, but thousands of Poles still lost their lives in the prisoner-of-war camps and mass shootings in the Rotunda, a ring-shaped fort 10 minutes from the Old Town. Many of the town's inhabitants were transported to the extermination camp at Bełżec 42 kilometres (26 miles) away and the Jewish population was completely wiped out.

Lublin's Old Town survived World War II relatively intact and many of the old buildings have been restored.

BELOW:
Lublin Castle.

Lublin

The region of Lublin in the northeastern part of Małopolska is an agricultural area, but with industry concentrated in the larger towns. The largest town in eastern Poland, **Lublin ⓴**, is an important centre for industry, culture and science. It has been a busy trading centre since medieval times and during several periods in its history has been a target for invaders. Its finest moment occurred in 1569 when the Polish and Lithuanian rulers met here to agree the Lublin Union. A period of prosperity followed, but this ended with the First Partition (*see page 30*). When Poland regained its full independence in 1918, the **Katolicki Uniwersytet Ludowy** (Catholic People's University), known as the KUL and the only Catholic university in the whole of eastern Europe, became the centre for Poland's Catholic intelligentsia. In July 1944, after liberation, Lublin was also the provisional capital of Poland and the seat of the transitional government that Stalin installed.

The small **Stare Miasto** (Old Town) is full of interesting sights: the market-place with its old town houses (16th–8th century); the cathedral (16th–17th-century) and the Dominican monastery (14th–17th century) are noteworthy. The Gothic church has 11 chapels and two are worth seeking out: the Firlej family chapel has a two-tier grave and the dome above the Tyszkiewicz family chapel has a large fresco depicting *The Last Judgement*. The first building on the hill to the east of the town was erected during the 9th century, but the tower that stands there now is 13th century. The Holy Trinity Chapel with its Russo-Byzantine paintings has survived the ravages of time. Recently restored, this 15th-century art treasure can now be admired in all its splendour. Western European Gothic architecture and Russian Orthodox frescos make strange bedfellows.

During the years of the German occupation, thousands of Poles were tortured and killed in the neo-Gothic prison (1823) and, following the war, Polish freedom fighters and anti-Communists were imprisoned here. Lublin used to have a large Jewish population and they mainly occupied the part of the Old Town around Grodzka street, where a few memorial plaques can be seen. During the 19th century, Lublin was also one of the centres of Hassidic Jewry and its Talmud school, the Jeschiwa, was among the most distinguished of its kind anywhere in the world. The school was closed by the Germans and its fine library plundered, but the building remains, now housing Lublin's medical faculty. All the synagogues and Jewish quarters were destroyed by the Nazis in 1943, but some graves from both the old and new Jewish cemeteries escaped destruction. In 1941 German forces established a ghetto in the north of the Old Town by the Lubartowska. In the same year they built one of their most terrible extermination camps in **Majdanek**, a suburb of Lublin. During the following year most of the 40,000 inhabitants of the ghetto were systematically murdered, if not in Majdanek, then in Treblinka or Bełżec. A monument on Plac Bohaterów recalls the victims of this atrocity. Lublin now has only a small Jewish community.

Between Lublin and the Vistula lies the region known as Plaskowyz Nałęczowski. The town of **Nałęczow** which gives this high plateau its name owes its existence to the mineral springs discovered here in the 18th century. It is still a popular health resort for patients suffering from circulatory disorders and heart disease. Many famous Polish writers and artists, including Bolesław Prus and Stefan Żeromski, often came to this spa during its heyday to relax and take the waters. Biographical museums have been erected in their honour.

The Majdanek Museum (open daily Oct–Apr 8am–5pm; May–Sept 8am–6pm) details the history of the death camp.

BELOW: alleyway off the Market Place in Lublin.

Map on page 220

Kazimierz Dolny Castle ruins on the River Vistula.

BELOW: the Market Place in Kazimierz Dolny.
RIGHT: Lublin, the cultural hub of Eastern Poland.

Kazimierz Dolny to Chelm

On the right bank of the Vistula lies the delightful town of **Kazimierz Dolny ㉑**. Founded by Duke Kazimierz II Sprawiedliwy (who died in 1370), Kazimierz Dolny originally earned its living from the grain trade and the town enjoyed great prosperity for many centuries. During the 16th century, the grain merchants built themselves some fine town houses – their naïve interpretation of Renaissance motifs seems quite touching nowadays. Stucco work covers the whole of the façades. Also worth looking out for are Kazimierz Dolny's three regional style 16th-century churches and the unusual grain stores.

A network of footpaths crisscross the landscape in the immediate vicinity of the town. Many visitors enjoy a relaxed walk up to the ruined castle and the watchtower. Kazimierz Dolny has also become a popular haunt with actors, writers and painters, particularly during the summer holiday period and at weekends. In the spring, orchards explode into flower all around this town on the Vistula. In June of each year a fair which includes a folk music competition is held in the town.

A short way downstream from Kazimierz Dolny is **Puławy**. This town can also look back on a rich cultural tradition. Towards the end of the 18th century, a centre for Polish culture and a focal point for political activity grew up here on the Czartoryski family estate. It was because of these seditious activities that the family's property around Puławy was confiscated by the Czarist authorities, the members of the family forced into exile and the name changed to New Alexandria.

During the time of Izabella Czartoryska (1789–1810), a fabulous palace with English gardens was built alongside the Gothic, Chinese and Alexander pavilions, the Temple of Sibylle and the small Palace of Marynka. The whole complex is well preserved and open to the public (open May–Nov: Tues–Sun; entrance fee).

The medieval town of **Chełm ㉒**, which was famous for many centuries for its chalk industry, lies at the eastern edge of the Lubelszczyzna. The town itself is perched on a 221-metre (722-ft) high chalk hill known as the Chełmska Góra, an easily defensible spot in the Middle Ages. At the highest point stands an impressive group of buildings including a cathedral, bishop's palace, monastery and gate. In order to mine the chalk on a commercial basis during the Middle Ages, a network of lengthy passageways and deep shafts was carved out of the soft stone. This multilevel labyrinth of chalk cellars some 40 kilometres (25 miles) long and 27 metres (89 ft) deep is open to the public (Przechodnia; tel: 082 65 25 30; open daily 10am–6pm; entrance fee; guided tours available in English or German via advance booking), warm clothing is advised.

To the north of the line connecting Lublin and Chełm is the **Polesie Lubelskie** region. This tranquil area is covered with woods, meadows and marshland. The variety of flora and fauna is protected by nature reserves and parks, with the most interesting being Jezioro Białe, Krowie Bagno and the newly-opened Polesie National Park. ❑

KARPATY

The mountainous Karpaty region is characterised by beautiful scenery, quaint timber houses and rustic churches. Culturally it is one of the best preserved regions in Poland

The outstanding natural beauty of the **Karpaty** (Carpathian Mountains), Europe's largest chain of mountains after the Alps, extends through the whole of southern Poland. The highest range in the Carpathians are the **High Tatras**, reminiscent of the Alps, which adjoin the **Bieszczady** and the **Beskidy**, characterised by woodlands, lakes and forests. Hiking trails and established tourist facilities make many areas within these mountain chains readily accessible. Meanwhile, fascinating historic towns, including some of Poland's most renowned spas, provide an ideal base from which to explore the surrounding area, and enable you to combine the urban with the rural.

This unique mountain terrain became a series of national parks in the 1920s–30s, to preserve the countryside from any prospect of industrial development. This foresight means that the natural landscape remains virtually unaffected, with rare animal and plant species thriving among its dense woodlands. The clean air, microclimates and mineral-rich spring waters, also provide a natural habitat for health spas (which date from the 18th and 19th centuries).

The western region of the Carpathian mountains is readily accessible to tourists, with convenient road and rail connections, and an established tourist infrastructure, including a wide range of hotels, resorts and guesthouses. The eastern region is far less populated, and consequently less developed. This appeals more to hikers who prefer heading off with a rucksack, tent and their own supplies, and who enjoy exploring rugged and beautiful countryside independently.

LEFT: wintertime in the Tatra mountains.
BELOW: typical country house.

Bieszczady National Park

The **Bieszczady**, a region of primeval forest at the southeastern tip of Poland, is one of those rare places in Europe that has scarcely been touched by tourism. The long, gentle slopes, covering a large part of the *województwa* (county) of Krosno, run along the border with Slovakia and the Ukraine. The highest peak here is the **Tarnica** (1,350 metres/4,500 ft). The steppe-like pastures (*połoniny*) are definitely worth exploring, using the extensive network of hiking trails, which do not present any great difficulties, but are quite long and often require considerable stamina.

More than half of this region is thickly wooded. Right in the middle of the mountain area is the **Bieszczadzki Park Narodowy** – a national park that is a haven for brown bears, herds of bison, lynx, wildcat, sparrow hawk, black stork and kingfisher. Even covering the area by car provides panoramic views from the roadside, with the Pętla Bieszczadzka (Bieszczady Loop) winding through the most interesting sections of the foothills, which is one of the most unusual landscapes in Europe.

With an area less than 3,000 hectares (7,413 acres) the Pieniny National Park is one of the smallest in Poland, but it makes up for its lack of size in scenic beauty and its enormous variety of plant species.

Another major attraction in Bieszczady is the **Jezioro Soliński** (Solina reservoir). Also known as the Sea of Bieszczady, this lake covers an area of 21 sq km (8 sq miles) and was created in 1968 when a dam was built. Pleasure boats cruise the lake, which also has numerous tourist and holiday centres providing accommodation and leisure activities.

Some of the original inhabitants of these mountains belong to two small ethnic groups, the Lemks (*Łemkowie*) and the Boyks (*Bojkowie*), Greek-Catholic and Russian-Orthodox respectively. These groups are now a minority, as many of the region's current inhabitants were resettled here by the government from other parts of Poland after World War II. Many of the originally Orthodox wooden churches which are typical of the area have now been converted into Catholic churches. The best known of these is in **Komańcza**.

Beskid Sądecki

Two main rivers, the Poprad and Dunajec, cross the next mountain region which is known as the **Beskid Sądecki**. Numerous hiking trails – all of them classified as "easy" and therefore suitable for less experienced hikers – cross the beautiful wooded slopes of the two main mountain ridges: the Radziejowa, which reaches a height of 1,261 metres (4,186 ft) and the Jaworzyna rising to 1,113 metres (3,677 ft).

Beskid Sądecki is best known for its numerous mineral-rich springs. The water from these streams, considered highly effective in treating stomach, kidney and rheumatic complaints, flows down the hillsides into the River Poprad, which rises on the southern Slovakian slopes of the Tatra Mountains, and then flows through rocks and woods into Poland.

The Beskid Sądecki region is also known for its lively folk traditions. However, the number of mountain villages in which the *Łemkowie* maintain their folk customs in their original form is rapidly diminishing. The foothills of this region are also home to the tiny ethnic group known as the *Lachowie Sądeccy*.

The administrative centre for this region is **Nowy Sącz ❶**. Founded in 1292 by the Czech king, Wenceslas II, it developed into a regional centre during the reign of King Kazimierz Wielki (1333–70). The original layout of the town is intact, with some buildings dating from the 15th and 16th centuries. The **Sądecki Museum** (Lwowska; open Tues–Fri 10am–5.30pm, Sat 9am–2.30pm; entrance fee) contains a collection of folk arts and crafts, as well as Orthodox sacred art. The town has a comfortable hotel, the Beskid (Limanowskiego 1; tel: 442 07 70), and a few other guesthouses to choose from.

To the south of Nowy Sącz ("New Sącz") is the small town of **Stary Sącz, ("Old Sącz") ❷** which dates from the 13th century. The town is linked historically with Kinga, a duchess beatified by the church, who founded a nunnery for the order of St Clare. The fortified convent complex and the town's historic fortifications, as well as several interesting churches, and medieval arcaded townhouses, have survived. With its peaceful setting, mild climate and wealth of cultural events, such as classical concerts in historic churches, and the Annual Festival of Ancient Music, Stary Sącz is thoroughly recommended for a longer stay in the region. Another great attraction is the excursions on the Radziejowa railway into the Poprad valley.

The most historic spa in the Beskidy is the small town of **Krynica ❸**, 45 km (28 miles) to the southeast of Nowy Sącz. This is also one of the most beautiful spas, being surrounded by wooded hills, with various sanatorium facilities

Map on page 238

BELOW: the iron water pump in the town square of Stary Sącz.

located on the mountain slopes. A cable car (daily in summer) provides access to the peak of the Góra Parkowa at a height of 741 metres (2,400 ft), from which there are magnificent panoramas and marked trails leading in various directions. It was during the 18th century that the springs, and the medicinal benefits of the waters, were discovered here. The waters continue to be used for drinking and bathing, as well as to treat stomach, intestinal, heart, kidney and respiratory disorders.

From the end of the 19th century, Krynica became increasingly popular as a retreat for famous Polish artists, writers and musicians. One such patient was the world-famous Polish opera singer Jan Kiepura, whose regular visits during the 1920s and 1930s helped to boost Krynica's international reputation. The renowned naïve artist Nikifor (1895–1968) was born here and continued to work here after World War II.

Touring by car, the region is best explored via the Pętla Popradzka (Poprad Loop), which extends through wonderful scenery from Krynica via the spas of Muszyna, Żegiestów and Piwniczna, all the way back to Stary Sącz. Also worth visiting is the Obrożyska linden tree reserve near Muszyna.

The town of **Szczawnica** ❹, situated on the River Dunajec, between the Pieniny and the Beskid Sądecki mountains, also has a sanatorium. This dates from the second half of the 19th century, and specialises in treating respiratory complaints, which includes inhalation therapy. The town was regularly visited by the novelist Henryk Sienkiewicz. Fascinating wooden buildings and long-standing folk traditions are among the town's other attractions. It is also recommended as a base for excursions into the Pieniny, an individual mountain range with a complex geological structure and varied climatic conditions.

BELOW: Topiary Jug in Kyrnica Park.

Almost the entire mountain range is within the **Pieniński Park Narodowy** (Pieniny National Park). The highest peak, **Wysoka**, at 1,000 metres (3,350 ft), is located in the southern part of the range, and can easily be reached from Szczawnica. The route to the peak passes the spectacular gorge known as **Wąwóz Homole**, which is cut deep into the rock. The mountain peak in the area that attracts most hikers, however, is **Trzy Korony** or the "Three Crowns", which rises to 980 metres (3,200 ft). If you want to reach the summit of Trzy Korony, the best starting point is undoubtedly Krościenko, a picturesque village by the River Dunajec.

Map on page 238

Sailing the River Dunajec

A raft ride on the River Dunajec, which winds through the dramatically beautiful Pieniny gorges, is one of the most popular tourist attractions in Poland. As the river flows rapidly between steep gorges up to 300 metres (980 ft) high, has many sharp turns and a couple of loops, rafting is not for the faint-hearted. It is more dangerous when water levels are higher, but the trips are led by experienced Góral guides. The two-hour excursion which covers about 15 km (9 miles), beginning in **Sromowce Wyżnie** and ending in Szczawnica, is an unforgettable experience.

The Pieniny region is divided between Poland and Slovakia, with the border running across the top of the mountains and along the Dunajec. Despite the ruggedness of this terrain, it has been a vital route for traders and armies for centuries. That's why castles and fortresses were built on various hilltops to protect the route, and to observe any enemy movements. Many ruined castles and strongholds now provide a poignant reminder of this era.

BELOW: raft-riding on the River Dunajec.

It is a mystery why the Niedzicka museum includes the will of the last Inca ruler, Tupac Amaru. Amaru's daughter Umina married the last owner of the castle, and his will is said to have been discovered within the castle by a descendant, who vanished in mysterious circumstances.

The remains of an ancient fortress known as **Zamek Pieniński** near the summit of Trzy Korony is open to the public. Further west are two 14th-century castles, **Czorsztyn** and **Niedzica** (first mentioned in records in 1325 as Dunajec Castle), which face one another on opposite sides of the Dunajec. Both were built on the ruins of pre-Christian fortresses, and were important territorial markers, frequently occupied by opposing warlords. Czorsztyn is now a ruin, while part of Niedzica castle serves as a folk art museum (open Tues–Sun).

The **Gorce** and **Beskid Wyspowy** mountain ranges form the region's northern boundary. Most visitors to this region are experienced mountain-hikers, who are undeterred by its remoteness, basic accommodation or the limited road and rail links.

Podhale

Between Gorce and the Tatra mountains lie the **Podhale** – an area which is of great ethnographic and historic interest. The largest town in Podhale is **Nowy Targ** , a settlement dating from the 13th century. It was traditionally the centre of the entire region, serving as the seat of the royal administration and judiciary. The town also became famous for its annual country fairs, a tradition that continues today. Additionally, the town market, selling livestock, local produce and domestic utensils every Thursday, is a principal attraction for locals and visitors. Among the historic buildings, of what is otherwise an unremarkable industrial town, are the Church of St Katharina in the town centre, and the small Church of **St Anna** by the town's cemetery, which dates from the 14th century and is thought to have been founded by brigands from the Podhale region (presumably trying to salve their conscience).

BELOW:
cultivation in Gorce.

GÓRALS

The Górals (*górale*) are a small ethnic group of highlanders, living in the Podhale and Pieniny regions. Traditionally farmers and shepherds, they speak their own dialect, and maintain their traditional customs and regional costumes – regardless of living among Poles, or, for that matter, the dominant influence of tourism. In fact, as the Górals are a major attraction of the region, tourism is actually helping to ensure the continuation of their culture.

A distinctive feature of Góral folk culture is the local architecture: ornately carved wooden houses and churches, many of which can be admired in the Tatra villages. These traditional houses are often well-maintained – one of the greatest ironies of recent Góral culture is that poverty forced generations of them to emigrate to the United States, but the money they sent back to their relatives was used to preserve the traditional farmhouses they left behind.

In additon to architecture, music and folk dancing are other easily accessible elements of Góral culture, and there are plenty of opportunities for visitors to enjoy performances by Góral choirs, string bands and dance troupes. Some restaurants in Zakopane have regular performances in the evenings.

The sculpture of the Madonna and Child in nearby **Ludźmierz** is revered throughout Podhale. Every year countless devout Catholics from the Polish and Slovakian foothills come to Ludźmierz for the festival on 15 August, celebrating the Feast of the Assumption of the Blessed Virgin Mary.

The village of **Dębno**, also near Nowy Targ, is renowned for its beautifully preserved larchwood church, dedicated to the Archangel Michael. Constructed during the 15th century using dowels in place of metal nails, the church was decorated with splendid paintings in the early Renaissance style by unknown artists. Similar paintings can be seen in the churches of **Harklowa** and **Grywald**, but these are not as well preserved.

Map on page 238

Zakopane

The small town of **Zakopane** ❼ at the foot of the Tatra mountains was originally a Góral village until it was "discovered" by a Warsaw doctor, Tytus Chałubiński. It became increasingly important in Poland from the 1870s. A growing number of Polish intellectuals and artists soon began to settle in what was then a village, drawn by the area's natural and rustic beauty. Moreover, the Górals' love of freedom and indomitable sense of independence became a source of inspiration for the entire country, and a symbol for the national struggle against Prussia, Russia and Austria. Consequently, Zakopane was elevated into a cultural and political centre.

After World War I this small town in the Tatra Mountains continued to be a meeting point for prominent politicians and artists, many of whom made Zakopane their permanent home. Elements of Góral culture and folk music also inspired various artists, such as the composers Karol Szymanowski, Mieczysław

Typical country house in the beautiful Podhale region.

BELOW: Góral souvenir seller.

Zakopane wooden chapel in Jaszczurówka, designed by the architect Stanisław Witkiewicz.

BELOW: Willa Pod Jodłami at Bystre, also designed by Stanisław Witkiewicz.

Karłowicz and Artur Maslawski; the writers Jan Kasprowicz, Kornel Makuszyński and Kazimierz Przerwa-Tetmajer, the Dutch pianist Egon Petri and the painter, architect and theoretician Stanisław Witkiewicz (*see page 247*).

Individual museums dedicated to the lives and work of Karol Szymanowski, (*see page 111*) Jan Kasprowicz and Kornel Makuszyński have been established in the town. A memorial also stands in the Old Cemetery, honouring many renowned figures who have contributed to public life in Zakopane.

Several artists, such as Stanisław Witkiewicz, built houses in the Zakopane style at the end of the 19th century. This is a synthesis of various types of folk art and was an attempt to integrate elements of local art and architecture with their Polish counterparts. The most beautiful example is the Dom pod Jedlami, built in **Koziniec** in 1897 for the Pawlikowski family. Equally worth seeing is the chapel in **Jaszczurówka**, built in 1908.

In Zakopane's **Muzeum Tatrzańskie** (Tatra Museum) there is an important collection of local folk art (Krupówki 10; tel: 0165-152 05; open Tues–Sun 9am–3.30pm; entrance fee), while the traditional Góral houses which have survived on Kościeliska street create the unintentional effect of an open-air museum of regional architecture.

Zakopane's reputation as a Bohemian town continues to attract artists, writers and composers, while various cultural events – such as the concerts held in the villa housing the Atma museum – underline the continued importance of art and culture to the locals, as well as visitors. Galleries, such as that run by the famous Polish artist Władisław Hasior, organise regular exhibitions of work by professional artists as well as devoted amateurs. The **Witkacy Theatre** at Chramcówki 15, has received critical acclaim and is very popular with visitors

– check with the Tourist Offices for details of performances. Zakopane also hosts the annual international **Festival of Highland Folklore** in mid-August, which attracts large crowds.

Map
on page
238

The Tatra Mountains

Zakopane is the gateway to one of Poland's greatest natural treasures, the beautiful High Tatras (Tatry) mountain chain, which have established the town as Poland's premier skiing resort. The highest mountains between the Alps and the Caucasus, the High Tatras extend to almost 800 sq km (300 sq miles), part of which is in Poland, while two-thirds are in Slovakia. The highest peak within Poland is the Rysy at 2,499 metres (8,200 ft). The Tatra area is totally enchanting, with alpine scenery and an abundance of attractive water features: streams, waterfalls and lakes, of which the **Morskie Oko** ("Eye of the Sea") is the largest. It can easily be reached by bus from Zakopane, followed by a short walk.

About three million annual visitors, many from western Europe, use the peaks for mountaineering and skiing. The most beautiful spots are connected by an extensive network of hiking trails, which range in difficulty from simple walks to skilful rock climbs. It must not be forgotten that this entire mountain area is part of the Tatra National Park, with its own strict regulations protecting the fauna and flora. If you want to trek in the mountains, it is strongly recommended that you seek the assistance of professional local mountain guides; there is also a volunteer rescue service looking after hikers in case of accidents. You can go hiking in the Tatras in both the summer and the winter, but make sure you take all the necessary precautions and equipment before venturing off, whatever the season, and inform rangers of where you are going.

BELOW:
woodcarver at work.

Map on page 238

Having once hosted the Winter Olympics, Zakopane's excellent winter sports facilities cater for skiers and winter sports enthusiasts of all grades. In addition to good ski slopes there are several ski jumps and over 50 ski lifts, which includes access to the most popular mountain, the **Kasprowy Wierch** at 1,985 metres (6,510 ft). Facilities for tourists are improving all the time; there are ever-more good-quality hotels, as well as hundreds of *pensions*, youth hostels and simple mountain huts.

The region is not only popular in winter. In recent years the Tatra have become a summer resort too, for mountain bikers and paragliders. There are now designated biking trails within the range.

Orawa and Babia Góra

To the north of Zakopane (which can be reached by car or by a four-hour walk) lies the extraordinary village of **Chochołów ❽**. The traditional wooden houses and church lining the main street provide some of the finest examples of the Podhale region's typical architectural style. A characteristic feature of these houses is the absence of any nails, with pieces of timber skillfully slotted together through joints.

From here the road leads on to **Orawa**, the least known of all areas in the foothills. From the gentle hills of this delightful countryside there are wonderful views of the nearby Tatra and Beskid Wysoki mountains. As the public transport system is limited, it is advisable to travel here by car, either from Kraków, Katowice or Zakopane. Although this area has only a few places of interest, these are certainly special enough (and refreshingly uncrowded) to make the effort worthwhile. Foremost among these is the small holiday village of

BELOW: the cable car to Mount Kasprowy in Zakopane.

Orawka, which dates from the 16th century. The exceptional wooden church of St John the Baptist, decorated with interesting paintings (including a *biblia pauperum*, an illustration of the Ten Commandments, on the chancel wall), was built in the 17th century. A little farther on from Orawka is the larger village of **Zubrzyca Górna ❾**, where many wooden buildings typical of this region have been preserved.

Definitely not to be missed is the **Orawski Park Etnograficzny** (Orawa Ethnographic Park; open Tues–Sun 9am–3pm during the summer months). This is a *skansen* (open-air museum) with rural buildings from the region, some of which date from the 17th century. This includes an entire farmstead that once belonged to a local mayor, as well as other farm buildings and stalls, each containing original traditional tools and household objects.

To the northwest of Orawa the mountain of **Babia Góra** rises to a height of 1,725 metres (5,690 ft). A number of hiking trails offering varying degrees of difficulty lead to the summit, and in clear weather it is well worth the climb for the unforgettable and all-embracing panorama it offers: of the Tatras, the Beskids, large areas of the foothills and, in the distance, Silesia. If you're tired after the climb why not recover by checking into the mid-market hotel Markowe Szczawiny, which is conveniently situated close to the summit. ❏

Witkacy

One personality who is closely linked with Zakopane is Stanisław Ignacy Witkiewicz (1885–1939). Generally known as Witkacy, he was one of the most original exponents of Polish culture, combining the roles of painter, art theoretician, philosopher, writer and dramatist. Although born in Warsaw, Zakopane became the centre of Witkacy's life: his father, Stanisław Witkiewicz, a painter, art critic and creator of the "Zakopane Style", which he applied to architecture and the design of everyday objects, had established himself here.

In 1890, at the age of five, Witkacy made his debut as an artist in the magazine *Przeglad Zakopianski*, and only a few years later his pictures were exhibited in Zakopane for the first time. Brought up to be an artist by his father, he enjoyed the companionship of many of the cultural élite who came to spend their holidays in Zakopane. After the suicide of his fiancée Witkacy fled Zakopane, travelling first to Australia, then to Sri Lanka and on to Russia, where he served as a soldier, surviving World War I. From 1918 he lived permanently in Zakopane, usually staying in one of the guesthouses run by his mother. In 1933, he moved to Witkiewiczowka on Antalowka Hill, and lived in a house built in the Zakopane Style; there are now plans to found a Witkacy Museum here.

Witkacy was a prolific artist. He produced several hundred portraits in his studio, often under the influence of alcohol or hallucinogenic drugs. Even as a young man his paintings were surreal, with visionary and Utopian elements. His early self-portraits reveal carefully chosen colour and psychological depth, but the sharp lines already show signs of the caricature of his later portraits, in which faces were distorted and grotesque.

His *Composition with Three Female Forms* (oil on canvas, 1917–20) is indicative of this development. It is also an example of the way in which he incorporated his impressions of the exotic Tropics and the horrors of the war. Most of his works are exhibited in the museums of Słupsk, Stolp and Warsaw, and in the Tatra Museum in Zakopane. He wrote the majority of his plays in the dramatic surroundings of the Tatra mountains. His major works, including *Matka* (*Mother*), *Szewcy* (*Cobblers*) and *Nowe Wyzwolenie* (*New Deliverance*), became popular in the 1960s. In 1925 he founded the Formistic Theatre and put on several productions in Morskie Oko's Eye of the Sea Room, such as *Wariat i Zakonnice* (*The Madman and the Nuns*) and *Nowe Wyzwolenie* (*New Liberation*). Witkacy was also involved in philosophy and art theory: before World War II he was one of the organisers of the General Vacation University in Zakopane. In conjunction with his belief in "catastrophism", the disintegration of civilisation, the Soviet army's invasion of Poland shocked him into committing suicide.

Witkacy is commemorated in Zakopane cemetery with a symbolic gravestone. The S I. Witkiewicz Theatre on Chramcówki was founded with the aim of producing his plays, so that people can continue to profit from the life and work of this brilliant outsider. ❏

RIGHT: *Composition with Three Female Forms* (1917–20) by Stanisław Witkiewicz.

SILESIA

Silesia offers the beauty of the Sudety Mountains, health resorts, sightseeing and the cosmopolitan city of Wrocław

Long established as the industrial heartland of Poland, Silesia's turbulent history has been dominated by Germany and the Austro-Hungarian Habsburg Empire – a legacy that can be traced throughout the region.

Silesia is thought to have been named after an early Slavic tribe of settlers, the Silings, and was ruled by the Polish Piast dynasty from the 11th century. In the 12th century the region was divided into two duchies: Lower Silesia, governed by Prince Bolesław, while Prince Mieszko controlled Upper Silesia. This historic division has remained, with Lower Silesia was surrounding the city of Wrocław in the northwest, and Upper Silesia, which includes Katowice, in the southeast.

As Silesia prospered during the 13th century, the population also began to diversify, with many new towns and villages principally settled by Germans. Moreover, the death of Bolesław III in 1348 brought the Piast's rule to an end, and Silesia became part of Bohemia. From 1526 Silesia was ruled by Ferdinand I, and remained a part of the Habsburg empire for 200 years. The Silesian wars of 1740–63 resulted in Frederick the Great annexing Lower Silesia and much of Upper Silesia, leaving only part of Upper Silesia under Habsburg rule.

Following World War I, the Treaty of Versailles incorporated a small area of Silesia within Czechoslovakia, and the rest was divided between Poland and Germany in 1921. After World War II Silesia was returned to Poland, after an absence of 600 years. The German population was replaced by those Poles who had been forced to leave the eastern areas of Poland, which had become part of the Ukraine.

Silesia's industrial prowess is, inevitably, an aspect of the region's heritage and character, with various museums depicting the evolution of key industries such as mining and steelworks. However, the region also has numerous attractions which can be visited without going anywhere near an industrial unit.

Wrocław is a fascinating and dynamic city, the Jasna Góra monastery in Czéstochowa is Poland's holiest shrine, while the Beskid mountains, part of the Carpathian mountain range, provide endless vistas of outstanding natural beauty. ❏

PRECEDING PAGES: the Cistercian monastery in Krzeszów.
LEFT: only a few masters of the art of instrument making remain in Poland.

UPPER SILESIA AND KATOWICE

*In the country's industrial centre, coal and steel
production have shaped the landscape
and its people for centuries*

Map
on page
254

U pper Silesia is the industrial heartland of Poland, offering "attractions" such as museums of mining or weaving – even industrial towns yield architectural and cultural gems. The surrounding countryside offers enormous natural beauty, as well as historic towns and villages.

During the Middle Ages, Silesia was a gold mining centre. However, the economic policies of Frederick the Great encouraged the mining of coal and iron ore, which led to the construction of iron and steel works. Industrialisation in Silesia made rapid strides. By the turn of the 19th century, it was a major competitor to the great industrial areas beside the Rhine and the Ruhr.

Upper Silesia's main natural resource is hard coal extracted in more than 50 mines. The Katowice steel works are the largest in Poland, while the iron, chemical and automobile industries are also major factors. In fact, it's a way of life. Of the region's 2½ million inhabitants almost one million are employed in industrial concerns. With such a large population concentrated into a relatively small area, many cities have merged to form conurbations.

The heavy industry located between Gliwice and Dąbrowa Górnicza created a serious pollution problem which culminated in it being declared a disaster area in the 1980s. The main reason for this was the Communist regime's planning policies, or rather lack of planning. Heavy industry was seen as the key to economic prosperity, which entailed misusing natural resources and ignoring environmental consequences. Once the Communist government was out of office, a major clean-up began, with environmentally harmful and unprofitable factories closed down, while modern technology was also introduced to prevent damaging emissions. An added impetus is the Polish government's determination to meet the environmental criteria established as a pre-condition for joining the European Union.

LEFT: evening in the Jura mountains.
BELOW: willow trees.

Katowice

The capital of Górny Śląsk (Upper Silesia) and centre of the Upper Silesian industrial belt, **Katowice ❶** is also a scientific and cultural centre. With a population of 360,000, Katowice was once a typical 19th-century industrial town, but now embraces some 70 small towns scattered across the southern highlands. The oldest of them, Bogucice and Dąb, were founded in the 13th and 14th centuries.

Urbanisation began in the 1860s and for this reason there are numerous examples of Revivalism, Art Nouveau and Modernism in the town's architecture; the theatre and the railway station in particular. Most of the churches date from around the turn of the century and were designed in the neo-Romanesque or neo-Gothic styles that were popular at the time.

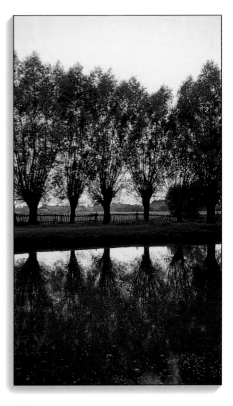

One particularly striking example of the ecclesiastical style that prevailed between the two world wars is the basilica of the Cathedral of Christ the King by Xavery Dunikowski. The sandstone structure is the largest 20th-century church in Poland. The Council Offices, representative of the secular architecture of this period, were a showpiece for Upper Silesia in the inter-war years.

Close by is a Monument to the Silesian Insurgents, commemorating the inhabitants who fought against the Germans in the uprisings of 1919–21 for Silesia to join the newly independent Poland. After World War I it required three uprisings and a plebiscite before Katowice finally joined Poland. Nearby is a giant sports and entertainment complex, the Wojewodzka Hala Widowiskowo-Sportowa, known locally as "the saucer" because of its shape. By the Market Square is the **Muzeum Śląskie** (Museum of Silesia; al Korfantego 3; tel: 58 56 61; open Tues–Sun; entrance fee). The collection of art and sculpture includes a section devoted to the works of Jan Matejko, Mojžesz Kisling, Jerzy Nowosielski and other 19th- and 20th-century artists. Among the exhibits at the **Archdiocesan Museum** (ul Jordana 39; tel: 51 67 03; open Tues–Sun; entrance fee) is an impressive collection of carved Madonnas. On the edge of the city is the Culture and Leisure Park, including a sports stadium, planetarium and observatory, and the Upper Silesian Ethnographic Park (open Tues–Sun; closed Mon and Sat; entrance fee), showing examples of local wooden buildings.

History and industry

In **Bytom**, 12 km (7 miles) north of Katowice, the Muzeum Górnoc Slaskie (Museum of Upper Silesia) (pl Jana III Sobieskiego 2; tel: 81 82 91; open Tues–Sun, entrance fee) has an interesting collection of Polish and European

Upper Silesia

painting, as well as folk arts and crafts, and discoveries from archaeological digs in the region. The town is also home to the Silesian Opera. A little further north is the mining town of **Tarnowskie Góry** ➋ which developed after rich deposits of silver and lead were discovered in the area during the 13th century.

While this form of mining ended in the 1920s, the ancient mine in the Bobrowiki district is a great tourist attraction, where you can follow a 1,500-metre (5,000-ft) long trail through chambers and galleries, at a depth of 40 metres (130 ft). Trolleys and tools have been deliberately left in place show to help conjure up the working atmosphere, with guides explaining the history of mining during escorted tours. The huge silver chamber is of particular interest. Another extraordinary attraction in this mining complex is the so-called Black Trout Gallery, a canal around 30 metres (100 ft) below ground level, bored out of dolomite rock. A boat takes you across the 600- metre (1,960-ft) wide canal, which separates two mine shafts.

The Regional Museum also details the history of mining in the area. The first steam-driven engine in Europe went into operation in the town in 1788, which also explains why there is a *skansen* (open-air museum) of steam engines.

Gliwice, one of Upper Silesia's oldest towns, has a significant place in the outbreak of World War II. In 1939 Hitler accused the Poles of attacking a German radio station in the town and used this as a pretext for invading Poland. The attack had, in fact, been carried out by SS troops. The main points of interest in the well-preserved medieval town are the Gothic All Saints Parish Church, the neoclassical Town Hall surrounded by restored townhouses, and the Piast Palace Museum.

Będzin is situated on the border between Silesia and Małopolska (Little Poland). In the 14th century it occupied a key position in the new Polish state's defensive system. The neo-Gothic Piast Palace, originally 13th-century and refashioned in the 19th century, is now a museum with archaeological and folk arts and crafts, as well as military exhibits. The industrial town of Dąbrowa Górnicza, east of Będzin, has the largest iron and steel works in Poland, known as the "Katowice", which began operating in 1976. This replaced the traditional local industry, the mining of precious metal ores, which ceased at the beginning of the 19th century. These tunnels and the Ore Mining Museum at Czarny Pstrąg are now a tourist attraction.

Since the 15th century **Piekary Śląskie** has been a shrine for Catholic pilgrims, and since the 17th century this has been focused on a painting of the Virgin Mary of Piekary. The painting's miraculous powers were said to heal people from the Black Death. The last Sunday in May sees the largest influx of pilgrims, worshipping in the 19th-century basilica situated on Cerekwica Hill.

Mining and spa towns

North of the Silesian highlands is the region of Rybnicki Okręg Węglowy, where **Jastrzębie-Zdrój** has been a spa town since 1861. However, it is also the site of a large modern coal mining centre, and the mass strikes held here in 1980 – together with strikes

Map
on page
254

TIP

A more colourful aspect of the mining tradition in Tarnowskie Góry is the annual Miner's Day Festival in September.

BELOW: a carpenter works on a house in a *skansen* (open air museum).

in Gdańsk and Szczecin – led to the founding of the Solidarity trade union movement (*see page 63*). Between Katowice and Bielsko-Biała, adjacent to a woodland region, lies the medieval town of **Pszczyna** ❸. Until 1945 Pszczyna Palace was the seat of the Hochberg-Fśürstenstein family, although it was originally constructed for the Piast dynasty, who made the town the capital of their Duchy. It was refashioned from the original Gothic into an exquisite, highly decorative neoclassical style during the late 19th century by the renowned French architect Hipolit Destailleur. It is now a Museum of Interiors (open Tues–Sun, May–Oct; Wed–Sun, Nov–Apr; entrance fee) with a superb collection of decorative arts and furniture from the Renaissance to the 20th century. There are also exhibitions of armoury and hunting trophies. Concerts of chamber music composed by the former court bandmaster Philipp Telemann, a resident of the town from 1704–8, are held in the Hall of Mirrors. The palace is surrounded by one of Silesia's most attractive and largest parks, totalling 44 hectares (109 acres). Laid out in an English style, the park is traversed by the River Pszczynka.

Interiors at the other end of the scale, though nonetheless beautiful, can be seen at the Zagroda Wsi Pszczynskiej (Pszczyna Village and Farm *Skansen*, al Parkowa; tel: 210 34 93; open Wed–Sun; entrance fee), where the local building style is shown through a collection of rustic homes with folk interiors.

To the Black Madonna

Częstochowa ❹ is a major industrial centre concentrating on metallurgy, textiles and chemicals, although the city is much better known for the **Jasna Góra Monastery** (tel: 65 38 88; open daily; entrance fee). This is the most important

Catholic shrine in Poland for the cult of the Virgin Mary. Pilgrims arrive here throughout the year from around the world, including those who walk from Warsaw, particularly on 15 August, the Feast of the Assumption of the Virgin Mary, and 26 August, the feast day of the Blessed Virgin Mary of Częstochowa. The object of veneration is a painting of the so-called Black Madonna, a miraculous icon of the Blessed Virgin Mary holding the infant Jesus.

This medieval Byzantine icon is believed to be a copy of a painting by St Luke, made on a piece of wood which came from the table on which the Holy family ate. Originating in the Ukraine, the icon was brought to Silesia by Pauline monks led by Prince Władysław of Opole in 1382, and in whose care the icon remained. The prince ordered that the icon be kept in a church and monastery constructed on a limestone hill above the town.

This resulted in a fortified 14th-century monastic complex, extended in the 16th and 17th centuries, which is now one of Poland's most important sacred buildings. The monastery even withstood a heavy siege during the Swedish invasions in the 17th century. When the Swedes inexplicably retreated from the monastery and were subsequently driven from the country, the cult of the Virgin Mary was intensified even further.

In 1717 King Kazimierz laid his crown before the icon and officially declared the Virgin Mary as Queen of Poland. The icon is hung above an early Baroque altar made of ebony and silver in the beautiful Chapel of the Virgin Mary of Częstochowa, which is high Baroque. It is uncovered every day before the first mass and covered again at midday. A poignant showcase in the chapel features walking sticks, crutches and other medical items left behind by people who have been miraculously cured here.

Map on page 254

BELOW: pilgrims queue to see the Black Madonna in Częstochowa.

The basilica is equally magnificent, with priceless votive offerings from several Polish kings exhibited in the treasury. The armoury includes rare weapons and suits of armour including Middle Eastern examples, which Jan III Sobieski brought back with him after his victory over the Turks at Vienna. The library contains numerous rare tomes, illuminated manuscripts and liturgical works. Other rooms which can be visited include the refectory, with its extraordinarily beautiful vaulted ceiling painted with religious scenes.

The **Muzeum Okręgowe** (pl Biegańskiego 45; tel: 24 44 24; open Tues–Sun; entrance fee) is housed in the Town Hall. Detailing the history of the Częstochowa region, the collection also includes local folk arts and crafts.

The **Krakówsko-Częstochowska Jura**, a rocky area running from Częstochowa to Kraków close to the border between Upper Silesia and Małopolska (Little Poland), is now a popular holiday region. The natural beauty, characterised by caves, wild gorges, gentle valleys and variegated woodland, is the attraction. The highest point is the Podzamcze Ogrodzienieckie at 500 metres (1,650 ft). In the Middle Ages this border area was defended by a series of imposing castles and fortresses, known as eagle's lairs because of their inaccessibility. Ruins of these old castles can still be seen today along the Eagle's Lair Route which starts with the Wawel in Kraków (*see page 216*) and finishes with Jasnogorski Castle in Częstochowa. Near Olsztyn beside the Eagle's Lair Route are the ruins of a castle built by Kazimierz the Great, which was badly damaged by the Swedes in 1655. Not far away, in **Potok Złoty**, is a palace formerly owned by the Raczynski family, and a manor house where the romantic poet Zygmunt Krasiński (1821–59) worked. In Mirów and Bobolice further castle ruins testify to the eventful history of this region.

Certainly worth a short detour are the ruins of Ogrodzieniec Palace, just to the south of **Zawiercie**. The palace was so sumptuously furnished by its owner, a wealthy merchant by the name of Boner, that it even rivalled the opulence of Kraków's Wawel. The oldest building in the Krakówsko-Częstochowska Jura is the small Romanesque Church of St John the Baptist, near Siewierz.

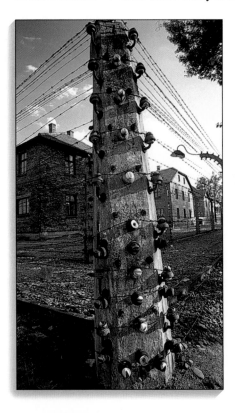

BELOW: Auschwitz.

Oświęcim (Auschwitz)

Located on the border between Silesia and Małopolska, where the River Sola flows into the Vistula, **Oświęcim** ❺ was the site of a 12th-century castle. In 1317 it became the capital of an independent principality, incorporated into Poland in 1457. In 1772, under the First Polish Partition, the town was ceded to the Habsburg Empire. It is now an industrial centre, but will always be synonymous with the Holocaust.

Built in 1940, Auschwitz-Birkenau was the largest Nazi concentration camp complex, with two camps covering an area of 40 sq km (15 sq miles).

Auschwitz was a slave-labour camp, largely reserved for political prisoners, members of the resistance and other "opponents" to the Nazi regime, while a second camp, Birkenau, was an extermination camp. A total of four million prisoners of 28 nationalities lost their lives here, brought by train from all over Europe. At the end of the unloading ramp new arrivals were divided into those capable of work, and those to be taken straight to the gas chambers. The great majority of the victims were European Jews, together with Poles, Russians and gypsies, who were forced to endure inhuman conditions. Many died as a result of slave labour, hunger, illness and torture, while the genocide reached a peak in 1942 with up to 24,000 people being murdered every day in the gas chambers. The corpses were burned in crematoria and then buried in mass graves.

In 1944 the Nazis began destroying the crematoria and some of the camp buildings before retreating, but they did not have enough time to destroy the gas chambers. The camp was liberated by the Red Army in 1945.

In 1947 Auschwitz-Birkenau was established as a National Museum of Martyrology (open daily; entrance fee). Visitors are taken on a guided tour of the camp – children under the age of 13 are not admitted. One of the films shown was taken by troops who liberated the camp in 1945. Other film footage and photos from the camp's archives can also be seen, while the museum depicts the struggle and martyrdom of daily life, with heart-breaking exhibits such as piles of spectacles and shoes belonging to the victims. A monument to the Victims of Auschwitz was unveiled in the grounds of the camp in Birkenau.

Map on page 254

Auschwitz concentration camp flag.

Around Bielsko-Biała

Situated by the River Skawa on the way to Wadowice (*see page 216*) is the town of **Zator**, which until 1494 was ruled by Silesian princes and subsequently became part of the Polish Republic. Places of interest are the Old Town walls, the Gothic Church of St George and a palace in an eclectic style but with numerous neo-Gothic features. An important place of pilgrimage in southern Poland

BELOW: Auschwitz camp gate with the inscription "*Arbeit Macht Frei*" ("*Work Makes Free*").

TIP

Within easy reach of
Wisła are two centres
of Beskid folk arts and
crafts. Koniaków and
Istebna are both
renowned for lace-
making, and Istebna
also has a museum of
sacred art, housed in
an 18th-century
church.

is the small town of Kalwaria Zebrzydowska. Up in the Wadowice Hills, is the most historic and renowned "Way of the Cross" (Road to Calvary). The route culminates at the Bernardine Monastery's Baroque Church of Our Lady of the Angels. This hill is also a setting for performances of a Passion play in Holy Week, leading up to Easter.

The West Beskid Mountains, in the Polish Carpathians, form the southern boundary of Upper Silesia, which includes the towns of Beskidy Śląskie, Maly, Żywiec, Makowski and Wysoki. The capital of the region is **Bielsko-Biała**, where the most impressive buildings are the 14th-century Gothic Kościół Św. Stanisława (St Stanislaus' Church), and the 17th-century wooden church Kościół Św. Barbary (St Barbara's Church). Dom Tkacza (Sobieskiego 51; tel: 291 76; open Tues–Sun; entrance fee) is a reconstructed weaver's house furnished in a 17th-century manner; the Muzeum Techniki Włokienniczej (Museum of Textile Technology) reflects the town's traditional status within the Polish textile industry (Sukiennicza 7; tel: 223 67; open Tues–Sun; entrance fee).

South of Bielsko-Biała is **Szczyrk**, Poland's second most popular ski resort after Zakopane (*see page 243*). Located at the foot of the Skrzyczne (1,257 metres/4,122 ft), this is the destination for some 30,000 winter sports enthusiasts every year. A chairlift takes skiers to the Czantoria mountain station at 854 metres (2,800 ft). The sources of the Czarna and the Biała Wisełka meet in Czarne and continue as the longest river in Poland, the Vistula. Wisła and Ustroń, two other popular holiday resorts, can be reached via the Salmo-polski Pass (934 metres/3,063 ft). An abundance of minerals in the spring water has led to the establishment of several spas in this district.

Near the border with the Czech Republic, on the banks of the Olza, is the

BELOW: hiking in
the Karkonosze
mountains.

historic town of **Cieszyn**. From 1282 to 1653 it was the capital of a duchy owned by the Silesian Piasts, which has left a rich architectural legacy, including the Piasts late 13th-century tower. The Chapel of St Nicholas is one of Poland's few remaining Romanesque rotundas, and there are several other medieval and Baroque churches to see. The Market Square features a Renaissance Town Hall and fine burghers' houses of the same period, while early 16th-century fragments of the town walls can be seen on Przykopa.

 Map on page 254

The Silesian Lowlands

Further to the west, beside the gently flowing Odra, are the fertile Silesian Lowlands, which become hillier further south. The climate is perfect for agriculture and the area continues to attract holiday-makers keen on outdoor pursuits.

Bordering the Upper Silesian industrial area to the west are the **Góra Św Anny** (St Anna mountains), which reach a height of 404 metres (1,325 ft). Mount St Anna was the site of a fierce battle between Polish insurgents and the German army in 1921. This mountain lies at the heart of the German-speaking region and mass is usually conducted in two languages. The town of Góra Św. Anny, situated on the Chelmer Ridge, has been the centre of the cult of St Anna since the beginning of the 17th century. A Franciscan monastic complex built here in the mid-18th century includes no less than 37 chapels, two devotional churches and the Basilica of St Anna. A Renaissance figure of St Anna with the Madonna and Child, can be seen in the parish church.

Opole was initially a fortified settlement inhabited by the Opole tribe, and the town was established on the River Oder in the 13th century; it soon became the capital of the Opole duchy. Reminders of the past include the mas-

BELOW: the marketplace in Opole.

Map on page 254

TIP

Every year in the third week of June Opole is flooded with visitors who come here to enjoy the Festival of Polish Songs.

BELOW: glass worker in the Karaonosze mountains.

sive Piast Tower, part of the former castle of the Opole dukes. Other elements of the town's fortifications include fragments of the town wall, and a bastion.

The town centre, on the banks of the Młynówka Canal, has retained a delightful Renaissance atmosphere. The Town Hall in the Market Square has a distinguished Italianate character, which isn't surprising as it was intended to be a copy of the Palazzo Vecchio in Florence. The surrounding buildings combine Gothic, Renaissance and Baroque elements. However, it is the town's sacral buildings which are the most impressive. The Gothic Church of the Holy Cross (now the cathedral) dates from the 15th century, while the 14th-century Franciscan Monastery complex includes a church with the St Anna Chapel, also known as the Piast Chapel, where the Piast dukes of Opole were buried.

The road to Wrocław (*see page 267*) leads past the Opole Village Museum, a *skansen* displaying farm buildings from the Opole region, including cottages, windmills, a forge and granaries from the 17th century.

Towards the Góry Opawskie

Nysa ⑦, to the southwest of Opole on the Nysa Kłodzka River, was the capital of Wrocław's bishops for several hundred years until 1820, with its most prosperous period during the 16th and 17th centuries when it was a centre of handicrafts. When the Red Army "liberated" the town in March 1945, around 80 percent of it was destroyed in the process. The town's original fortifications, comprising 28 bastions and four towers, were reduced to a couple of 14th- and 15th-century town gates and a fragment of the town wall. The postwar expansion followed the opening of a factory producing pick-up trucks. The town's sacred buildings are well worth seeing, with the **Church of St Jacob** in the town centre a wonderful example of Gothic architecture, with numerous Gothic, Renaissance and Baroque sculptures. Comprising three naves, 19 chapels, three porches and a belfry (added in the 16th century), the monumental proportions are impressive considering it was built in the 13th century. The Church of SS Peter and Paul, built in the 1720s, contains one of finest Baroque interiors in Silesia. The man-made Nysa Lake to the west of town provides various watersports.

A few miles further west, at the foot of the Gold Mountains, is **Paczków ⑧**, a town which is popularly known as "Poland's Carcassonne" because of its perfectly preserved medieval fortifications, comprising stone defensive walls, 18 turrets and four city gates. In the Market Square is the fortified Church of St John, a massive triple-naved Gothic church with a carved portal adorning the west wall and an ornamental Renaissance attic. The Renaissance altar is a work of art, with the interiors also featuring Gothic sculptures. The surrounding burghers' houses provide fine examples of various architectural genres. Up in the Góry Opawskie hills beside the border lie some picturesque little towns such as the historic spa **Głuchołazy**. In the Market Square stands a linden tree surrounded by burghers' houses. The town's other impressive features are the Baroque twin-towered Church of St Lawrence and the Lower Gate Tower, part of the original defensive system. ❑

Teutonic Knights

The Order of St Mary of the Germans in Jerusalem was the last of the religious-military orders. It was founded in 1198 as part of the Hohenstaufen emperors' crusades and employed as an auxiliary force against infidel armies. It won territory in Palestine, Greece, Italy and Germany.

The order greatly expanded its power base under the fourth Grand Master, Hermann von Salza, when the Teutonic Knights began expanding in central Europe with the backing of German overlords. In 1211, the knights defeated the Cumans in Transylvania but when they became too powerful for the Hungarian king they were expelled. In 1226 Duke Konrad of Mazovia employed the knights in his struggles with the Prussians, a pagan tribe that repeatedly invaded and laid waste to the north of the principality. Konrad gave the knights land north of Toruń in exchange for their protection and the conversion to Christianity of the Prussians. The duke wanted to retain sovereignty over the land he entrusted to the knights, but the agreement turned sour. The conflict between Germans and Poles would continue for 250 years. Instead of being converted, the native Prussians were simply wiped out and their names passed to their exterminators. Bismarck's Prussians were in fact descendants of the people who had eliminated the original tribe and whose ethnic origin was quite different.

One important element was the signing of the "Golden Bull of Rimini", ratified in 1226, which allowed Emperor Friedrich II to call upon the knights in any lands that he had conquered. This papal edict encouraged him to extend his empire further, and the knights captured regions around the Baltic. In 1308, the order won control of the region around Gdańsk and moved its headquarters to the castle at Marienburg, now Malbork.

At the head of the knights' hierarchy was a Grand Master, elected for life, who had five regional commanders-in-chief. The dioceses were led by knight-priests. Knights and priests had equal status, but they were all sworn to obedience, poverty and chastity.

The white cloak with the black cross became the knights' uniform. The achievements of the Teutonic Order can be attributed to their expansionist policies, cultivation of farmland and the resettlement of Germans. This was underpinned by an efficient bureaucracy and the cities it controlled in the Hanseatic League such as Gdańsk, Toruń and Königsberg, which traded cereals, timber and amber. This wealth encouraged architects and craftsmen – Pomerania and Mazuria have magnificent castles and churches from this period.

After the unification of Poland and Lithuania the order started to decline and the rivalry came to a head in the Battle of Grunwald in 1410. The order's Grand Master, Ulrich von Jungingen, died in the battle. Under the Second Peace of Toruń of 1466 the knights ceded Gdańsk and Malbork to the Poles. Marienburg Castle was captured in 1457 and their headquarters moved to Königsberg.

The order was finally dissolved in Germany by Napoleon. The surviving branch of the order has headquarters in Vienna. ❏

RIGHT: the gates of Malbork Castle.

POLAND'S LIQUID ASSETS

Spa towns throughout Poland specialise in treating specific illnesses and provide a wide range of reviving and relaxing treatments

The earliest Polish health spas were established in the 12th century and entered a golden age during the 18th and 19th centuries when it was fashionable for high society from France, Germany, Austria and the United States, to "take the waters" and mingle.

Today there are more than 40 spas in Poland, offering a range of treatments including mud baths, inhalations, hydrotherapy, kinetic therapy, and of course drinking mineral water, with each spa's water having its own mineral profile. Individual spas specialising in treating specific illnesses include Połczyn Zdroj, renowned for treating rheumatism, and Ciechocinek, the first choice for curative baths in the treatment of respiratory illnesses. The range of resort locations also means that spas can be chosen on the basis of their setting and surrounding attractions, as well as their range of facilities. On the Baltic Coast for example, there is a clinic in Sopot, while the largest spa on the coast is in Kołobrzeg.

There are a few spas in central Poland such as Inowrocław and Nałęczów, while the greatest concentration of spas is in the south, along the Carpathian mountain range.

△ **SALT WONDER WORKS**
Ciechocinek's amazing salt-filtering graduation towers extend to a total of 1,750 metres (5,741 ft) with the earliest tower dating from 1824.

▷ **TAKING THE WATERS**
Mineral waters smell worse than they taste. The traditional way to "take the waters" is to drink from a porcelain tankard while walking slowly.

HEALTH FROM A BOTTLE

◁ **CURATIVE EFFECTS**
In the past, the saline mist produced during the filtration process was inhaled by respiratory patients walking through the tower for its high level of iodine.

△ **SWIMMING POOL**
In between Ciechocinek's towers is a natural salt water swimming pool, also used as part of a range of treatments.

◁ **SEASIDE SPA**
The clinic at the delightful 19th-century seaside town of Sopot is perfectly located right by the sandy beach and the pier.

▷ **HAND PUMP**
The traditional way of filling your glass, the old fashioned hand-pump, is a feature of some Polish spa towns – many are still in working order although some are purely decorative.

Each spa resort has a water source with a different mineral profile. Some spas such as Kudowa Zdrój in the south of Poland have three separate water sources, each offering variations on the theme, including hydro-carbon-calcium-soda, chalybeate and boron, which is quite a mouthful in more ways than one. Numerous spas also bottle and distribute their waters throughout Poland. Ciechocinek for example has been bottling the Krystynka brand since 1903, and the Kujawianka brand since 1962. Similarly, the Kołobrzeg spa markets the Perła Bałtyku (Pearl of the Baltic) mineral water, while Polanica Zdrój is the source of Staropolanka (Old Polish). Other spas market mineral water under their own name, such as Kryniczanka, bottled since 1808 in the spa town of Krynica.

WROCŁAW AND LOWER SILESIA

Wrocław's long and turbulent history provides a packed sightseeing itinerary which contrasts with the relaxed scenic beauty of the surrounding Lower Silesian countryside

Map
city: 268
area: 274

Warsaw

Wrocław

The most important city in Silesia, Wrocław is characterised by broad thoroughfares and imposing buildings, which are handsome and robust rather than beautiful. And despite the city's varied architecture, with definitive examples of every genre, there is a distinct sense of harmony. This is not due to some master plan, but to their character: big, bold and beckoning. The buildings make you want to look longer and closer. Arriving in Wrocław by train means you get the picture straight away. The railway station's late 19th-century neo-Gothic white stucco building, with various gables, turrets and castellations, houses a main hall that is 200 metres (650 ft) long. But then it was built as one of the largest stations in Central and Eastern Europe.

And yet, even within the city it is easy to escape, with quiet walks through parks or riverside greenery, and around the city's islets, linked by small bridges.

Changing rulers and artistic heyday

Wrocław's location, close to the borders with both Germany and the Czech Republic, is one reason why the city frequently changed hands, and nationalities, during its long history.

Wrocław dates from the 9th century, with the earliest settlement established on small islands within the River Odra by a Slavonic tribe called the Sężanie. This settlement was already recorded in the 9th century by the so-called "Bavarian Geographer". During the 10th century this developed into a Slavic trading post, benefiting from its advantageous position on the routes between western Europe and Russia and between the Baltic and Mediterranean.

Briefly taken over by a 10th-century Bohemian prince called Wrotisłav, after whom the city takes its name, the Piast prince who became the Polish King Mieszko I incorporated Silesia into Poland in AD 990. In the year 1000 the first Silesian episcopal seat was founded in Wrocław. The town recovered quickly from the Tartar invasion in 1241, and in 1259 became the capital of a Piast dukedom. After joining the Hanseatic League, Wrocław prospered during the 14th and 15th centuries under Bohemian and then Austrian rule, developing into one of Central and Eastern Europe's largest cities.

The city's varied architecture reflects its varied rulers. Romanesque dominated during the Piast era, with Gothic established by the Bohemians, which includes the magnificent late-Gothic Town Hall. The Austrian Habsburg dynasty ruled during the Baroque, with Silesia coming under 200 years of Prussian rule during the partitions of Poland, and becoming part of Germany between the two world wars. During this

LEFT: ornately decorated house in Wrocław's market square.
BELOW: statue of Alexander Fredro.

period the painter Adolph von Menzel (1815–1905) and Ferdinand Lassalle (1825–74), the founder of social democracy, lived in Breslau, the German name for Wrocław.

An industrial centre

In 1939, with a population of 700,000, **Wrocław ❶** was one of the Third Reich's largest cities. However, 75 percent of the town, including many historic buildings and monuments, were destroyed during World War II, with a massive rebuilding programme beginning in May 1945 within days of the Polish authorities regaining control of the city. Having expelled the German population, the city was resettled by Poles from Polish territories which had, in turn, been lost to the Ukraine. With a current population of 640,000, Wrocław is now Poland's fourth largest city, with the university one of Poland's most historic and prestigious. Together with ten further education colleges this also ensures a high youth quota, and the inevitable accompaniment of student and alternative cultures. Meanwhile the city's cultural events include the annual Festival of Polish Contemporary Music (February), Jazz on the Odra festival (May), and the Festival of Modern Polish Plays (June).

Ostrów Tumski

During the 9th century, the earliest settlement was established on what is now **Ostrów Tumski** (Cathedral Island). Around 1000 the episcopal church was built here and, until the Tartar attack of 1241, this was also the site of the Piast dukes' original residence. Ostrów Tumski continues to be the city's spiritual centre, with several churches, and although it ceased technically to be an island, after a tributary of the River Oder was filled in during the 19th century, Ostrów Tumski continues to feel isolated from the bustle of the city. An evening stroll is particularly delightful, with gas lamps still lit to illuminate the views.

The **Katedra Św. Jana Chrzciciela** (Cathedral of St John the Baptist) Ⓐ (open daily 10am–3pm), dating from the 13th century, is the largest and most important church on Ostrów Tumski. The three chapels in the ambulatory provide contrasting styles: the Italianate Baroque of St Elizabeth's; the Gothic chapel of Our Lady Mary; and the Duke's Chapel, designed by the Viennese master architect Fischer von Erlach. Other outstanding features include an impressive Renaissance stone portal, a triple-winged altarpiece dating from 1522, and an alabaster pulpit.

To the right of the cathedral's main portal stands the neoclassical **Pałac Arcybiskupa** (Archbishop's Palace) Ⓑ, now the home of the Papal Institute of Theology. It is the first in a series of historic buildings along Katedralna ("Cathedral street"). The archbishop now resides at Number 11 Katedralna. The second largest church on Ostrów Tumski is the Gothic **Kościół Św. Krzyżai Św. Bartolomeja** (Church of the Holy Cross and St Bartholomew) Ⓒ (open daily), also an architectural rarity. The building actually comprises two churches. The elegantly appointed Gothic Kościół Św. Krzyża (Church of the Holy Cross) is on the ground floor. Meanwhile, the crypt houses the Greek-Catholic (Uniate) Church of St Bartholomew, which is the final resting place for two of Wrocław's most renowned bishops, Nanker and Lubusz.

The impressive **Most Tumski** (Cathedral Bridge) Ⓓ was constructed from iron in 1889. The bridge displays figures of St Hedwig and John the Baptist and links Ostrów Tumski with the **Wyspa Piaskowa** (Sand Island).

Maps
City: 268
Area: 274

Cathedral Bridge was constructed at the end of the 19th century. It joins Cathedral Island to the Old Town.

BELOW: restored houses in the marketplace at Wrocław.

Church of St Mary on the Sand has a Piast vault (the aisles have an asymmetrical tripartite rib) which is only seen in this region.

BELOW: the Aula Leopoldina of Wrocław University.

Wypsa Piaskowa is dominated by the Gothic **Kościół NMP na Piasku** (Church of St Mary on the Sand) ❸ (open daily). Built over a 12th-century Romanesque chapel, this lofty edifice has an interesting 16th-century icon of the Blessed Virgin Mary in the north aisle, originating from east Poland.

Around the Old Town

A monumental white Baroque façade, dating from 1811, forms the main building of the **Uniwersytet** (University) ❺ (open Mon, Tues, Thurs, Sun 10am–3.30pm; entrance fee). Situated on the leafy banks overlooking the River Oder, it was established on the site of a medieval castle which guarded the ford across the river. The façade's elegant Astronomical Tower is crowned by a globe, encircled by statues personifying the four academic sciences: law, theology, astronomy and medicine. The interiors are all eclipsed by the magnificent Aula Leopoldina Assembly Hall (pl Uniwersytecki 1; tel: 340 22 71; open Thurs–Tues; entrance fee). This is one of Poland's most beautiful Baroque halls, where the flamboyant architectural details, *trompe l'oeil* paintings, frescos and sculptures all harmonise perfectly. Nearby is the Baroque **Biblioteka Ossolińskich** (Ossoliński Library) ❼ (tel: 344 44 71; entrance fee) erected on the site of a former Augustinian monastery. Its collection of illuminated manuscripts includes the Florentine publication of Dante's *Divine Comedy* of 1481 and original manuscripts of Polish writers such as Adam Mickiewicz and Henryk Sienkiewicz.

Passing the 19th-century red brick **Hala Targowa** (Covered Market) ❽ (open daily), formerly a tram depot, you can head to the **Muzeum Narodowe** (National Museum) ❶ (pl Powstanców Warszawy 5; tel: 342 56 46; open

Tues–Sun; entrance fee except Thurs). Overlooking the River Oder on one side and a wooded park on the other, this neo-Renaissance building dates from the 1880s. An extensive collection of Silesian art includes ultimate examples of Gothic, including a sarcophagus from the Church of the Holy Cross, bearing a Latin inscription: "Prince Henryk IV passed away in the year 1290 after years of superb leadership in Silesia, Kraków and Sandomierz." Reliefs on the side of the sarcophagus depict two eagles, representing the Polish crown and the principality of Silesia. There is also an extensive collection of Polish paintings from the 17th to 20th centuries, including plenty of modern, conceptual and avant garde Polish art.

A stroll across the **Park J. Słowackiego** (Słowacki Park) **J** (open daily) leads to an ugly modern building resembling a giant circus tent. Nevertheless, this purpose-built rotunda houses the city's most popular tourist attraction, the **Panorama Racławicka** (Panorama of the Battle of Racławice) **K** (Purkiniego 11; tel: 44 23 44; open daily; entrance fee). The exteriors are totally forgotten once you climb a circular staircase to the dome, which displays this painting in the round. Depicting the victorious battle won by Kościuszko's Polish army against Russian forces in 1793, it is 114 metres (370 ft) long and 15 metres (50 ft) high, and took nine months to complete. It is a truly spectacular painting: incredibly life-like and, despite the fact that you view it from a special platform, it is easy to become totally lost in the view and the historic struggle between opposing forces.

This genre of painting, hung in the round to heighten the three-dimensional qualities, was very popular during the 19th century, until overtaken by cinema. Painted in Łwów in 1893 by the artists Wojciech Kossak and Jan Styka to mark the 100th anniversary of the battle, it was first exhibited in Lwów (part of Poland between the two world wars). In 1939 it was put into storage, which is where it remained after the war – the symbolic significance of the painting being the struggle for independence. Only in 1980 when the Solidarity movement began to gain ground and could exert some pressure on the Communists, was it decided to restore the painting, which took five years.

Around the Market Square

After the Tartar invasion of 1241, a new town on the left bank of the Odra began to emerge. The **Stare Miasto** (Old Town) was laid out in a chequerboard style around the **Ratusz** (Town Hall) **L** (open Mon, Wed–Fri 10am–4pm, Sat 12am–6pm, Sun 10am–6pm, entrance fee except Wed), with the circular Kazimerza Wielkiego following the course of the town's original fortifications.

The Town Hall is one of the finest examples of Gothic in Central and Eastern Europe, while definitive of Silesian Gothic style. The flamboyant façade is decorated with tracery as well as fine carvings, with an arched roof crowned by a spire and featuring a turret on each corner. The central gable features an ornamental 16th-century astrological clock, with clocks on each façade of the spire too. Next-door cafés allow you to marvel at the façade at leisure.

Map on page 268

The entry to the Piwnica Świdnicka (the 13th century beer cellar) in Wrocław Town Hall.

BELOW: the Town Hall, Wrocław.

TIP

Some rooms in the Town Hall are used for temporary exhibitions, such as the highly successful Lego exhibition of famous buildings from around the world, popular with children.

Equally impressive interiors feature inlaid panelling, paintings and Renaissance portals, as well as The Grand Hall and the Prince's Room. The **Muzeum Historyczne** (Historical Museum) is housed in the Town Hall's upper floors, while the 15th-century cellar, **Piwnica Świdnicka** serves local beers including the eponymous Świdnicki beer.

The **Rynek** (Market Square) is truly extraordinary, for the range of architectural styles and the sheer scope, number and layout of the buildings. Unusually, the Town Hall is not situated in the centre but on one edge of the Market Square. The prime location would be too much for one building, and indeed it is shared by a group of buildings arranged as an "inner square". One side of this inner square is taken up by the Nowy Ratusz (New Town Hall), which continues the Gothic theme but is an example of more subtle 19th-century neo-Gothic. Moreover, there are more buildings within the inner square, with a few alleyways providing access to what were originally artisans' workshops.

The perimeter of the Market Square includes numerous burghers' houses, with Numbers 2–11 dating from the 13th century. Pod Gryfami ("Under the Griffins") at Number 2 has an amazing portal with a crest bearing griffins, while a series of griffins also ascend the top five storeys of this building in a *tour-de-force* of Mannerism.

The southwest corner of the Market Square opens onto another market square, **Plac Solny** Ⓜ which is lined with Renaissance buildings and the early 19th-century neo-Gothic Nowy Giełda (New Stock Exchange). In addition to the Market Square's civic buildings, the Gothic **Kościół Św. Elżbiety** (St Elizabeth's Church) Ⓝ, in the northwest corner, dates from the 14th century. The 86-metre (282-ft) tower makes this the city's tallest church.

BELOW: the view from the top of the town hall tower.

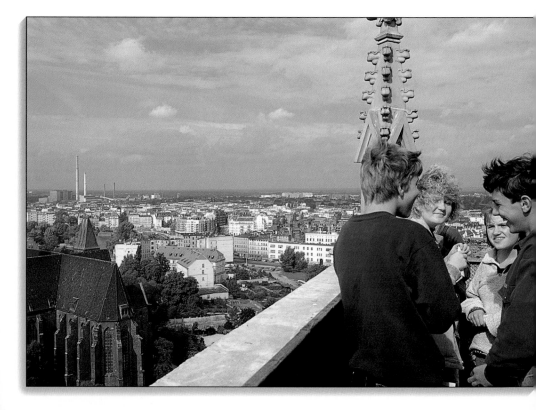

The most outstanding feature of **Kościół Św. Marii Magdaleny** (Church of St Mary Magdalene) is something older rather than taller, in nearby Szewska. This triple-naved Gothic basilica has a 12th-century Romanesque portal, from a Benedictine abbey formerly in the vicinity, which was built into the south wall during the 16th century.

For a change of ambience, from secular to civic, and from Gothic to multi-period, continue to **Świdnicka** ℗. This is the city's principal thoroughfare, just as it has been since the mid-13th century. It offers prime shopping opportunities, with department stores and boutiques, while wide pavements and the mostly pedestrianised street provides plenty of space for street traders, and performers. It is also one of the city's most architecturally varied streets, the oldest building being the 14th-century **Church of St Dorothy**. The elegant neo-classical **Opera House** ℚ was completed in 1840, while the Centrum Department Store dates from the 1920s. Its many other department store rivals date only from the 1990s.

The former palace of the Spaetgen family houses the **Muzeum Etnograficzne** (Museum of Mankind) ℝ (Kazimierza Wielkiego 33; open Tues–Sun; entrance fee) with a large collection of dolls dressed in various national costumes. Next door is the **Muzeum Archaeologiczne** (Archaeological Museum). Housed in the city's former arsenal, dating from the 15th century, it is encircled by medieval fortifications, and is now predominantly an arms and weapons museum (open Tues–Sun; entrance fee).

North of Wrocław

One of the oldest Silesian towns**, Oleśnica** ❷ stands on a hill 30 km (19 miles) northeast of Wrocław. It was the seat of the Oleśnica dukes between the 14th and

Map
city: 268
area: 274

On H Modrzejewska, is one of Poland's most renowned hotels, the Monopol. Built in 1892 in the Seccesionist style, it is full of exquisite original features, though in need of renovation to restore its former splendour, when guests such as Marlene Dietrich stayed there.

BELOW: the wooden Church of Peace in Świdnicka.

18th centuries, with the 14th-century castle one of Poland's most beautiful and best preserved Renaissance examples. In addition to an entrance gate decorated with heraldic motifs, the inner courtyard features arcaded galleries.

Trzebnica ❸ is situated in a shallow valley of the Wzgórze Trzebnickie (Trzebnickie Hills) north of Wrocław. The mild climate means that grapevines were cultivated here during the Middle Ages. The town is also renowned for its mineral springs, though the principal reason for visiting is the monastic complex of the former **Cistercian Abbey**. Founded in 1202 by Prince Henryk Brodaty (Henry the Bearded), the church was built around a Romanesque basilica and is now one of Poland's most precious monuments. The showpiece in the basilica is the early-Gothic Chapel of St Jadwiga to the right of the chancel. It was built in 1680 in memory of Princess Jadwiga, wife of the founder. Canonised in 1267 for contributing to the advent of Christianity and numerous charitable works, she is the patron saint of Silesia. On 15 October every year pilgrims arrive to celebrate St Jadwiga's feast day, just as they have done for centuries.

West of Wrocław

Środa Śląka ❹ is one of the most historic settlements on the trade route between Germany and Russia. Its medieval town centre has been preserved, with particular points of interest being the unusual, oval-shaped marketplace, fragments of the town walls and the Parish Church of St Andrew, which has retained its late-Gothic interiors, despite repeated alterations.

About 50 km (31 miles) north-west of Wrocław is the village of **Lubiąż**, where the large Baroque monastery complex was the first Cisterican settlement in Silesia. The oldest of the monastery churches, which dates from the 13th century, was the first of its kind to be built in brick, and the largest of its kind in Europe. The main building measures 223 metres (724 ft) in length, and is one of the finest examples of Baroque. Michael Willmann, a famous painter and a team of artists were commissioned to work on the project. Another fine example of Baroque is the three-aisle St Walenty church, dating from the 1740s.

Further along the Odra, near the confluence with the River Kaczawa lies **Prochowice**, where the walls of a ruined 13th-century castle have survived more or less intact. As early as the 10th century, **Głogów 5**, about 40 km (25 miles) upstream, was the seat of the Piast princes and one of Poland's strongest fortress towns. After 1745, the town played a key role in Prussia's military strategy. Destroyed during World War II, the late Baroque church and the Corpus Christi College, the work of the Italian architect Simonetti, were subsequently rebuilt. So, too, was the town's most important monument, the **Piasts' Castle**, detailed in the town's Archaeological and Historical Museum (open Wed–Sun; entrance fee). Princes of the Piast dynasty resided here from the 13th century, but the current style of the castle reverts to its Baroque 17th-century incarnation, except for the cylindrical Gothic tower.

Since 1957 the area between Legnica and Głogów has been the centre of the region's copper industry, but the cost to the environment has been disastrous. Atmospheric pollution is high and this is now regarded as one of the most blighted areas in Poland. At the heart of this region lies the former trading settlement of **Lubin**, a charming town with several examples of Gothic architecture, fragments of town wall, a fortified tower, a church and castle ruins.

The copper industry brought rapid economic expansion to **Legnica 6**, (which can be followed in the town's Copper Museum), but the town is also renowned

Map on page 274

BELOW: examples of typical Silesian woodcarving.

for producing some of the country's finest pianos, and for once having the largest garrison of the Red Army in Poland. Legnica was originally the capital of the Trzbovites, a Slavic tribe, before becoming a Polish episcopal seat and, due to its favourable location on the River Kaczawa, an important trading centre. As the capital of the Piast duchy until the 17th century, the town has some suitably grand architecture. The duke's early Gothic Castle also has Romanesque elements and a Renaissance portal by Johannes von Amberg. After a serious fire in 1835, it was refurbished according to a design by Karl-Friedrich Schinkel, the architect responsible for many of Berlin's neo-classical buildings.

The delightful Old Town includes the Academy for the Nobility and the "herring" tenement houses, so-called because of their narrow stature. Other important buildings are the Church of SS Peter and Paul, principally Gothic with a Romanesque font, and the former presbytery of the Baroque **Church of St John**, which contains the Mausoleum of the Legnica and Brzeg Piasts.

Not far from Legnica is **Legnickie Pole**. This was the scene of a fierce battle in 1241, when an army composed of Silesian knights fought bitterly against the Tartars. The mother of Henryk II the God-fearing, who led the European army and was killed in battle, founded a church in honour of her son. Subsequently, it was in her memory that the Benedictine Abbey, comprising the Church of St Jadwiga was founded in the 18th century. The vaults of the Baroque church, the work of Kilian Ignaz Dientzenshofer, are decorated with frescos by the Bavarian master Cosmas Damian Asam.

In the town of **Chojnów** stands a Renaissance palace, built during the reign of the Prussian King Friedrich III. Subsequently extended, it now houses a museum. You can also see a Gothic church and the impressive remains of medieval fortifications.

BELOW:
craftsman at work.

From the 12th century onwards the town of **Złotoryja** prospered from the mining of local gold deposits. Once these had been exhausted, the inhabitants began producing textiles instead. A number of medieval buildings have survived: fragments of the original town walls, including a bastion, the Romanesque Gothic Parish Church of the Virgin Mary, the Church of St Hedwig and the Gothic-Baroque Franciscan monastery.

Świdnica-Jawór region

Jawor was the capital of the Świdnica-Jawór duchy, ruled by the Piasts for a short period during the 14th century, and the Market Square is still overlooked by imposing town residences. A Regional Museum is housed in the Franciscan Monastery. The **Protestant Church of Peace** is also worth seeing for its half-timbered exteriors, and wooden interiors hung with unusual paintings dating from 1710.

Perched on top of a basalt hill is the town of **Strzegom**, one of Silesia's oldest settlements. Even before the birth of Christ there was a castle here, which was subsequently used by the Poles as a fortress. The medieval **Church of SS Peter and Paul** features elaborately carved portals with gable windows, and Mannerist interiors. Until 1456, the Church of St Barbara was a Jewish synagogue. Beyond the original town walls, with their ancient Beak Bastion, lie numerous historic quarries and mines which were once an important source of basalt and granite.

In the centre of the medieval town of **Bolków** on the Nysa Szalona stands Poland's oldest stone castle (13th-century), with a tower that provides a fine view over the surrounding region. The marketplace also occupies the highest point of a hill, where you can stroll beneath historic arcades, past the Town Hall and the Parish Church of St Jadwiga.

Situated on the Bystrzyca river, **Świdnica ❼** was originally a fishing settlement that developed into a trading centre from the 12th century, being on the key route between Kiev and Germany. Between the 13th and 14th centuries it was the capital of the Piast's Świdnica-Jawór duchy (which extended to the suburbs of present-day Berlin) and developed into a fortified town. During the 15th and 16th centuries, under the Piast dynasty, the town was renowned for linen and brewing beer (with grapevines also cultivated around the town).

Świdnica's **Market Square** is surrounded by 16th- to 18th-century burghers' houses, while the town walls are as decorative as they are defensive, bearing beautiful stone sculptures. The Church of SS Stanisław and Wacław, a blend of Gothic and Baroque, has the highest church tower in Silesia (100 metres/340 ft), and one of the most splendid interiors, with an ornate organ and various sculptures and paintings.

In the former cemetery stands the beautiful half-timbered **Evangelical Church of Peace**. This dates from the end of the Thirty Years War in 1648, when Silesian Protestants were allowed to build three "churches of peace" in Świdnicka, Jawor and Głogów (this last church has not survived). However, this included significant restrictions: the churches had to be located outside the

Map on page 274

Near the town of Bolków is the former concentration camp of Rogoxnica. It is now a mausoleum and an exhibition on the site remembers the victims of crimes committed here by the Nazis.

BELOW: flowers and shutters of a house neighbouring the Wang Church.

Details of hunting frieze on a door in Brzeg.

town, they could not be constructed from stone or have a tower, and must be completed within a year. Even these "concessions" were grudgingly made by the Habsburg authorities (Silesia was then part of the Austro-Hungarian Empire). Nevertheless, this didn't mean modest churches – far from it. Gilded interiors, wooden balconies, frescos and an imposing altar create a splendid effect, within a fascinating half-timbered façade.

The **Scenic Park of Ślęża,** criss-crossed by mountain streams flowing into the Ślęża, which then joins the Odra northwest of Wrocław, contains the **Góra Ślęża**, the highest peak (720 metres/2,360 ft) in Poland north of the Sudety mountains. Two thousand years ago this isolated mountain rising from an immense plateau became a sacred site for the Slenzane (an early Slav tribe), who performed pagan rites on the peak. Remains of sculptures can still be seen here, while clearly marked tourist trails lead to archaeological digs in the area, yielding stone dykes and cult statues.

Sacred objects and sculptures dating from the 3rd to 1st centuries BC can also be seen in the museum in **Sobótka**, a small town situated at the foot of the Góra Ślęża. The town's other attractions, such as the 14th-century churches of St Anna and St Jacob, ensure that it's a popular destination all year, particularly as a weekend break from Wrocław.

South from Wrocław

Between the rivers Odra and Oława, to the southeast of Wrocław, lies the former episcopal town of **Oława**. By the marketplace is a 14th-century Town Hall, later converted into neoclassical by the renowned Berlin architect, Karl-Friedrich Schinkel. **Brzeg**, further south, has a superb Renaissance castle housing the

Museum of the Silesian Piasts (open Tues–Sat; entrance fee). This dynasty was instrumental in the history of lower Silesia. Resembling the Wawel in Kraków (*see page 209*), the castle features an arcaded courtyard. There is more Renaissance architecture to be seen in the Market Square, with a fine Town Hall, while a delightful park incorporates the medieval town walls.

The foothills of the Sudeten mountains begin around **Strzelin**, about 45 km (28 miles) south of Wrocław, and these hills provide most of Poland's granite. Within the town, the **Church of St Gotthard**, a Romanesque rotunda dating from the 12th century, certainly merits a visit.

Heading southwest, **Henryków ⓽** is one of Silesia's oldest Cistercian monasteries, founded by Henryk Brodaty in the 13th century. This complex includes the Monastery Church of St Mary, with Gothic and Baroque features that include elaborately carved monks' stalls, valuable sculptures and paintings. The **Henrykówa Book**, Poland's oldest manuscript containing the earliest example of written Polish, was completed in the abbey during the 13th century. In the abbey garden is the largest yew tree in Poland – the trunk measures 12 metres (39 ft) in diameter.

Ziębice, at the source of the River Oława, has retained its medieval town centre and fortifications. The Church of St George has fascinating interiors reflecting various architectural styles. Next to the former monastery hospital stands the Church of SS Peter and Paul, laid out in the shape of a Greek cross.

On the edge of the **Kotlina Kłodzka** (Kłodzko Basin) is the town of **Ząbkowice Śląskie**, renowned for its glassworks. The town's bastions and fortified towers, the Gothic Church of St Anna and the Dominican Monastery are among the historic attractions. Of Poland's first Renaissance palace only ruins

Map on page 274

BELOW: landscape at Ogorzelecon near Jelenia Góra.

now remain, with a romantic cloistered courtyard. The former Cistercian monastery is worth visiting in **Kamieniec Ząbkowicki**, together with the ruined neo-Gothic **Hohenzollern Palace**, poignantly set on a hill within an English-style park. Built between 1838–63 by Karl-Friedrich Schinkel, this palace was one of the final but also most remarkable works by this renowned Berlin architect. The ruins were destroyed by fire during World War II, but a British-based Polish émigré has now pledged to restore the palace.

The Kłodzko region provides a natural habitat for the protected yellow European globe plant, known as the "Kłodzko rose", which flowers in June on mountain meadows.

On the border between Silesia and Bohemia at the foot of the mid-range Sudetens in the Nysa Kłodzka valley lies the beautiful episcopal town of **Bardo**. In the early Middle Ages, pilgrims came to the town in large numbers to pay homage to the Virgin Mary, and the single-nave Baroque church contains a wood-carving as well as a Gothic sculpture of *Our Lady of Sorrows*.

Around Kłodzko

Adjoining the foothills of the Sudeten is the large basin through which the Nysa Kłodzka, Bystrzyca, Ścinawka and Biała Lądecka rivers flow. At the centre of this basin is **Kłodzko ❾**, founded in 1223. Its oldest feature is the Gothic stone bridge, built around 1390 and decorated with Baroque reliefs. There is also a citadel, as well as three large monasteries belonging to the Franciscans, the Order of St John and the Jesuits. The Franciscan St Mary's Church is decorated with paintings and frescos by the the Prague maestro Scheffler. A feature of the twin-towered parish church is the Baroque altar designed by Tausch.

The Kłodzko region is a beautiful part of Silesia surrounded by forest-covered mountains. Other aspects of the region's natural beauty are the **Jaskinia Niedźwiedzia** (the "Bear Cave") with almost 2 km (1 mile) of tunnels, as well as the labyrinths and fascinating rock formations known as **Błędne Skały** ("Erratic Rocks"). However, this region is best known for its mineral water springs. The earliest recorded mention of these waters' medicinal benefits date from 1272, with the earliest spas established during the 17th century in the towns of Polanica, Duszniki, Kudowa and Ladek.

The oldest of the Sudeten spas, **Lądek-Zdrój**, was known for its curative mineral springs even before it was granted a town charter in 1282. The spa of Kudowa-Zdrój is on the Czech border, with nearby Czerna having a macabre Baroque chapel, the floor and walls of which are covered with some 3,000 human skulls.

Chopin stayed in **Duszniki-Zdrój ❿**, one of the most beautiful spas on his journey through Poland that eventually led to his permanent exile in Paris. To commemorate the visit the town holds an annual Chopin Festival. The 17th-century paper mill, where some fine frescos were recently discovered, is now a museum devoted to the history of paper production, for which the town was once known. Another attraction in this area is **Wambierzyce**, at the foot of Góry Stołowe. On a hill in the centre of the town, a staircase leads up to a monumental Baroque basilica and a group of calvary chapels which has been the site of pilgrimages since 1218. Near the church is a delightful exhibition of mechanical Christmas cribs.

BELOW: Kłodzko on the River Neisse.

Westwards along the Sudetens

Wałbrzych, the largest town in the region, has little to offer tourists, being an important industrial and mining centre. However, the town does have a neo-classical Evangelical Church with an oval galleried interior, designed by K.G. Langhans, whose work includes the Brandenburg Gate in Berlin. The Museum of Industry and Technology covers mining installations, minerals, fossils and porcelain. Soon after the Communist government was ousted, several large industrial plants were closed in the area, and in parts the landscape makes a pitiful sight, though the scenery beneath the Sudetens in the west makes a marked contrast.

Map on page 274

Moreover, not far from the outskirts of Wałbrzych is Silesia's largest castle, **Książ** ⓫ (open daily; entrance fee). Constructed by Bolko I, the prince of Świdnica in the 13th century, the castle is set in a park surrounded by multicoloured rhododendron bushes, while a ravine with a small river isolates the castle on three sides. Up until the 15th century the palace belonged to the Piasts of Świdnica, and later to the German Hochberg family, who converted the castle into a Baroque citadel. The Nazis began to convert the building into a headquarters for Adolf Hitler, and by excavating a giant bunker destroyed parts of the original building. However, remains of the medieval stone tower and the Renaissance wing have survived, while the museum's collection includes ceramic tiles and decorative glassware. An English-style garden laid out on the slopes around the palace, planted with exotic trees, is a very pleasant place for a stroll. Among various terraces in this garden is the Water Terrace, with a grand total of 27 fountains.

The Town Hall in Jelenia Góra stands out among the pastel-toned façades of the burghers' houses.

BELOW: preparations for Corpus Christi in Krzeszów.

Of special interest in **Kamienna Góra** are the ruins of a large Renaissance palace, a row of Baroque houses with arcades on the Market Square, and an interesting exhibition detailing the history of weaving in the town's small Museum of the Silesian Textile Industry.

The Cistercian abbey of **Krzeszów** ⓬ is one of the most outstanding examples of late Baroque architecture in Silesia. Behind the ornamental and monumental façade, with its twin towers, the white and gold interiors are laid out in a circular manner, decorated with wall-paintings, canvases and sculptures. It is thought that the renowned architect, Kilian Ignaz Dientzenhofer, was involved in the initial work. The neighbouring Church of St Joseph is famed for its frescos, attributed to Michael Willman, a painter often referred to as the Silesian Rembrandt.

In nearby **Chełmsko Śląskie**, a street of centuries-old weavers' cottages has been preserved, among them the House of the Twelve Apostles. The River Bóbr and its tributaries, the Kamienna and the Łomnica, flow through the densely populated and heavily industrialised area of **Kotlina Jeleniogórska**. The former episcopal town of **Jelenia Góra** ⓭, situated in a low valley surrounded by mountains, is now the region's administrative and cultural centre. From the Middle Ages it was an important regional trading centre, and developed rapidly as it became industrialised. But the town has also long been a major tourist attraction, with numerous historic sights.

At the centre of Jelenia Góra is the Market Square with its imposing **Town Hall** dating from the 17th century, surrounded by colourful arcaded burghers' houses of the same period. An unusual feature of the **Grace Church** is not so much the huge 18th-century organ, but the theatrical three-storeyed gallery. The Parish Church of St Erasmus and St Pancras has a Renaissance tower, subsequently refashioned in a Baroque style, while the impressive main altar is the work of two Norwegian sculptors, Weisfeld and Kretschmer. Beyond the fragments of the medieval town walls stands the Protestant **Church of the Holy Cross**, dating from 1718, which was, designed by the Swedish architect Franz. The interior is decorated with frescos painted by the Prague master A. F. Schaffler, assisted by local artist J. F. Hoffmann. There is also a museum exhibiting 17th- and 18th-century glass, ranging from everyday functional glassware to works of art.

The spa town of **Cieplice**, one of Poland's most historic, now falls within Jelenia Góra's town boundaries. It once belonged to the Order of St John, and records from 1281 show that the monks used waters from hot sulphur springs to treat various illnesses such as skin complaints. During the 18th- and 19th-century Cieplice was established as an essential rendezvous for the fashionable and wealthy, who easily outnumbered the minority of genuine patients looking for a cure. Of special interest are the monastery, with its Church of St John the Baptist, the former Schaffgotsch Family Palace dating from the late 18th-century, and a park housing the **Museum of Nature** (open Tues–Sun; entrance fee), with an extensive collection of birds and butterflies. The town also has a reputation for producing excellent cut glass, as well as being a centre for manufacturing paper. The town of **Lwówek Śląski** on the River Bóbr, dates from 1217. The first town on Polish soil to adopt the Magdeburg laws, it was formerly a centre of gold mining. Some splendid Gothic monuments give the town its essential character, including well-preserved defensive walls and turrets, the twin-towered Church of the Assumption with superb portals, and the Town Hall, which incorporates Renaissance elements and has a vaulted vestibule.

BELOW:
a performance of a religious play outside the Wang wooden church.

The Karkonosze

The main mountain range, the **Karkonosze**, sometimes known by its German name, the Riesengebirge (meaning Giant Mountains), stretches for 36 km (22 miles) between **Przełęcz Szklarska** (885 metres/ 2,900 ft) in the west and **Przełęcz Kowarska** (727 metres/2,384 ft) in the east. These mountains are known for their unusual rock formations and two lakes **Mały and Duży Staw** ("Large" and "Small" lakes) which were formed in the Ice Age, as well as romantic waterfalls, alpine meadows and peat-bogs.

The highest mountain is the **Śnieżka** (1,602 metres/ 5,254 ft), followed by the Szyszak and the Szrenica, with the peak of Śnieżka also the site of two man-made features: St Laurentius' Chapel dating from the 16th century and, dating from the 1960s, the saucer-shaped meteorological observatories. Reaching the top of this mountain doesn't necessarily entail a long hike, as a chair-lift can do much of the work for you.

Pines and mountain ash grow up to a level of 1,250 metres (4,000 ft). Beneath this the vegetation consists of dwarf pines and Carpathian birches. Deer, mouflons and owls are plentiful on the hillsides. The **Karkonosze National Park** covers an area of 5.5 hectares (13 acres) and is well supplied with guesthouses for those wishing to explore it on foot. However, some of the thickly wooded mountain slopes have been affected by atmospheric pollution, largely caused by power plants on the Czech side and in what was the German Democratic Republic. **Szklarska Poręba**, at the foot of **Mount Szrenica**, occupies a picturesque spot on the banks of the Kamienna. Skiers can reach the pistes on the nearby **Szrenica** via chair lifts, leading to trails catering for various standards of expertise. Moreover, the microclimate means that the snow often remains here until the end of April.

The most popular skiing and holiday resort is **Karpacz ⑭**, at the foot of Śnieżka mountain. This makes a good starting point for excursions and skiing along various trails in the Karkonosze, with the town's cultural attractions including the Toy Museum exhibiting dolls from all over the world. In the Karpacz Górny district is the **Wang**, a 13th-century wooden church, which was sold by the village of Wang in Norway at the beginning of the 19th century, because the congregation had become too big for the church. Dismantled, it was brought here in sections and reassembled in 1842. It is a traditional Norwegian "*stave*" church, with a vast sloping roof, a design that was typical in Norway during the 12th and 13th centuries. Two dragon's heads looking down from the gable are claimed to be made from Viking long ships. Some of the beams feature detailed carvings of mythical creatures, while carved figures on the portal narrate a Nordic saga. ❑

An example of Lazarus carving at the Wang Church.

BELOW: Wang Church interior.

WIELKOPOLSKA – GREATER POLAND

Wielkopolska isn't famous for its scenery, but its fascinating history makes up for anything it lacks in landscape

One of Poland's largest provinces, Wielkopolska, literally "Great Poland", is also the most historic. Situated in the west of the country, along the central and lower reaches of the River Warta (the main tributary of the Oder), Wielkopolska provided the foundation for the first sovereign state of Poland.

It was the Piast dynasty who united the scattered territories of the Polan tribe into a single dominion, which they ruled from Lednica, between Poznań and Gniezno.

Gniezno subsequently became the capital of this state, and also the centre of Catholicism. The archdiocese founded in the town in 1000 resulted in the magnificent cathedral. This is an important sacral building, exemplifying Romanesque architecture, which is also intrinsically linked with the evolution of the early state of Poland. Although Kraków and then Warsaw assumed Gniezno's role as the capital city of the country, Gniezno is still considered to be the spiritual centre of Poland.

The region's principal city, Poznań, has always been an important trading centre, and continues this historic role by hosting the largest trade fairs in Central and Eastern Europe. An attractive city to visit, and one of Poland's greenest, Poznań also makes a good base from which to tour the surrounding countryside.

Among the attractions within easy reach of the city are the Lednica Piast Museum, which includes the remains of the Piast's ducal castle, the Gothic Kórnik Palace, the French Renaissance Gołuchów Palace, and the neoclassical Rogalin Palace, which are all museums set in magnificent parks. And if you want to get away from it all there are plenty of secluded villages, lakes and forests in which to enjoy tranquillity and natural beauty. ❏

PRECEDING PAGES: the Cathedral Island in Wrocław.
LEFT: the early Slavic settlement of Biskupin.

POZNAŃ

*The industrial centre and trade-fair city of Poznań comes second
only to Warsaw in Western Poland from an economic,
cultural and historical point of view*

Map
on page
290–91

Warsaw
Poznań

Poznań divides quite naturally into four equally interesting sections, that can
easily be navigated on foot, and which are never far from a park or some
other greenery. The most historic part of the city, Ostrów Tumski, is full
of Romanesque and Gothic architecture. The Old Town is characterised by
Renaissance and Baroque, while the "New Town" district contains 19th-century
neoclassical "statement" buildings. Further west is the most modern part of
town, with generic contemporary European architecture, spreading out past the
main railway station to the international trade halls, which host the largest international trade fairs in Central and Eastern Europe.

This combination ensures that the city has as many business visitors as
tourists, with an established infrastructure to handle both, and the town is
continually being smartened up – although it is very attractive it is not yet a
"showpiece" on the same level as Kraków. There are numerous business and
tourist hotels, which tend to be outside the historic centre, but these are in great
demand when the numerous trade fairs are on, so dates and accommodation
need to be checked well ahead.

LEFT: feeding the
birds in Poznań's
Old Town.
BELOW: a fountain
outside the
Renaissance
Town Hall.

The history of Poznań

As the capital of the Wielkopolska (Greater Poland)
region, in the centre of western Poland, Poznań is a
thriving industrial and commercial hub, with a long
history as a major trading centre.

One of Poland's oldest cities, Poznań dates from
the 9th century, when a fortified settlement was established on an island in the River Warta. As this
expanded it became the main capital of the Polish
state, Polonie, in the late 10th century, which also
included Gniezno and the surrounding region (*see
page 301*). Duke Mieszko I, later Poland's first king,
was baptised here in 966, converting the Slavs from
pagans to Christians, and Poznań became a bishopric
in 968. In 1253 Poznań was granted its town charter
under the Magdeburg Laws.

As trade flourished the town prospered, particularly
during the 16th century, with Poznań a key "transit
point" on numerous European trade routes: from western Europe to Russia and Lithuania, and from the
Balkans to Scandinavia. However the Swedish invasion in the 17th century devastated the city, and during the partitions Wielkopolska, together with Silesia,
was annexed by Prussia. In towns and villages patriotic organisations were formed to resist the "Germanisation" policies being actively exerted on the
region. Poznań played an important part in the battle
for Poland's full independence, with the Wielkopolska
Uprising, which began in Poznań on 27 December

1918, overthrowing the Prussians (*see page 37*). Wielkopolska subsequently rejoined a newly-independent Poland. During World War II more than half of the city was destroyed, but a rebuilding and restructuring programme got underway immediately, and Poznań's population was soon twice its pre-war total. Since 1925 international trade fairs have been held in Poznań, which developed from the city's medieval tradition of holding a major midsummer fair. The main event, the Industry Fair, takes place in June, with ten additional specialist fairs, such as Salmed for medical equipment, Polagra (agricultural) and Multimedia. The reason for the success of these fairs is the "bridging" function they perform between Central and Eastern European markets, as well as their suitability for small and medium-sized companies.

In addition to the university, Poznań has ten institutes of Higher Education, a branch of the Polish Academy of Sciences and numerous scientific institutes, including the Western Institute which provides links between Poland's industry and the European Union, particularly Germany.

As well as historic churches and civic buildings, palaces and specialised museums, this highly cultured city has several theatres including the Teatr Narodowy (National Theatre), a Philharmonic Orchestra, three well-known boys' and male-voice choirs, not to mention hosting the renowned Henryk Wieniawski Violin Competition which takes place every five years.

The Baroque spires on the two towers of the Cathedral of SS Peter and Paul in Poznań were reconstructed after World War II.

Ostrów Tumski – Poznań's heart

The earliest settlement and site of Christian worship was established on Ostrów Tumski (Cathedral Island), the peninsula between the River Warta and the River Cybina, which continues to be the city's religious and spiritual centre. Just beyond the River Cybina is the late Romanesque **Kościół Św. Jana** (St John's Church) **Ⓐ** (open daily), one of the first brick-built churches in Poland. The neighbouring **Kościół Św. Małgorzaty** (St Margaret's Church) **Ⓑ** (open daily) stands in what was until the 18th century the independent municipality of Śródka, a district which has retained a distinct atmosphere.

Crossing the River Cybina to Ostrów Tumski, the most important of several sacred buildings is **Katedra Św. Piotra i Pawła** (Cathedral of SS Peter and Paul) **Ⓒ** (open daily). The foundations of the first Romanesque church built here in 968, and even pre-Romanesque fragments can be seen in the crypt, with the building continually extended and refurbished until the 16th century. Reconstructed after World War II, the cathedral now resembles a Gothic basilica with three naves and radiating towers. Two Baroque towers dominate the entrance, and while it is certainly imposing, this geometric façade is no preparation for the grandeur within. The Gothic main altar with a beautiful triptych dating from 1512, crafted in a Silesian workshop, is often cited as the most outstanding feature. But there are also 12 impressive chapels, including the magnificent neo-Byzantine Golden Chapel, dating from the 19th century, containing the tombs of the nation's founder and first king, Mieszko I, as well as his successor, Bolesław Chrobry. Polish rulers were buried here from the 10th to 13th centuries, which gives the cathedral immense national status.

Nearby are two churches, **Kościół Najswiętszej Mariji Panny** (Church of the Blessed Virgin Mary) **Ⓓ** (open daily), dating from the 15th century, which has survived entirely in its original form, and the early 14th century **Psałteria**, the house where cathedral choristers once lodged. Also near the cathedral on Mieszka I are the **Pałac Biskupow** (Bishop's Palace) and canons' homes. To the

Map on page 290–91

BELOW: Cathedral of SS Peter and Paul – the Golden Chapel.

The interior of Poznań's Parish Church has a painting hanging over the altar which details an episode from the life of Saint Stanisław.

BELOW: horse and cart in Poznań.

north stands a building that houses the present Lubrański Academy (1518), with an attractive arcaded courtyard, once the site of Poznań's first university. The neighbouring **Muzeum Archidiecezjalne** (Archdiocesan Museum) has an interesting collection of sacred art from the Wielkopolska region (ks Ignacego Posadzego 2; tel: 852 61 95; open Mon–Sat; entrance fee). The modern architecture of the adjoining seminary, where priests are trained to work in Polish émigré parishes around the world, is a sharp contrast to the other buildings in this historic part of the city.

Around the old town

In 1253 two Wielkopolska dukes, Przemyśl I and Bolesław Pobożny, founded a new town on the left bank of the River Warta. This revolved around what is now the **Stary Rynek** (Old Market Square), which is one of the finest medieval urban complexes in Poland.

The **Kościół Dominikanów** (Dominican Church) **E** (open daily) in Dominkańska is one of the city's finest churches. It was the Dominicans who introduced the techniques of Gothic brick architecture to Poland, and fragments of the original monastery and Rosary Chapel can still be seen in the south wing. Retaining an impressive Gothic brick portal, dating from the 13th century, the church was subsequently rebuilt in a magnificent Baroque style.

A 19th-century former Masonic Lodge houses the **Muzeum Etnograficzne** (Museum of Mankind) **F** (Grobla 25; tel: 852 30 06; open Tues–Wed, Fri–Sun; entrance fee except Fri). It doesn't take long to see a lot here, with an extensive but compact collection of folk arts and crafts from the Wielkopolska region, as well as the paraphernalia involved in traditional celebrations such as Easter.

Now acting as the principal church in the city, as well as being one of the finest Baroque churches in Eastern Europe, **Kościół Farny** (Parish Church) **G** (open daily) on Gołębia, was built by the Jesuits in the second half of the 17th century. Massive ornate columns lining the walls do not support the building, they are purely decorative which is typically Baroque. Being purely aesthetic and inspirational, and together with elaborate stucco work, the effect is as palatial as it is religious. The neighbouring building is the Jesuit College.

While Ostrów Tumski and both banks of the River Warta may seem dominated by churches, the Market Square is entirely a case of civic showmanship, with the Town Hall, ornate palaces and highly individual burghers' houses with polychrome decorations creating an impressive effect, particularly stunning when floodlit at night. By one corner of the Market Square is the **Muzeum Archeologiczne** (Archaeological Museum). The exhibits, ranging from the Stone Age to the Middle Ages, are housed in a beautifully restored former palace, which is also Poland's second oldest museum (Pałac Gorków, Wodna 27; tel: 852 82 51; open Tues–Sun; entrance fee). One of the city's most unusual museums is the **Muzeum Instrumentów Muzycznych** (Musical Instruments Museum) **H** (Stary Rynek 47; tel: 52 08 57; open Tues–Sun; entrance fee except Fri). Housed in a beautiful burgher's house which needn't take long to negotiate, there are more than 2,000 historic instruments from Poland and other parts of Europe, including a room dedicated to Chopin with pianos that he played. Even if you're not musical, the instruments are impressive for their craftsmanship alone, and qualify as works of art beyond their musical status. The most outstanding building on the Market Square is the **Ratusz** (Town Hall) **I**. Built between 1550–55, this is one of Europe's finest Renaissance buildings,

TIP

An annual highlight in Poznań's Market Square is the Swietojanski Fair (St John's Fair) in June, which sees colourful market stalls as well as street performers out in force.

BELOW: the Musical Instruments Museum, Poznań.

with the façade comprising three floors of arcaded loggias surmounted by a high ornamental attic and turrets, above which extends an ornamental tower. The exquisite harmony and unmistakeably Italianate style stem from the architect being Giovanni Quadro of Lugano. Original Renaissance interiors are also exhibits in themselves, particularly the splendid Great Hall's coffered ceiling resting on two impressive pillars (concerts are held in the hall during the summer), and the Courtroom with decorative portraits, while more portraits can be seen in the Royal Chamber.

The Town Hall also houses the **Muzeum Historii Miasta Poznania** (Historical Museum of the City of Poznań; tel: 852 56 13; open Fri–Wed; entrance fee except Fri). A daily attraction at noon sees two mechanical kid goats, made from metal, emerge from above the clock on the tower and playfully lock horns to the sound of a bugle call. Locals are just as enchanted by this as tourists. In front of the Town Hall is an ornate rococo fountain of Proserpinae, and a copy of the 16th-century pillory formerly used for floggings.

The Town Hall is one of several buildings in the central area of the Market Square, with fortunately only one "intrusion" in the form of a small 1960s-style "concrete block" tucked among historic neighbours. A terrace of arcaded 16th-century vendors' houses, from which herrings were sold, are smaller and simpler than the ornamental burghers' houses lining the square, but equally interesting, and street traders still vie in front of them for pole positions. Behind the Town Hall is the neoclassical white stucco single-storey Odwach (Guard House) housing the **Wielkopolskie Muzeum Historyczne** (Historical Museum of the Wielkopolskie region), which has various temporary exhibitions (Stary Rynek 3; tel: 852 94 64; open Tues–Sun; entrance fee). While this is a small

BELOW: the Town Hall in Poznań.

museum, with modest interiors and exhibits generally comprising documents, pictures, photographs and other ephemera, they provide a very personal insight into regional life and history. An exhibition of the region's officers killed in the Katyń massacre (*see page 50*) is particularly moving.

The life and works of the renowned Polish author, who won the Noble Prize for Literature in 1905 with *Quo Vadis*, are detailed in the eponymous **Muzeum Literackie Henryka Sienkiewicza** (Literary Museum dedicated to Henryk Sienkiewicz) ❶ (Stary Rynek 84; tel: 852 24 96; open Mon–Fri; entrance fee except Fri, reservations required for groups) Even if this author is unknown to you, his "museum home" is still worth visiting to see how this type of burgher's house was decorated at the beginning of the 20th century and to gain some idea of what life was like for its resident.

Being the heart of the Old Town, the Market Square is a key rendezvous and place to promenade. Burghers' houses feature smart boutiques and galleries, together with numerous restaurants and cafés ranging from expensive to fast food outlets. Additionally, **Park F. Chopina** is only 250 metres (270 yards) from the Market Square, and is an ideal spot for a picnic among greenery.

Przemysł Castle to Freedom Square

While most of the city walls were pulled down at the beginning of the 19th century, medieval fragments, including a tower, have survived on Przemysław Hill to the northwest of the Market Square, in the vicinity of **Zamek Przemysła** (Przemysł Castle) ❸ (open Mon–Wed, Fri–Sun; entrance fee except Fri). This impressive castle houses the Muzeum Rzemiosł Artystycznych (Museum of Decorative Arts). Arranged over two floors, the extensive collec-

Map on page 290–91

TIP

One of the most atmospheric restaurants in the Market Square is Stara Ratuszowa at Number 55. A *fin-de-siècle* Bohemian townhouse, complete with antique interiors, it serves traditional Polish food (including regional dishes).

BELOW: enjoying a beer outside a café.

Shimmering copies of classic icons for sale.

tion is concentrated without being time-consuming, providing the finest examples of Gothic and Renaissance sacred art and furniture, Gobelin rugs, Limoges porcelain and decorative enamelwork, together with crystal and glassware, and silver and gold *objets d'art*, many of which were formerly owned by eminent Poles. The 20th-century galleries also provide definitive examples of Secessionism and Art Deco (Góra Przemysława 1; tel: 85 22 035; open Wed–Sun; entrance fee). Beyond the square at the foot of this hill are two churches facing each other, and both merit a visit. The façade of **Kościół Św. Józefa** (St Joseph's Church) is classic early Baroque. The Gothic façade of **Kościół Św. Wojciecha** (St Adalbert's Church) may seem to tell the whole story, but the interiors include wonderful Seccessionist polychrome. Moreover, many renowned Poles have been laid to rest here, including Józef Wybicki (1747–1822), who composed the Polish national anthem. Heading for **Plac Wolności** (Freedom Square) marks a change of character, with this area dominated by 19th-century neoclassical "statement" buildings, not to mention a modern urban buzz (which the pedestrianised Market Square area is blissfully free from). This area is also more ragged and not yet as manicured as the Old Town. Plac Wolności is actually a vast rectangle rather than a square, harbouring skateboarders as well as locals chatting on benches, overlooked by several important buildings.

The **Muzeum Narodowe Galeria Malarstwa i Rzeźby** (National Museum, Painting and Sculpture Galleries) ❶ (Marcinkowskiego 9; tel: 852 80 00; open Tues–Sun; entrance fee except Fri) is housed in a neoclassical building. It contains one of the most comprehensive collections of Polish paintings, including works by Jan Matejko, Poland's greatest historical painter (*see page 112*). European masters such as Ribera, Bellini and Bronzino can also be seen, together

BELOW: relaxing in front of etchings stall.

with a range of folk arts and crafts. At the opposite end of the square is the neoclassical Arkadia building, currently a casino, though its provenance is more cultural, with concerts given here by Paganini in 1829 and Liszt in 1843.

Biblioteka Raczyńskich (Raczyński Library) takes the form of an outstanding neoclassical building, dating from 1829, with the sublime colonnade featuring 24 Corinthian columns. Modelled on the Louvre in Paris, it reflects the initially peaceful Prussian regime, which changed over the following decades as the Prussians attempted to "Germanise" the city.

A centre of the Polish Nationalist Movement against the Prussians was the nearby **Hotel Bazar** at Marcinkowskiego 10. Dating from the 1840s, this is one of Europe's oldest hotels, with the neoclassical atmospheric style being the work of renowned Berlin architect Schinkel.

Poznań art and culture

On **Plac Adama Mickiewicza** (Adam Mickiewicz Square) are two interesting monuments, one to the eponymous romantic poet and the other in memory of the worker's uprising of 1956, known as the "Poznań June". Like the Berlin Uprising of 17 June 1953, this was a spontaneous insurrection against the injustices of Communism, and one in which many people lost their lives.

This square is overlooked by the distinctive neo-Gothic architecture of **Collegium Minus** (Minus College) (open Mon–Fri 8am–8pm), the university concert hall which is renowned for the quality of its accoustics. This is a regular venue for the city's Philharmonic Orchestra and the Poznań Ballet, while also hosting the Henryk Wieniawski International Violin Competition. Opposite Plac Adama Mickiewicza is the **Pałac Kułtury** (Palace of Culture) **O** (tel: 853

BELOW: the Raczyński Library.

Map on page 290–91

60 81; open Mon–Fri 10am–8pm, Sat 11am–6pm). This *fin-de-siècle* neo-Romanesque building, originally known as the Kaiserhaus, was the German Emperor Wilhelm II's former palace, and now houses various institutions. Although its appearance can seem like a grey bulk, it is worth visiting for its programme of interesting temporary exhibitions covering a wide range of subjects. Its location on **Święty Marcin** (St Martin's Street) means that, the Palace of Culture is also on the prime shopping street, which has all the atmosphere of a modern, lively city. Parallel to this street is Aleksandra Fredry, which is also retail terrain and includes the extraordinary Okrąglak Dom Towarowy ("Roundabout" Department Store), a 1950s glazed rotunda. Further along Fredry is the wonderfully grand neoclassical S Moniuszko Teatr Narodowy (S Moniuszko National Theatre).

Poznań's parkland

You are never far from a park in Poznań, with 20 percent of the city being green. North of the city centre lie the remains of a large citadel which was almost completely destroyed in 1945. Today, the **Park Cytadela** occupies this site, together with a cemetery for Red Army soldiers who died during World War II, and the Poznań Citadel Museum (open Tues–Sun), which details the struggle against the Prussians during the partitions, as well as other aspects of military history, including the city's wartime fate.

Wilson Park, in the Lazarz district, includes Poland's (and one of Europe's) largest palm houses. A number of pavilions totalling 4,000 sq metres (4,700 sq yards) contain around 17,000 tropical plants, including 700 species from subtropical and tropical countries. An adjoining aquarium contains plenty of local and exotic fish. The city limits to the southwest of this park see the start of the Wielkopolski Park Narodowy (Wielkopolski National Park), with diverse landscapes, woods, hills and lakes to explore, together with *skansens* and agricultural museums.

BELOW: exhibit in the Poznań Citadel Museum.
RIGHT: gnomes on the road to Poznań.

Adjoining the northern outskirts of Poznań is a large area of park and woodland with a series of four lakes. Part of **Lake Strzesyńskie** is an open-air swimming pool, with a motel and a camp site also on its shores. **Lake Kierskie**, which covers an area of 300 hectares (740 acres), is very popular with sailing enthusiasts who find the wind conditions to be near perfect.

Also within easy reach of the city centre past Ostrów Tumski is **Lake Maltańskie**, one of the finest rowing and canoeing regatta courses in Europe, created on this lake between 1985–90. The world canoeing championships were held here in August 1990. In sunny weather the lakeside is very popular for a stroll, with walking and cycling trails encircling the lake, while cafés and beer gardens provide refreshments. On the eastern edge is an artificial ski slope, for practising at any time of year.

East of the lake is Wielkopolska Zoo, Poland's largest and most comprehensive. The animals are kept in spacious compounds under conditions that closely resemble their natural habitat. If you don't want to walk that far, a miniature railway runs along the lakeside (from Kościół Św. Jana, May to September). ❑

AROUND POZNAŃ

This chapter features one day trip that can be made from Poznań
to the beautiful lakeland landscape and quiet bucolic
villages that surround the city

Map
on page
302

Poznań is situated in the centre of a large agricultural region, which includes forests and nature reserves, with good road and rail links making it easy to visit historic towns and villages – and to enjoy the pastoral views on the way. Nor do you have to go far to escape the city, and be in the midst of fascinating countryside. In fact, on the southern outskirts of **Poznań ❶**, only 15 km (10 miles) from the city centre, lies the **Wielkopolski National Park**, which covers an area of about 10,000 hectares (24,750 acres). This has the archetypal characteristics of the Polish lowlands: deciduous woods with many different types of vegetation, moraine hills and lakes. The most beautiful part of the park is Lake Góreckie, where the ruins of a castle remain on one of its islands.

Kórnik to Szamotuly

Two popular destinations around 20 km (12 miles) south of Poznań are Kórnik and Rogalin. The small town of **Kórnik ❷**, with a three-nave Gothic church on the Market Square, is idyllically set on the shores of Lake Kórnickie. An impressive arboretum can be seen in the adjoining park (open daily; entrance fee), laid out in an English style. (It contains 3,000 species of trees and shrubs from around the world, which is the most extensive collection in Poland). The centrepiece of the park is **Kórnik Palace**. Originally built in the 16th century, it was redesigned in an English neo-Gothic style in the mid-19th century by the aristocratic owner Tytus Działynski, incorporating designs by the famous Berlin architect, Karl-Friedrich Schinkel. Gothic features, which include a bridge over the moat, were intended to recall Poland's historic splendour, with the refurbishment also providing a suitable home for the owner's collection of historic books and paintings. Bestowed to the nation in 1924, the castle houses a museum (Zamkowa 5; tel: 817 00 81; open Tues–Sun; entrance fee) including furniture, paintings, military weapons and armour. The library has one of the most valuable collections of Polish books in the country, with over 350,000 volumes, including one by Napoleon. A neighbouring building houses historic horse-drawn carriages.

The main attraction in **Rogalin ❸**, a village beside the River Warta, is the beautiful park and palace on the edge of an oak forest. Laid out in the late 18th century in a French Baroque style, with an English-style landscaped park laid out at the beginning of the 19th century, this is home to the greatest number of ancient oak trees (over 1,100) of any forest in Europe, some of which are 800 years old. The most famous are three oaks named after the legendary Slav brothers Lech, Czech and Rus, the founders of Poland, Bohemia and Russia. The late Baroque–early neo-

LEFT: boat on Lake Kórnickie in Kórnik.
BELOW: sculpture in Rogalin park, overlooking the Palace.

The Rogalin Chapel, built in pink sandstone, serves as a parish church and a mausoleum for the Razcyńskis family.

classical **Rogalin Palace**, formerly owned by the Raczyński family is now a museum (tel: 813 80 54; open Tues–Sun; entrance fee). The collection includes a range of clocks, furniture, tapestries, porcelain and 18th- and 19th-century Polish paintings. Separate pavilions house an exhibition of 20th-century Polish and European art, and horse-drawn carriages.

Superb Gothic architecture can be seen in the small town of **Szamotuły ❹**, 35 km (22 miles) northwest of Poznań. The Gothic Collegiate Church has magnificent interiors, with the late 15th-century **Zamek Górków** (Górków Castle) now a museum (Wroniecka 30; tel: 218 13; open Tues–Sun; entrance fee). In addition to the castle's interiors, the collection includes Poland's most comprehensive collection of icons and Russian Orthodox sacred art. The castle is adjoined by fragments of a moat and defensive system, with the superb three-storey late-Gothic Halszka Tower housing an exhibition of the region from ancient times to World War II. Around the Market Square are numerous late 19th- and early 20th-century burghers' houses, with another interesting 19th-century building formerly used by the mounted postal service.

An essential detour, less than 10 km (6 miles) northeast of Szamotuły, brings you to **Słopanowo**, where a stunning wooden church dating from 1699 features beautiful folk interiors, 16th- and 17th-century sculptures and late 17th-century wall polychrome.

The origins of the Polish state

The **Szląk Piastowski**, a road that leaves Poznań in a northeasterly direction, passes several places marking the origins of the Polish state. Consequently, this road is named after the first dynasty of Polish kings, the Piasts.

The first place of interest along this route is the village of **Lednogóra** ➎, located on Lake Lednica. On Ostrów Lednicki, the lake's largest island, is a fascinating archaeological site, the **Muzeum Pierwszych Piastów na Lednicy** (Museum of the First Piasts in Lednica; open Tues–Sun 9am–5pm during the summer; entrance fee). This has the oldest architectural fragments of brickwork in Poland, and includes the remains of Palatium, the Pre-Romanesque late 10th-century residence of Mieszko I, founder of the Polish state and the first Polish king. Massive earthworks mark the site of a castle built here in the 11th century. The island was originally connected to the shore by a series of bridges with a total length of about 700 metres (2,300 ft).

On the opposite shores of the lake is the **Wielkopolski Park Etnograficzny** (Wielkopolski Ethnographic Park; open Tues–Sun 9am–5pm during the summer; entrance fee). This *skansen* (open-air) museum has plenty to see with around 50 primarily wooden buildings, such as an 18th-century Wielkopolska farmstead, a manor house, and the oldest Polish windmill dating from the late 16th century.

Further along this route is the hilltop town of **Gniezno** ➏, Poland's first capital. The earliest inhabitants settled here in the 7th century, with a fortified settlement built in the 9th century and the first church founded around 970, after Poland converted to Christianity in 966. Gniezno's 14th-century **cathedral** is the grandest Gothic church in Poland, and the seat of Polish archbishops since the year 1000. A three-naved basilica with 14 chapels, featuring ornate portals and grilles, this is also the final resting place for the first Polish martyr and one of the country's most important saints, St Wojciech (Adalbert). His silver sarcophagus is in the centre of the main nave. The cathedral's magnificent pair of

Map on page 302

Statue of Bolesław Chrorby (The Brave).

BELOW: sculptures on the roof of Gniezno Cathedral.

Details of bronze doors of Gniezno's Cathedral, one of the finest surviving examples of Romanesque decorative art.

BELOW: the Old Fort at Biskupin.

Romanesque bronze doors date from 1170, and illustrate the life of St Adalbert through a series of panels on each door. The saint is shown leaving teh St Alexis Monastery in Arentine, Italy and arriving in Gniezno in 996. The following year he baptised the pagan Prussians, before being killed by them. King Bolesław Chrorby is shown buying his body from the Prussians, with the final scenes showing the saint being laid to rest inthe cathedral.

Collections of ancient books and works of art, some dating from the 10th century, are kept in the church archives and the **Muzeum Archidiecezi Gnieneźnieńskiej** (Museum of the Archdiocese of Gniezno; Kolegiaty 2; tel: 26 37 78; open Tues–Sun; entrance fee). It doesn't take long to see the Gothic and Baroque sacred art here, together with various ecclesiastical items, and it's certainly worth it.

A delightful stroll past various historic churches and buildings, past a lake surrounded by greenery, leads to the **Muzeum Początków Państwa Polskiego** (Museum of the Origins of the Polish State; Kostrzewskiego 1; open daily 10am–4pm; entrance fee). This ugly modern building hides a treasure trove of archaeological fragments covering the history of the Piast Dynasty. An audio-visual display may seem a bit dated, but it does the job effectively, detailing the town's history up to the Middle Ages. Once Kraków became the capital in the 14th century, Wielkopolska's nobility tried to reverse the town's declining status, but to no avail – the town gradually fell into provincial obscurity.

North of Gniezno is **Biskupin ❼** (open daily, Apr–Oct; entrance fee), an archaeological reserve where in the 1930s an early Slav settlement on the Biskupin Lake peninsula was discovered, with artifacts from the Bronze Age in well-preserved wooden buildings going back 2,500 years. Part of the settlement has been reconstructed , offering an insight into prehistoric Slav life. Continuing along the Śzląk Piastowski from Gniezno lie the five towns of Trzemeszno, Mogilno, Strzelno, Kruszwica and Inowrocław. In **Trzemeszno** sections of the magnificent church show its 10th-century origins, although it is essentially Baroque in character. In the vicinity of Trzemeszno are several lakes, most of which have a rather unusual, elongated shape. This is because they fill glacial channels created during the Ice Age.

One of the first Benedictine monasteries in Poland was built in **Mogilno** ❾ during the 11th century. A Romanesque church was built at the same time, and although repeatedly refashioned, it has retained many original elements including the crypt. Further points of interest along the Śzląk Piastowski are described in the chapter on Gdańsk and the surrounding area (*see page 302*).

East of Poznań

The eastern part of the Wielkopolska region is a flat, exclusively agricultural area with sparse woodland. One of the country's major trunk roads, the E30 International Expressway, leads through it from Poznań to Warsaw. It remains an expressway until Września, and is subsequently a motorway as far as Konin.

About 50 km (30 miles) from Poznań is **Września** ❿, where several monuments commemorate the local people's heroic struggle against the Prussians' attempted "Germanisation" during the partition of Poland. The school where pupils went on strike to demand religious education in the Polish language in 1901, which led to a chain of protests throughout Wielkopolska, is now the **Muzeum Regionalne im Dzeici Wrześińskich** (Regional Museum dedicated to the Children of Wrześien; Dzieci Wrzesińskich 13; open Mon–Sat; entrance

TIP

There is an interesting narrow-gauge and steam engine rail link between Biskupin and nearby Wenecja. Here there is also a delightful railway museum (open Apr–Sept) from where you can take a "historic" train ride.

BELOW: rural modes of transport.

fee), with reconstructions of the original classrooms.The small town of **Miłosław**, 16 km (10 miles) south of Września, is famous for the battles that took place here during the revolution of 1848. Its 18th-century church and neo-classical palace, both in the attractive setting of a large park, are well worth visiting. In the chapel in the neighbouring village of **Winna Góra** is the grave of the Polish general Jan Dąbrowski, a national hero from the time of the Napoleonic Wars, while the palace (open Tues–Sun; entrance fee) has an exhibition detailing his life.

The village of **Ląd** on the Warta River is one of the most important sites of the Cistercian order in Europe, with an extensive monastery. Built in the 13th century and remodelled in the mid-17th century, this is now one of the most beautiful examples of Gothic and Baroque architecture in Poland. The monumental architectural style, with its splendid interiors and fine collection of 14th-century wall paintings, is an impressive sight. The Passion Plays staged at Easter attract people from across the country.

Konin ⓫, on the River Warta, has retained a medieval urban layout in the Old Town, which includes the **Stary Rynek** (Old Market Square) with numerous 19th-century buildings. There is also a late 14th-century Gothic church set in a garden that includes a 2.5 metre (8-ft) high sandstone mile post dating from 1151. The postwar area of Konin contains sports and cultural centres hosting large-scale events such as the annual Children's Song and Dance Festival in June. But this is also an industrial centre, with power plants and factories (including an aluminium smelter) taking advantage of the area's deposits of brown coal. It is also rapidly expanding, and the town's population has increased sevenfold since 1960. A palace in the **Gosławice** district of Konin houses the

BELOW: sheep herd on the move.

Map on page 302

Regional History Museum (Muzealna 6; open Tues–Sun; entrance fee) with a good collection of jewellery, Polish coins and 19th- and 20th-century Polish paintings. As Konin has a long history of mining, there is also a gallery of paraffin lamps. Next door is a small *skansen* (open Tue–Sun; entrance fee) with 19th-century farm buildings, and a Gothic church dating from 1444.

The countryside around Konin is popular with holiday-makers, with the area's towns also providing aesthetic sights. Stary Licheń, 13 km (8 miles) northeast of Konin attracts numerous pilgrims, who come to the mid-19th-century neo-Gothic church to see the small painting of St Mary of Licheń. **Ślesin**'s triumphal arch, erected in 1811 in honour of Napoleon Bonaparte, is the only monument of its kind in Poland.

Koło and Uniejów are two interesting small towns on the River Warta. **Koło** is home to an architectural rarity: a Gothic church with Art Nouveau interiors, while **Uniejów**'s main attraction is a Gothic castle. This can also be experienced as a resident, having been converted into a comfortable hotel, with the surrounding park providing various walks among a variety of trees and bushes.

Around Poland's oldest towns

Picturesquely located between moraines on the edge of the Warta valley, en route to Kalisz, are Żerków and Śmielów. The main feature of the quiet town of **Żerków** is a delightful Baroque church. The renowned Polish poet Adam Mickiewicz stayed in the village of **Śmielów** on a number of occasions, which helped to put the place on the map. The village and surrounding area features in Mickiewicz's *Pan Tadeusz*, one of Poland's most significant poetic works. The neoclassical Śmielów Palace, dating from 1800, is an appropriate location for the A Mickiewicz Museum (open Tues–Sun; entrance fee), detailing his life and the Romantic era.

By the village of **Gołuchów** ⓬ is the magnificent late 16th-century French Renaissance Gołuchów Palace (open Tues–Sun; entrance fee). In addition to rooms decorated with interesting furniture, porcelain and Polish and European paintings from the 16th and 17th centuries, there is an exquisite collection of Ancient Greek vases. The palace is set in Wielkopolska's largest landscaped park, which includes a Forestry Museum within an outbuilding, while the outlying of the park are a reserve for European bison. An unusual sight worth visiting in the Gołuchów woods is the "Erratic", a huge boulder left over from the Ice Age with a circumference of 22 metres (71 ft) and a height of 3.5 metres (12 ft).

As the second largest town in the region is **Kalisz** ⓭ is also one of Poland's oldest, retaining its medieval layout of narrow streets. The town was first mentioned 1,800 years ago in the writings of the Roman traveller Ptolemy. Formerly an important stop on the amber trade route from the Baltic, Kalisz is now an equally important Polish textiles centre.

The Old Town's most interesting buildings include the **Cathedral of St Nicholas**, dating from 1253, with its splendid late Renaissance stucco work and Baroque altar; the late-Baroque Collegiate Church of St Joseph, as well as the Bishop's Palace and Town

BELOW:
European bison.

Hall, both neoclassical. The **Franciscan church and monastery** dating from the 13th century, was rebuilt during the Baroque era, while fragments of the defensive walls can also be seen. The avant garde design of two modern churches in the **Asnyka** district provide an interesting contrast to the town's wealth of traditional architecture.

Idyllically located on the banks of the River Prosna is the Wojciech Bogusławski Theatre, a sublime confection of white stucco neoclassicism. This adjoins the Town Park, one of the country's oldest public parks founded in 1798. Some of Poland's greatest writers, such as Adam Asnyk, Maria Konopnicka and Maria Dąbrowska lived and wrote in Kalisz. The town's cultural calendar also includes several festivals such as the Mieczyław Kalisz International Jazz Pianists Festival. The **Kalisz Regional Museum** (Kościuszki 12; tel: 736 62; open Tues, Thurs, Sat–Sun 10am–2pm, Wed, Fri noon–6pm; entrance fee) has a good collection of archaeological, historical and ethnographic exhibits, while also detailing the history of the town's textile trade.

Wielkopolska's southern border is formed by the Ostrzeszowskie Hills. The park in **Autonin**, a village on the busy road from Poznań to Silesia, contains many ancient oak trees and an extraordinary neoclassical wooden hunting palace. Odd, perhaps, but why have a mere shooting lodge if you're a distinguished aristocrat who can afford a four-storey hunting palace? Considered one of the most remarkable buildings in Europe at that time, the body of the palace is a large hexagonal tower (containing a circular galleried staircase), from which four short evenly spaced wings extend. The intention was to create an entirely new architectural form, and it certainly succeeded. Built at the beginning of the 19th century, it was designed by the renowned Berlin architect Karl-Friedrich

BELOW: lush and green pastures.

Schinkel. Frédéric Chopin was a guest at the palace, which explains the Chopin concerts every Sunday. Moreover, every September a festival called "Chopin in the Colours of the Autumn" is held here.

Map on page 302

Southern and western Wielkopolska

The intensively cultivated agricultural region of South Wielkopolska has the highest concentration of farms of any region in Poland. The area is, however, equally rich in architectural monuments and places of historical interest.

Dating from the Middle Ages, the Market Square in **Leszno** ⓮ has numerous imposing 17th- to 19th-century burghers' houses. But they are still over-shadowed by the elegant Baroque Town Hall, dating from the 1780s, with a striking colour co-ordinated façade of sienna, yellow and white. It was designed by the Italian architect Pompeo Ferrari, who also designed the splendid Baroque parish church. The Regional Museum (pl Metziga; tel: 206 781; open Tues–Sun; entrance fee) has an impressive collection of coffin portraits, which were very traditional in Poland, as well as folk art. The town is also well known for the Akwawit indoor swimming pool, the largest in Poland, which includes a 52-metre (170-ft) chute.

On a hill in **Lubiń** around 30 km (19 miles) to the northeast of Leszno, stands a Benedictine monastery built in the early 18th century, with neighbouring buildings housing a Regional Museum covering local history and folk arts.

One of Poland's most beautiful and striking sacred buildings is the Church of the Philippians on the **Holy Mount** by the town of Gostyń, a replica of the Santa Maria della Salute church in Venice. Beneath a massive dome, the interiors include a painting of the Madonna dating from 1540. A view of the town forms

BELOW: haymaking in Jelenia Góra.

TIP

In Strzyzewice, a
suburb of Leszno,
there is an airfield for
gliders, where the
world gliding
championships have
twice been held.

the background of the painting – almost certainly the earliest example of its kind in Polish art. Also worth seeing in the nearby village of **Pawłowice** are the Gothic church with Renaissance interiors and the neoclassical Palace set in a beautiful park with several lakes. Near Leszno in the direction of Wrocław (*see page 267*) is the small town of **Rydzyna** ⑮, which is registered in its entirety as a historical monument of outstanding quality. The 18th-century layout includes the Market Square surrounded by burghers' houses, while the rococo monument to the Holy Trinity dates from 1760. The Baroque Rydzyna Castle, dating from the 17th century, houses a museum, hotel and restaurant.

Some of the lakes near **Boszkowo**, a village northwest of Leszno, are well worth exploring. The largest of the area's numerous convalescent homes (many of which are open to tourists) is situated by the clear waters of Lake Dominicki.

The town of **Grodzisk Wielkopolski**, lying midway between Poznań and Zielona Góra, is renowned for brewing a strong wheat beer. This also has a superior flavour attributed to the local spring water, whose special qualities were discovered in the 14th century. Monuments to Grodzisk's glorious past, including a fine Renaissance church, can be seen throughout the town.

Wolsztyn, on the River Obra, is a popular with watersports enthusiasts, particularly canoeists, as the surrounding area contains many lakes. Moreover, the lakes are linked by either the river or small canals. The choice of accommodation includes an irresistible opportunity to live like a prince for a fraction of the price, with a tourist hostel located in what was once a neoclassical palace (tel: 384 33 75). The town was formerly a centre of woollen cloth production, and includes an 18th-century Baroque church, while the Regional Museum is housed in the former workshop of the outstanding Polish sculptor Marcin Rożek.

BELOW:
country girls pose
for the camera.

Around Zielona Góra and Ziemia Lubuska

The western part of Wielkopolska includes a densely wooded region with many rivers and lakes, extending along the border with Germany, which follows the Odra and Nysa-Tuzycka rivers.

Attractively situated close to the Odra valley at the foot of a chain of hills, is the region's administrative centre, **Zielona Góra** . This was traditionally a wine-growing area, with a vine-covered hill in the centre of town the only symbolic remains of this practice, where a palm house also houses a restaurant. However, this tradition is celebrated in the colourful September Days of Zielona Góra Harvest Festival, also called "a Holiday of Vine Gathering". The **Lubuska Regional Museum** (Niepodłegłości 15; open Wed–Sun; entrance fee) documents the history of wine production in the area, with a collection of tools and pots used by vine growers, as well as archaeological and ethnographic exhibits. The town also has one of Poland's most renowned distilleries, with Polmos Zielona Góra producing a wide range of clear and flavoured vodkas.

Much of Zielona Góra's original layout dates from the town's charter, granted in 1323. The most impressive sights include the **Cathedral of St Jadwiga** with its monumental Gothic architecture dating from the 13th century, the neoclassical Town Hall with an elegant clock tower, and 15th-century fragments of the defensive walls. Despite the name, the **Church of the Virgin Mary of Częstochowa** is actually Evangelical, with this half-timbered building dating from the mid-18th century. There are also various early 20th-century buildings, providing a wide range of Secessionist and eclectic styles.

There are a number of interesting towns in the southern part of Ziemia Lubuska, a region which formerly belonged to Lower Silesia. In **Kożuchów**, for

BELOW:
resting tired legs.

example, large sections of the medieval town walls have survived, while the 13th-century church with Baroque interiors is also particularly impressive.

Żagań, situated on the River Bóbr, was the capital of an independent Piast duchy from 1270s, and has preserved its original medieval town structure including fragments of the 12- to 14th-century town ramparts. The neoclassical Town Hall is surrounded by 17th- and 18th-century burghers' houses, while the Augustinian Monastic Complex, including a 15th-century parish church, monastery and a granary, offers a wide range of architectural styles. The monastery houses an early 18th-century library used by the astronomer Kepler, while another part of this complex is a hotel. The town also has the ruins of a Franciscan monastery, dating from the 13th century and refashioned in the 18th century. However, Żagań's finest architectural monument is the early 18th century **Wallenstein Palace**, approached by a bridge over a moat, and picturesquely situated on the banks of the Bóbr, in a park with many rare species of trees.

Until the end of the Communist regime the town of **Żary**, originally founded in 1260, had a long history of producing the finest cloth and linen in the country. Recalling the town's medieval heyday are the 14th-century Town Hall with a Renaissance portal, a few 13th- and 14th-century Gothic churches, and sections of the ramparts and watchtowers from the 14th century. The Dewins-Biberstein late 18th-century palace and burghers' houses by the Market Square provide prime examples of other architectural styles.

By the banks of the Warta lies **Gorzów Wielkopolski**, a town granted its municipal charter in 1257. As the principal town of this region it has a current population of 120,000 and several large textile factories.

BELOW: the Palace of the Order of St John in Łagów,

Particularly interesting is the 13th-century Gothic cathedral, with a substantial defensive tower dating from the 14th century, a 15th-century presbytery and a Renaissance altar. The imposing half-timbered granary on the banks of the River Warta was built in the 1770s, and is now a museum of historic and modern paintings. The town's main museum is housed in a *fin-de-siècle* Seccessionist Palace (Warszawska 35; tel: 32 28 43; open Tues–Sun; entrance fee), with a collection of decorative arts and crafts, and Polish portraits. Every August the town sees gypsy groups converge for the annual international meeting for the Romane Dyvesa festival of gypsy musical groups.

South of Gorzów, surrounded by beautiful woodland and lakes, is the holiday resort of **Lubniewice**, while heading northeast brings you to **Strzelce Krajeńskie**, where the medieval fortifications, built of uneven blocks, have been preserved almost entirely intact.

The north German-Polish border

Along the historic border between Wielkopolska and Ziemia Lubuska, to the north of the main Berlin to Poznań road, are several places worth visiting. **Łagów** is set in a particularly beautiful location, between high moraines and two lakes. Its most outstanding architectural monument is a castle, built in the 15th century for the Order of St John, with a watchtower providing a wonderful view of the surrounding area. The castle now houses a hotel and restaurant. Łagów is still protected by a medieval wall, interrupted only by two gates leading into the town. The nearby lakes offer good leisure facilities, and not surprisingly are popular in the summer months. On the western border of Wielkopolska lies the small town of **Międzyrzecz** ⓱, a good base from which to tour the area.

Map
on page
302

Dating from the 10th century, the town is perched on a small hill above the River Obra. The carefully preserved ruins of a 14th-century Gothic castle are worth seeing, with the grounds including the 18th-century House of the Starosts (town governors), now a museum with historical and ethnographic exhibits, including some unique 17th-century coffin portraits. The neoclassical Town Hall, built in 1813, has a neo-Gothic clock tower, while the 16th-century Gothic parish church with a wooden spire and beautiful star vaulting, also has thoroughly modern interiors.

North of Międzyrzecz, in the hilly area close by the lakes, is **Rokitno**, the site of a Baroque church, which is the destination for countless pilgrims who worship its image of the Virgin Mary. Surrounded by woodland, the village of **Gościkówo** is situated 10 km (6 miles) south of Międzyrzecz. The main attraction is a former Cistercian monastery, dating from the 13th century but with Baroque additions.

To the west and southwest of Międzyrzecz is an extensive system of **fortifications**, which the Nazis constructed from 1934–8. One of the world's largest military fortifications, the complex consists of 55 individual defensive shelters, with walls of reinforced concrete up to 2.5 metres (8 ft) thick. The fortifications are connected by a network of underground corridors totalling 30 km (19 miles)

BELOW: fishing on the lake in Łagów.

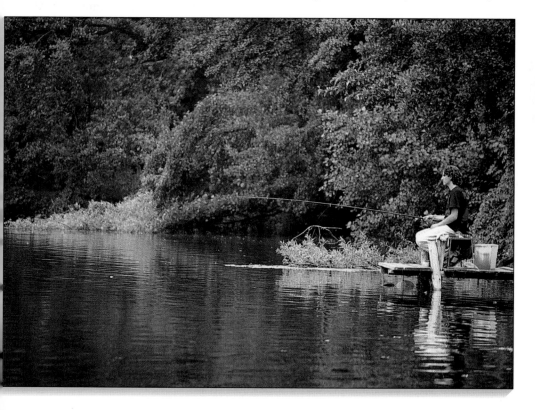

in length, through which electric trains ran. Part of the underground area also housed armaments factories. In January 1945, the entire complex was captured by Soviet tank units and large sections were blown up. The ominous remains can be visited, though it is a rather hazardous undertaking if unescorted. The best place to enter the complex is at **Kaława**, a village 8 km (5 miles) south of Międzyrzecz. If you do, you won't be alone. Some of the tunnels have become a winter shelter for huge colonies of bats, up to about 30,000 in total, which includes 10 different species of these flying mammals. Consequently, this has been declared the Nietoporek nature reserve.

The Warta lakes

One of Wielkopolska's most scenic areas, the Międzychódzko-Sierakowskie Lakes, extends northwest of Poznań beside the lower reaches of the Warta. With over 100 lakes, moraines, woods, footpaths and recreational facilities, it has become a very popular area with holiday-makers.

There is a large holiday centre on the shores of **Lake Jaroszewskie**, while Lake Lutomskie, with its steep banks and impressive beech forest, forms part of a nature reserve. A route called the "black path" leads to the town of **Sieraków**, located 3 km (2 miles) away. By the altar of the town's Renaissance church is a painting that originated from Rubens' studio. Another attraction is the stud farm, which raises a horse breed unique to the region and offers riding holidays. A large holiday centre by the side of Lake Mierzynskie also attracts many visitors during the summer.

BELOW: horseback riding holidays are popular with visitors.

The town of **Międzychód** ⓲, situated between the River Warta and Lake Kuchenne, has a delightful Old Town with gabled houses. Between the Warta and the Noteća lies one of the country's largest forest areas, densely covered of pines, which is the **Noteća Primeval Forest**. In the autumn mushroom-pickers from all over the country flock to this hilly area.

Map on page 302

North Wielkopolska

North Wielkopolska is a hilly, mainly wooded region with many lakes. One of its beauty spots is the **Noteć Valley**. Nestling among the hills and between three lakes, Chodzież occupies a picturesque site. This town has three factories producing porcelain, making it one of the main centres of this industry in Poland.

On the banks of the River Gwda, a tributary of the Noteç, lies the 15th-century town of **Piła**, the administrative centre for North Wielkopolska. The elegant Rodlo Hotel is recommended as a base from which to make day trips to the many different points of interest in this part of Wielkopolska and Pomerania. Piła was badly damaged during World War II, but the town has an early 20th- century neo-Gothic church of St Stanisław Kostka and the modernist 1920s church of St Anthony, which are both worth seeing. This is also the home town of Stanisław Staszic, a priest, scientist, and politican who reformed the Polish economy at the end of the 18th and early 19th centuries. His family house is now a museum detailing his life and works. The town's lakes include beaches and recreational areas, while Lake Rudnicki is part of a nature reserve, harbouring wild boars and various species of birds and trees.

North of Piła, and over the border into Pomerania, are the remains of the German-built Pomeranian Wall, a defensive line crossing an area of forests and lakes. This World War II relic is described in greater detail in the chapter on West Pomerania (*see page 321*). ❏

BELOW: the woods provide natural habitat for many wild animals and their young.

THE NORTH

The well-forested countryside that surrounds the post-glacial lakes of the north is gentle and undulating, while the city of Gdańsk provides an urban centre for the region.

The Baltic coastline, with its secluded beaches fringed by pine trees, includes many attractive resorts and spa towns, as well as major ports such as Gdańsk and Szczecin.

As the capital of Pomorze Zachodnie (Western Pomerania), which borders Germany, Szczecin's historic importance is demonstrated by monumental buildings such as the Castle of the Pomeranian Prince's and the Pomeranian Parliament Building. The city is also a gateway to other Hanseatic towns such as Starogard Szczeciński, as well as national parks and seaside resorts. The surrounding countryside also features vast expanses of agricultural land, with potatoes the most important crop.

The tri-city of Gdańsk, Sopot and Gdynia is the largest municipal area in northern Poland. The historic centre of Gdańsk, with numerous buildings that were designed to impress, reflects its long history as the most important Polish port. Sopot has remained a delightful seaside resort, characterised by 19th century pavilions and *fin-de-siecle* villas, while Gdynia is a modern marina and port with dockyards, essentially dating from the 1920s.

A lasting legacy of the Teutonic Order of Knights, who dominated this region from the 13th to the 15th century, are a large number of castles. Some are now picturesque ruins on hillsides, while others are museums. The most impressive is the vast castle in the town of Malbork, south of Gdańsk, and there are well-preserved fragments of a Teutonic castle in the delightful town of Toruń, the birthplace of Copernicus. The town also has prime examples of Gothic architecture. To the east the area is bordered by Warmia i Mazury, which includes the Masurian lake district – with over 1,000 lakes it's Poland's most popular holiday destination. ❏

PRECEDING PAGES: Gnieyno Cathedral.
LEFT: the wandering dunes at Łeba.

WEST POMERANIA AND SZCZECIN

*Western Pomerania is the top sea and sun destination in Poland,
while the capital of the region, Szczecin, has all the buzz
of a busy port town and a fascinating past*

West Pomerania's 200-km (124-mile) stretch of coastline means a choice of secluded beaches as well as seaside resorts with various facilities. Similarly, the Pomeranian lake district provides tranquil havens, with its series of inter-connected lakes surrounded by forests, as well as attractive resorts. Among the national parks are the islands of Uznam and Wolin, while the Słowin National Park is renowned for its "wandering dunes". With numerous historic towns and villages, the region provides a versatile range of attractions.

Elbe Slavic tribes, ruled by various dukes, first settled in this part of Pomerania in the 9th and 10th centuries. At the end of the 10th century the area was unified by the Piast dynasty, the first Polish kings, though control of the region fluctuated between the early Polish state and the Brandenburg Margraves (German nobles). In the 12th century the Margraves were forced to cede territorial claims to the Polish king, Bolesław Krzywousty, who once again united the region's leaders. However, in league with the Danes, the Margraves subsequently re-established control, with the Greifen family, originally Slavic but then "Germanised", ruling from the early 13th–16th centuries.

LEFT: sheaves of corn after the harvest.
BELOW: tug-boat in Szczecin harbour.

In the 17th century, the region was annexed by Sweden and then by Prussia in 1720, after which the region was again "Germanised" and not returned to Poland until after World War II. The region's postwar prosperity rests on a combination of industry, fishery, agriculture and forestry.

Szczecin

The capital of West Pomerania, **Szczecin ❶**, is near the border with Germany on the River Odra (Oder). This river, and the fact that Szczecin is only 65 km (40 miles) from the Baltic, has ensured its status as the largest Polish port and a junction for land traffic.

Szczecin evolved from a 9th century Slav settlement. In 1237 the city was granted its municipal charter, and joined the Hanseatic League in 1251. Establishing the city as the capital of their duchy, the Pomeranian dukes began to build their magnificent castle in 1346. Between the 13th and 18th centuries the harbour developed into an important commercial centre, particularly for fish and grain, trading with the major Baltic ports, including Lubeck, Tallin, Stockholm and Gdańsk. Sixty percent destroyed by Allied bombing during World War II, the city was rebuilt and expanded after the war. As a cultural and educational centre, it has a university, five institutions of higher education and the Higher Maritime Academy, a Philharmonic orchestra and several theatres.

The city's attractions are concentrated in the centre, and can easily be seen on foot, with broad boulevards, river banks, parks and squares providing various settings for historic architecture. While Szczecin is an attractive city, sightseeing is a case of robust, handsome "highlights", rather than continual, refined aesthetics. A prime example of Pomeranian ecclesiastical architecture, located on the banks of the River Oder, is **Kościół Św. Jana Ewangelisty** (St John the Evangelist's Church) **A** (open daily). One of the few buildings to survive the war, the 14th-century façade yields simple interiors with fragments of the original wall paintings in the right-hand aisle.

Further along by the banks of the Oder is the **Ratusz Staromiejski** (Old Town Hall) **B** (open Tues–Sun; entrance fee). Originally Baroque, dating from the 17th century, it was burned down in 1944, and reconstructed in its original Gothic style. This includes an extraordinary gabled roof, while the decorative terracotta façade is typical of Hanseatic towns around the Baltic. The building now houses the **Muzeum Historii Miasta Szczecina** (Museum of the History of the City of Szczecin) with a collection that dates from the 8th century (open Tues–Sun; entrance fee). Nearby are the elegant **Kamiennica Loitzów** (Loitz House) **C** (open daily) formerly the residence of a wealthy 16th-century merchant family, and the far more majestic **Zamek Książąt Pomorskich** (Castle of the Pomeranian Princes) **D**. Built between the 14th and 17th centuries, it was reconstructed after World War II in a Renaissance style, retaining Gothic elements. Originally housing the dukes' valuable art collection, it comprises five wings and two inner courtyards which are an impressive sight. In addition to a library, there is a concert hall within the former chapel, while the belfry's observation tower provides a magnificent panorama of the city and the harbour. The

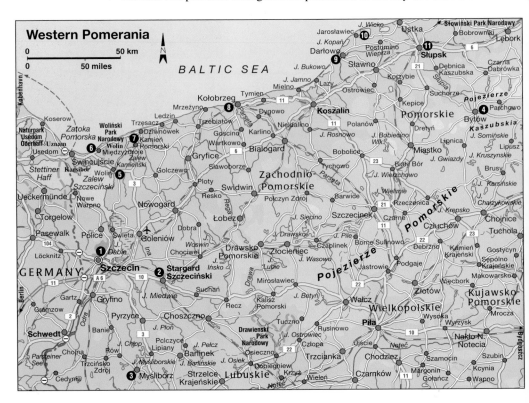

east wing houses the Castle Museum (open Tues–Sun; entrance fee) which details the castle's history. Among the most interesting exhibits are six sarcophagi of Pomeranian princes from the early 17th century. At the foot of the castle are fragments of the town's medieval defences, the **Baszta Panieńska** (Maiden's Tower) **E** (summer months open 10am–6pm; entrance fee), also known as the Bastion of Seven Cloaks.

Walking along **Wały Chrobrego** (Chrobry Embankments) **F** takes you past an eclectic group of red-brick buildings. Dating from the early 20th century and built on the site of the former town walls, these buildings house the Maritime Academy and the **Muzeum Morskie** (Museum of the Sea; open Tues–Sun; entrance fee) including maritime, ethnographic, and archaeological exhibits. Proceeding further north brings the harbour into view, from where boats leave on sightseeing tours of the river, and cruise further north to the port of Świnoujście by the Baltic. Strolling through **Park Zeromskiego** **G** (Zeromskiego Park; open daily) takes you through wooded greenery, including numerous trees and shrubs from around the world, as well as the **Pomnik Adama Mickiewicza** (Mickiewicz Monument) **H** honouring Poland's most romantic poet (*see page 108*).

The north of the city

The streets and squares of the northern part of the city are laid out in a star-shaped pattern, with the radial roads meeting at **Plac Grunwaldzki** (Grunwald Square). Unlike the city centre, which was badly damaged during World War II, the surrounding area was relatively unscathed. If perhaps ready for refurbishment, the area's houses are, nevertheless, attractive.

Maps:
Area 322
City 323

The reconstructed Castle of the Pomeranian Princes. Climb the bell-tower for a great view of the city.

BELOW: the Church of SS Peter and Paul, Szczecin.

The ornate and ceremonial **Brama Królewska** (Royal Gate) ❶, also known as the Gate of Prussian Homage, is one of the city's landmarks. Replacing an earlier Gothic gate, this was built by the Prussians at the beginning of the 18th century as a reminder of the Prussian purchase of the city from the Swedes in 1720. This highly artistic gate now houses an art gallery.

The **Kościół Św. Piotra i Pawla** (Church of SS Peter and Paul) ❶ (open daily) is a superb example of Pomeranian Gothic sacral architecture, with an ornate façade featuring an impressive rose window. The façade is decorated with glazed terracotta mascarons, while the interiors include an 18th-century wooden ceiling, buttresses and an historic portal from a monastery in Grabów.

The Baroque Parliament Building of Pomeranian States on Plac Zolnierza Polskiego (Square of the Polish Soldiers), built in the 1720s, now houses the **Muzeum Narodowe** (National Museum) ❸ (tel: 433 50 66; open Tues–Sun; entrance fee). A fascinating collection encompasses medieval sculptures from eastern Pomerania, Polish paintings from the 18th to the early 20th centuries, the history of Szczecin and Pomerania, silver, folk arts and crafts. Among the sacred art are some beautiful altarpieces. Modern Polish art is displayed at the museum's annexe across the road in the neoclassical Pałac pod Głowami (Palace under the Heads), named after the busts which decorate the windows. This is one of several neoclassical buildings in the immediate area.

The **Pałac Pod Globusem** (Pod Globusem Palace) ❶ (open daily) was built in the 1720s for the President of the Province of Pomerania, and features a decorative tympanium. Opposite the 18th-century Baroque **Pomnik Flory** (Statue of Flora) ❹, is one of Pomerania's largest Gothic churches, Katedra Św. Jakuba (St James' Cathedral). After the war, only the bomb-damaged tower and the

The tune that now traditionally accompanies all brides down the aisle, The Wedding March, *was first played by its composer Felix Mendelssohn-Bartholdy in 1827 at Szczesin's St James' Cathedral.*

BELOW: detail of brick heads on the Church of SS Peter and Paul.

choir remained, until reconstruction began in 1971. Few of the original features have survived, though the 14th-century altar triptych and Baroque epitaphs are worth seeing. The Baroque **Fontanna z orłem** (Fountain with the eagle) is indeed crowned with a majestic sandstone eagle. Erected in 1723, it also served as a well, being part of the city's newly established water system. The willows surrounding the fountain really do make this a "green oasis", and the best view of the fountain is with the Pod Globusem Palace as the backdrop.

Brama Portowa (Harbour Gate) **O** was also built by the Prussians at the start of the 18th century, on the site of an earlier Gothic gate. Among the ornate inscriptions and carvings is a panorama of Szczecin. The late 19th century neo-Gothic **Kościół Św. Jana Chrzciciela** (St John the Baptist Church) **P** (open daily) is arranged in the form of a cross. It is often known as the "Polish church" as even during the Prussian regime mass was occasionally celebrated in Polish. The early 20th century **Kościół Św. Wojciecha** (St Adalbert's Church) **Q** (open daily) pays homage to Poland's most famous saint, with stained-glass windows depicting his life. As the garrison church, there are also monuments to Polish troops who lost there lives in various uprisings and wars.

Further north is Jasne Błonia where a monument was erected to commemorate the dramatic events of 1970, when many dockers were killed during an uprising against the Communist regime. Directly adjoining the woodland of the Wrkrzanska Heath is **Jan Kasprowicz Park** (open daily).

Founded in the late 19th century, it includes an amphitheatre together with various rare trees and shrubs. The southern districts of Zdroje and Dąbie, both originally villages, border onto delightful countryside. The Emerald Lake, created on the site of a former chalk quarry, is named after the colour of the water.

Map on page 323

The Gothic Cathedral of St James was badly damaged in 1945: restoration was completed in 1982.

BELOW: the Old Town, Szczecin.

A comprehensive tram service operates in Szczecin. A local map (from the tourist office) details tram routes.

BELOW: writing postcards home.

Around the lake are marked trails through the **Puszcza Bukowa** (Beech Tree Heath), with the highest hills providing a wonderful panorama of the city and surrounding lakes and forest.

South and east of Szczecin

One of the most popular and interesting towns, situated by the River Ina about 35 km (16 miles) to the east of Szczecin, is **Stargard Szczeciński** ❷. It provides a great day out and a leisurely stroll will take you past all the Gothic and Renaissance attractions, set amid a delightful "country town" atmosphere.

The Market Square includes the ornate late Gothic Town Hall, with a wonderful flourish of mascarons on the façade, neighboured by Gothic and Renaissance burghers' houses and the former police station, which houses the Regional Museum covering local history. The twin-towered **Kościół Najświętszej Marii Panny** (Church of the Blessed Virgin Mary), was designed by Henryk Grunsberg, one of the most renowned Gothic architects. Construction began in 1292, but continued until the end of the 15th century. The 15th-century Gothic **Kościół Św. Jana** (St John's Church) has Pomerania's tallest tower at almost 100 metres (328 ft), not to mention an impressive vaulted nave.

The town's powerful defensive system has survived remarkably well. Dating from the 13th and 14th centuries, the city walls enclose the Old Town, with attractive parks laid out along the walls. Several gates and towers provided aesthetics as well as defence. The oldest tower is the imposing red-brick Brama Pyrzycka, dating from the 13th century, set among wooded greenery. One of the most unusual is the 15th-century Mill Gate. The tallest is the Morze Czerwone Tower (Red Sea Tower) at 34 metres (111 ft), while the Harbour Gate crosses

Map on page 322

a tributary of the River Ina, with a tower on each bank. The village of **Chojna**, originally a 10th-century Slav settlement, is also a popular destination. The remains of the 15th-century **Kościół Najświętszej Marii Panny** (Church of the Blessed Virgin Mary), is currently being restored, while the Augustinian Monastic complex dates from the 13th century, and the Town Hall is 15th-century. Fragments of the defensive walls and two splendid gates are 15th century.

There are more defensive walls and impressive 15th-century gates to be seen in **Trzcińsko Zdrój**, set by the picturesque Trzyglowskim lake and park. Traditionally a cattle and sheep trading town, a spa was established in 1895. The church dates from the 13th century and has a vast stone tower, while the 15th-century Town Hall includes an ornamental façade and vaulted interiors.

Heading south are a number of towns which played a prominent role during the war, with forts by the Oder erected by Polish and Russian soldiers in April 1945, shortly before the capture of Berlin. A monument on a hill near Cedynia, Poland's most westerly town, recalls the battle between Mieszko I, Poland's first king, and German Margraves in 972. The town also has a 13th-century church and the remains of a 14th century abbey. The Cedyński National Park, which includes a reserve for rare plants, is within easy reach of the town.

Myślibórz ❸, a small town close to a number of lakes, is encircled by the remains of a medieval wall. The walls of the late 13th-century parish church are also worth seeing, being constructed of loose stones arranged on top of one another, a building method typical of early-Gothic churches in Pomerania. The grand Town Hall is Baroque. Among various sights in **Pyrzyce** are the well-preserved town walls with three medieval gates, and the early 16th century Church of the Blessed Virgin Mary, with notable stained glass windows.

BELOW: landing a catch.

TIP

During summer there is a varied programme of cultural events: in Swinoujscie there is an Arts Festival (June), Days of the Sea (July) and Polish Songs of the Sea (September); In Międzyzdroje the annual International Festival of Choral Music and the Comedy Film Festival.

To the east, by the lower reaches of the River Drawa, large wooded areas extend across Drawska Heath. This countryside is perfect for outdoor pursuits, such as hiking and cycling. Meanwhile, the section of the River Drawa between Czaplinek and Krzyż is a kayaker's paradise.

The Pomeranian Lakes

West Pomerania's landscape is dominated by lakes, most of which are ringed by delightful wooded hillsides. The **Pojezierze Drawskie** (Drawski Lakes), including the towns of Drawsko Pomorskie, Połczyn Zdrój and Szczecinek, is the most attractive region. The largest and most beautiful of the 200 lakes is Lake Drawsko, with the popular tourist town of **Czaplinek** on its southeastern edge.

Travelling northwards through the picturesque Valley of the Five Lakes leads to **Połczyn Zdrój**. This popular spa town has been renowned for the medicinal benefits of its waters since the 14th century. Nestling between high moraine hills, the town's attractions include a castle dating from the 13th century and the Gothic Church of the Blessed Virgin Mary. The **Wał Pomorski** (Pomeranian Wall) stretches from Szczecinek through Wałcz and Tuczno to Krzyż. This defensive barrier built of reinforced concrete by the Germans in the 1930s was part of an ambitious system of fortifications. It was only in February 1945 that Polish soldiers managed to break through. Monuments and military museums in Podgaje near Jastrowie, in Wałcz and in Mirosławiec serve as memorials to the fierce battles waged in this part of West Pomerania. The best preserved fragments of the wall can be visited near Wałcz. This town, on the shores of two lakes, also has a vast military cemetery where victims of World War II are buried. The **Pojezierze Bytówskie** (Bytów Lakes), found among wooded hills, begin east of the Drawa Lakes. **Bytów ❹**, on the edge of the Bytów Lake District, has a Gothic castle built by the Teutonic Knights which is now a Regional Museum of Western Kashubia, with a collection that includes folk arts and crafts. The castle also houses a hotel and restaurant. The town's other attractions include the Gothic tower of St Catherine's church, the 18th-century neoclassical former post office, and a half-timbered 19th-century granary.

Along the Baltic Sea coast

Świnoujście occupies three islands: Uznam, Wolin and Karsibór. While this is a major port for cargo ships and passenger ferries to Hamburg, Copenhagen and Ystad, it is also a tourist centre.

The western end of Świnoujście has long sandy beaches, with Poland's tallest lighthouse (68 metres/220 ft), and being a long established spa town there are various Seccessionist spa buildings.

The town of **Wolin ❺**, in the south of the island, was one of the oldest Slav settlements, flourishing during the 9th and 10th centuries. A Slav burial mound and cemetery both date from the 9th century. However, it was also a Viking stronghold, which accounts for the annual Viking Festival. Part of the island is a national park, established to protect the unusual geological formations, cliffs and offshore rocks. The remote eastern edge of the park has several

BELOW:
statue guarding the ruins of the church in Wolin.

lakes which link to form a small lake district. This includes Lake Turkusowe at the southern end of the park, with Lake Gardno close to the seashore. Eagles, water fowl and other protected species such as wild boar can be seen in the woods surrounding the lakes, with a small bison reserve at the edge of the park.

Having attractive sandy beaches, impressive cliffs, and dense forests on either side, makes **Międzyzdroje** ❻ one of the most popular Baltic resorts. In addition to numerous sports facilities, the spa operates from attractive wooden buildings dating from the 19th century.

Kamień Pomorski ❼, a town which joined the Hanseatic League in the 14th century, is situated by the Kaminski Lagoon about 10 km (6 miles) from the sea. This was once an important trading centre, with a mint issuing Pomeranian coins in the late 12th century. Retaining its original medieval lay-out, the town's most important building is the Romanesque-Gothic cathedral. Elegant features animate the red-brick façade, while the interiors include a 12th-century baptismal font, a 17th-century wrought-iron screen and Baroque organ, which can be heard during the town's Summer Festival of Organ Music. The late Gothic Bishop's Palace, the 14th-century Church of St Nicholas, now housing the Regional Museum, and St Mary's Church, built in the 18th century, are also prime examples of sacred architecture. Fragments of the town walls include the 15th-century Wolin Gate, which leads into the Old Town and the late-Gothic Town Hall. To explore the lagoon, boats can be hired by the day at the harbour.

The coast is lined with numerous holiday villages such as Dziwnów, Dziwnówek, Mrzeżyno, and Dźwirzyno, which are renowned for their recreational facilities. Parts of the coast have suffered from erosion, which is particularly evident in Trzęsacz, where the ruins of a 14th-century Gothic church, originally

Map on page 322

European bison in a reserve at the Wolin National Park.

BELOW: fishing boats at low tide.

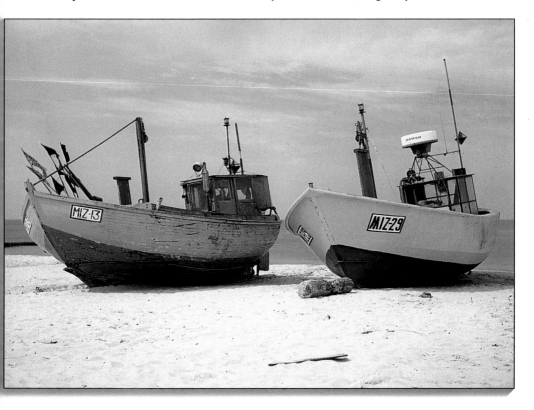

built 2 km (1 mile) from the coast, have been lapped by the sea since 1901. Founded in the 13th century, **Trzebiatów,** beside the River Rega, has managed to preserve its delightful medieval character. The main sights are the Gothic St Mary's Church, dominated by a stately 90-metre (295-ft) steeple which is typical of West Pomeranian architecture and contains one of Poland's heaviest bells (7.2 tons). Scaled-down Gothic can be seen at the delightful Holy Ghost Chapel. Fragments of the town walls include the late-Gothic Kaszana tower. A great way to see the surrounding countryside is from a narrow-gauge passenger train which operates between Trzebiatów and other coastal towns.

Kołobrzeg ❽, at the mouth of the River Parsęta, is both a port and major holiday spa resort. The town dates from AD 1000, when King Bolesław Chrobry established an episcopal see and prospered as a member of the Hanseatic League. A great asset was salt production, which also fostered production of salted herrings. Almost 90 percent of Kołobrzeg was destroyed in World War II, but the Old Town has now been rebuilt, much of it very recently. The Gothic Collegiate Church of St Mary is the town's most impressive building, with leaning columns supporting a vaulted ceiling. These pillars may give the impression that the church is about to collapse, but they have leaned at an angle since the 16th century. Various Gothic features include a bronze font, a vast chandelier, and beautifully carved stalls. It's an effort to climb to the top of the brick steeple, but the reward is a magnificent panorama of Kołobrzeg and its surroundings. Fragments of the medieval city wall include the **Wieża Prochowa** (Gun Powder Tower), while the Military Museum exhibits weapons and other items salvaged in 1945 (open Tues–Sun; entrance fee). Lying beyond the dunes east of Kołobrzeg are more holiday villages, with Ustrońie Morskie,

BELOW: strolling in the woods.

Map
on page
322

Sarbinowo and Mielno popular with tourists especially during the summer. Around this area the countryside has an extraordinary beauty, combining lakes and flooded meadows.

The sleepy fishing village of **Darłowo** ❾, by the mouth of the River Wieprza, was granted its municipal charter in 1270. The Pomeranian Duke Eryk I, who also ruled Denmark, Sweden and Norway, established the 14th-century castle as the capital of his dukedom. This magnificent castle is now a museum (open Tues–Sun; entrance fee) with an interesting collection of folk arts and crafts, furniture, armour, sacred art and portraits of Pomeranian princes. Duke Eryk also founded the Scandinavian Gothic-style St Gertrude's Chapel, which is a rarity, being twelve-sided. He is buried, together with other Pomeranian dukes, in the Gothic St Mary's Church. The Old Town has retained a medieval character, which includes the town walls and one of the Gothic town gates. A Baroque Town Hall overlooks the market square.

The neighbouring village of **Darłówko** is another popular seaside resort, as is the small town of **Sławno**, 20 km (12 miles) from Darłówko, which has several monuments that are well worth a detour, including the medieval town wall, the huge Gothic St Mary's Church, and various burghers' houses.

Jarosławiec ❿ is one of Poland's most attractive seaside resorts, partly due to its proximity to Lake Wicko. The traditional fishermen's cottages and half-timbered houses surrounding the lake, and the 17th century lighthouse, create a delightful atmosphere. At the mouth of the River Słupia is Ustka, a small port and popular resort. The harbour was built to serve **Słupsk** ⓫, a busy town situated some 20 km (12 miles) inland. One of the largest coastal resorts, Słupsk's attractions include the 14th-century Gothic Parish Church and the Renaissance Castle of the Pomeranian Dukes. This houses the **Museum of Central Pomerania** (open Tues–Sun; entrance fee) as well as a gallery devoted to the works of Witkacy (*see page 247*). The castle's grounds also include the Dominican Church of St Jacek, with its ducal tombs and Baroque organ.

The **Słowin National Park** encloses four lakes: Łebsko (the third largest in Poland), Gardno, Dołgie Wielkie and Dołgie Małe. Separated from the sea by a small beach, the lakes are a refuge for numerous birds. However, the park is most renowned for the "moving" sand dunes, along the coastline between Rowy and Leba, which are a rarity in Europe. In some areas the dunes are moved up to 10 metres (30 ft) per year by the wind. Considering that the tallest dune is just over 40 metres (130 ft) high, and the largest extends to around 300 hectares (740 acres), it's quite a phenomenon. In the western part of the park are the remains of V-2 rocket launch pads, abandoned by the Nazis at the end of World War II, which now attract a lot of visitors. **Kluki**, a remote fishing village on the edge of Lake Łebsko, has some fine half-timbered houses and a *skansen* (open-air museum) with a collection of historic regional buildings. Most of the local inhabitants are descended from the Slavic Slovincian tribe. The coastal village of **Łeba** is an attractive seaside destination and a fishing port, and is a good base from which to explore the Słowin National Park. ❏

BELOW: the shifting dunes at Łeba.

GDAŃSK

Gdańsk was reduced to rubble during World War II, but it has been reconstructed and today looks much the same as in the Hanseatic era when it was built by rich shipowners and merchants.

Map on page 334

The most important city along the Baltic Coast is actually a "Tri-City", comprising Gdańsk, Sopot and Gdynia, which together extend along the Bay of Gdańsk for 20 km (12 miles). Originally separate towns, the suburbs of each have linked to create a conurbation inhabited by almost 800,000 people, which is well connected by road, rail, ferry, bus and tram links.

These three cities have nevertheless retained their own distinct characters. Gdańsk is the historic and cultural centre, with outstanding examples of Gothic, Renaissance and Baroque architecture. Sopot is a traditional seaside resort, which developed in the 19th and early 20th centuries, and is characterised by Art Nouveau villas, while the maritime character of Gdynia dates from the 1920s, when the city was "purpose-built" to provide a modern harbour and docks.

Historic pearl of the Baltic

Gdańsk has long been an important port and trading centre. Originating as a Slavic fishing village, a defensive settlement was established in the Gdańsk area during the 9th century. From the 10th century this was a seat of the Pomeranian dukes, with Poland's most important saint, Adalbert, baptising the local inhabitants in AD 997. The earliest recorded mention was in 999, within *The Life of Saint Adalbert* written by a Benedictine

LEFT: the Golden House. **BELOW:** the Neptune Fountain, symbol of the city of Gdańsk.

order. Being a river port on the Vistula also meant that Gdańsk was an important link in the early Middle Ages with the historic capital of Kraków (*see page 201*), with grains, furs, leather and amber among the most important commodities.

The region's evolution was also dictated by Polish-Prussian rivalry. In 1225 the Mazovian Duke Konrad Mazowiecki asked the Teutonic Order of Knights (*see page 22*) to help in his struggle against the heathen Prussians, in order to control the area around Toruń in East Pomerania. The Teutonic Knights agreed, but it soon created another problem, as the Knights used this as an opportunity to strengthen their presence in East Pomerania. Gdańsk and East Pomerania came under the control of the Teutonic Knights in 1308, the same year in which the Main Town district received its town charter. The Knights also founded the Młode Miasto (New Town) in 1380, which subsequently merged with the Main Town, while also incorporating the neighbouring East Pomeranian town, now known as the Old Town district. The Knights also transferred their capital from Venice to nearby Malbork.

As a member of the Hanseatic League, Gdańsk developed into a prosperous town during the 14th century, and the town's burghers set about constructing major civic buildings, with St Mary's Church intended to be the largest brick-built church in the world.

The princes of East Pomerania and Wielkopolska (Greater Poland) attempted to resist the growing dominance of the Teutonic Knights, and a Polish triumph in 1454 brought Gdańsk and East Pomerania under Polish rule. This was further ratified by the Teutonic Knights agreeing to the Second Peace of Toruń in 1466. Being granted exclusive rights to Poland's maritime trade in the 15th century resulted in Gdańsk enjoying even greater prosperity, with two-thirds of Poland's external trade passing through the town. Gdańsk continued to have the status of an independent town until the partitions of Poland brought it under Prussian control in 1792, regaining its original status as a free town during the Napoleonic era. Between the two World Wars, Gdańsk was under the protection of the League of Nations.

It was in the Westerplatte region of Gdańsk that the first shots of World War II were fired, and Gdańsk remained in the active war zone for longer than any other region, with the occupation lasting until the Nazis surrendered on the Hel peninsula in May 1945. By the end of the war Gdańsk was reduced to rubble, though much of this was inflicted by the "liberating" Red Army, who thought of Gdańsk as "Danzig", in other words German.

Following the end of World War II, Gdańsk became a part of Poland and, despite the town's devastation and Poland's precarious economic situation, there was never any question that the city would be reconstructed. The question was how this should be done. It was suggested that a new, modern city be built on this site, but it was eventually decided to reconstruct the city in its historic style. This presented a huge challenge for architects and planners. Although some fragments of the original buildings, such as church walls, towers and gates, could be retrieved from the rubble, many of the landmarks were totally

The most famous chronicle of the wartime years is The Tin Drum, *by the German writer Günter Grass. Born in Gdańsk (or Danzig as it is known in German) in 1927, he describes this period through the eyes of a child.*

destroyed. It was a massive undertaking, and it wasn't until 1975 that the reconstruction programme was completed. Indeed, St John's Church was only finished in the 1990's. The historic granaries are still waiting their turn.

In 1997, Gdańsk, now with a population of 500,000, commemorated its millennium, and the city continues to be Poland's largest port as well as an important industrial, scientific and cultural centre, not to mention a major tourist attraction. Among the city's varied cultural repertoire is the Baltic Philharmonic, with annual events including the Festival of Organ Music, the Film Festival and the Dominican Fair in August. First established during the mid-13th century and revived in 1972, this market offers numerous folk arts and crafts, antiques and bric-a-brac, amber jewellery and various other local specialities, with various concerts and events organised to coincide with this fair.

 Map on page 334

Gdańsk's historic centre

Much of the historic centre was originally constructed as a showcase of the city's prosperity. The buildings were designed to impress. From grand and imposing to flamboyant and ornamental, the city is beautiful but never ostentatious. The burghers had that rare combination: wealth and style. As much of the historic centre is pedestrianised, a walking tour is the best way to explore, with the numerous cafés, boutiques and galleries providing plenty of refreshing stops en route. Nine principal thoroughfares each link to a waterside gate that provides access to the harbour, so you are never far from a sea view.

The principal thoroughfare, Długa (literally "Long street"), is best approached through the **Złota Brama** (Golden Gate) **Ⓐ**. Designed by Abraham van den Blocke between 1612-14 in a Renaissance style, it was inspired by a triumphal

The statues on the Golden Gate are copies of the orginals made in 1648.

BELOW: Solidarność plaque, Gdańsk.

CRADLE OF SOLIDARITY

Gdańsk is now best known as the birthplace of the trade union movement *Solidarność* (Solidarity), which challenged the Communist regime and shaped Polish history during the 1970–80s. Lech Wałęsa, the union's leader and President of Poland (1991-95), wrote:

"Visitors… have no trouble finding their way to the monument… outside the Gdańsk shipyard. Striking workers were murdered here in December 1970, in a hail of fire from the militia. They sacrificed their lives for more than Gdańsk – even at a time when nobody had foreseen what far-reaching effects their struggle would have on the future of all of Europe. Their resistance and deaths were experiences from which we learned lessons…

"The resounding slogan of 1980 was 'good bread for good work'. Of course, the call for freedom was within everyone's heart all over Poland, but it was also clear to every one of us that such a cry at that time could have triggered off a swift Soviet intervention.

"And yet 10 years later, we have attained our goal – in a revolution without force and without bloodshed, a revolution which overthrew the Communist regime and set an example for democratic freedom initiatives throughout central and eastern Europe."

The Gdańsk Town Hall clock and tower. The statue at the top of the tower is of King Zygmunt August.

BELOW: the historic Mariengasse.

Roman arch, and the view along Długa is equally triumphant. As this was the route along which Polish kings paraded when attending events in the city, it's hardly surprising that Długa features numerous impressive buildings. An immediate example is the neighbouring Dwór Bractwa Św. Jerzego (Court of the Fraternity of St George). This Gothic mansion was built in the late 15th century, as the seat of this fraternity.

Before continuing along Długa, turn left into Tkacka to see the **Wielka Zbrojownia** (Great Armoury) **B**. A magnificent example of Renaissance architecture, the intricate symmetry of its four-gabled façade was designed by Dutch architect Anthonis van Opbergen. He was highly regarded in Gdańsk, and also built the Kronborg in Helsingor, Denmark, more popularly referred to as "Hamlet's Castle". The armoury now houses the Państwowa Wyższa Szkoła Sztuk Plastycznych (the Academy of Fine Arts; open Tues–Sun; entrance fee).

The **Ratusz** (Town Hall) **C** is unusual in not occupying a central position in a square, but forming part of a terrace of buildings at the far end of Długa. Nevertheless, this red brick 14th-century Gothic building stands out as the largest building in the street, with its elegant Renaissance tower crowned by a gilded statue of King Zygmunt August, dating from 1561. Needless to say, the view from the top of the tower is magnificent. The interiors are equally impressive, and the Red Room, originally the setting for the Town Council's debates, is truly a showpiece. Set against a vivid red and gilded background, this room's wealth of sculptures and ornamental carvings, are dominated by numerous paintings – 25 on the ceiling alone, while a series of seven allegorical paintings are the work of Jan Vredean de Vries. Many of the furnishings are original, having been shipped from Gdańsk prior to the outbreak of war for safekeeping.

Map on page 334

Housed amid these sumptuous interiors is a stylish restaurant and the **Muzeum Historyii Miasta Gdańska** (Historical Museum of the City of Gdańsk, Długa 47; tel: 301 48 71; open Tues–Sun; entrance fee except Sun). At this point Długa broadens out to form Długi Targ ("Long Marketplace"). The architectural magnificence is also heightened, as this is where the very wealthiest merchants and ship-owners built their residences. The beginning of this street is marked by the decorative **Fontanna Neptuna** (Neptune's Fountain) **D**. Enclosed by its original wrought iron railings, this statue of Neptune, symbolising the city's maritime links, dates from 1613.

Another impressive building is **Dwór Artusa** (Arthur's Court) **E** , the traditional seat of the Gdańsk Merchants' Guild and Poland's first stock exchange. The highly individual Mannerist architecture includes windows that dominate the main façade (equal to three storeys of the neighbouring houses). The vaulted entrance hall contains various historic features, including an ornate tiled stove. One of the few buildings not to be totally destroyed during World War II, this is now a museum (open Tues–Sun; entrance fee).

Façades of neighbouring buildings are equally definitive of other architectural genres. Baroque *in extremis* is the only way to describe the **Złota Kamiennica** (Golden House) **F**. Dating from the early 17th century, this four-storey house was built for the Mayor of Gdańsk and was named after its gilded bas reliefs, comprising historical figures including Achilles and Cleopatra. Home to the Cunard Line between the world wars, this is now the Maritime Institute.

The marketplace culminates in another gateway, the ornate quadruple arched **Zielona Brama** (Green Gate) **G**. Designed in a Flemish Renaissance style, this was also an official residence of Polish kings when visiting the city.

In the 14th century Europe became fascinated with the stories of England's King Arthur and Camelot, and many towns such as Gdańsk attempted to emulate the chivalrous spirit in their self-styled courts.

BELOW: relief detail the Golden House.

Gdańsk's waterfront

The Green Gate opens onto the wharf by the Motława estuary, formerly the site of the town's harbour. Boats leave from here for trips along the coast to Sopot, Gdynia and Westerplatte, or across the Bay of Gdańsk to the popular holiday resort of Hel on the Gdańsk peninsula (*see page 345*). Across the estuary on **Wyspy Spichrzów** (Granary Island) are numerous historic granaries, some of which are still awaiting restoration. Part of this area is also being re-developed as the city's modern commercial and banking centre. Turning left leads to the Brama Chlebnicka (Bread Gate), with the waterfront featuring numerous galleries selling souvenirs, antiques and above all, "Baltic Gold" or amber, alongside cafés and bars. Amber is almost the only thing you can buy, together with antiques, in the boutiques and galleries along the street **Mariacka** , entered through the Brama Mariacka (St Mary's Gate). One of the city's most beautiful streets, with its original granite cobblestones, it is also one of the most individual, characterised by "*perrons*". A feature of grander houses in numerous Baltic cities, this comprises a small but ornate flights of steps from the pavement to a terrace by the entrance to each building (rather like a box at the theatre). This was a prime place for the residents to sit and watch passers-by, as well as being seen themselves. Totally rebuilt after World War II, the first task was to determine exactly which fragments could be used where, as masonry was scattered all over the street. Furthermore, there was little documentation to draw upon as the archives were destroyed during the war, which meant the architects frequently resorted to photographs as their source material. There was at least one surviving *perron*, which was an invaluable starting point.

At the end of Mariacka is the transcendent **Kościół Mariacki** (St Mary's

Mariacka provided a location for the film version of Thomas Mann's novel Buddenbrooks – *as no such street could be found in post-war Lubeck, where the novel is set.*

LEFT:
Mariacka Street.
BELOW:
St Mary's Church,
Piwna Street.

Map on page 334

Church) **J**. This monumental red-brick Gothic building is thought to be the world's sixth largest church, able to accommodate a congregation of 25,000 (or crowds of tourists). Not surprisingly, it took more than 150 years to complete, from 1343–1502. Austere through its simplicity, but undoubtedly beautiful, the initial impact is provided by the scale and height of the three-naved arrangement. It is certainly worth looking up at the Baroque organ, and the magnificent vaulting, much of which was reconstructed following a fire in 1945.

While many original treasures were looted by the Nazis (or ended up in Polish museums), this still leaves plenty to see: 13 Gothic altars, over 30 Renaissance and Baroque epitaphs and a stunning sculpture of the so-called Beautiful Madonna. An astrological clock, the work of Hans Duringer in 1470, is one of the world's largest medieval clocks, revealing the phases of the moon as well as the positions of the sun and the moon. Another outstanding feature is a triptych by Hans Memling entitled *The Last Judgement*, dating from 1466–73. This painting was actually en route to a church in Tuscany when it was intercepted by the citizens of Gdańsk. A copy now hangs in the church, with the original in the Muzeum Narodowe (National Museum). If you feel like climbing the lofty tower a wonderful view across the historic centre is your reward.

Neighbouring the church is the elegant **Royal Chapel**, built in 1678–81. Founded by King Jan III Sobieski, it is thought to be the work of Tylman of Gameren, the Dutch architect responsible for many of Poland's most beautiful Baroque buildings; sculptures decorating the façade are by Andreas Schluter.

Returning to the riverfront, the 15th-century **Zuraw Gdański** (Gdańsk Crane) **K** was meticulously restored after World War II. Housed in the largest double-towered gate on the waterfront, it handled cargos as well as raising ships masts. Capable of lifting up to 2,000 kg (2 tonnes), it is one of the largest industrial constructions to have survived from the Middle Ages, and seeing the crane in action is a major attraction. This building now houses the Centralne Muzeum Morskie (Central Maritime Museum, Szeroka 67–8; tel: 31 86 11; open Tues–Sun; entrance fee). Adjoining the crane is a restaurant of the same name, which provides a panoramic view of the Motława. There are two prime examples of sacred Gothic architecture on Swiętojańska. The **Kościół Św. Jana** (St John's Church) **L**, which has only recently been reconstructed after its wartime devastation, has an impressive altar and various tombs of city dignitaries. The **Kościół Św. Mikolaja** (St Nicholas' Church) **M** was one of the few buildings to survive the war intact. The Gothic façade gives way to highly gilded Baroque interiors, with a beautiful altar where a central painting is surrounded by gilded figures.

It is claimed that the St Mary's Church Astrological Clock has only lost three minutes in the first hundred years of service.

BELOW: the riverfront with the Gdańsk Crane.

The Old Town

Although the **Stare Miasto** (Old Town) district was not rebuilt to the same extent as the Główne Miasto, there are numerous historic buildings and architectural styles. It has a different character: less densely built up, and providing greater variety, with broader streets and more open spaces interlaced with greenery. The parish church Kościół Św. Katarzyny (St Cather-

Map on page 334

ine's Church) on Wielkie Młyny has a magnificent Gothic tower with unusual ornamentation soaring above the façade, while the interiors feature late Gothic vaulted ceilings and Baroque details and monuments. This includes the tomb of the renowned Gdańsk astronomer, Jan Heweliusz, also known as Johannes Hevelius (1611–86), who published one of the first detailed maps of the moon and stars. However, earning little money from astronomy, he was also a successful brewer, with profits from the brewery providing funds to establish an observatory (the Hevelius beer brand continues to be very popular). Immediately behind this church is Kościół Św. Brygidy (St Bridgets's Church), which played a significant role in Poland's recent history, being known as the "Solidarity church". During martial law in 1981–3 anti-Communist groups met here to worship, which was then considered an act of "political opposition". This church is also unusual in not having recreated period interiors. Instead a modern layout, in a form of "sacred minimalism" creates a poignant setting for contemporary works of art, including a monument to Fr Jerzy Popiełuszko, the outspoken supporter of Solidarity who was murdered by the Communists.

Both St Brigitte's and St Catherine's Church are part of a cluster of buildings around the **Kanał Raduni** (Raduni Canal), at the heart of the Old Town. The combination of a small park and other stretches of greenery, canals and delightful cascades, gives this area a distinct, relaxed identity. **The Wielki Młyn** (Great Mill) **N** completed in 1595, and the Mały Młyn (Small Mill) are both prime examples of medieval architecture, with the former housing an elegant shopping centre (open daily 11am–7pm). The 16th-century **Ratusz Starego Miasta** (Old Town Hall) **O** (tel: 301 10 51; open Mon–Sun 10am–8pm; entrance fee) with its distinct Dutch appearance, has splendid interiors; although not on the same scale as the main Town Hall it is certainly worth seeing, with some beautiful paintings and fine examples of the Gdańsk chests.

Heading further north in the direction of the shipyards is the poignant Pomnik Poległych Stoczniowców (Monument to the Shipyard Workers). Three huge crosses, on which much smaller anchors are attached, soar above Gate 2 of the entrance to the Gdańsk shipyards, commemorating the 28 people who died when the December 1970 strike was suppressed. The crosses symbolise Faith and the anchors Hope, while metal figures of dockyard workers feature at the base of the crosses. The monument was unveiled in 1980 by the Solidarity movement, the year in which the trade union movement was legally recognised by the government. The Communists did not dare touch the monument because of its powerful significance.

South of Długi Targ is **Stare Przedmieście** (The Old Suburb). Among the area's most important buildings are the Kościół Św. Trójcy (Church of the Holy Trinity) built at the beginning of the 16th century, with a former Franciscan monastery housing the **Muzeum Narodowe** (National Museum) **P** (Toruńska 1; tel: 301 68 04; Tues–Sun 9am–4pm; entrance fee except Sat). The extensive collection includes Polish paintings, *objets d'art* and furniture, such as the renowned Gdańsk chests, which were exported across the world. ❑

BELOW: Gdańsk Shipyard Monument.

Amber

Fondly referred to as "the gold of the north", amber is Poland's national stone and a visible element of daily life, whether it's in the form of rings, earrings, necklaces, bracelets or cuff-links, not to mention various decorative items for the home such as lampshades and jewellery boxes. Amber varies enormously in terms of shape and size, while the colour ranges beyond the eponymous amber from yellow to white, red and green. Being transparent, amber is usually streaked with various colour-ways, while the inherent flaws add character.

Artificial amber can be convincing and inexpensive (if sold honestly), prepared from substances such as camphor. The genuine article is actually fossilised resin that seeped from deciduous and coniferous trees and has solidified and "matured" over thousands of years. The resin frequently trapped insects and flora, resulting in numerous pieces of amber containing perfectly preserved specimens of prehistoric life. Polish amber has even included fragments of date trees and tea bushes from the primeval forest which originally occupied the Baltic coastline.

Beyond the technical explanation, various legends define amber as the solidified tears of the passing of time, and more specifically as the tears of the Heliades, the sisters of Meleager, who couldn't stop weeping after his death.

Another version attributes the tears to the sisters of Phaeton. His father was Helios, god of the sun, who drove the chariot that dragged the sun across the sky from sunrise to sunset. One day Phaeton drove the chariot, but brought the sun too close to the earth: mountains burned and seas evaporated into deserts. Phaeton's punishment was to be struck by a fatal thunderbolt by Zeus. To stop his sisters from weeping the gods turned them into willows on the banks of the River Edrin, into which their tears continued to flow. En route to the Baltic the teardrops turned into amber. Locals who collected the amber on the beach assumed it was a gift from the gods.

Amber continues to be collected from beaches as the sea washes it up from beneath the surface of the sand. The best time to go amber-hunting is after a storm. The region between Chlapów and the Sambian peninsula yields the largest amounts.

Amber was prized by the Ancient Egyptians who called it the stone of "life and health" as it was thought to promote youthfulness and longevity. In fact, the world would be a far healthier place if amber fulfiled all the claims made for it.

There is no shortage of amber boutiques throughout Poland. Gdańsk is the historic centre, with a guild of amber craftsmen established in the 15th century. The city still has hundreds of shops selling amber jewellery and decorative items. Some of the finest are along Motława Quay and Mariacka, where the Archaeological Museum also has an amber collection. Outside the city is the Bakowo Forest, which includes an amber mine. The most extensive collection of historic amber can be seen at the castle in Malbork (*see page 347*). ❏

RIGHT: shopping for amber in Gdańsk.

AROUND GDAŃSK

*To follow the route around Gdańsk to the historic towns of Toruń,
Frombork and Chełmno is to journey through the 1,000-year
history and culture of the country.*

Map
on page
344

At the entrance to the harbour, about 5 km (3 miles) from the city centre, is
the Westerplatte peninsula. It was here, at 4.45am on 1 September 1939,
that 210 Polish soldiers and officers came under fire from the
Schleswig-Holstein, a German battleship. The garrison held out for seven days
before surrendering, after 3,000 Nazi soldiers landed here. The site has become
a memorial, with some of the ruins left exactly as they were after the bombardment, and there is a modernistic monument commemorating the bravery of
the garrison.

Oliwa is one of Gdańsk's most attractive suburbs, with a large Cistercian
monastery complex including the Oliwa Cathedral. The incredibly slender,
twin-towered façade actually houses the longest church in Poland. The
Romanesque-Gothic style, dating from the first half of the 13th century, was
partly remodelled in the 18th century, adding rococo elements. The 23 side
altars date from the 16th and 17th centuries, with a marble tomb of Gdańsk
princes who were buried here in the 13th century. Many famous musicians have
performed on the cathedral's rococo Oliwa organ. The work of J. Wulf at the end
of the 18th century, the organ has an amazing 1,876 pipes and 110 voices. Organ
concerts are a regular attraction at the cathedral, and the adjoining park is a
delightful place for a stroll.

LEFT:
Szerova Street,
Toruń Old Town.
BELOW:
fountain in front of
the abbey in Oliwa.

Sopot ❷ is full of greenery, open perspectives
along tree-lined streets, boulevards and parks. As there
was little damage to the town during World War II,
many buildings are original 19th-century Seccessionist, with wooden villas providing a "bourgeois"
character in contrast to the "showcase" architecture
of Gdańsk.

The original settlement of Sopot was established
by Oliwa's Cistercian monks. During the 16th century the Gdańsk burghers decided that sea air was
beneficial to their health and began turning the village into a spa. This received a much greater impetus
at the beginning of the 19th century, mainly due to
the fact that Napoleon's former doctor, Jean Haffner,
erected bathing pavilions by the sea in 1823.

It's easy to see why Sopot became so popular: a
park runs the length of its wide, sandy beaches which
provide an ideal setting for sun bathing. Some highly
eclectic spa buildings can still be seen around the
seafront. The pier is the longest in Poland, extending 516 metres (1,693 ft) into the sea, which is a
favourite place to promenade while also providing an
embarkation point for boat trips to Gdańsk, Gdynia
and the Hel peninsula.

Another favourite place to promenade is the adjacent main thoroughfare, Bohaterów Monte Cassino
(Heroes of Monte Cassino street): lined with pave-

The modern assembly hall beside the road from Oliwa to Sopot was the venue for the first and second regional Solidarity conferences, both important milestones on Poland's road to democracy.

ment cafés, trendy boutiques and galleries, it encapsulates Sopot's relaxed spirit. The Grand Hotel is a reminder of Sopot's traditional grandeur. Built in an Art Nouveau style in 1926 and renovated in 1990, the hotel offers a beachside terrace, tea dances, gourmet meals and Poland's most elegant, not to mention most historic casino.

Gdynia, 9 km (6 miles) north of Sopot, is Poland's second-largest port. A small fishing village until 1921, it was transformed into a "purpose built" port to ensure that Poland would not be entirely dependent on Gdańsk. Tourist attractions reflect the maritime character. The museum ships *Błyskawica*, a World War II destroyer, and *Dar Pomorza*, a three-masted frigate, are moored at the dockyard and have exhibits tracing the history of the Polish navy. The city also has an excellent Oceanographic Museum and Aquarium (Zjednocazenia 1; tel: 21 70 21; open Tues–Sun; entrance fee), and a Naval Museum (Sędzickiego 4; tel 26 37 27; open Tues–Sun; entrance fee). Climbing the 50-metre (165-ft) Kamienna Góra (Stone Hill) provides a great view across the harbour.

The Bay of Gdańsk and Kashubian Lakes

Curving almost 35 km (20 miles) across the Bay of Gdańsk is the narrow **Mierzeja Helska** (Hel Peninsula). This is an idyllic area, with fishing villages including Jastrzębia Góra, the romantic port of Władysławowo, Chalupy, Kuźnica, Jąstarnia, Jurata and, on the tip of the peninsula, the old village of Hel, whose fascinating history is documented in the local fishing museum.

At the beginning of the peninsula is the quiet port of **Puck**, which developed from a Slavic settlement into a naval base for the Polish fleet in the 16th and 17th centuries. The town's buildings are mainly 16th to 18th century with an 18th-century half-timbered former hospital housing the Museum of the Puck region. Southwest of Puck, **Wejherowo ❸** has a distinctly religious character, with the 16th-century governor establishing the *Kalwaria Wejherowska* (the Wejherowo "Road to Calvary") over the nearby hills. It includes some 26 17th- to 19th-century chapels in total. To the west of the tri-city is the **Pojezierze Kaszubskie**, an extraordinarily scenic combination of lakes and hills, the highest point of which is the Wieżyca at 329 metres (1,080 ft). These uplands are also the source of the rivers Radunia, Wierzyca, Wda, Słupia and Łeba, all of which flow into the Baltic Sea.

The largest lake is the Wdzydze, and around it is **Wdzydze Kiszewskie ❹**, a superb *skansen* (open-air ethnographic museum), which extends over an area of 21 hectares (52 acres). This collection of traditional buildings from the Kashubian region, including an exquisite wooden church painted with rustic motifs, provides a wonderful insight into the region's heritage (open Tues–Sun; entrance fee). **Kartuzy ❺**, surrounded by lakes and woods, is the capital of Kashubia. The Carthusian abbey complex has a fascinating 14th-century Gothic church, with a roof shaped like a coffin. The Kashubian Museum's rich collection of folk arts and crafts also details the history and lifestyle of this historic West Slavic tribe (open Tues–Sun, May–Sep; Tues–Sat, Oct–Apr; entrance fee).

A little further southwest is the 1,000-year-old city of **Kościerzyna**, the main centre of Kashubian culture. In June the popular Kashubian tradition of floating wreaths on the lake is followed by a procession around other lakes in the region. With numerous sporting facilities to hand, this makes an ideal base from which to explore the region's towns, such as Chmielno. A popular holiday destination and one of the most historic Kashubian settlements, it is located on the banks of three lakes, the Białe, Kodno and Rekowskie. Traditionally a pottery centre, the renowned Necel workshop can be seen on request. The Kashubian Country Park was established at the centre of this lake district in 1983.

Further south on the River Wierzyca is **Pelplin ❻**, where you can see one of Poland's most beautiful Gothic cathedrals. Originally the church of a Cistercian abbey, this vast triple-naved basilica includes Gothic stalls, as well as Renaissance, Baroque and rococo works of art by Herman Han and Bartlomiej Strobel. The Diocesan Museum's prized possession is a medieval manuscript of the only Guttenberg Bible in Poland, and an amazing collection of musical

Map on page 344

TIP

There is a wonderful cultural programme in Sopot. The Opera Leśna (Opera in the Woods), a delightful al fresco auditorium set in a wood, hosts various annual events including the Opera Festival in July, and the International Song Festival in August.

BELOW: Hel beach.

Altar detail in Malbork Castle chapel.

manuscripts (ks Biskupa Dominikana 11; tel: 36 12 21; open Tues–Sun; entrance fee). **Gniew** ❼ is situated on a steep cliff at the confluence of the Wierzyca and Vistula rivers. Originally settled by the Cistercians, it was subsequently controlled by the Teutonic Knights – the remains of the knights' Gothic castle is perched on a hilltop near the town. The original medieval layout includes churches and town walls, some dating from the 16th century, while the arcaded burghers' houses are the finest in Pomerania. South of Gniew, and also on the Vistula, is Nowe. Now a centre of the furniture industry, the outline of this medieval town with its small castle and two Gothic churches rises high above the river.

The **Wysoczyzna Świecka** (Świecka Uplands) run to the south of the Starogard Lakes, with the main town being **Świecie**. From 1309 to 1466, Świecie was the headquarters for a local commander of the Teutonic Knights, with the ruins of the knight's castle, together with a Gothic church, standing above the fork of the Wda and Vistula. One of Poland's largest forested areas, the **Bory Tucholskie** (Tuchola Heath), lies to the north and northwest of Świecie beside the rivers Wda and Brda, which are very popular with watersports enthusiasts. Distinctive features in this landscape are the narrow "channel" lakes, with countless man-made lakes, such as Lake Kornowskie near Koronowo.

In an isolated and wooded area, the **Cisy im L. Wyczólkowskiego** nature reserve near Wierzchy and the Kręgi Kamienne (Stone Circles) archaeological biological reserve (the megalithic site has been dated at the first or second century) in Odry north of Czersk, are of particular interest. At the western tip of the heath lies **Tuchola**, the area's main tourist centre, with medieval buildings and remnants of the town's fortified walls drawing visitors.

BELOW: Frombork Cathedral.

On the right bank of the Vistula

Poland's most northerly holiday region lies east of the Vistula estuary, where resorts are typically separated from the beach by narrow strips of dunes and woodland. However, resorts such as Mikoszewo, Jantar and Stegna are directly by the beaches of the Mierzeja Wiślana spit. The nearby town of Sztutowo was the site of a concentration camp in which 85,000 people of various nationalities died. Near the Russian border, overlooking the Vistula lagoon, is the fishing town of **Frombork ❽**, which has an outstanding 14th-century Gothic cathedral. This fortified complex includes defensive walls, and a bastion where the famous astronomer Nicolaus Copernicus lived from 1512–43, while writing his celebrated work *De Revolutionibus Orbitium Coelestium* (*On the Revolutions of the Celestial Spheres*). The bastion now houses the Copernicus Museum, with his early treatises and scientific instruments (open Tues–Sun; entrance fee).

A chain of hills covered with beech and oak forests runs alongside the Vistula Lagoon (Zalew Wiślany). To the south lies **Elbląg**, the region's second largest city after Gdańsk, and an important centre for industry, culture and tourism. Established in the 9th century, it developed into a flourishing port during the 16th and 17th centuries. Despite devastating losses in World War II, a number of interesting monuments have survived. The Market Gate (1319) includes fragments of the town wall, the Dominican St Mary's Church from the 13th–14th centuries (now an art gallery) and the Gothic Church of St Nicholas, with its 95-metre (312-ft) tower are the main highlights. Just below Elbląg lies Jezioro Drużno, a nature reserve that harbours around 150 species of waterfowl.

The town of **Malbork ❾**, on the Nogat river southwest of Elbląg, is dominated by the monumental Malbork Castle (open Tues–Sun; entrance fee), the

Map
on page
344

A strawberry festival is held in June on a hill 2km (1 mile) from Kartuzy, when local strawberry farmers show off their produce.

BELOW:
Malbork Castle on the River Nogat.

largest fortification in Europe. Built by the Great Masters of the Teutonic Knights in the late 13th century, it is actually a castle within a castle, with various chapels, church and refectories. This fascinating museum includes extraordinary interiors, sacred art and Poland's finest collection of amber.

There is another Teutonic castle, with an attractive courtyard, further south in **Kwidzyń** , also now a museum (open Tues–Sun; entrance fee). This is part of a Gothic complex including a two-tier chancel, a tower and a triple-naved fortified cathedral. Massive columns support the cathedral, which also has fine 14th-century frescos. At the northwestern edge of the triangle formed by the rivers Vistula, Osa and Drwęca lies the small and significant town of **Chełmno** ⓫. The medieval city walls including several bastions and the Grudiądz Gate, enclose about 200 monuments of historic interest within the Old Town, perched high up on the banks of the Vistula. Among the most impressive are the 16th-century Italian Renaissance Town Hall with ornamental attics. The design also turns conventional proportions upside down, with the largest windows at the top of the building, diminishing in size as they reach the ground floor. The Town Hall now houses the Regional Museum (open Tues–Sun; entrance fee). The Gothic parish church of St Mary's, also on the Market Square, features beautiful frescos in the choir and the apostles on pillars.

About 30 km (19 miles) to the north of Chełmno lies Grudziądz with its medieval town centre. The Gothic parish church, several Baroque Jesuit churches, and a group of warehouses joined by a complex system of defensive walls on the banks of the Vistula, deserve special attention. Near Grudziądz is Radzyń Chełmiński, noted for its 14th-century Teutonic Knights Castle, an architectural masterpiece for this era. About 6 km (4 miles) to the east is Rywałd,

BELOW:
Toruń Old Town.

Map on page 344

where a 15th-century sculpture of the Virgin Mary in the Capuchin monastery draws numerous pilgrims. In the Drwęca valley at the eastern edge of the Chełmno region about 35 km (22 miles) east of Toruń lies the town of Golub-Dobrzyń. At the top of the steep valley walls is a Gothic castle originally built by the Teutonic Knights, though its present appearance reflects Baroque additions. Every July the castle hosts the International Knights' Tournament, re-enacting medieval jousting. By the river's upper reaches is Brodnica, a gateway to Brodnicki Krajobrazowy country park. Parts of the town's medieval fortifications, including the Mazurian Tower and Chełminski Gate, have survived, while overlooking the Drwęca are the ruins of a Teutonic castle with an 85 metre (278 ft) tower. The remains of medieval architecture can also be seen in nearby Nowe Miasto Lubawskie.

Toruń – a Gothic haven

Toruń ⓬ is one of Poland's most interesting cities, with on-going restoration work also turning it into one of the most attractive. Numerous buildings that largely survived the Nazis intact provide variations on a historic theme: Renaissance and neo-Renaissance, Gothic and neo-Gothic, not to mention some splendid Baroque and the occasional Secessionist flourish. In fact, the city is full of delightful architectural surprises: a decorative frieze here, a stained glass window there. You have to keep looking, but you'll be rewarded. Comprehensive and compact, Toruń is easily covered on foot, with a day's walking tour taking in all the sights, though you obviously need longer to visit museums.

As the largest city in the Chełmno region, with a population of 200,000, Toruń was founded on the right bank of the River Vistula in 1233 by the

BELOW: Old Town Hall, Toruń.

Teutonic Knights. This order effectively ruled the town for the next 260 years, as it developed into an important trading centre within the Hanseatic League. In the 17th century Toruń became a centre for the Protestant movement, and subsequently for the Polish nationalist movement against Prussia after the partitions of Poland. Becoming part of an independent Poland in 1920, Toruń is now an educational and cultural centre, with the Mikołaj Kopernik University one of Poland's finest institutions.

The Old Town and New Town have retained their medieval layout, with the 14th-century **Ratusz** (Town Hall) **Ⓐ** at the centre of the Rynek Staromiejski (Old Town Market Square). One of Europe's finest Gothic civic buildings, it houses the Muzeum Okręgowe (Regional Museum; Rynek Staromiejski 1; tel: 270 38; open Tues-Sun; entrance fee except Sun), with a superb collection of Gothic sacred art, exhibited amid Gothic interiors with vaulted ceilings, a portrait gallery of Polish monarchs and impressive 18th- and 19th-century Polish paintings. Climbing the Town Hall Tower is an experience in itself, and the observation terrace at a height of 42 metres (140 ft) provides great views of the Old Town. To the side of the town hall, the Mikołaj Kopernik (Nicholas Copernicus) Monument states "*ruszyłziemie, zatrzymal slonce i niebo*" ("*he put the earth in motion and stopped the sun and sky*"). Every 19 February the University Rector places a bouquet here, honouring his status as the university's patron.

Among the surrounding buildings are Dwór Artusa (Arthur's Court) a late 19th-century neo-Renaissance building, formerly the seat of the town's burghers and now a cultural centre, while one of the most extravagant is **Kamiennica Pod Gwiazdą** (House under the Star) **Ⓑ** (tel: 652 11 33; open Tues–Sun; entrance

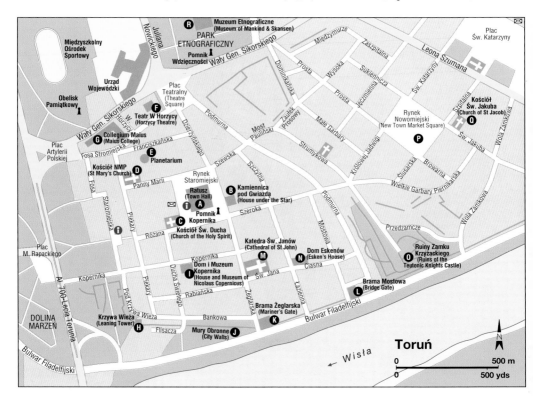

fee except Sun). Its Baroque architecture, featuring a flourish of fruit and floral motifs culminating in a wonderful gabled roof crowned with a star, dates from 1697. This is now a museum exhibiting the arts and crafts of the Far East (Rynek Staromiejski 35; tel: 211 33; open Fri–Tues; entrance fee). The neo-Baroque, mid-18th century **Kościół Św. Ducha** (Church of the Holy Spirit) **C** (open daily) is next door to the late 19th-century neo-Renaissance main post office. By the edge of the Market Square is the vast **Kościół Najswiętszej Maryii Panny** (St Mary's Church) **D** (open daily). Built in 1351, it incorporates fragments of two earlier churches and is approached through a cloistered courtyard. In addition to the Baroque altar, the church has an amazing vaulted ceiling, while the walls bear poignant frescos of Christ.

The city's other attractions include Poland's most modern **Planetarium** **E** (Franciszkańska 15-21; tel: 250 66; open Tues-Sun; entrance fee), while the most impressive of several theatres is the neo-Baroque **Teatr W. Horzycy** (Theatre dedicated to W. Horzyc) **F** (guided tours available tel: 252 22). It was built in 1904 by the renowned Viennese architects Ferdinand Felner and Herman Helmer, who specialised in theatres and concert halls. Meanwhile, the most historic part of the university is **Collegium Maius** (Maius College) **G** (not open to the public), dating from 1594.

Local explanations for how the **Krzywa Wieża** (Leaning Tower) **H** acquired its 1.5-metre (5-ft) tilt vary. It may have resulted from a Teutonic Knight caught fraternising with a townswoman. As this monastic order stipulated celibacy, his penance was to build a leaning tower, to remind him of having "deviated" from the rules. A more technical (and probable) explanation is that the foundations are on clay soil. **Dom i Muzeum Kopernika** (House and Museum of

Map on page 350

BELOW: Church of the Blessed Virgin Mary in Toruń.

The three roofs of the Cathedral of St John date from the 14th century. The Beautiful Madonna statue on the north wall of the apse is a copy of the original statue which disappeared during World War II.

BELOW: the River Vistula and Toruń.

Nicholaus Copernicus) **①** (M Kopernika 15-17; tel: 267 48; open Tues-Sun; entrance fee) is a fine red-brick Gothic house, documenting the life and work of this great astronomer, born here in 1473. The well-preserved **Mury Obronne (City Walls) ②** dating from late 13th century have been preserved virtually in their entirety along the river, with four bastions and three gates including the **Brama Żeglarska** (Mariner's Gate) **③** built in 1432 and **Brama Mostowa (Bridge Gate) ④**. Formerly the parish church of the Old Town, **Katedra Św. Janów** (Cathedral of St John) **⑤** (open daily) dates from the 15th century, built on the site of a church dating from 1250. A combination of restraint and extravagance, Gothic murals and a chapel in which Copernicus was baptised are among the features, together with Baroque and rococo elements. The Renaissance palace **Dom Eskenów** (Esken's House) **⑥** (Łazienna 16; tel: 286 80; open Tues-Sun; entrance fee) includes 20th-century Polish paintings and military effects from the 15th–19th centuries.

Loathed as a symbol of oppression, the Teutonic castle was pulled down by the town's inhabitants in 1454. However the **Ruiny Zamku Krzyżackiego** (Ruins of the Teutonic Knights' Castle) **⑦** still show what an important building this was. Constructed between 1250–1450, it is now a picturesque, romantic spot (Przedzamcze; open Tues-Sun, summer only).

Rynek Nowomiejski (New Town Market Square) **⑧** includes a delightful café, Pod Modrym Fartuchem ("Under the Bright Blue Apron"), first established in 1489 and still going strong. The original Baroque interiors once hosted Polish kings such as Jan Olbracht and Kazimierz Jagiellończyk. The neighbouring 19th-century **Kościół Św. Jakuba** (Church of St Jacob) **⑨** (open daily) includes beautiful arches, together with Gothic sacred art, including crucifixes.

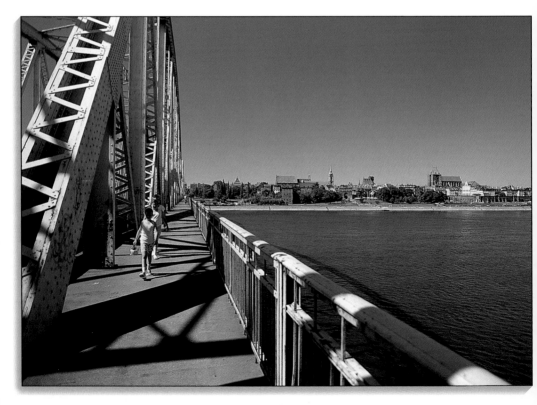

The **Muzeum Etnograficzne** (Museum of Mankind and *Skansen*) (Wały Gen Sikorskiego 19; tel: 280 91; open daily; entrance fee) comprises two museums. One is housed within the former Arsenal, built in 1824, and has an incredible collection of fishing items, a traditional occupation in the city. In the *skansen*, you forget the city-centre location as this enchanting village enclave transports you back to 18th- and 19th-century village life. Various farmsteads and households are furnished with period furniture and effects. A roadside shrine, fire station, forge and windmill complete the scene. There is also a museum shop and café housed in traditional wooden buildings.

Maps:
Area 344
City 350

Bydgoszcz and surroundings

Nearby **Bydgoszcz** ⓭ has always had a sense of "rivalry" with Toruń, and the inhabitants of both typically deride each others' city. Toruń is infinitely more attractive to visit, although Bydgoszcz has its moments. An administrative centre with a population of 400,000, it was founded by Casimir the Great in 1346. The city's heyday was in the 15th and 16th centuries, when its warehouses and breweries supplied the entire region, with barges being the mode of transport along the River Vistula to Gdańsk. Destroyed during the Swedish invasion, Bydgoszcz flourished under Prussian rule, but paid the price of being thoroughly "Germanised". Nevertheless, the Nazis were met by fierce resistance from the inhabitants and when the city surrendered mass executions were carried out – some 50,000 by the end of the war.

The city has a fragmented atmosphere. The most interesting area is the Old Town, where the River Brda meanders and cascades to provide a backdrop for the half-timbered 18th- and 19th-century granaries, a 15th-century late-Gothic

BELOW: the mist rolls in across the River Vistula.

Map on page 344

The Hollywood actress Apolonia Chalupiec (1896–1987) was born in Lipno about 23 km (14 miles) to the north of Włocławek. She made her name in the silent movie era as Pola Negri and remains a Hollywood icon.

BELOW: lake and tree dwellers.

parish church, and the 17th-century Jesuit College. The neoclassical and Baroque Public Library, built in the second half of the 18th century, is renowned for its valuable collection of historic books. The Regional History Museum (Gdańska 4; tel 22 16 08; open Tues–Sun; entrance fee), named after the painter Leon Wyczółkowski, contains many of his works alongside other Polish painters. West of Bydgoszcz stretch the Pojezierze Krajeńskie (Krajna Lakes), where deep gorges cutting through the moraine hills provide attractive views, with Sępólno Krajeńskie and Więcbork especially popular holiday destinations. The few historic buildings are mainly churches, combining Gothic and Renaissance architecture.

Kujawy Region

Always one of Poland's wealthiest regions, **Kujawy** played an important role in Poland's early history, becoming part of the Polanie State at the beginning of the 10th century.

The spa town of **Inowrocław** , the administrative centre for West Kujawy, has a few interesting buildings, including the triple-naved, Romanesque St Mary's Church built from stone, and the Gothic-Baroque Church of St Nicholas.

To the south, on the large Lake Gopło, is the town of **Kruszwica**. Among the ruins of the 14th-century castle is an ornate Romanesque collegiate church in the form of a basilica, and the Mysza Wieża (Mouse Tower). According to legend, Kruszwica was the centre of an empire ruled by Popiel, but the prince was apparently eaten by a pack of mice, which accounts for the name.

A wide variety of waterfowl are protected by the Nadgoplański Park Tysiąclecia nature reserve. The banks of the countless lakes provide excellent breeding grounds for the birds.

Nearby **Strzelno** has an interesting monastery. The village church here is a combination of the circular, early-Romanesque Church of St Procopius, dating from around 1160, and the interesting Church of the Holy Trinity (1133–1216), where you can see highly artistic 12th-century sculpted pillars and a tympana.

In the eastern part of Kujawy, on the left bank of the Vistula, is the former episcopal see of **Włocławek** ⓯. Now an industrial town with a population of 120,000, the most interesting monument is the brick Church of the Assumption, dating from 1411. Baroque elements and chapels were subsequently added around the church. This includes the Chapel of the Mother of God, with late-Gothic carvings by the renowned Wit Stwosz dating from 1493. Soft light from a magnificent window designed in an Art Nouveau style by Józef Mehoffer illuminates the chancel. Try to set aside time to make a visit to the Gothic Church of St Vitalis (dating from 1330) with its famous 1493 triptych depicting the coronation of the Virgin Mary. The 14th-century Church of St John dominates the historic Market Square.

Stretching between the towns of Włocławek and Płock is the vast Gostynińsko-Włocwławski Country Park, established in 1979. The pretty Dobrzyński lakes are to be found to the north of Włocławek, between the Vistula, Drwęca and Skrwa rivers. ❏

Nicholas Copernicus

One of the most influential astronomers, Mikołaj Kopernik (Nicolas Copernicus) was born in Toruń in 1473, the son of a prosperous merchant. The house in which Copernicus was born is now a museum detailing his life and works (*see page 352*). The collection includes the original edition of De Revolutionibus Orbium Coelestium, Copernicus's revolutionary theory that the sun and not the earth was the centre of the universe, and that the earth and planets revolved around the sun.

Copernicus studied at the Jagiellonian University in Kraków from 1491–95. As central and eastern Europe's second oldest university (after Prague), it was already renowned for its astronomy and mathematics faculties. Collegium Maius, the oldest college, includes a Copernicus Room, with a collection of astronomical instruments from the 1480s including astrolabes and handwritten sections of the *De revolutionibus* manuscript.

In 1497 Copernicus went to Italy, studying under renowned Italian astronomers including Domenico Maria Novara. It was after arriving there that he witnessed a lunar eclipse, which first led him to question whether the earth was the centre of the universe. Meanwhile, he studied cannon law at Bologna and lectured on astronomy in Rome, before studying medicine at Padua and becoming a doctor of cannon law at Ferrara in 1503.

Returning to Poland in 1503, he was appointed administrator and physician at the Bishop's Castle of Lidzbark Warminski in the Mazurian lake district, where his uncle was Bishop of Warmia. This Gothic castle, built between 1350–1401, is now a museum with part of the collection devoted to Copernicus and his work.From 1510 he was based in Frombork, where he was appointed cannon, although between 1510–19 he spent regular periods of time in Olsztyn. It was in Olsztyn's Gothic Cathedral Chapter and Castle that he created an astonomical table on the walls of the cloisters, where he recorded his findings.Olsztyn's Copernicus Planetarium now provides the opportunity to "experience" outer space from the perspective of an astronaut. Continuing to study astronomy, it was here that he wrote a treatise questioning the belief that the earth was the centre of the universe. This was the foundation of his famous book, completed in 1530. Popular phraseology in Poland (which every schoolchild learns) sums this up as: "he stopped the sun, and set the earth in motion." However, the book was not published until 1543 in Nuremberg. Copernicus only saw a copy as he lay dying in Frombork, having suffered a brain haemmorage. He was buried in Frombork cathedral.

Copernicus dedicated the book to Pope Paul III, but the Roman Catholic church still considered his theories to be "subversive" and the work was banned until 1757. Yet it provided a basis for subsequent theories by distinguished astronomers including Galileo.

The Nicholaus Copernicus Museum in Frombork exhibits among other items astrological instruments and an edition of his book inscribed by the 17th-century astronomer Jan Hevelius who lived in Gdańsk. ❏

RIGHT: Copernicus monument in Toruń.

THE NORTHEAST

One of the best ways to explore the "Land of the Great Masurian Lakes" is by a locally-hired yacht, canoe or kayak

An area of outstanding natural beauty, the Masurian Lake district includes more than 1,000 lakes, many of which are linked by rivers and canals, and surrounded by several national parks that shelter various rare species of flora and fauna. Extending across three separate regions of northeastern Poland – Warmia, Mazury and Suwalszczyzna – this area is also known as the "green lungs" of Poland, reflecting the absence of any industrial development. With numerous lakeside resorts in the area, this is the most popular holiday destination for Poles.

Warmia is named after the ancient Prussian tribe known as the Warms, with Mazury also originally part of East Prussia. It was the constant threat to Polish territories posed by the Prussians, that led Duke Konrad Mazowiecki to seek help from the Teutonic Order of Knights in the mid-13th century. However, this resulted in the Order establishing its own territories in the process. Being extremely well-organised and industrious, the Teutonic Knights built a chain of heavily fortified castles to consolidate their presence, and continued to extend their territory through military conquests.

It was only in 1410, during one of the greatest European battles of medieval times, that a combined Polish and Lithuanian army succeeded in defeating the Tuetonic Knights, around the town of Grunwald. Consequently, part of this northeastern region was returned to Poland, and the remainder of the knights' territory became a Polish fiefdom.

Following the Swedish invasion of the 17th century the region came under Swedish rule, and under the partitions of Poland, these regions were annexed by Prussia. Suwalszczyzna was returned to Poland after World War I, and Warmia and Mazury after World War II. ❑

PRECEDING PAGES: a rural estate in Łabędnik near Bartenstein.
LEFT: a trip along one of the canals in northeast Poland.

THE MAZURIAN LAKES

The "Land of a Thousand Lakes" is the ideal place for watersports enthusiasts, anglers and hikers, or visitors who just want to get away from it all

Map on page 362

A region of outstanding natural beauty, the Mazurian landscape is characterised by countless lakes, gentle hills, deep valleys and flat depressions, as well as sandy plains, wooded areas and extensive forests, formed after the Ice Age. Popularly referred to as the "land of a thousand lakes", this is in fact Europe's largest complex of wetlands, with a series of national parks and primeval forests providing a sanctuary for an amazing range of flora and fauna. Many of the region's lakes are linked by rivers and canals, which means you can travel for days entirely on water. Almost the entire region is fully protected, with no industrial development allowed, and even agriculture is strictly monitored to be eco-friendly. Nevertheless, a range of hotels, guesthouses and campsites offer leisure facilities, while organic farms provide a novel and inexpensive option, with board and lodging partly paid by helping out with the work. Moreover, many historic towns throughout the region provide an interesting contrast to "nature's architecture".

Olsztyn

Olsztyn ❶, on the banks of the River Łyna, is an ideal base with various lakes within easy reach. There is also plenty to see in this engaging town – although renovation is on-going, the important buildings are well maintained.

LEFT: typical country road.
BELOW: milking in the fields, Talty.

The Old Town, granted its municipal charter in 1353, was largely destroyed by the Red Army in 1945. The key sights are the neo-Renaissance New Town Hall, which is early 20th-century, while several impressive churches include the Gothic Katedra Św. Jakuba (St James's Cathedral). A monumental tower sets the tone of this grand building, and the interior features vaulted ceilings, the altar of the Holy Cross, with its mid-16th-century Renaissance triptych depicting the crucifixion, and the neo-Gothic altar to the Madonna of Ostrobrama, which is late 19th-century. One monument that survived the war intact is the Wysoka Brama (High Gate), a handsome brick construction that continues to provide an "official" entrance into the Old Town. Beyond the Old Town there are wonderful examples of Prussian, Seccesionist and eclectic early 20th-century architecture.

However, Olsztyn's most important historical building is the 14th century Gothic **Castle of the Cathedral Chapter**, a fortified residence of the Bishops of Warmia. Between 1516 and 1521, the astronomer Nicolaus Copernicus was in residence here, in his capacity as the town administrator (*see page 355*). Fragments of an astronomical chart drawn by him can be seen in the courtyard, and his study has been re-created complete with astronomical instruments.

The Castle is now the Warmia and Mazurian Regional Museum (open Tues–Sun; entrance fee). Atmospheric interiors provide a setting for a fine collection of regional art, sculpture, decorative arts and furniture, as well as folk arts and crafts, the earliest dating from the 17th century. Archaeological finds recovered from ancient burial sites in the area can also be seen here.

Several idyllic lakes heighten the appeal of the nearby landscape. The largest, Lake Ukiel, has a good beach, as do lakes Skanda and Kortowskie. If you prefer to be on the lake rather than in it, there are cruises following various itineraries, or you can hire a boat and travel independently.

West of Olsztyn

The delightful lakeside scenery in the Ostróda and Iława regions is very popular with holiday-makers from Warsaw, Gdańsk and Germany. The peak summer months, July and August, see the most popular beaches crowded, the campsites often full and boat-hire companies booked up.

In addition to aqua- and eco-pursuits, the region's sightseeing options include the delightful town of **Morąg ❷**. Key sights include a Gothic Town Hall, fragments of the town walls and the Baroque Dohn Palace where the German philosopher and writer, Johann Gottfried Herder, was born in 1774; a museum exhibits details of his life and works (open Tue–Sun; entrance fee). The nearby Jezioro Narie (Narie lake), with almost 20 islands, is a beautiful sight.

A principal attraction of **Olsztynek**, located on the northeastern edge of town, is the *skansen* (open-air ethnographic museum; open Tues–Sun; entrance fee). Set in prime countryside, the traditional timber cottages and farmsteads exemplify the Warmia and Mazurian style, together with buildings from the Vistula

Bust of Olsztyn poet Michael Lengowski.

Valley and Lithuania. Among the most interesting are a water mill, a Mazurian farmyard, a wooden church and three windmills. To the east of Olsztynek is an attractive forest with numerous small lakes.

Grunwald, 20 km (12.5 miles) southwest of Olsztynek, is chiefly known as the site of one of Poland's most famous battles and one of the greatest battles of the Middle Ages, fought by almost 80,000 men. On 10 July 1410, a combined army of Polish and Lithuanian troops defeated the Teutonic Knights (*see page 263*). A monument erected in the town in 1960 commemorates this victory, which effectively broke the knight's dominance in Poland, while an amphitheatre houses a museum detailing the battle (open daily; entrance free).

The **Elbląg Canal**, linking Elbląg and Ostróda, is a fascinating feat of engineering, completed in 1860. A journey along this almost 130-km (80-mile) stretch is a major tourist attraction and takes around 12 hours. Comprising a network of lakes, canals and locks, there are also special platforms on wheels used to transport ships of up to 50 tonnes across tracts of land with major height differentials of up to 100 metres (330 ft) onto the next stretch of water. This is the only operational system of its kind in the world. The views are also spectacular, with the large and shallow Lake Drużno, outside Elbląg, an ornithological reserve, and numerous lakes and forests between Iława, Ostróda and Morąg.

Being a Baltic port meant that Elbląg was always a priority for invading armies, with each invasion, including World War II, reducing the town to rubble. Now known chiefly as a brewing centre, a limited area of the original Old Town is slowly being recreated in its historic style, with the surrounding area rebuilt using ultra-modern designs. While no longer an important port, Elbląg is still the key departure point for the nearby Russian territory of Kaliningrad.

The beauty of the Mazurian countryside can be enjoyed on Lake Ukiel near Olsztyn.

BELOW: country cottage.

The Great Mazurian Lakes

The Mazurski Landscape Park embraces the central Mazurian Lake district. The peaceful town of **Mrągowo ❸** is an ideal base, with its 18th- and 19th-century buildings including the Town Hall and Evangelical Church. The park has the largest number of lakes in the region, with almost a third of its 50,000 hectares (124,000 acres) accounted for by water, including Lake Śniardwy, surrounded by the primeval Piska forest. Lake Łuknajno, near Mikołajki, is listed as a World Biosphere Reserve, and is a nesting ground for mute swans among other rare breeds. Only marked trails can be followed in this protected area.

Near Mrągowo, on the edge of Lake Dejnow, is **Święta Lipka ❹**, where the church is an important shrine for Roman Catholic pilgrims. This dates from the 13th century, when a roadside wooden statue of the Madonna appeared to have miraculous powers and was moved to a nearby church. During the 16th century the statue and chapel were destroyed by the Protestants who ruled this region, then part of Prussia. However, at the beginning of the 17th century the Polish king was allowed to build a Catholic church on the site where the statue had originally stood. A hundred years later (1687–93), the present Italianate Baroque church was designed by Georg Ertly, a native of South Tyrol who spent nearly all of his working life in Vilnius. Ertly also used his skills as an illusionist: painting frescos to simulate a dome, and the wood chancel to resemble marble. When the organ plays, small gilded figures depicting saints and angels are activated. Organ concerts are held here during the summer season.

The ruins of the **Wolf's Lair**, Adolf Hitler's former headquarters in the Gierłoz Forest near Kętrzyn, are a chilling reminder of the Nazi occupation. Around 70 buildings were constructed here, including seven massive bunkers

BELOW: the castle of the Teutonic Knights in Olsztyn.

with walls up to 8 metres (25 ft) thick. With only a few short intervals, Hitler directed much of his military strategy from here between 1941–44, particularly the eastern front. On 20 July 1944, Count Claus von Stauffenberg made his courageous, though unsuccessful, assassination attempt on Hitler. Although the bomb exploded, Hitler was not close enough for it to harm him.

A major centre for various watersports, **Giżycko ❺** is located on the edge of Lake Niegocin. The town also has a church designed by the renowned German architect Karl-Friedrich Schinkel and a castle built by the Teutonic Knights.

The delightful town of **Mikołajki ❻** is set on the edge of Poland's largest lake, Śniardwy – so large that its also referred to as the Mazurian Sea, while the town is frequently described as the "Venice of Mazuria". This is an exaggeration, but the small 19th-century houses, delightful fountain and long quayside with pleasure cruisers and sailing boats, create an inviting atmosphere.

Boat excursions

As many of the smaller lakes surrounding Augustów, Ostróda and Iława, not to mention the Great Mazurian Lakes, are linked by a network of canals, an ideal way of seeing them is by taking a pleasure cruise.

One of the most popular cruises covers the main lakes in five separate stages. A passenger service operates between Giżycko and Węgorzewo (25 km/16 miles), between Giżycko and Mikołajki (40 km/25 miles), between Mikołajki and Ruciane-Nida (20 km/12 miles), and between Mikołajki and Pisz (25 km/16 miles). Various circular sightseeing trips via Ruciane-Nida can be booked in Giżycko and Mikołajki. One of the most attractive sections of the canal network connects Mikołajki and Ruciane-Nida, with the woodland of the Puszcza Piska

Map on page 362

It is sometimes possible to spot a tarpan from the zoological station in Popielno, near Mikołajki. Europe's only wild horse, the tarpan became extinct in the wild in the 18th century. However, some farmers continued using them as work-horses, which provided a means of breeding.

BELOW:
sailing on one of the Great Lakes.

Map
on page
362

lining almost the entire route. The lock in Guzianki compensates for the difference in water levels between the Beldany and Guzianka lakes.

If you'd rather explore in your own boat, an interesting route that extends for 90 km (55 miles) begins in Sorkwity between Biskupiec and Mrągowo, and ends in Lake Bełdany. The River Krutynia changes its name between the various lakes, with a large section running through the untamed woodland of the Puszcza Piska, past several camping and rest areas, and close to nature reserves.

Sorkwity has one of Masuria's few Protestant churches, an attractive brick and white-washed building with a carved baptismal angel suspended above the congregation in the nave. Using a block and tackle the angel can be lowered at christenings, and the head of the child anointed with holy water from the silver dish held by the angel. Another neighbouring attraction is the impressive Sorkwity Palace, a 19th-century neo-Renaissance confection, which is set in a landscaped, wooded park, near Lake Lampackie.

The eastern region

The route along the Czarna Hańcza River (97 km/60 miles) is one of the most attractive and popular in Poland, particularly for kayak enthusiasts. Beginning on the eastern bank of Lake Wigry in Stary Folwark, the river meanders through the beautiful Augustów forest.

The Augustów Canal is also a popular route for boat trips. Engineered in the first half of the 19th century, it linked the Vistula and Niemen rivers in order to transport Polish goods to Baltic ports. Constructed between 1822–39, the Augustów Canal begins in Biebrza and extends through the lakes of the Augustów forest for 100 km (60 miles), reaching Hrodna in Belarus. A total of 18 sluice gates regulate different water levels. The engineers were led by the Polish general Ignacy Prądzyński, and the canal is now considered a historic monument. It is also a great tourist attraction, with canoes, sailing boats and yachts, not to mention pleasure steamers, cruising the waters. The surrounding area is also able to offer a variety of facilities and accommodation.

The Suwałki lake district includes the **Wigierski Park Narodowy** (Wigry National Park) ❼, of which almost two-thirds is forest, mainly fir and pine, with some trees more than 200 years old. It's a natural habitat for rare species including the mute swan, wild boar, wolf, elk and the white-tailed eagle.

Lake Wigry, Poland's second deepest lake, is outstandingly beautiful with a meandering shoreline – if you feel like strolling all the way around it's a 70-km (45-mile) hike. The park also has Poland's deepest lake, Hańcza, at 110 metres (360 ft), while Lake Jaczno is renowned for its amazing malachite coloured water.

The River Biebrza flows into the narrow valley around Sztabin, where it twists and divides to create a stunning vista. Overflowing during the spring, the river floods the surrounding bogs and meadows supporting a community of beavers, though the area is best known for rare birds, including ruffs, the spotted eagle, whooper swans and the double snipe. ❏

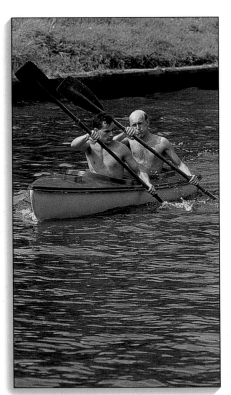

BELOW: canoeing on the canal near Giżycko.
RIGHT: boat on Lake Mamry.

INSIGHT GUIDES

Travel Tips

TIMBUKTU   KALAMAZOO

AT&T Direct® Service

AT&T Direct Service access numbers are the easy way to call home from anywhere.

www.att.com/traveler

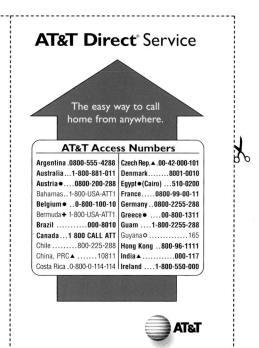

AT&T Direct® Service

The easy way to call
home from anywhere.

AT&T Access Numbers	
Argentina .0800-555-4288	Czech Rep.▲.00-42-000-101
Australia...1-800-881-011	Denmark........8001-0010
Austria●....0800-200-288	Egypt●(Cairo) ...510-0200
Bahamas..1-800-USA-ATT1	France.....0800-99-00-11
Belgium● ..0-800-100-10	Germany ..0800-2255-288
Bermuda✦ 1-800-USA-ATT1	Greece● 00-800-1311
Brazil 000-8010	Guam 1-800-2255-288
Canada...1 800 CALL ATT	Guyana○ 165
Chile 800-225-288	Hong Kong ..800-96-1111
China, PRC▲ 10811	India▲ 000-117
Costa Rica .0-800-0-114-114	Ireland 1-800-550-000

AT&T

AT&T Direct® Service

The easy way to call
home from anywhere.

AT&T Access Numbers	
Argentina .0800-555-4288	Czech Rep.▲.00-42-000-101
Australia...1-800-881-011	Denmark........8001-0010
Austria●....0800-200-288	Egypt●(Cairo) ...510-0200
Bahamas..1-800-USA-ATT1	France.....0800-99-00-11
Belgium● ..0-800-100-10	Germany ..0800-2255-288
Bermuda✦ 1-800-USA-ATT1	Greece● 00-800-1311
Brazil 000-8010	Guam 1-800-2255-288
Canada...1 800 CALL ATT	Guyana○ 165
Chile 800-225-288	Hong Kong ..800-96-1111
China, PRC▲ 10811	India▲ 000-117
Costa Rica .0-800-0-114-114	Ireland 1-800-550-000

AT&T

connection
with the AT&T
Network

AT&T
direct
service

The best way to keep in touch when you're traveling

overseas is with **AT&T Direct**® Service. It's the

easy way to call your loved ones back home from just

about anywhere in the world. Just cut out the wallet

card below and use it wherever your travels take you.

For a list of AT&T Access Numbers, cut out the attached wallet guide.

AT&T

Israel 1-800-94-94-949	Portugal▲..........800-800-128
Italy ● 172-1011	Saudi Arabia ▲ 1-800-10
Jamaica ● 1-800-USA-ATT1	Singapore 800-0111-111
Japan ● ▲ 005-39-111	South Africa 0800-99-0123
Korea, Republic ● ...0072-911	Spain 900-99-00-11
Mexico ▽ ● ..01-800-288-2872	Sweden.............020-799-111
Netherlands ● ..0800-022-9111	Switzerland● 0800-89-0011
Neth.Ant.▲✪001-800-USA-ATT1	Taiwan.............0080-10288-0
New Zealand● 000-911	Thailand❮......001-999-111-11
Norway.............800-190-11	Turkey● 00-800-12277
Panama 00-800-001-0109	U.A. Emirates● 800-121
Philippines ● 105-11	U.K. 0800-89-0011
Poland● ▲...00-800-111-1111	Venezuela 800-11-120

FOR EASY CALLING WORLDWIDE

1. Just dial the AT&T Access Number for the country you are calling from.
2. Dial the phone number you're calling.   *3.* Dial your card number.*

For access numbers not listed ask any operator for **AT&T Direct**® Service.
In the U.S. call 1-800-222-0300 for **AT&T Direct** Service information.
Visit our Web site at: **www.att.com/traveler**
Bold-faced countries permit country-to-country calling outside the U.S.

●   Public phones require coin or card deposit to place call.
✚   Public phones and select hotels.
▲   May not be available from every phone/payphone.
○   Collect calling only.
▽   Includes "Ladatel" public phones; if call does not complete,
     use 001-800-462-4240.
✪   From St. Maarten or phones at Bobby's Marina, use 1-800-USA-ATT1.
❮   When calling from public phones, use phones marked Lenso.
*   AT&T Calling Card, AT&T Corporate, AT&T Universal, MasterCard®,
     Diners Club®, American Express®, or Discover® cards accepted.

When placing an international call *from* the U.S., dial 1-800-CALL ATT.
WW   © 6/00 AT&T

Israel 1-800-94-94-949	Portugal▲..........800-800-128
Italy ● 172-1011	Saudi Arabia ▲ 1-800-10
Jamaica ● 1-800-USA-ATT1	Singapore 800-0111-111
Japan ● ▲ 005-39-111	South Africa 0800-99-0123
Korea, Republic ● ...0072-911	Spain 900-99-00-11
Mexico ▽ ● ..01-800-288-2872	Sweden.............020-799-111
Netherlands ● ..0800-022-9111	Switzerland● 0800-89-0011
Neth.Ant.▲✪001-800-USA-ATT1	Taiwan.............0080-10288-0
New Zealand● 000-911	Thailand❮......001-999-111-11
Norway.............800-190-11	Turkey● 00-800-12277
Panama 00-800-001-0109	U.A. Emirates● 800-121
Philippines ● 105-11	U.K. 0800-89-0011
Poland● ▲...00-800-111-1111	Venezuela 800-11-120

FOR EASY CALLING WORLDWIDE

1. Just dial the AT&T Access Number for the country you are calling from.
2. Dial the phone number you're calling.   *3.* Dial your card number.*

For access numbers not listed ask any operator for **AT&T Direct**® Service.
In the U.S. call 1-800-222-0300 for **AT&T Direct** Service information.
Visit our Web site at: **www.att.com/traveler**
Bold-faced countries permit country-to-country calling outside the U.S.

●   Public phones require coin or card deposit to place call.
✚   Public phones and select hotels.
▲   May not be available from every phone/payphone.
○   Collect calling only.
▽   Includes "Ladatel" public phones; if call does not complete,
     use 001-800-462-4240.
✪   From St. Maarten or phones at Bobby's Marina, use 1-800-USA-ATT1.
❮   When calling from public phones, use phones marked Lenso.
*   AT&T Calling Card, AT&T Corporate, AT&T Universal, MasterCard®,
     Diners Club®, American Express®, or Discover® cards accepted.

When placing an international call *from* the U.S., dial 1-800-CALL ATT.
WW   © 6/00 AT&T

CONTENTS

Getting Acquainted

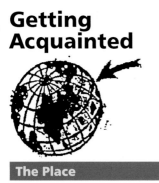

The Place

Area: Poland is 690 km (430 miles) east-west and 650 km (400 miles) north-south. The total land area encompasses 312,680 sq. km (120,720 sq. miles).
Population: 37.8 million.
Language: Polish.
Capital: Warsaw.
Religion: 97 percent Roman Catholic. The remaining population is composed of about 575,000 Russian Orthodox, 267,000 Protestants, 80,000 Old Catholics, 5,200 Muslims and 5,000 Jews. Throughout the country there are more than 12,500 churches.
Time Zone: GMT plus one hour. When it is noon in Warsaw it is 6am in New York and 8pm in Tokyo. Daylight Saving is in effect May–October when one hour is added.
Currency: Polish złoty (zł or PLN), divided into 100 groszy (gr).
Weights & Measures: Metric.
International dialling code: 48.
Electricity: 220 volts. Sockets take two round pins.

Geography

Poland is locked in the middle of Europe and is a border between western and eastern Europe.

In places, the eastern border with Russia, Lithuania, Belarus and the Ukraine (1,244 km/771 miles in length) follows the River Bug, while the Czech and Slovakian border along the Carpathian and Sudeten mountains to the south is 1,310 km (812 miles) in length. In the west, the border with Germany follows the Odra, Poland's second-largest river, and the Nysa Lużycka for a total of 460 km (285 miles).

The Polish coastline on the Baltic Sea to the north is over 524 km (325 miles) long. It consists of sandy beaches, dunes and cliffs. Lakes and woodland dominate the landscapes of northern Pomerania and Mazuria, while the lowland region between the Odra and the Bug is used mainly as arable land. The Sudeten and Carpathian mountains run along Poland's southern borders. At the heart of the Polish section of the Carpathians are the High Tatras, an alpine chain of mountains with towering peaks and steep sides.

Warsaw is situated on the largest river, the Vistula, which flows northwards from the mountains to the Baltic. The country's main ports are Gdańsk, Gdynia and Szczecin.

Topography

Poland has a varied topography but most of it is low-lying country. To the north, the Baltic Sea coastline is composed of sandy beaches backed by dunes, steep slopes and cliffs. Picturesque lowland plains dotted with lakes, forests, rivers and canals make up the typical moraine landscape of the Northern Pomeranian and Mazurian Lakelands. Lake Śniardwy, the largest lake in this area, measures 109,700 hectares (271,075 acres). The central-Polish lowlands between the Odra and Bug rivers are cultivated extensively for agricultural purposes. The Sudeten and Carpathian mountains stretch along Poland's southern borders. The Sudeten belong to the oldest mountain massifs in Europe, with the highest peak Mount Snieżka (1,602 metres/5,255 ft). The Carpathians are have a shorter history. The Tatra range makes up their central part and is alpine in character. It contains Poland's highest peak, Mount Rysy, which is 2,499 metres (8,200 ft).

Climate

Due to the country's lengthy coastline, the climate in Poland varies between oceanic and

The People

Of the total Polish population of 37.8 million, around 300,000–500,000 are German, 300,000 Ukrainian, 200,000 Bela-russians, with Slovaks, Sintis, Romas, Lithuanians, Czechs, Greeks and Macedonians making up the remainder. The average population density was calculated in 1992 at around 122.9 people per sq. km (318.3 per sq. mile).

About 9.5 million people of Polish descent live abroad, the majority of them in the USA (about 7 million), but over a million live in the former Soviet Union and about the same number in Germany. Large Polish communities also live in France, Canada the UK and Brazil.

continental. Therefore, weather conditions are subject to change. From May until October Poland enjoys beautiful weather. In March spring begins – a little windy and rainy and averaging -1–15°C (30–60°F). In May to June temperatures rise to 21°C (70°F) and remain as such through the summer. August can be very warm with temper-atures often climbing beyond 30°C (86°F).

The traditional "golden Polish autumn" in September is usually sunny and dry, with temperatures around 15°C (60°F). In November the first foggy and cold days begin, complemented by shorter days. Winter lasts about three months (December–February), but can be so severe that in many northern regions temperatures drop to -30°C (-22°F). Snow in the mountain regions makes for excellent skiing. It remains in the mountains until around Easter.

Economy

Growth rates in Poland have been good since 1992 (despite the recent slow-down in the Russian economy) and it is now reckoned to be the new "tiger economy" of eastern Europe. Most economic activity comes from the private sector but Poland has a long way to go before it has a "true" market economy both economically and socially. It's two biggest industries, the steel mills and coal mines, are still not privatised but the government plans to increase the overall rate of privatisation over the next decade. Its prime target for privatisation will be the steel mills which currently employ 40 percent of workers, account for a third of industry sales but only return 5 percent of profits. The antiquated agricultural sector is high on the government's list for modernisation. Other government plans include an increase in the level of domestic savings and a reduction in the amount of money spent on welfare.

In 1995 the National Bank of Poland announced that old bank notes would be replaced by new ones. Unlike the old currency, the five new notes (for 10, 20, 50, 100 and 200 złoty) come in different sizes and are easily recognisable. The nine coins are as follows: 1, 2, 5, 10, 20 and 50 groszy and 1, 2 and 5 złoty. All new notes and coins have a picture of an eagle with a crown above its head.

Constitution and Government

The constitution drawn up by the Communist government in 1952 was significantly amended for the first time in 1989. The main elements in the new constitution included the establishment of a bicameral legislative system and the introduction of direct presidential elections. After a referendum in which over half of the electorate voted in favour of the amendments, in 1997 the *Sejm* or Polish parliament approved the new constitution. However, there are still certain aspects of it that arouse controversy, in particular the powers of the president and the role of the Catholic church. The current president, Aleksander Kwaśniewski (independent),

defeated the preceding incumbent, Lech Wałęsa, in the elections of November 1995.

The parliament consists of the 460-seat lower house (*Sejm*) and the 100-seat upper house (Senate). Both the Senate and the president have the power to veto the *Sejm*, but both their vetoes can be overriden by a two-thirds majority vote in the *Sejm*.

In the parliamentary election of 1993, the Democratic Left Alliance (SLD) and the Polish Peasant Party (PSL) – both of which had been satellites of the ruling Communist party pre-1989 – commanded a substantial majority of the *Sejm*, but the elections of 1997 saw the pendulum swing back to the right-leaning Solidarity Electoral Action (AWS) coalition, and in October 1997 Jerzy Buzek was appointed prime minister.

Local Government

Poland is divided into 17 counties known as *województwa*. These administrative districts vary in size and density. In area, Olsztyn is the largest (12,327 sq. km/4,758 sq. miles) and the smallest Lódź (1,523 sq. km/587 sq. miles), but the latter has the highest population density in the country.

Planning the Trip

Passports and Visas

Visas can be obtained from a Polish consulate in your country of residence or from Warsaw airport on arrival. Visa extensions can be obtained from the offices of the Ministry of Internal Affairs, Foreign Visitors' Department, 11 Floor, 47a/49 Wspólna Ulica, Warsaw. Children on their parents' passports are not charged for visas.

Transit visas are valid for 48 hours. If you want a transit visa, you will need a visa for your destination country. Passport and visa regulations can change quite quickly so it's wise to check with the Polish consulate in your country of residence before setting off.

British visitors can stay in Poland for six months without a visa but passports must be valid for at least six months after the date your departure. Passport holders from most European countries, the USA and the Commonwealth can stay for up to 90 days without a visa. Visitors from Bulgaria, Estonia, Macedonia, Mongolia and Romania can remain for up to 30 days without a visa, while visitors from Hong Kong are allowed two weeks. Visas remain valid for six months from the date of issue.

Visitors to Poland are obliged to register their stay within 48 hours after crossing the border. Registration is performed by the hotel or camp site reception desk.

Customs Regulations

The following articles may be imported into Poland duty-free:
Alcohol: 2 litres of wine, 5 litres of beer, 1 litre of spirits.

Tobacco products: up to 200 cigarettes or 50 cigars or 250g of tobacco (for people aged 18 and above).

Food: up to 200g of coffee, up to 1 kg of chocolate products and presents to the value of $100.

Two cameras and one video camera can be imported duty-free. Expensive articles such as photographic, film or hi-tech equipment, jewellery and furs should be declared on entry. The importation of weapons is not permitted.

Dogs and cats may be imported, but they must have been immunised against rabies at least three weeks before arrival at the border. The official vaccination certificate (not older than 12 months) must be produced. Many hotels accept dogs, but will make a surcharge.

Works of art purchased in Poland, such as antiques and books printed before 9 May 1945, can only be exported as long as an authorisation from the relevant Curator of Art Works or the National Museum in Warsaw is produced.

Polish customs regulations are subject to frequent alterations. Before buying anything of value, check that customs will issue an export licence and whether any special documentation is required.

Warsaw Customs Headquarters
Hotel Marriot
Al. Jerozolimskie 65/69
Tel: 630 5162.

Health

The Polish authorities do not require any special inoculations, but protection against tetanus, polio and diphtheria (the latest booster should have been carried out within the past 10 years) is recommended. If, however, you are planning to spend a lot of time in country areas, particularly those close to the Russian, Lithuanian or Belarus border, then it is wise to see your doctor about the symptoms and treatment of Lyme Disease before leaving home.

It is also advisable to take out a private health insurance policy.

Warsaw Banks

Narodowy Bank Polski
Plac Powsta Dcw 4
Tel: (022) 620 0321.
Bank Polska Kasa Opieki S.A.
Plac Bankowy 2
Tel: (022) 637 1061;
Ul. Czackiego 21/23
Tel: (022) 661 271.
Bank Gda Dski S.A.
Ul. Karowa 20
Tel: (022) 826 0461.
Bank Handlowy
Ul. Cha Bubi Ds kiego 8
Tel: (022) 630 0304.
Powszechny Bank Kredytowy
Aleje Jerozolimskie 7
Tel: (022) 621 0066.

Money Matters

Currency and Exchange

The currency is Polish *złoty* (*zł*). Since the economic reforms of 1990, złoty can be changed in privately run *bureaux de change* (*kantor*). Some travel agents and hotels will change money too. Eurocheques (maximum amount per cheque – 500 new złoty) are not accepted in all change offices, so it may be necessary to go to a bank. Banks are plentiful in Poland (*see page 375* for opening times), but with the increasing number of cash dispensers you can easily go your whole stay without entering one. There are often long queues in banks, so be prepared for a wait.

A *kantor* is usually the best place to make a straight exchange of foreign currency, and these almost always offer a better rate for cash than the banks. Sterling, USA dollars and German marks can attract a better rate than less frequently traded currencies. These offices rarely accept travellers cheques. Most *kantor* can be found in hotels, main railway and bus stations and in main streets.

Credit cards & Travellers' cheques

Most hotels, petrol stations, car rental firms, good quality restaurants, luxury goods shops

and large supermarkets will accept payment with credit cards (check for appropriate signs on entrance). American Express, Visa, Eurocard, MasterCard, Diners' Club and JCB credit cards are the most commonly accepted. Cash against Visa cards can be obtained in banks or in cash dispensers (*bankomat*).

Travellers' cheques are accepted all over Poland. These can be cashed at the foreign exchange desk only of banks.

Loss or theft of credit cards can be reported at the following credit card hot lines:
American Express:
Tel: (022) 625 4030
Diners' Club, Master Card, EuroCard and Visa:
Tel: (022) 515 3000 or 513 3150
Visa and Master Cards:
Tel: (022) 659 2713.

Cash dispensers

There are 24-hour cash dispensers, accepting credit and bank cards (with pin numbers) on many main streets in larger cities.

The machines usually offer a choice of three languages in which to conduct your transaction, but they issue only Polish złoty. There may be a few day's delay in the transaction reaching your home account.

What to Bring

The type of clothing you bring on your trip will depend on the time of year and where you plan to visit. In general, the climate during the summer months is similar to that of the UK with less humidity. The winter, however, is cold with heavy falls of snow in the mountains and temperatures falling below 0°C (32°F). In winter it is necessary to bring a thick coat, boots and especially hat and gloves. In autumn it rains often so don't forget a raincoat and good water resistant footwear.

Photography

Most international brands of camera film are available throughout Poland. Developing and repairs are also quite cheap. Some shops in the larger cities will process films in one hour. Film and video cassettes are generally available in larger shops or specialist stores, where you can also develop film. Camera film is also available at many petrol stations. If you're looking for special materials, or want to have a camera repaired, you'll need to track down an expert.

Those buildings and locations that the authorities regard as strategically important, such as stations, bridges, port installations, police and military buildings, may not be photographed. If you wish to take photographs of people, it is courteous to ask permission first: "*Czy mogę zrobić zd ęcie?*"

Getting There

By Air

The flight time from the UK to Poland is approximately two-and-a-half hours; from Paris, two hours and 15 minutes; from New York, just under 10 hours. Poland has regular connections to almost all capital cities of Europe.

Okęcie Airport, 6 km (4 miles) from the centre of Warsaw, is the hub of most Polish National Airlines worldwide services. There are daily flights to and from London, New York, Chicago and Montreal. Warsaw has regular direct flights to the main cites of former republics of Soviet Union, as well as Minsk, Riga and Vilnius. Most international flights are on B767s and 737s. Some flights are seasonal. From the UK, the three scheduled carriers are Polskie Linie Lotnicze LOT, British Airways and British Midland. International flights land at Warsaw, Kraków and Gdańsk; internal flights land at the following city airports: Kraków, Gdańsk, Katowice, Poznań, Rzeszów and Szczecin. Okęcie Airport is comfortable and compact, servicing 3.5 million passengers per year. You will find international airline offices, banks, post offices and car rental companies within the terminal.

Warsaw International Airport (Okęcie): Arrivals tel: (022) 650 4220; Departures tel: (022) 650 3943, 846 1700/31, 846 5603.
Reservations and tickets:
Tel: (022) 846 9645/952/953; business class tel: 0-800 225757.
Domestic flights:
Tel: (022) 650 1750.

Travel to and from the airport

Okęcie Airport is situated only 6 km (4 miles) from the centre of Warsaw. To reach the main city, you could take buses 175 or 188, which take you to the centre. Buy a ticket at the kiosk and validate it immediately on entering the bus. Always watch your luggage, as these routes are more exposed to theft than other regular lines. For large luggage you need to purchase an extra ticket.

Okęcie Airport also has its own bus line, **City Line**. The bus stops at the all the larger hotels and operates every 20 minutes between 6am–11pm. (On Sunday and public holidays every 30 minutes.) Buy a ticket on board the bus. It's a little more expensive than the regular buses.

LOT also organises a luxury car service **Fly&Drive** into the centre of the city. Or you could phone for a taxi – do not take a taxi from the taxi station at Okęcie unless you must because they are far more expensive than ordering by phone.

By Train

There are regular daily services from London's Liverpool Street Station. On Saturdays in season charter couchettes are available. The journey time from England is about 31 hours.

EuroCity trains connect Warsaw

Airline Offices

Polish Airlines (LOT) Offices
Information and reservation centres are located in all main cities throughout Poland. To call to a particular city for information you should dial the national code followed by 952 or 953.
Kraków: 15 Basztowa Ul.
Tel: (012) 952/953.
Gdańsk: 2/4 Waly Jagiellonskie Ul.
Tel: (058) 952/953. Fax: 301 2621
Poznań: 6/1 Piekary Ul.
Tel: (061) 952/953. Fax: 852 2847
Warsaw: 65/79 Aleje Jerozolimskie
Tel: 952/953.

LOT offices Overseas:
Amsterdam: Overtoom 60, 1054 HK, Amsterdam. Tel: (020) 616 9266, fax: (020) 616 9666.
Berlin: Budapester Strasse 18. Tel: (030) 261 1505/06 Fax: 265 0806.
Chicago: 333 N Michigan Avenue, Suite 916. Tel: (312) 236 3388/ 5501.
London: 313 Regent Street. Tel: (020) 7580 5037 Fax: (020) 7323 0774.
Los Angeles: 6100 Wilshire Blvd., Suite 1450. Tel: (213) 934 5151 Fax: (213) 934 5262.
Montreal: 2000 Peel Street Tel: (514) 844 2674/75 Fax: (514) 844 7339.
New York: 500 Fifth Avenue, Suite 408. Tel: (212) 869 1074, toll free (800) 223 0593.

Paris: 18 rue Louis-le-Grand, 75002 Paris. Tel: (01) 4742 0560 Fax: (331) 4017 0297.

Overseas Airlines in Warsaw
Air Canada: Tel/fax: 822 5477.
Air France: 21 Krucza Ul.
Tel: 628 1281/3.
American Airlines:
20 Aleje Ujazdowskie.
Tel: 625 0517, 625 3002
Fax: 625 3146.
British Airways: 49 Krucza Ul
Tel: 628 9431/3991.
KLM: Swirkii Wigury 1 (Airport)
Tel: 622 8000.
Fax 622 9685.
Lufthansa: 19 Nowy Zwiat Ul.
Tel: 826 150.

with Berlin. Passengers who use this connection also have links with Cologne, Wiesbaden, Karlsruhe, Hamburg, Frankfurt and Munich. Travelling from Germany to Poland by train is relatively cheap. It is not worth obtaining the reduced Interail Pass for people under 26 as travel within Poland is so cheap. Most trains to Poznań and Warsaw pass through Berlin and Frankfurt.

All fast and express trains run on international links. Trains have first and second class carriages, berths, sleepers and restaurant cars. Almost all international trains arrive at Warsaw Central Station, located in the city centre.

International and domestic information:
Tel: 9436;
Reservations:
Tel: 8256033

Direct trains to Poland

Paris–Cologne–Düsseldorf–Hanover –Berlin–Poznań–Warsaw;
Cologne–Hanover–Leipzig–Wrocław–Warsaw;
Frankfurt–Bebra–Wrocław–Warsaw;
Munich–Dresden–Wrocław–Katowice;
East-West Express: London–Hoek van Holland–Berlin–Warsaw–Moscow;
Chopin Express: Vienna–Warsaw.

For further information on train times contact:
POLRES
Al. Jerozolimskie 4400-024 Warsaw
Tel: (022) 827 2588.

By Sea

Regular passenger ferry services link the Polish ports of Świnoujśie and Gdańsk with Denmark and Sweden.

By Road

Coach Services

Regular weekly services are run most of the year in luxury air-conditioned coaches, with bar and toilet facilities. The Polski Express leaves either from London via Amsterdam to Poznań and Warsaw; or from London, Manchester or Birmingham to Wrocław, Katowice and Kraków. The journey time is about 30 hours, with fare reductions for students, senior citizens and children.

Coach operators throughout Poland run many services to and from German cities, such as Cologne, Dusseldorf, Essen, Dortmund, Hanover and Braunschweig.

By Car

It is possible to drive to Poland via the Channel (or with the ferry to Hook of Holland or Ostend) and via Holland and Germany to reach the Polish border. At the point of entry you must show your car registration documents, driving licence and Green Card (international insurance). There is no limit on buying petrol and no restriction on travelling within Poland. Petrol costs

around £0.45 a litre.

From the Hook of Holland or Ostend, the driving time to the Polish border is about 12 hours. Be prepared for queuing at the border (sometimes for few hours) and for a luggage check, as this is a border between EC and non-EC countries.
The **Polish Motoring Association** (PZM) can provide information about travelling around Poland and maps.

Vehicles towing caravans require an additional insurance document. Drivers who do not possess the necessary third-party insurance papers will have to obtain them from the Polish Motoring Association (PZM) at the border crossing. Fully comprehensive insurance is, however, recommended.

Main Crossing Points

Germany–Poland:
Ahlbeck–Świnoujście (foot passengers only); Linken–Lubieszyn; Pomellen–Kołbaskowo (near Szczecin); Schwedt–Krajnik Dolny; Frankfurt-am-Oder–Slubice and Swiecko; Guben–Gubin); Forst–Olszyna (motorway to Wrocław); Bad Muskau–Łęknica; Gürlitz–Zgorzelec; Zittau–Porajów/Sieniawka; Hohenwutzen–Osinów Dolny.

Poland–Czech Republic:
Jakuszyce–Harrachov, Kudowa–Słone Nachod; Głuchosłazy–Mikulovice; Chałupki Stary–Bohumin; Porajów–Hradek n. Nisou; Lubawka–Kralovec; Boboszów–Dolni

Polish Tourist Offices Abroad and websites

Germany: Polnisches Informationszentrum fr Touristik, Waidmarkt 24, 50676 Köln. Tel: (0221) 230545. Fax: 210465.
Netherlands: Pool Informatie-bureau voor Toerisme, Leidsestraat 64, Amsterdam 1017 D. Tel: (020) 625 3570 Fax: 623 0929.
Sweden: Polska Statens Turistbyra, Kungsgatan 66, Box 449, S-10128 Stockholm. Tel: (08) 216075, 218145 Fax: 210465.
UK: Polish National Tourist Office,

1st floor, Remo House, 310–312 Regent Street, London W1R 5AJ. Tel: (020) 7580 8811.
USA: Polish National Tourist Office, 333 N Michigan Avenue, Suite 224, Chicago, IL 60601. Tel: (312) 236 9013 Fax: 236 1125.

Websites
Poland's shop window on the net contains useful tourist information, including visa requirements:
http://www.polska.com
an introductory site, with maps,

places, situation in Poland.
http://www.explorepoland.pl
large, general guide to Poland.
city.net/countries/poland-city
small guide to Poland, including a useful on-line hotel reservation system.
http://www.polshworld.com
list of guides and ISPs.
http://www.hotelspoland.com
hotels in Poland; on-line reservation system.
http://www.polhotels.com
secure on-line hotel reservation system; car rental.

Lipka; Cieszyn– Cesky Tesin.
Poland–Slovakia:
Chyxne–Trestena; Piwniczna–
Mnisek; Zwardoý–Skalite; Cysa
Polana–Javorina.
Poland–Ukraine:
Medyka–Mostiska; Dorohusk–
Jagodin; Hrebenne–Rawa Ruska.
Poland–Lithuania:
Ogrodniki–Lazdijai.
Poland-Belarus:
Terespol–Brest.
Poland–Russia:
Bezledy–Bagrationowsk.

Maps

Note that several words are
frequently abbreviated on Polish
maps. Aleja (abbreviated as Al.)
means avenue, Ulica (abbreviated
as ul.) means street, Plac means
square, and Rynek is Market
Square. In addresses, house
numbers usually follow the name of
the street.

Specialist Tour Operators

UK Tour Operators
PolOrbis Travel Ltd
82 Mortimer Street
London W1N 7DE.
Tel: (020) 7636 2217 or 7637
4971, fax: (020) 7436 6558.
Fregata Travel Ltd
100 Dean Street, London W1V 6AQ.
Tel: (020) 7734 5101.
**New Millennium Holidays and
Travel Ltd**
20 High Street, Solihull
West Midlands B91 3TB.
Tel: (0121) 711 2232
Fax: (0121) 711 3652.

US Tour Operators
Happy Holidays Travel
5324 W Lawrence Avenue
Chicago, IL 60630.
Tel: (312) 282 1188.
American Travel Abroad Ltd
250 West 57th Street
New York, NY 10107.
Tel: (212) 586 5230
Fax: (212) 581 7925;
4801 W Peterson Ave
Chicago, IL 60646.
Tel: (312) 725 9500
Fax: (312) 725 8089.

Practical Tips

Business Hours

Offices are generally open Monday
to Friday 9am–6pm. Shops open
10am–6pm Monday to Friday and
9am–2pm on Saturdays. In general
shops are closed on Sundays, but
more and more larger stores are
staying open all week. There are
plenty of small neighbourhood
shops open 24 hours a day.

Banks open Monday to Friday
8am–6pm without lunch break. Post
Offices open Monday to Saturday,
8am–8pm. The main post office in
Warsaw is open 24 hours.

Shop Opening Hours

Opening times vary. Whatever the
time, whatever the day, you will
almost certainly find a shop open
somewhere. In general, the bigger
the town, the longer the opening
times. Most shops open at 8am
(some food shops at 6am) and
close at 7pm, on Saturday a little
earlier. Department stores generally
close at 6pm. Most shops are
closed on Sunday.

Media

In recent years Poland has greatly
increased the amount of newspapers, magazines and books that
it publishes and television and radio
have more interesting channels,
especially independent stations.

Newspapers

In March 1990, the government's
monopoly on the press was lifted
and the powerful state-owned Ruch
publishing co-operative dissolved.
Within four months of the introduction of a market economy, some
90 magazines had ceased trading.

In October 1990, the press was
privatised and over 100 magazines
sold off, in most cases to foreign
companies. About 70 titles passed
to newly formed co-operatives, one
of which was the respected Warsaw
weekly magazine *Polityka*. The daily
Gazeta Wyborcza, once the mouth-
piece of the Solidarity trade union,
increased its circulation to about
650,000 copies, becoming the
country's largest and most
influential daily paper. During the
presidency of Lech Wałęsa, it
frequently incurred his wrath for
criticising his style of government.

By 1999, the Polish media
published 76 daily newspapers (19
national and 57 regional) and more
than 150 magazines. Many of these
magazines are international titles
published in Polish, such as
Playboy, *Elle*, *Marie Clare*, *Hustler*
or *Cosmopolitan*.

International newspapers and
magazines are available from hotel
kiosks, good bookshops, EMPIK'S (a
special bookshop network found at
www.@empik.com.pl). British
newspapers usually arrive a day
after publication. *Gazeta Wyborcza*
and *Życie Warszawy* produce
weekend supplements in English.
The *Warsaw Voice* is probably the
most authoritative English-language
publication. It gives a good insight
into Polish politics, business and
culture and also has a listings
section for tourists. The second
important publication in English is
Business Journal Magazine.

Public Holidays

- **January** New Year's Day (1)
- **March/April** Easter Monday
  (variable)
- **May** Labour Day (1);
  Constitution Day (3)
- **June** Corpus Christi (variable)
- **August** Feast of the
  Assumption (15)
- **November** All Saints' Day (1);
  National Independence
  Day (11)
- **December** Christmas Day (25);
  St Stephen's Day (26)

Radio and Television

In October 1992 the monopoly on radio and TV was abandoned and the private broadcasters who had been working illegally since 1990 were legalised. Polish radio now offers four main stations, the most important being Polskie Radio. There are also numerous local channels. During the summer, Polish Radio 1 provides a summary of the news and weather in English.

Polish television consists of two state-run and several private stations; in addition, a range of regional programmes is also produced. Large hotels in the main cities have satellite receivers and most of the western satellite channels can be seen. These channels are also very popular among Poles. It is reckoned that one in every four households now has a satellite dish or at least access to one. Since 1998 two digital broadcast TV platforms have been available between them offering up to 100 TV channels.

Tourist Guides

Unfortunately, there are not many English-language city guides. There are only a few magazines in English which inform about current cultural events, important hotels and what is going on in the main cities, particularly in Warsaw. These are: *Warszawa What, Where, When*; *Welcome to Warsaw*; *Spotkania z Warszawa* and *Warsaw Insider*. Other good sources for details outside Warsaw and the cities include: *Poland, what, where, when*; *Business News From Poland*; *Airport Magazine Okęcie*; *Club Tourist Magazine*; *Coastal Times* and *The Polish Business Monthly*. These are available at hotel kiosks, travel offices and in the airport.

The Worldwide Web is another practical source of information on arts, news, restaurants, etc.

Postal Services

Post offices (*poczta*) are marked by a blue sign with the white letters POCZTA POLSKA, and are usually open Monday to Saturday 8am–8pm, earlier on Saturdays. Services at the *pocztas* include stamps, tokens and cards for public phones, postcards, sending letters, faxes, etc. Stamps, postcards and phone cards are available from most kiosks as well.

To send a letter within Europe costs 1 zł, postcards 70 gr. Airmail letters to European destinations take about a week to arrive, two to three weeks elsewhere.

Telecommunications

Public telephones

In Poland the telephone service belongs to Telekomunikacja Polska. There are both token (*leton*) and card (*karta*) public phones. There are now plenty of public phone boxes, although many of them still don't work, so it is often better to head for a post office if you need to make a call. For a long-distance call it is better use a credit-card phone. There are credit-card phones at airports and in the foyers of almost all hotels. These are considerably cheaper than making calls from your room. To call abroad from Poland, first dial 00 and then the country code, eg UK = 44. To call Poland from abroad, dial 00 48 then the number required.

It is advisable to purchase one of the recently introduced phone cards (remove a corner before use), available from post offices and kiosks. If you have to use coin phones you will need to buy one or more of the tokens (A = 1 unit, C = 6 units) from a post office or kiosk.

Until recently, it was often necessary in smaller towns to dial out via the operator, but now almost everywhere has its own dialling code. A leaflet listing dialling codes can be obtained at post offices.

Useful Numbers
Roadside Assistance (PZM): Tel: 9637 (981 in Kraków).
Long-distance Operator: Tel: 900.
International Operator: Tel: 901.
Telegrams: Tel: 905.
International Directory Enquiries: Tel: 908.
Inland Directory Enquiries: Tel: 913.
Radio Taxi: Tel: 919.
Speaking Clock: Tel: 962.
International Area Dialling Codes: Tel: 930.

Dialling Codes

You don't need to dial the area code if you are telephoning from within that area. If calling from abroad, drop the first "0".

Białystok 085	**Olsztyn** 089
Bielski-Biała 033	**Opole** 077
Częstochowa 034	**Poznań** 061
Elbląg 055	**Sopot** 058
Gdańsk 058	**Szczecin** 091
Gliwice 032	**Szczyrk** 033
Jelenia Góra 075	**Toruń** 056
Katowice 032	**Warsaw** 022
Kazimierz Dolny 081	**Wrocław** 071
Kołobrzeg 09 4	**Zakopane** 018
Kraków 012	
Lublin 076	
Łańcut 017	If dialling abroad from Poland, the international dialling codes for the following countries are:
Łeba 059	**Australia** 0-061
Łódź 042	**Canada** 0-01
Malbork 055	**Ireland** 0-0353
Nowy Sącz 018	**New Zealand** 0-064
	USA 0-01
	UK 0-044
	Dial 00 and then the country code, followed by the number.

Mobile Phones

Large numbers of Poles now have mobile phones – at the last count there were more than three million users. The main reason for this is the increasing speed of life and the frustration of using private and public phones. Although the telephone network is still being developed, there remain some areas where only mobiles work.

There are currently three GSM operators that provide roaming facilities for foreign tourists with their own telephones. Plus GSM or PL01 (on telephone display) operates in almost the entire country. Era GSM or PL02 also operates almost everywhere. Idea or PL03 (using the DCS system) operates only in Warsaw, Gdańsk, Szczecin, Katowice, Kraków, Pozań and Wrocław. It is advisable to contact your local GSM dealer to get information about facilities and roaming costs.

Fax Services and Telegrams

You can send and receive faxes from the larger hotels and main post offices. The best hotels also provide a secretarial service, which includes access to a computer and printer. Enquire at reception.

Telegrams can be sent from any post office. The number of words and speed (normal or express) determine the cost.

Internet Services

There is a special phone number (tel: 0 202122) that provides an internet link from any point in Poland without a subscription fee. The user name and password is PPP.

Embassies & Consulates

Australia:
3/5 Estońska Ul, 03 903 Warsaw
Tel: 617 6081/5
Fax: 617 6756.
Austria:
34 Gagarina Ul, 00-748 Warsaw
Tel: 841 0081/4
Fax: 841 0085.
Belgium:
34 Senatorska Ul, 00-950 Warsaw

Local Tourist Offices

Bielsko-Biała:
2 Piastowska Ul, 1 Warszawska Ul, 43-300 Bielsko-Biała.
Tel: (033) 25844
Fax: 22406.
Chełm:
20 Lubelska Ul, 22-100 Chelm.
Tel: (082) 53667
Fax: 54185.
Częstochowa:
65 Aljea NMP,
Częstochowa 42-200.
Tel: (034) 241360
Telex: 037686.
Gdańsk:
27 Heweliusza Ul, Gdańsk 80-861
Tel: (058) 314355/ 316637
Telex 0512733.
Katowice:
11 Młyńska Ul, Katowice 40-098.
Tel: (032) 539787/566.
Kielce:
12 Piotrkowska Ul, Kielce 25-510.
Tel: (041) 48666.
Kraków:
8 Pawia Ul, 31-154 Kraków.
Tel: (012) 226091
Fax: 220471.

Lublin:
Ul Krakowskie Prezmie, cie 78, Lublin 20-400.
Tel: (081) 24412/25339
Telex: 0643229.
Nowy Sącz:
46a Jagiellońska Ul,
Nowy Sącz 30-300.
Tel: (018) 23724
Telex: 0322663.
Płock:
38 Aleja Jachowicza, Płock 09-400.
Tel: (024) 629497.
Poznań:
Stary Rynek 59, Poznań 61-772.
Tel: (061) 526156.
Szczecin:
Ul. Kardyna Ba Wyszy Dskiego 26,
Tel: (091) 4340440.
Toruń:
1 Rynek Staromiejski (Town Hall), Toruń 87-100.
Tel: (056) 6210931.
Warsaw:
1/13 Plac Zamkowy,
Warsaw 00-297.
Tel: (022) 6351881.

Tel: 827 0233/5
Fax: 635 5711.
Canada:
1/5 Matejki Ul, 00-481 Warsaw
Tel: 629 8051
Fax: 629 6457.
Denmark:
19 Rakowiecka Ul, 02-517 Warsaw
Tel: 848 2600
Fax: 848 7580.
France:
1 Piękna Ul, 00-477 Warsaw
Tel: (022) 628 8401/4
Fax: 629 6480.
Germany:
30 Dabrowiecka Ul, 03-932 Warsaw
Tel: (022) 617 3011
Fax: 617 3582.
Italy:
6 Dabrowskiego Pl,
00-055 Warsaw
Tel: (022) 826 3471
Fax: 827 8507.
Japan:
AL. Jana Pawła II 23, Warsaw
Tel: (022) 621 4231
Fax: 628 0938.

Norway:
2a Fryderyka Chopina Ul,
00-559 Warsaw
Tel: (022) 621 4231
Fax: 628 0938.
Russia:
49 Belwederska Ul, 00-761 Warsaw
Tel: (022) 621 5575
Fax: 625 3016.
Switzerland:
Al. Ujazdowskie 27, 00-540 Warsaw
Tel: (022) 628 0481, 621 0548.
Spain:
4 Myliwiecka Ul, Warsaw
Tel: (022) 622 4250
Fax: 622 5408.
Sweden:
3 Bagatela Ul, 00-585 Warsaw
Tel: (022) 640 8900
Fax: 640 8983.
UK: Al. Rox 1, 00-556 Warsaw
Tel: (022) 628 1001/5
Fax: 621 7161.
USA: 29/31 Al. Ujazdowskie,
00-540 Warsaw
Tel: (022) 6283041
Fax: 6288298.

Emergency Numbers

Ambulance (public): 999
Police: 997
Fire: 998
Please note: do not expect
anyone at these numbers to be
able to speak English.

Religious Services

A large majority of the Polish
population is Roman Catholic, and
Poles attend church regularly.
Services in English can be found at
the following places of worship in
Warsaw:
Warsaw International Church:
Christian Theological Academy,
21 Ul. Miodowa Protestant, Sunday
worship at 11am (summer 10am).
Mokotwska Christian Fellowship:
6 Zbawiciela Square. New
Testament. Sunday 6pm.
**Roman Catholic Service for
Catholics Abroad:** Caritas,
14 Ul.Radna Sunday 11am.
Basilica of St John the Baptist:
6 Ul Kanonia (Old Town). Holy mass
at 11am.
**Augsburg Evangelical Church of
the Holy Trinity:** 6 Ul.Kreytowa
Confession 10.15am on Sunday,
service and holy communion
10.30am
Reform Evangelical Church: 74 Al.
Solidarno, ci. Sunday 10am.
Warsaw Eastern Orthodox Church:
52 Al. Solidarno, ci. Sunday 10am.
Nożyków Synagogue: 6 Ul. Twarda
Saturday service at 10am.
Warsaw Mosque: 103 Ul.
Wiertnicza Friday prayers at 1pm
(summer); 12 noon (winter).

Health

In an emergency, you will be taken
to a hospital where you will receive
immediate treatment, but for any
course of treatment or hospital stay
you will be expected to pay in cash.
Make sure you take out medical
insurance to cover all eventualities.

Chemists

Chemists are open from 10am to
7pm. An emergency system
operates in most towns. The
address of the chemist providing
out-of-hours service is usually
posted in chemists' windows. To be
on the safe side it is advisable to
bring a supply of any special medi-
cation you might need on your trip.

Chemists serve as the first place
to ask for help in minor medical
problems. There is a rota system
with one chemist (*Apteka*) in the
area staying open 24 hours for
emergencies. Most standard drugs
are available in Poland without a
prescription, but are sometimes
marketed under different names. It
is always a good idea to show the
chemist the empty container to
ensure you get the right drug.

Doctors and dentists

Most of the doctors and dentists in
the cities speak English and are
trained to western standards. Most
four- and five-star hotels have a
doctor on call to deal with
emergencies.

Hospitals and ambulances

Hospitals in Poland do not always
meet western standards of nursing
and accommodation, but medical
care is usually sufficient in an
emergency.

There are public and private
ambulance companies operating in
major cities and a public ambulance
service covering the whole country.
Ambulances are usually equipped
according to western standards.

Depending on their speciality
different hospitals cover different
emergencies. Patients are referred
to an appropriate hospital by a
doctor or ambulance crew. Self
referral is also possible via the
Accident and Emergency depart-
ments (*Izba przyj*).

Warsaw Hospitals and Clinics

Szpital Damiana: Ul WaBbrzyska 46
Tel: (022) 853 1644, 847 3313.
CM Medical Centre: Al. Jerozolim-
skie 65/79 (LIM Hotel Mariott)
Tel: (022) 630 5115, 621 0646.
FALCK: Ul. Prosta 69. Tel: (022) 534
5263/64; emergency tel: 9675
Ambulance service, not a clinic.
KLINIKA ProMed: Ul. Uniwersytecka
5 at Pl.Narutowicza. Tel: (022) 822
1811. Open: Mon–Fri 7.30am–8pm;
Sat 9am–5pm.

British Embassy Medical Centre:
Al. Ról 1 Tel: (022) 628 1001.
Mon–Fri 8.30am–4.30.
For foreign diplomats and British
nationals. Appointments only.
German Embassy Medical Centre:
Ul. Katowicka 31. Tel: (022) 617
3021/3011 ext. 240. Mon–Thurs
8am–1pm; 2pm–5pm. For all
foreigners; appointments only.

Dental Treatment
Austria Dental Centre: Ul. Zelazna
54. Tel: (022) 654 2116; 821
3184. Mon–Fri 9am–9pm; Sat
9am–1pm. English- and German-
speaking dentists.
Eurodental: 8–20 Ul. Andersa 15
Tel: (022) 831 3161/2090;
Ul. Nowowiejska 37
Tel: (022) 825 7800/9709;
Ul. Zniadeckich 14
Tel: (022) 625 7800/7808.
English-speaking dentists.
Perfect-Med:
20–8 Pl. D browskiego 12
Tel: (022) 826 6060.
Dental Centre: 20–8 Ul. Radiowa 1
Tel: (022) 638 9746.

Security & Crime

Theft is not unusual in places
frequented by tourists. It is better
to keep any valuables and jewellery
in the hotel safe. If you are
travelling by car, it is essential to
park it for longer periods or overnight in a guarded car park – even
the smaller towns have them. If you
are the victim of a theft, report it
immediately to the reception desk
at your hotel or to the police. The
emergency police number is 997. If
you lose all your money or your
passport, you will have to seek
advice from your nearest consulate
or embassy (*see page 377*).

Tipping

It is usual to leave about 10
percent of the total bill as a tip in a
restaurant, hairdressers and for
taxi drivers.

Getting Around

By Air

The Polish airline LOT operates flights from Warsaw to Gdańsk, Katowice, Koszalin, Kraków, Poznań, Szczecin and Wrocław (*see page 373*). Flights also link Gdańsk, Katowice, Kraków, Poznań and Wrocław with main Polish towns.

On arrival the Airport City Bus Service runs from the airport to major hotels in downtown Warsaw. Tickets are available from the Orbis desk at the airport, the LOT desk at the Marriott Hotel or from the driver (*see page 373*).

By Train

With over 26,500 km (16,450 miles) of railway lines, the Polish railway network covers the whole country, but regular, non-express trains can be slow and overcrowded.

Express trains run between the major cities. Non-stop express trains complete with restaurant cars run between Warsaw and Gdańsk/Gydnia, Poznań and Kraków. For information about connections, enquire directly at the railway station or in the PKP (Polish National Railway) offices.

Rail fares are still reasonable. Tickets can be purchased from the Orbis offices or in the POLRES offices (Warsaw, tel: 365055). It is well worth booking a seat particularly on express services and paying 50 percent extra for a first-class ticket. You may also wish to consider buying a POLRAIL pass. Valid on all PKP railway lines, these are issued for 7, 14, 21 or 30 days. Users named on the non-transferable ticket, are entitled to unlimited rail travel during this period.

Most stations have left-luggage offices (*przechowalnia bagazu*).
http://www.pkp.com.pl information and reservations.
http://www.it.com.pl/pkpdc/eng Warsaw Central Station schedules.
http://www.walden.mo.net/jdobek/pkptrav.html Polish rail page with extensive details about Polish trains.

Getting around towns

Buses and trams are the main forms of public transport in the larger towns (although in Warsaw it is the metro). They usually operate between 5.30am and 11pm, (Warsaw's metro closes around 11.30pm). In some cities there is a night service, but fares are more expensive.

Tickets (*bilety*) can be purchased at a RUCH kiosks or from machines at bus and railway stations. Tickets are not available from bus drivers. Tickets must be validated immediately on entering the vehicle in the metal boxes on the bus or tram wall. When you change vehicles, you must punch a new ticket. All-day tickets and one-week tickets are available in kiosks or at the ZTM-Transport Authority (pl. Unii Lubelskiej or ul. Senatorska 37, Warsaw). Route maps are usually displayed inside buses and at stops.

By Coach

There are two possibilities to choose from: the state-owned **PKS** or the private **Polski Express**.

The **PKS** runs both stopping and express services. Tickets can be bought at bus stations, Orbis offices, travel agencies and, if there are spare seats, from the driver. In the Tri-City (Gdańsk-Gdynia-Sopot) and in the Upper Silesia industrial region, a zonal system operates. The biggest private coach company Polski Express provides several shuttle services between major cities in Poland. Prices are higher than PKS, but the standard is relatively high (buses with air-conditioning, TV, toilet and coffee bar). For information about all available connections you may ask in any travel office or at PKS coach stations.
Polski Express tel: 620 0330 (open 7am–9pm).
PKS tel: 9433.

Cruises

In the summer season (1 May to 15 October), the following cruises along the Baltic coast are available: Gdańsk Sopot Hel; Gdynia Jastarnia; Gydnia Hel; Szczecin Świnoujście and Szczecin Midzyzdroje. Also possible are excursions on the Vistula between Warsaw and Gdańsk, on the Mazurian Lakes and on the Elblag-Ostróda Canal.

By Taxi

When available for hire taxis display an illuminated sign. The best places to find one at taxi ranks in city centres and outside hotels, railway stations and airports. It is also possible to phone for a radio taxi (ask in your hotel for details). This usually works out cheaper, as independent drivers, who are not linked to companies, are more likely to overcharge their passengers. At night, and for journeys into the outlying countryside, fares are usually 50 percent higher.

To overcome the problems of inflation, taxi meters show only a base unit. To calculate your fare, the driver multiplies the number of units by a number on an authorised list (normally this factor is shown on a sticker on the passenger door). Check that the taxi meter is switched on as soon as your journey starts.
Taxi Telephone Numbers
MPT- Radio Taxi 919
Taxi Plus 96 21
Super-Taxi 96 22
Halo-Taxi 96 23
Korpo-Taxi 96 24
Volfra-Taxi 96 25
Express-Taxi 96 26
O.K. Taxi 96 28
Wa wa Taxi 96 44

Super Taxi 2 96 66
Sawa Taxi 644 44 44

Hitchhiking

Hitchhiking is a perfectly acceptable way of travelling in Poland. The normal method of signalling to drivers that you are looking for a lift is to wave the whole arm. The thumbs-up signal is, however, understood by drivers. Sometimes, a small contribution is expected.

Driving

The road network in Poland covers 220,000 km (135,000 miles) and even remote tourist attractions are relatively easy to reach. Roads have internationally recognised signs, and you should drive on the right-hand side of the road. Outside built-up areas, traffic levels are generally lower than in western Europe, but drivers should always be on the look-out for motorcyclists, carts and tractors. In main towns during peak hours you will find traffic jams and slow traffic. At night on country roads it is often difficult to spot pedestrians. The main streets and most side roads are usually in good condition. You may also expect heavy traffic during summer weekends.

Petrol Stations

The majority of petrol stations along main routes are open 24 hours a day. They offer similar services to those in western Europe, including small shops and tea and coffee facilities. In small towns, however, you may expect petrol stations to open from 6am to 10pm.

Lead-free petrol is available in all stations. Ten litres (2 gallons) of petrol can be imported into Poland or taken out in fuel containers.

Breakdown Services

The Polish Motoring Association (PZM) is the main breakdown service but there are many other roadside assistance stations. The breakdown emergency service centres usually operate from 7am to 10pm, some closing at 3pm. Membership of the PZM secures assistance to members of automobile clubs affiliated with the Fédération Internationale de l'Automobile (FIA) and the Alliance Internationale de Tourisme (AIT), holders of insurance policies issued by the Intermutuelle Assistance, Assistance Internationale and SOS, and ADAC club members. Members should contact the Autotour Motoring Tourism Bureau to check whether they are affiliated.

If your car model has a producer assistance programme (such as Mobilo with Mercedes-Benz), call your dealer and ask for correct telephone numbers in Poland to contact local assistance services.

Polish Motoring Association (PZM), Tel: 981.

ADAC (Warsaw)
Tel: 290374, 24 hours.

Autotour Motoring Tourism Bureau, 63 Aleje Jerozlimskie, Warsaw 00-697.
Tel: 621 0789, 628 6255
Fax: 628 6254.

Rules of the road

Maximum speed limits are: in built-up areas 60 kmh (37 mph); motor-ways 130 kmh (80 mph); express roads (specially signed) 110 kmh (68 mph); outside built-up areas 90 kmh (56 mph). Motorists caught exceeding speed limits (radar traps are very frequent) can expect a substantial fine. The maximum fine for speeding is 500 złotty.

From 1 November to 1 March, it is necessary to keep dipped head-lights on throughout the day. Motorcyclists should leave their headlights on throughout the year.

Many traffic lights have green arrows, which permit filtering to the right on a red light as long as there are no pedestrians crossing the road. However it's necessary to stop before the lights, and continue turning right after checking that the road is clear. Vehicles on round-abouts have priority over joining traffic. Where priority is not clearly stated, trams always have priority over other road users. Stopping within 100 metres (330 ft) of a level crossing is not permitted. Many of the main trunk roads have slow lanes to allow faster traffic to pass.

The permitted blood alcohol level is virtually zero, so do not drink at all when driving. The penalties are severe. Seat belts must be worn by the driver and front-seat passenger at all times. If belts are fitted on rear seats, they must be worn as well. Children can travel in the car only in special child-seats.

Car and Bus Hire Companies in Warsaw

Ann,
Okęcie Airport
Tel: 650 3261/2; and
Hotel Marriott-Terminal LOT
Tel: 630 5683.
Avis,
65/79 Aleje Jerozolimskie,
Hotel Marriott
Tel/fax: 630 7316; and
Okęcie International Airport
Tel: 650 4871/2.
Budget,
65/79 Aleje Jerozolimskie,
Hotel Marriott
Tel: 630 7280
Fax: 630 6946; and
Okęcie International Airport,
Terminal 1, Arrivals Hall
Tel/fax: 650 4062.

Five, 44/46 Z Bota Ul
Tel: 625 4094/7515.
Hertz,
Okęcie International Airport
Tel: 650 2896; 621 0239, 621
0238/9; 0800 143789.
National Car Rental,
Okęcie International Airport
Tel: 6504733, 6069202,
8687574

Bus and Minibus Hire:
Europe Tour,
Ul. Mokotowska 222/10
Tel/fax: 621 0508, 622 0424,
628 6462.
Mazurkas Travel, Ul. Nowogrodzka
24/26 – Hotel Forum
Tel: 629 1878, 629 1249.

Parking

In larger towns and cities, only leave your car in secure car parks and make sure nothing of any value is visible to passers-by. If possible, remove the car radio. Coded radios or a detachable front panel are not enough to stop theft. Car thieves are particularly interested in German models, such as BMWs, Mercedes and VW Golfs.

Car hire

Branches of the main car rental companies are to be found at airports, stations, leading hotels and in the major cities. The following conditions apply: drivers should be at least 21 years old, have a valid passport and a full driving licence. In addition, they must either pay a substantial deposit or leave security in the form of a credit card imprint. Daily rates are similar to those in western Europe.

Tour Operators & Travel Agents

Polorbis, the tour operating and travel agency arm of Orbis, a private hotel chain (*see page 375*), produces a varied and imaginative brochure. There is a Warsaw Opera Weekend, Activity Holidays and Health Spas; and a Tribute Tour taking in ghettos, castles and the Pope's birthplace.

Tourists can obtain information from the Orbis offices in Poland, good-quality hotels and tourist information offices, identified by the "it" symbol.

Orbis can arrange for English-speaking guides to accompany groups or individuals on day trips or longer excursions. At main tourist sights, such as Malbork, guides are usually on hand, but their English may be of variable quality.

Organised tours

The Polish Association for Tourism and Culture (PTTK) organises hiking, canoeing, sailing and motorcycling tours, as well as excursions on foot, on skis and in the mountains. Local tour guides are available on request. Contact:
PTTK,
36 Swiętokrzyska Ul.,
00-116 Warsaw
Tel: 208241
Fax: 240071.

Sports-Tourist offers sporting events, sailing, canoeing and horse-riding in its programme. **Almatur**, the travel agency run by the Polish Student Association, arranges reasonably priced individual or group tours for students, including educational and cultural pro-grammes, international student lodgings along the coast, on lakes and in the mountains. They also organise tours for film, fishing and horse-riding enthusiasts. Contact:
Almatur,
15 Kopernika Ul.,
00-359 Warsaw
Tel: 826 5381
Fax: 826 2353.

Juventur is another organisation that specialises in organising tours of Poland and visits to cultural events for students and young people. Contact:
Juventur Travel,
01-002 Warsaw,
Nowolipie Ul. 25
Tel: 384586, 383127, 635 9967
Fax: 384586.

Other useful tour operators include:
Polish Travel Quo Vadis Ltd.,
Ul. Ptasia 2, Warsaw.
Tel: (22) 652 1458/60
Fax (22) 652 1461.
Email: ptqv@polishtravel.com.pl
Open: Mon–Fri. 9am–5pm.
English-speaking guides, organised tours of Poland.
Mazurkas Travel,
Ul. Nowogrodzka 24/26 –
Hotel Forum, Warsaw.
Tel: 629 1878/1249, 635 6633.
Email: Euromic@mazurkas.pol.pl
Open: Mon–Fri. 8.30am–8pm.
Tour operator and travel agency for groups only.

Where to Stay

Hotels and Private Rooms

During the height of the season, basic hotels, youth hostels and campsites in the main tourist regions are hopelessly overcrowded, so it is a good idea to reserve accommodation well in advance. However, it is not usually a problem finding a bed in the higher-price range hotels, even in mid-summer. If you find yourself facing a night under the stars, do not despair. Ask at the local tourist information office or rooms agency (*biuro zakwaterowania*) for a list of private houses where overnight guests are welcome. By the coast or in the Mazurian Lakes district, houses with beds available show signs with the words *pokoje* or *noclegi*. If you arrive in a town late at night, ask a taxi driver about likely vacancies.

Hotels are divided into five categories: 1-, 2-, 3-, 4-star and luxury hotels. Luxury hotels provide the same standards of comfort as the international hotel chains of western Europe and the USA, such as Marriott and Holiday Inn. The now privatised tourist organisation Orbis also manages some very good hotels. The number of stars beside the hotel name can be misleading, however, as many have recently taken to reducing their star rating for tax reasons.

Hotels that target business people and tourists will offer guests spacious rooms, translation and secretarial services, fitness suites, bars and restaurants. Prices are comparable with similar hotels in western Europe.

The number of hotels and *pensions* is still growing and many of them do not yet have star ratings, but generally offer good facilities. Almost all hotels and boarding houses accept major credit cards.

UK: PolOrbis Travel Ltd, 82 Mortimer Street, London W1N 7DE. Tel: (020) 7637 4971/580 8028 Fax: 436 6558.

USA: 342 Madison Avenue, New York, NY 10173. Tel: (212) 867 5011 Fax: 682 4715.

Hotel Listings

WARSAW

In the capital of Poland you can find various places to stay. There are a few hotels with luxury accommodation (Bristol Hotel) some international chain hotels (Holiday Inn, Sheraton, Marriot, Mercure), and many inexpensive options as well. Many hotels have been renovated and are therefore in good condition.

It's a good idea to choose a hotel in the centre of Warsaw, only a short distance from the interesting sights in the Old Town and other places of interest. You should make reservations in advance, particularly in June, July, September and October. Christmas time is also very busy.

Budget
Belfer
Wybrzel e Kołciuszkowskie 31/33.
Tel: (022) 625 5185/0571.
Fax: (022) 625 2600.
Twenty minutes' walk from the city centre, on the banks of the Vistula. Not all rooms are ensuite. **$**

Garnizonowy
Ul. Mazowiecka 10.
Tel: (022) 683 3565.
Situated in the city centre. Of the 48 rooms none have ensuite bathrooms but there is a bar and restaurant. **$**

Saski
Plac Bankowy 1.
Tel: (022) 620 4611.
The location (close to Saxon Gardens and Old Town) and price are the best reason for choosing

this hotel, currently undergoing renovation. It is set in a 19th-century house and on the ground floor there is a restaurant and cocktail bar. **$**

Moderate
Cytadela
Ul. Krajewskigo 3/5.
Tel/fax: (022) 391024.
In the city centre, within walking distance of the Old Town. Rooms (single, double, twin) have bath-rooms, clean and in good order. **$$**

Harenda
Krakowskie Przedmiecie 4/6.
Tel: (022) 826 0071.
Fax: (022) 826 2625.
Excellent location on one of the finest streets in town. Only a few minutes' walk to the Old Town. In the same building as one of the city's best-known restaurants (of the same name). Not all of the 40 rooms are ensuite; some can take an extra bed. **$$**

Karat
Ul. Słoneczna 37.
Tel: (022) 601 4411.
Fax: (022) 849 8454.
Close to Lazienski Park, in a quiet location but near Puławska Street – one of Warsaw's main thorough-fares. Newly renovated, the hotel offers 30 ensuite rooms at a reasonable price. **$$**

Maria
Jana Pawłall 71.
Tel: (022) 384062.
Fax: (022) 383840.
Just outside the city centre, a small hotel (22 rooms) in very good condition. Rooms have ensuite bathrooms; parking, restaurants, bar. **$$**

Expensive
Belwederski
Belwederska 46/50.
Tel: (022) 841 60 21.
Fax: (022) 841 6029.
A modest-sized hotel (44 rooms), situated on the same street as the President's Palace. Excellent view of park. All rooms with bath. Sport facilities, bar, restaurant. **$$$**

Dom Chłopa
Plac Powstańców Warszawy 2.
Tel: (022) 827 9251.

Similar to the Grand, with renovated apartments which still retain something of their Communist-era appearance. The majority of the rooms are ensuite and the location is good, not far from the city centre and Old Town. There are health facilities, a restaurant and a café. **$$$**

MDM
Plac Konstytucji 1.
Tel: (022) 621 6211.
Fax: (022) 621 4173.
Situated in the centre, on one of the biggest streets in Warsaw. The architecture of MDM and surrounding buildings was created in the Communist era, so the local Burger King is a mark of newfound capitalism. The 111 pleasantly renovated apartments are ensuite; the hotel is air-conditioned and has business and disabled facilities. **$$$**

Polonia
Al. Jerozolimskie 45.
Tel: (022) 628 72 41.
Fax: (022) 628 6622.
City centre hotel with 234 rooms – all with bathroom/WC, satellite TV; restaurant, café, dancing. One of the oldest hotels in Warsaw (1913), still awaiting renovation. **$$$**

Solec
Ul. Zagórna 1.
Tel: (022) 625 4400.
Fax: (022) 625 4424.
Located in quiet area of Warsaw, only 20 minutes walk to city centre, close to the River Vistula and parks. This two-storey building has 147 ensuite rooms. The restaurant serves Polish and international dishes. Guarded parking. **$$$**

Luxury
Bristol
Krakowskie Przedmiecie 42/44.
Tel: (022) 625 2525.
Fax: 625 2577.
One of the most elegant and oldest hotels in the city. Art Nouveau, recently renovated. 155 beds (double and single rooms), 43 apartments – all ensuite, with satellite TV. Excellent cuisine in three separate restaurants; café, bars. Health club with indoor swimming pool, sauna, solarium;

suitable for the disabled, facilities for children. **$$$$**

Europejski
Krakowskie Przedmiecie 13.
Tel: (022) 826 5051.
Fax: (022) 826 11 11.
Situated in one of Warsaw's main streets, this is the oldest working hotel in the city. Although in need of some renovation, it is a pleasant place to stay. Restaurants and café, information desk, hairdresser, shop. **$$$$**

Forum
Ul. Nowogrodzka 24/26.
Tel: (022) 621 0271.
Fax: (022) 625 0476.
Situated on the junction of two main streets, in the heart of the commercial district. The tallest hotel in Warsaw, there are 733 rooms with panoramic views of the city. Small rooms with interesting decor. Restaurant "Soplica" offers international cuisine and "Maryla" specialises in traditional Polish dishes. Shops, hairdresser. **$$$$**

Holiday Inn
Zlota 48/54.
Tel: (022) 620 6534.
Fax: (022) 300 569.
Located between the main railway station and the Palace of Science and Culture, close to the business and shopping centres. There are 336 room, air-conditioned, with satellite TV; sports, health and disabled facilities; indoor and outdoor parking. **$$$$**

Jan III Sobieski
Plac Zawiszy 1.
Tel: (022) 658 4444.
Fax: (022) 659 8828.
Located on the way to the airport, this is one of the most modern hotels in Warsaw. The apartments are comfortable and smart, with all standard facilities. Restaurant, café, shop, guarded underground car park. **$$$$**

Marriott
Aleje Jerozolimskie 65/79.
Tel: (022) 630 6306.
Fax: (022) 630 0311.
Situated in Warsaw's centre. It has 521 rooms with luxurious facilities, including health club and indoor swimming pool. On the top floor the Panorama restaurant has a

wonderful view of Warsaw. On the first floor there are other restaurants, bars and a nightclub. Guarded car park. Casino. In this building is also the LOT-Polish Airlines Terminal, expensive shops, galleries, boutiques and hairdressers. **$$$$**

Mercure-Fryderyk Chopin
Aleja Jana PawIalI.
Tel: (022) 620 0201.
Fax: (022) 620 8779.
In the city centre, close to the Palace of Science and Culture; 250 rooms, all ensuite with satellite TV. Two restaurants (French and international), bar, sauna, guarded car park. Modern furnished rooms. Children's, disabled and health facilities. **$$$$**

Sheraton
Prusa 2.
Tel: (022) 657 6100.
Fax: (022) 657 6200.
The newest hotel in Warsaw, with 350 comfortable, well-equipped rooms. Excellent location, between Łazienki Park and the Old Town. Health club, swimming pool, business and conference facilities. Restaurant, café, jazz bar. **$$$$**

Victoria Intercontinental
Ul. Krolewska 11.
Tel: (022) 657 8011.
Fax: (022) 657 8011.
With 365 rooms, situated in the city centre near Opera and Saxon Gardens; walking distance to the Old Town. In the rooms there are minibars, air-conditioning, satellite TV, ensuite facilities. Business centre, perfume counter, shop, rooms for disabled, restaurants with Polish and international cuisine. **$$$$**

OUTSIDE WARSAW

Felix
Ul Omulewska 24.
Tel/fax: (022) 813 0255.
All rooms en suite. Good standard. **$$$**

Gromada
Ul 17 Stycznia 32a.
Tel: (022) 846 5822.
Fax: (022) 846 1580.
Close to the airport, 30 minutes

from the city centre by bus. 127 clean rooms, all with bathrooms. Guarded parking. **$$$**

Konstancja
Konstancin Jeziorna yródlana 6/8.
Tel: (022) 756 4325.
Fax: (022) 756 4367.
One of the few nice places in the surrounding area, 15 km (9 miles) from the city centre, on the way to Wilanów and near parks and forests. 44 comfortable rooms with air-conditioning; sport facilities. **$$$**

Novotel
Ul 1 Sierpnia 1.
Tel: (022) 846 40 51.
Fax: (022) 846 36 86.
Situated 4 km (2 miles) from the city centre, on the way to the airport. 144 rooms with bath. Health and disabled facilities, in summer a swimming pool and terrace. Restaurant, cocktail bar. **$$$**

Sokrates Hotel
Ul Smyczkowa 9.
Tel: (022) 843 9551.
Under the auspices of Warsaw University. Located 25 minutes from city centre by bus, or faster by metro. Tourist standard, clean. Rooms with bathroom, small restaurant/ bar. **$$**

Vera
Bitwy Warszawskiej 1920r 16.
Tel: (022) 622 74 21.
Fax: (022) 623 6256.
Located 30 minutes from the city centre by bus. The standard and price are similar to Novotel and Hotel Solec. **$$$**

Zajazd Napoleoński
Płowiecka 83.
Tel: (022) 15 30 68.
Fax: (022) 15 22 16.
The architecture of this place is a little similar to a Polish mansion. Located one hour by bus from the city centre. 24 rooms with bath, all in good condition. Restaurant

serves Polish cuisine, bar, parking, business facilities. **$$$**

CENTRAL POLAND

Bydgoszcz
Chemik
Al. Wojska Polskiego 48.
Tel: (052) 374 8913.
Fax: (052) 361 1822.
Five km (3 miles) from city centre.
20 rooms (single, double) with bathroom, satellite TV. **$**
Ikar
Ul. Szubińska 32.
Tel: (052) 379 1788.
Close to the centre, some ensuite rooms, recently renovated. **$**
Ratuszowy
Ul. Długa 37.
Tel: (052) 22 8861.
Located in the Old Town, in the city centre. Old architecture and stylish rooms, sauna, solarium, bar.
Intimate atmosphere. **$$**
Hotel Pod Orłem
Ul. Gdańska 14.
Tel: (052) 22 1861/9.
Fax: (052) 22 8988.
Probably the best hotel in town.
Renovated to its original splendour of 1896. Surrounded by attractive gardens, 1.3 km (about 1 mile) from the station. The 80 rooms are all ensuite, some with private balcony. Three restaurants, cocktail bar, nightclub, fitness centre, facilities for children and disabled, satellite TV. Some shops, travel service, car hire, guarded car park. Horse riding 6 km (4 miles) away, yacht charter and fishing 30 km (15 miles) away, watersports 3 km (2 miles) away. **$$$**
Hotel Brda
Ul. Dworcowa 94.
Tel: (052) 22 4061/9.
Fax: (052) 22 5655.
Located right in the centre of the city. 250 rooms, sauna, solarium, exchange bureau, car hire, guarded car park. **$$$**
City Hotel
Ul. 3. Maja 6.
Tel: (052) 325 2500.
Fax: (052) 325 2505.
Email: mailto:city@cps.pl
A modern, luxurious hotel located in the city centre, 3 km (2 miles) from the station, 5 km (3 miles) from the airport. Family atmosphere and excellent restaurant. 130 rooms all with bathroom/WC, satellite TV, Viennese coffee house, fitness suite, guarded car park, dogs allowed. **$$$$**

Kazimierz Dolny
Góralski Domek
Ul. Krakowska 47.
Tel: (081) 881 0263.
Rooms in this wooden house with garden have a view of the Vistula, but not all are ensuite. Dogs allowed. Disco, cinema and museum nearby. **$**
Aaznia
Ul. Senatorska 21.
Tel: (081) 881 0298.
Fax: (081) 881 0249.
In the city centre, near the Town Square; 13 ensuite rooms with satellite TV; restaurant and café; dogs allowed. **$$**
Dom Architekta
Rynek 20.
Tel/fax: (081) 881 0544.
Close to Town Market Square; the favourite place in Kazimierz Dolny to stay; 106 beds with bath; restaurant. **$$**
Zajazd Piastowski
Ul. Sloneczna 3.
24–120 Kazimierz Dolny.
Tel: (081) 881 0351.
Only 1 km (half a mile) from the Vistula riverside, ensuite rooms with satellite TV. Horse riding and swimming pool. Dogs allowed. **$$**

Łódź
Centrum
Ul. Kilińskiego 59/63.
Tel: (042) 632 8640.
Fax: (042) 636 9650.
In the city centre, close to the station; newly renovated, with 90 ensuite rooms. **$$**
Swiatowit
Al. Kołciuszki 68.
Tel: (042) 636 3817.
Fax: (042) 636 5291.
City centre hotel; 212 rooms (96 singles, 113 doubles); restaurant, café, guarded car park; suitable for the disabled. **$$**
Grand

Ul. Piotrkowska 72.
Tel: (042) 633 9920.
Fax: (042) 633 7876.
Located on the main historical street in the city centre. The hotel was built in 1888 and has retained its authentic atmosphere. Most of the 300 rooms are ensuite; restaurant, café, bar, disco, children's facilities, dogs allowed, guarded car park. **$$$**

Toruń
Trzy Korony
Rynek Staromiejski 21.
Tel/fax: (056) 622 6031/32.
Excellent location on the Market Square; 60 rooms, not all ensuite; restaurant, bar. **$**
Helios
Ul. Kraszewskiego 1/3.
Tel: (056) 655 5416/21.
Fax: (056) 655 5429.
Located in the city centre, close to the Old Town, the smartest hotel in town and completely renovated; 180 beds; (double rooms, single rooms, apartments) all ensuite with satellite TV; restaurant, café, dancing, sight-seeing service, dogs allowed, guarded car park. **$$$$**

Price Guide

Prices are for a double room per night during the high season.
$$$$ = above $100
$$$ = $50 to $100
$$ = $30 to $50
$ = below $30

THE COAST

Gdańsk
Dom Nauczyciela
Ul. Uphagena 28.
Tel: (058) 341 9116.
Located in the district of Wrzeszcz, pleasant rooms in a Seccessionist style house. **$**
Bartan Hotel
Ul. Turystyczna 9A.
Tel: (058) 530 80779.
Fax: (058) 530 80999.
Lovely hotel located on Sobieszewska Island, only 15 km (10 miles) from the city centre.
Family-run boarding house which

ensures peace and quiet. Some of the 34 rooms are ensuite, with a balcony; sauna, billiards table, conference room, bar, restaurant, car park, on-site mountainbiking, fishing, tennis. **$$**

Jantar
Ul. Długi Targ 19.
Tel: (058) 301 9532.
Fax: (059) 301 2716.
Situated in the heart of the old town within walking distance of all the attractions. **$$**

Kadyny Palace
Tolkmicko.
Tel: (055) 231 6120.
Fax: (055) 316 200.
Located 90 minutes southeast of Gdańsk Airport, close to the national park. 40 bedrooms all ensuite, restaurant, sauna, tennis, mountain biking, horse-riding. **$$$**

Novotel
Ul. Pszenna 1.
Tel: (058) 531 5611.
Fax: (058) 531 5619.
Near the city centre, within walking distance of the Old Town, 3 km (2 miles) from the station; 154 double rooms with bathroom/WC, satellite TV, some of them overlooking the Old Town. Restaurant, café, car park, dogs allowed. **$$$**

Hanza Hotel
Ul. Tokarska 6.
Tel: (058) 530 52427.
Fax: (058) 530 80999, email: Hotel@hanza-hotel.com.pl
Located in the Old Town, with wonderful views of the Motława River. The newest hotel in the city, 104 air-conditioned rooms, car park, health facilities, casino. **$$$$**

Kolobrzeg

Awangarda
Ul. Rubinowa 2/4.
Tel: (094) 351 6781.
Fax: (094) 351 6555.
Ten minutes by bus from the city centre, new hotel, 60 beds; rooms all with bath/ WC, sauna, solarium, swimming pool, bar, restaurant. **$**

Bisnesmen Klub
Ul. Morska 7C.
Tel: (094) 354 5709.
Fax. (094) 352 6679.
Situated on the seaside on the

Baltic. Not all the 65 rooms are ensuite; car park; watersports. **$$**

Hotel Centrum
Ul. Katedralna 12.
Tel: (094) 352 2905.
A new hotel in the city centre, 70 ensuite rooms with satellite TV; fitness centre; disco, restaurant. **$$**

Solny
Ul. Fredry 4.
78–100 Kolobrzeg.
Tel: (094) 354 5700.
Fax: (094) 354 5828.
Two km (1 mile) from the station and 1 km (half a mile) from the beach; 150 double rooms with bathroom/WC, satellite TV; restaurant, café, bars, disco, sports facilities, fitness suite, facilities for children, guarded car park. **$$$**

Leba

Arkun
Ul. Wróblewskiego 11.
Tel: (059) 866 2419.
Fax: (059) 866 2495.
In the city centre, near the beach and station; 60 ensuite rooms with satellite TV; guarded car park, fitness centre; watersports. **$**

Wodnik
Ul. Nadmorska 10.
Tel: (059) 866 1366.
Fax: (059) 661542.
Close to the beach; 300 double rooms and apartments, all with bathroom/WC, satellite TV; restaurant, café, bar, indoor swimming pool, sauna. **$$**

Neptun
Ul. Sosnowa 1.
Tel: (059) 866 1432.
Fax: (059) 866 2357.
Situated on the beach; 75 ensuite rooms; guarded car park; tennis court, billiards, fitness centre, playground; watersports, swimming pool. **$$$**

Słupsk

Staromiejski
Ul. Jedno, ci Narodowej 4.
Tel: (059) 842 8464.
Fax: (059) 842 5019.
Located in town centre; 77 ensuite rooms, satellite TV; restaurant, bar, dogs allowed, guarded car park. **$$**

Zamkowy
Ul. Dominikańska 4.

Tel/fax: (059) 842 5294.
In the town centre; 66 beds (double rooms, single rooms, apartments), satellite TV; restaurant, bar, dogs allowed, guarded car park. **$$**

Sopot

Pensjonat Eden
Ul. Kordeckiego 4.
Tel: (058) 551 1503.
On the beach; close to the town; rooms with shared bathrooms. **$**

Maryla
Ul. Spia 22.
Tel: (058) 551 0035.
All 34 rooms are ensuite in this clean and pleasant hotel. **$$**

Grand
Ul. Powstańcow Warszawy 12/14.
Tel: (058) 551 0041.
Fax: (058) 551 6214.
This hotel was built in 1926 in the Art Nouveau style; near the town centre, it overlooks the beach; 65 double rooms, 43 single rooms, 4 apartments – all ensuite; restaurant, café, bar, casino, suitable for the disabled, art and craft gallery, dogs allowed, guarded car park. **$$$**

THE NORTHEAST

Białystok

Hotel Garnizonowy
Ul. Akademicka 26.
Tel: (085) 677 7357.
22 rooms, some with bathrooms. **$**

Hotel Turkus
Al. Jana Pawła II 54.
Tel: (085) 651 3278.
100 ensuite rooms, with restaurant, café, bar and parking. **$**

Pensjonat Guliwer
Ul. Celownicza 29.
Tel: (085) 744 3837.
Fax: (085) 744 3451.
Near the city centre, single, double and family rooms. Horse riding. **$**

Hotel Leny
Al. Jana Pawła II 77.
Tel: (085) 651 1641.
Fax: (085) 651 1701.
Six km (4 miles) from the city centre, near the forest. 82 rooms and suites, satellite TV, restaurant, guarded car park, dogs allowed. Trips to nearby sights arranged. **$$**

Hotel Mosir
Ul. Wołodyjowskiego 5.
Tel: (085) 742 6229.
Newly built six-storey hotel with 93
en suite rooms, restaurant,
nightclub, fitness centre. Next door
to the athletic stadium with tennis
and watersports facilities. **$$**

Hotel Cristal
Ul. Lipowa 3.
Tel: (058) 742 5061.
Fax: (058) 742 5800.
Situated in the city centre. Pleasant
atmosphere and quality service, 80
rooms and suites, satellite TV,
health facilities, nightclub, casino,
car park. **$$$**

Hotel Gołbiewski
Ul. Pałacowa 7.
Tel: (085) 743 5435.
Fax: (085) 653 7377.
412 ensuite rooms and
apartments, restaurant, nightclub,
car park, swimming pool, disabled
facilities. **$$$**

Elblag
Stadion Hotel
Ul. Brzeska 41.
Tel: (055) 234 4042.
Fax: (055) 234 4042 ext 23.
40 rooms, pets allowed, car park.
Facilities include grill, solarium.
Museum and watersports 3 km
(2 miles) away. **$**

Wodnik Hotel
Tel: (055) 232 6720.
Thirty rooms (not all ensuite),
disabled facilities, watersports,
children's playground. **$**

Elzam
Pl. Slowiański 2.
Tel: (055) 234 8111.
Fax: (055) 232 4083.
Located in the town centre; 112
rooms with bathroom/WC, satellite
TV; restaurant, nightclub, sauna,
disabled facilities, car park, travel
agency. **$$**

Suławy
Ul. Królewiecka 126.
Tel: (055) 234 5711.
Fax: (055) 234 8338.
Conveniently located in the city
centre, 50 attractive, ensuite rooms
with satellite TV. Facilities include
sauna, billiards table, ticket
reservation, restaurant. Sailing
20 km (10 miles) away. **$$**

Malbork
Parkowy
Ul. Portowa 3.
Tel: (055) 272 2413.
Near to the Teutonic Knights' castle
in the park; 40 beds (double, single
rooms) in hotel and 10 camping
houses. All rooms and camping
places have bath/WC. **$**

Zamek
Ul. Starościńska 14.
Tel: (055) 272 3367.
Fax: (055) 272 2738.
Close to the castle; 80 ensuite
rooms; two restaurants, café,
guarded car park. **$$$**

Olsztyn
Kormoran
Pl. Konstytucji 3. Maja 4.
Tel: (089) 534 5864.
Fax: (089) 534 6330.
In the town centre; 100 double
rooms, 2 apartments – all ensuite,
satellite TV; restaurant, café, bars
and guarded car park. **$$**

Novotel
Ul. Sielska 4a.
Tel: (089) 527 4081.
Fax: (089) 527 5403.
Situated on the bank of Ukiel Lake,
close to the forest, with 97 double
rooms with bath/WC and satellite
TV; rooms for disabled people; car,
bicycle rental; guarded parking,
pets allowed, watersports (sailing,
windsurfing), horse riding, biking
and hiking nearby. **$$$**

Willa Palace
Ul. Zołnierska 4.
Tel: (089) 535 0115.
Fax: (089) 535 9915.
A new hotel, close to the Old Town,
with 60 rooms. Restaurant, bar,
fitness centre, car park. **$$$**

NORTHWEST

Poznań
Dom Turysty
Stary Rynek 91.
Tel: (061) 852 8893.
Located on the Old Market Square,
in an old palace; 83 rooms,
restaurant. **$$**

Merkury
Ul. Roosvelta 20.
Tel: (061) 855 8000.

Fax: (061) 855 8955.
In the city centre, close to business
areas; 100 double rooms, 197
single rooms, 11 apartments – all
with bathroom/WC, satellite TV;
restaurant, café, nightclub, casino;
suitable for the disabled, dogs
allowed, guarded car park. **$$$**

Vivaldi
Ul. Winogrady 9.
Tel: (061) 853 2177.
High standard hotel close to the city
centre; all rooms ensuite; rest-
aurant, café, swimming pool. **$$$**

Pałac Krzelice
Pobiedziska.
Tel/fax: (061) 815 3370.
Located 25 km (16 miles)
northeast of Poznań, the palace is
one of the magnificent examples of
19th-century architecture in Poland.
The 30 rooms are of a high
standard, with fitness centre,
stylish dining room, mountainbiking, skiing, hot-air ballooning,
horse riding and watersports. **$$$$**

Polonez
Al. Niepodleglosci 36.
Tel: (061) 869 9141.
Fax: (061) 852 3762.
Located in the city centre, near to
the historical part; 203 single
rooms, 192 double rooms, 12
apartments – all with
bathroom/WC, satellite TV;
restaurant, café, bar, dancing,
casino; guarded car park, dogs
allowed. **$$$$**

Szczecin
Marina
Ul. Przestrzenna 9a.
Tel/fax: (091) 461 4350.
Close to airport and 20 minutes'
drive from the city centre; 40 rooms
but not all ensuite; restaurant. **$**

Victoria
Pl. Batorego 2.
Tel: (091) 434 3855.
Fax: (091) 433 7368.
Set in an old house in the city
centre; 60 ensuite rooms. **$$$**

Neptun
Ul. Matejki 18.
Tel: (091) 488 3883.
Fax: (091) 488 4117.
In city centre, close to the Old Town
and business district; 179 double
rooms, 96 single rooms, 8

apartments, all ensuite with satellite TV; restaurant, bar, nightclub, outdoor swimming pool, casino, horse riding and downhill skiing 5 km (3 miles) away; dogs allowed. **$$$**

Radisson Sas
Pl. Rodła 10.
Tel: (091) 359 5595.
Fax: (091) 359 4594.
Situated in the city centre; 370 rooms all with satellite TV; two restaurants, café, bars, nightclub, casino, fitness suite, indoor swimming pool, guarded car park. **$$$$**

Relax
Maciejewo.
Tel: (091) 418 1285.
Fax: (091) 418 1130.
Located 20 km (13 miles) northeast of Szczecin. Excellent location on the bank of the Lechicki Lake, surrounded by old park. Sixty ensuite rooms; restaurant, bar, horse riding, tennis, watersports. **$$$**

SOUTHEAST

Lublin
Garnizonowy
Ul. Spadochroniarzy 7.
Tel: (081) 533 5121.
Close to city centre; 116 rooms all ensuite; restaurant, billiards. **$$**

Unia
Aleje Raclawickie 12.
Tel: (081) 533 2061.
Fax: (081) 533 3021.
Located in the city centre; 3 km (2 miles) from the station, 70 double rooms, 35 single rooms, 5 apartments, all ensuite with TV; restaurant, café, bar, dancing, guarded car park, dogs allowed. **$$$$**

Nowy Sącz
Max Motel
Ul. Graniczna 95.
Tel: (018) 443 9715.
24 bedrooms, all ensuite with satellite TV; restaurant, guarded car park. **$**

Beskid
Ul. Limoanowskiego 1.
Tel: (018) 443 5770.

Fax: (018) 443 5144.
In the town centre; at the junction of three rivers Dunajec, Poprad and Kamienica. 56 double rooms, 8 single rooms, 10 apartments – all with bathroom/WC; restaurant, café, dancing, dogs allowed, guarded car park; downhill skiing 20 km (12 miles) away, fishing 5 km (3 miles) away. **$$$**

THE SOUTHWEST

Jelenia Góra
Park
Ul. Sudecka 42.
Tel: (075) 726942.
Fax: (075) 26021.
One km (half a mile) from the railway station, near the museum and theatre; 40 rooms, not all with bathrooms, some with disabled facilities, sauna, car park, accepts credit cards; bar, café, grill. **$**

Venus
Ul. Cervi 19.
Tel: (075) 755 2096.
Situated in the district of Jelenia Góra-Cieplice, 7 km (4 miles) from the city centre. Quiet, old villa in the park, 26 ensuite rooms, car park, café, grill. **$**

Europa
Ul. Zmaja 16/18.
Tel: (075) 764 7231.
Fax: (075) 752 4495.
In the city centre. 115 beds, not all ensuite, near the museum and concert hall. Sailing 30 km (19 miles) away. **$$**

Jelenia Góra
Ul. Sudecka 63.
Tel: (075) 764 6480.
Fax: (075) 762 6269.
Near the town centre; 152 double rooms, 30 single rooms, 4 apartments, 2 rooms for disabled,

all ensuite with satellite TV; restaurant, brasserie, bars, fitness suite, guarded car park. **$$$$**

Wrocław
Panorama
Pl. Dominikański 8.
Tel: (071) 443 6819.
Fax: (071) 443 1125.
In the city centre; 70 double rooms, 34 single rooms, 8 apartments – all with bathroom/WC, satellite TV; restaurant, café, dancing, dogs allowed, guarded car park. **$$**

Monopol
Ul. Modrzejewskiej 2.
Tel: (071) 343 7041/49.
Fax: (071) 343 5103.
In the city centre; 45 double rooms, 24 single rooms, 3 apartments – most with bathroom/WC, satellite TV; restaurant, café, suitable for the disabled, dogs allowed, guarded car park. **$$**

SOUTH POLAND

Kraków
In high season Kraków is overcrowded so it is advisable to make a reservation a month before your stay.

Hotel Saski
Ul. Sławkowska 3.
Tel: (012) 421 4222.
Fax: (012) 421 4830.
In the centre of the Old Town, in a 16th-century townhouse; some rooms ensuite. **$$**

Krystyna Hotel-Pension
Ul. Lusińska 9B, Kraków-Swoszowice.
Tel: (012) 654 7165.
Fax: (012) 654 7856.
Boarding House-hotel located 15 km (7 miles) from Kraków, in a health resort. Offers four single, 20 doubles, four triples, all ensuite with satellite TV. Lounge with fireplace, bar, restaurant. **$$**

Letni e Studio Hotel
Ul. Kamionka 11.
Tel/fax: (012) 644 3722 ex. 139.
Located 3 km (1.5 miles) from the city centre, in two renovated buildings of the Jagielonnian University. Rooms with bathrooms and TV, Polish restaurant, billiards. **$**

Luna Hotel
Na Skarpie 18 Complex.
Tel: (012) 644 6309.
Fax: (012) 644 2219.
In Kraków suburbs, 47 rooms.
Café/bar, parking. **$**

Pod Białym Orłem
Ul. Pijarska 17.
Tel: (012) 422 1144.
Located in the historic centre of
town. Small but pleasant; 90
rooms, restaurant. **$$**

Pod Rół
Ul. Floriańska 14.
Tel: (012) 422 1244.
Located in a renovated building in
the Old Town. Family atmosphere,
ensuite rooms. **$$**

Rycerski
Pl. Na Groblach 22.
Tel: (012) 422 6082.
Small but smart boarding house,
close to the Royal Castle Wawel;
16 double rooms and 2 suites.
Restaurant. **$$**

Francuski
Ul. Pijarska 13.
Tel: (012) 422 5122.
Fax: (012) 422 5270.
Traditional hotel dating from 1912,
recently renovated, located in
historic centre of Kraków; 80 rooms
all with bathroom/WC, satellite TV,
some with view of the Old Town;
restaurant (Polish and French
cuisine), café, dogs allowed,
guarded car park. **$$$**

Pollera
Ul. Szpitalna 30.
Tel: (012) 422 1044.
The Pollera Hotel in the centre of
Kraków offers large rooms, some
suitable for disabled. Family
atmosphere, hotel taxi service, car
park, restaurant. **$$$**

Continental Hotel
Al. Armii Krajowej 11.
Tel: (012) 37 50 44.
Fax: (012) 37 59 38.
Close to motorway (E40), in
residential district of the town.
Offers traditional European comfort
and peaceful atmosphere; 302
double rooms, 2 suites. From some
rooms there is a view of the park
and private garden. Air-conditioned,
satellite TV, sauna, swimming pool,
tennis courts; restaurant, cocktail
bar, summer grill bar, casino

watersports in Kryspinów Lake
15 km (10 miles) away, horse riding
2 km (1 mile) away. **$$$$**

Cracovia
Al. F. Focha 1.
Tel: (012) 422 8666.
Fax: (012) 421 9586.
In the city centre, 5 minutes' walk
from the Old Town; single, double
and suites all with bathroom and
satellite TV; restaurant, café, bars,
disco, pets allowed; guarded car
park, car hire, travel service office,
currency exchange. **$$$$**

Ester
Ul. Szeroka 20.
Tel: (012) 429 1188.
Fax: (012) 429 1233.
In the city centre, close to the Old
Town; 24 ensuite double rooms with
TV, phone. **$$$$**

Forum
Ul. M. Konopnickiej 28, 30-302
Kraków.
Tel: (012) 266 9500.
Fax: (012) 266 5827.
Situated on the Vistula River, with
views of the Wawel, 4 km (2 miles)
from the station; 530 ensuite
rooms, with TV; restaurant, café,
bar, nightclub, indoor swimming
pool, sauna, casino. Dogs allowed,
guarded car park, business centre,
currency exchange, hairdresser,
boutique, travel agent. **$$$$**

Częstochowa

Vegas
Ul. ZW. Rocha.
Tel: (034) 362 0530.
Located close to the city centre,
some rooms ensuite. **$**

Hotel Skałka
Al. Wojska Polskiego 82.
Tel: (034) 363 2466.
Fax: (034) 363 2408.
Located 5 km (3 miles) from the
city centre, with 30 rooms.
Restaurant, car park. **$$**

Motel Orbis
Ul. Wojska Polskiego 281, 42-200
Częstochowa.
Tel: (034) 61 02 33.
Fax: (034) 65 56 07.
A perfect place to stay while
travelling, next to the Warsaw-
Katowice motorway and 1.5km
(1 mile) from the railway station;
76 double rooms, 30 singles, all

ensuite, overlooking meadows.
Restaurant, café, bars, car hire,
parking. Downhill skiing 10 km
(5 miles) away, tennis court 3 km
(1.5 miles) away. **$$$$**

Patria
Ul. Ks. Popieluszki 2, 42-200
Częstochowa.
Tel: (034) 24 70 01.
Fax: (034) 24 63 32.
Located in the town centre, on the
E16 (Lódź and Warsaw direction),
near the Jasna Góra Monastery;
30 single rooms, 66 double rooms
with bathroom/WC and satellite TV.
Restaurant serves Polish, French
and Hungarian cuisine, bars, disco,
facilities for the disabled, currency
exchange, guarded car park, dogs
allowed. Tennis courts, volleyball,
basketball. **$$$$**

Price Guide

Prices are for a double room per
night during the high season.
$$$$ = above $100
$$$ = $50 to $100
$$ = $30 to $50
$ = below $30

Gliwice

Argenteum
Ul. Sowińskiego 5.
Tel: (032) 238 0480.
Fax: (032) 231 6933.
Near the railway station, 30 ensuite
rooms, with car park. Sailing and
fishing 10 km (6 miles away). **$**

Piast
Ul. Chodkiewicza 33.
Tel/fax: (032) 231 2632.
132 ensuite rooms with satellite TV.
Car park, hairdresser, ticket
reservations on-site. **$$**

Diament
Ul. Zwycięstwa 30.
Tel: (032) 231 2244.
Fax: (032) 231 7216.
The 49 rooms are ensuite with TV;
restaurant, café, bar, dogs allowed.
Tennis court and disco 1 km (half a
mile) away; sailing, fishing 10 km (6
miles away). **$$$**

Katowice

AWF Katowice
Ul. Mikołowska 72C.

Tel: (032) 251 0225.
In the city centre. Not all rooms are ensuite. Restaurant, tennis court and fitness centre. **$**
Uniwersytecki
Ul. Bytkowska 1A.
Tel: (032) 599 271.
Outside the city centre. All rooms ensuite with satellite TV. **$$**
Silesia
Ul. P. Skargi 2.
Tel: (032) 596 21121.
Fax: (032) 596140.
In the city centre; all rooms ensuite with satellite TV; restaurant, café, cocktail bar, dogs allowed, guarded car park. **$$$$**
Warszawa
Ul. Rozdzieńskiego 16.
Tel: (032) 596 01118.
Fax: (032) 587066.
In the city centre; 297 double rooms, 5 apartments – all with bathroom/WC, satellite TV; restaurant, café, nightclub, indoor swimming pool, sauna, dogs allowed, guarded car park. **$$$$**

Opole
Festival
Ul. Oleska 86.
Tel: (077) 455 6011.
Ten minutes' walking distance to the city centre; 104 rooms with bath/WC; restaurant. **$$**
Opole
Ul. Krakowska 59.
Tel: (077) 453 8651.
Fax: (077) 453 6075.
Newly renovated, in the town centre; 34 double rooms, 59 single rooms, 5 apartments – all with bathroom/WC; café-restaurant, garages and guarded car park. **$$$**

MOUNTAINS

Bielsko-Biała
Hotel Ondraszek
Ul. Warszawska 185.
Tel: (033) 812 2037.
Fax: (033) 812 2037.
Email: ondrasze@pol.pl
Two km (1 mile) from the station and 4 km (2 miles) from the city centre. 39 comfortable rooms. **$$**
Hotel Prezydent
Ul. 3 Maja 12.

Tel: (033) 812 7211.
In the city centre, in a restored 19th-century building, one of the best hotels in town. 74 ensuite rooms. Smart restaurant. **$$$**
Magura
Ul. Sywiecka 93.
Tel: (033) 814 6545.
Fax: (033) 814 5874.
email: magura@orbis.pl
Situated 4km (2 miles) from the station, beside the Beskidy Mountain; 8 suites, 44 doubles, 88 singles, all ensuite, with wonderful views, satellite TV. Restaurant offers traditional Polish and international cuisine, Vegetarian food available. Business centre, hairdresser, café, bar, disco. Outdoor guarded car park. Pets permitted. Sixteen km (10 miles) to Szczyrk, well known resort for downhill skiing. **$$$**

Promnice
Norma Residence
Tel/fax: (032) 219 4678.
Located about 50 km (30 miles) north of Bielsko-Biała. Built in 1861, this neo-Gothic hunter's castle is one of the best architectural sights from the 19th century. A traditional atmosphere, with 24 rooms. Horse riding, balloon flights, sailing and mountain biking. **$$$$**

Szczyrk
Pensjonat Czak
Ul. Kampingowa 7.
Tel: (033) 032 2202.
Fifteen minutes' walk from the city centre; 25 rooms with bath/WC; bar, small restaurant. **$**
Włókniarz
Ul. Willowa 12.
Tel: (033) 817 8978.
Fax: (033) 817 8380.
All 260 rooms are ensuite with satellite TV; restaurant, sports facilities; guarded car park. **$$**
Meta
Ul. Sko[na 4.
Tel: (033) 817 8874.
A wooden house close to the city centre; 20 ensuite rooms; high standard, restaurant, car park. **$$$**
Klimczok
Ul. Poziomkowa 20.

Tel: (018) 817 8673/8906.
Fax: (018) 817 8907.
Two km (1 mile) from the city centre; 270 beds, high standard, two restaurants, Scottish pub, nightclub, casino, indoor tennis court, indoor swimming pool, fitness centre. **$$$$**

Roadhouses & Hostels

The many, often rustic-style, roadhouses (*zajazd*) on the main arterial roads offer good-quality accommodation. In recent years many new motels have sprung up beside the main highways. They do not claim to provide luxury accommodation but, after a long car journey, they offer a comfortable overnight stay.

The Polish Association for Tourism and Culture (PTTK) arranges holiday accommodation in tourist-class overnight hostels for those interested in activity holidays. They are located in the mountains, along canoeing and sailing routes, as well as in several cities, including Kraków, Poznań, Płock, Sandomierz, Sanok, Sopot, Szczecin, Szczyrk, Walbrzych, Warsaw and Zakopane. Some of the larger hostels have restaurants and cafés.
PTTK, Warsaw, Ul. Senatorska 11 tel: (022) 826 2151.

Student Hotels & Youth Hostels

Between the months of July and October, Almatur, a travel agency run by the Polish Student Association, offers bargain accommodation in student residences. If you have an International Student Card (ISIC), you'll receive a discount. The names of these hotels, further information and bookings are available from Polorbis, all Orbis offices, or at **Almatur**, 06-116 Warsaw, Ul. Ordynacka 9, tel: 265381.

During the summer holidays, the Polish Youth Hostel Association (PTSM) arranges accommodation in converted school buildings. The PTSM is a member of the International Youth Hostel

Federation (IYHF). Travellers bearing a valid IYHF card will receive a discount of 25 percent. You can obtain a listing of Poland's 200 or so youth hostels and an official IYHF card either at any IYHF office, or directly in Warsaw, from the **PTSM** at Ulica Chocimska 28, tel/fax: 498354. The hostels promoted by the PTTK are very similar.

Youth Hostels

Warsaw:

Ul. Smolna 30.
Tel/fax: (022) 827 8952.
Lockout 10am–4pm. In the city centre.
Ul. Karolkowa 53a.
Tel: (022) 632 8829, fax. (022) 632 9746.
Lockout 10am–5pm.

Kraków:

PTSM
Ul. Oleandry 4.
Tel: (012) 633 8822.
Al. Kasztanowa 49.
Tel: (012) 425 2312.

Zakopane:

Dom Turysty PTTK
Ul. Zaruskiego 5.
Tel: (018) 206 3281.
Located in the city centre in a 19th-century building; 640 beds, price depends on the standard, restaurant, bar, shop, TV room, billiards.
Schronisko Mlodzielewe
Ul. Marusarzówny 15.
Tel: (018) 201 5606.
Fifty beds; tourist standard but nice atmosphere.

Camping

The Polish Camping and Caravanning Federation (PFC) operates 240 campsites. The organisation grades the campsites into three categories. All have access to running water, sanitary facilities and electricity. In addition to these amenities, camp sites in Category II have washrooms, those in Category III hot running water in the washrooms and restaurants. Don't

expect luxury from these relatively inexpensive alternatives to hotels. Many campsites also rent out modestly furnished bungalows. It is worth seeking out sites that have guarded car parks (Category III).

Information about the various campsites is available from the **PFC**, Ul. Grochowska 331, 03838 Warsaw, tel/fax: 106050. Polorbis (*see page 375*) will also supply a list of Polish campsites. The regularly updated map entitled *Campingi w Polsce* is also very useful (available in bookshops and kiosks). The camping season lasts from 15 June to 30 September.

A number of unsupervised sites (*miejsca biwakowe*) are located in picturesque lakeside spots or in the forests, but no sanitary amenities whatsoever are provided. Independent camping is not permitted, but often the authorities turn a blind eye. It is always advisable to check with the forestry office or landowner before erecting your tent. Sometimes a small fee is requested.

Camp sites

Warsaw
Camping No 212
Al. Jana Pawła II 77
Tel: (085) 651 1641
Fax: (085) 651 1701.
First class. Open: 1 Jun–30 Sept.
All facilities.
Bielsko-Biala
Ul. Karbowa 15.
Tel: (033) 814 6080.
First class. Open: 1 May–30 Oct. All facilities.
Łeba
Intercamp 84
Ul. Turystyczna 6.
Tel: (059) 866 1206.
One of the largest campsites in Poland. Open: 15 June–30 Aug.
Poznań
Malta
Ul. Krałcowa 98.
Tel: (061) 876 6155
Fax: (061) 876 6283.
Situated overlooking the Malta Lake. Open all year round.

Where to Eat

What to Eat

Polish cuisine ranges from rich and substantial to light and elegant. Poles allow themselves a generous amount of time in order to enjoy their meals.

A typical lunch is usually composed of at least three courses, starting with a soup, such as *barszcz* (beet) or *żurek* (sour rye), followed perhaps by an appetiser of salmon or herring (prepared in either cream, oil or vinegar). Other popular appetisers are various meats, vegetables or fish in aspic. For the main course you may want to try the national dish, *bigos* (sauerkraut with pieces of meat and sausage) or *kotlet schabowy* (breaded pork chops). Finish on a sweet note with ice cream or a piece of *makowiec*, poppy seed cake, or *droż dzówka*, a type of yeast cake.

Other Polish specialities include *chłodnik* (a chilled beet soup), *golonka* (pork knuckles cooked with vegetables), *kołduny* (meat dumplings), *zrazy* (slices of beef served with buckwheat) and *flaki* (tripe).

What to Drink

Coffee or lemon tea follow a meal, Poles prefer to drink vodka or *piwo* (beer) with their meals. Among the best known brands are: EB, Sywiec, Okocim and Warka. Most restaurants offer a selection of German and Czech beers. Stronger alcoholic drinks, usually brands of vodka such as Subrówka, Wyborowa, Premium and Sytnia, are invariably present on every festive table. Finding good wine is easy but it tends to be expensive.

Where to Eat

It is common that good, smart, well-managed restaurants are located in the Old Town of major cities. More and more restaurants are also serving foreign specialities, particularly Italian, Chinese, Japanese, Vietnamese and French cuisine. A few restaurants serve traditional kosher Jewish fare. Most hotels have details of nearby restaurants.

A service charge is usually included in the price at restaurants, but it is customary to pay a figure rounded up by 5–10 percent in recognition of good service.

Milk bars (bar mleczny) are now almost a thing of the past but if you can find one, they make a good alternative to restaurants and are excellent value for money. Mainly self-service, they occupy simple premises and have a limited choice of basic dishes. There are also a number of popular Oriental food bars (usually run by Chinese or Vietnamese) located in the city centres. During the summer season in the tourist resorts along the Baltic Sea coast, stalls sell freshly caught baked or smoked fish.

You will find most of the international fast food chains, like McDonalds, KFC and Burger King represented in the major cities.

Restaurant Listings

All listed restaurants have a varied menu including starters, soups, main courses and salads. All of them have a good choice of wine, beer or vodka and non-alcoholic drinks. Most of them (other than the budget venues) accept major credit cards.

WARSAW

Adler
Ul. Mokotowska 69.
Tel: (022) 628 7384.
Nice setting, one of the few places offering typical German food. Very good wine and beer from all over the world. **$$**

Almo Steak House
Al. Jerozolimskie 119.
Tel: (022) 629 3969.
Open: noon–11pm.
American and Mexican cuisine dominate. Great variety of steaks. Speciality is grilled beef. **$$**

Belvedere
Lazenski Królewskie.
Tel: (022) 841 2250/4806.
Open: noon–late.
Located in the Orangery in the park, an impressive setting surrounded by exotic greenery. Sophisticated French and Polish menu, including *Iurek* (a Polish soup) with ham and mushrooms, sirloin steak cooked to the recipe of King Stanisław August's chef. In the summer there is an open-air café where you can simply order a coffee and cake if your budget can't stretch to the restaurant proper. **$$$**

Montmartre
Ul. Nowy Zwiat 7.
Tel: (022) 628 6315.
Open: noon–late.
Delicious French cuisine at a relatively low price. Menu includes frogs legs, snails, fresh oysters, and apple tart for dessert. **$$$**

Blue Cactus
Ul. Zajczkowska 11.
Tel: (022) 651 2323.
Open: noon–11pm (Mon–Sat); 11am–3pm (Sun).
Mexican style cuisine. Always crowded, so it is wise to make a reservation. **$$**

Casa Valdemar
Ul. Piekna 7/9.
Tel: (022) 628 8140.
Open: noon–last customer.
Excellent restaurant serving Spanish cuisine. Tastefully arranged interior, magnificent clay oven. Great atmosphere. **$$$**

Ciao Maurizio
Ul. Wolska 50.
Tel: (022) 632 6917.
Open: 1pm–last customer.
One of the best places in Poland for Italian cuisine. Risottos and pastas with freshly made sauces. **$$**

99
Al. Jana Pawa II 23.
Tel: (022) 620 1998.
Open: 9am–10pm.
Excellent for lunch, crowded in the evening. Chef's speciality is beef steak with a cheese filling and mushroom cream soup. **$$$**

Flik
Ul. Puławska 43.
Tel: (022) 849 4434.
Open: 10am–last customer.
Good restaurant serving Polish cuisine at reasonable prices. Delicious meat dishes with herb sauces and dumplings; good wine list. **$$$**

Fukier
Rynek Starego Miasta 27.
Tel: (022) 831 1013.
Open: noon–midnight.
Polish and Jewish cuisine in the heart of the Old Town, in an old wine cellar; lovely atmosphere. **$$$**

Bazyliszek
Rynek Starego Miasta 5/7.
Tel: (022) 831 1841.
Open: 11am–11pm.
Noted for its "duck with apples". Whether you order duck or not, the magnificent view over the Market Square is just as impressive. **$$$**

Malinowa
Ul. Krakowskie Przedmiecie 42/44.
Tel: (022) 625 2525.
Open: 6pm–11pm.
French and Polish restaurant in the Hotel Bristol (see page 382).
Excellent menu prepared by chef Bernard Lussiana. **$$$**

Santorini
Ul. Egipska 7.
Tel: (022) 672 0525.
Open; noon–11pm.
Traditional Greek restaurant outside the city centre. **$$**

Tokio
Ul. Dobra 17.
Tel: (022) 827 4632.
Japanese restaurant popular with resident Japanese. **$$**

Wilanów
Ul. Wiertnicza 27, Wilanów.

Tel: (022) 842 1852.
Traditional Polish cuisine in a stylish setting. The restaurant located close to Wilanów Palace. **$$**

CENTRAL POLAND

Bydgoszcz
Lotos
Ul. Gdańska 32.
Tel: (052) 228041.
Small restaurant serving Oriental cuisine, one of the best places in town to eat at a reasonable price. The Thai shashlik, duck and orange and soya bean noodles are particularly recommended. **$**
Bosfor
Ul. Niedzwiedzia 11.
Tel: (052) 224981.
Open 11am–11pm.
Turkish cuisine. Specialities are doner kebab and cheese and potato "fingers" in garlic sauce. **$$**
Torbyd
Ul. Chopina 12.
Tel: (052) 340 0064.
Open: 9am–10pm.
Traditional Polish cuisine. The speciality of the house are sautéed cutlets with mushrooms, pork shoulder with plums, as well as fine desserts and wines. **$$**
Chopin
Ul. 3 Maja 6.
Tel: (052) 335 2553
Fax: (052) 225266.
Open: 6.30am–10am; noon–11pm.
Polish and French cuisine in the centre of Bydgoszcz; the speciality is fried Norwegian salmon, but also try the beef medallions in various sauces, vegetables à la chinoise, and a wide selection of wines and desserts. **$$$**

Kazimierz Dolny
Obiady Domowe
Ul. Tyszkiewicza 22.
Tel: (081) 881 0731.
Open 1pm–5pm.
Homemade hot meals, delicious ravioli, pancakes. **$**
Staropolska
Ul. Nadrzeczna 14.
Tel: (081)881 0236.
Open: 9am–last customer
Inn-style, excellent food, reportedly

one of the best in the city. Polish cuisine. **$**
Zielona Tawerna
Ul. Nadwizlana 4.
All decorated in green. *Ruskie pierogi* (Polish ravioli) and sirloin steak with pumpkin are the specialities. **$**
Gril i bar sałatkowy
Ul. Nadrzeczna 24.
Open: from 1pm.
Range of salads, meats and soups. The ribs and trout are recommended. Good wines. **$$**

Price Guide

The following price categories are an indication only, based on a two-course meal for one, without alcohol.
$$$ = $15–$30
$$ = $8–$15
$ = $5–$8

Łódź
Łódź Kaliska Bar
Ul. Piotrkowska 102.
Tel: (042) 630 6955.
Tasty, traditional Polish dishes, and popular meeting place. **$**
BeRo Ko
Ul. Piotrkowska 64.
Tel: (042) 632 5063.
International cuisine. Located in the main street of the city. Wide range of grilled meat. **$**
In Centro
Ul. Piotrkowska 153.
Tel: (042) 636 9992.
Open: noon–10pm.
Reportedly the best pizza in town. **$**
Dworek
Ul. Rogowska 24.
Tel: (042) 659 7640.
Open: noon–11pm.
Polish cuisine outside the city centre. Speciality is sirloin steak with mushrooms. Wide variety of wines. **$$$**
Maharaja
Ul. Traugutta 4.
Tel: (042) 633 4045.
Open: noon–11pm.
Indian cuisine. Huge menu, with particularly good chicken and mutton dishes. **$$$**
Irish Pub 77

Ul. Piotrkowska 77.
Tel: (042) 632 4876.
Open: noon–3am.
Polish cuisine. The speciality is pork knuckle. **$**

Toruń
Staropolski Zajazd
Ul. Seglarska 10/14.
Tel: (056) 622 6060/3.
Open: 7am–10pm.
Traditional Polish cuisine. Located in the Old Town in a Gothic building. *Lurek, pierogi* and a selection of meat dishes. **$**
Hungaria
Ul. Prosta 19.
Tel: (056) 622 4189.
Open: 10am–10pm.
Polish and Hungarian cuisine. Located in the Old Town. Specialities include goulash soup and Hungarian style poultry delicacies. **$**
Staromiejska
Ul. Szczytna 2/4.
Tel: (056) 622 6725.
Open: 10am–10pm
Italian and Polish cuisine – perhaps the best Italian food in Poland. Delicious tortellini pasta with cheese and spinach, various good wines. **$$**

THE COAST

Gdańsk
Pod Złotym Kurem
Ul. Długa 4.
Tel: (058) 301 6163.
Open: 11am–10pm.
Polish and European cuisine. Quick, tasty and inexpensive. **$**
Molo
Ul. Jantarowa 8.
Tel: (060) 162 2707.
Open: 10am–10pm.
Located at the seaside, close to the new pier. Wonderful view of the sea. Mainly fish dishes.
Kubicki
Ul. Wartka 5.
Tel: (058) 301 0050.
Open: noon–9pm (in summer until the last customer).
Traditional Polish restaurant in the Old Town on the banks of the Motława River. Pork knuckle,

smoked eel and duck are recommended. Vodka is served in flasks. **$$**

Tawerna
Ul. Powróznicza 19/20.
Tel: (058) 301 4114.
One of the few restaurants reflecting on the maritime atmosphere of the city, decorated with model ships. Try the duck or fish with a large jug of beer. **$$**

Retman
Ul. St Giewna 1.
Tel: (058) 301 9248.
Open: noon–midnight.
Traditional Polish cuisine, with particularly fine fish dishes. **$$**

Pod Lososiem
Ul. Szeroka 54.
Tel: (058) 301 7652.
Open: 11am–last customer.
Old, elegant setting, and known for its excellent cuisine, mainly fish, but also for its "golden water" – pieces of gold leaf floating in a herbal liqueur. **$$$**

U Hubertusa
Ul. Piwna 59.
Tel: (058) 301 0322.
Fax: (058) 305 7671.
Open: noon–last customer.
Polish cuisine, with an emphasis on game. Located in the Old Town. Speciality is wild boar chop. **$$$**

U Szkota
Ul. Chlebnicka 9/12.
Tel: (058) 301 4911.
Polish cuisine. Try the duck, or fried trout. **$$**

Kołobrzeg

Smalalnia ryb
Ul. Morska 6.
Excellent fresh fish. **$**

Monte Christo Inn
Ul. Morska 7c/6.
Tel: (094) 354 5319.
Open: from 2pm.
Traditional Polish cuisine. Close to the lighthouse. Speciality is trout and cod "à la Baltic". **$**

Bachus
Ul. Mariacka 4.
Italian and French cuisine. Homely atmosphere, good food. **$$**

Skandynawia
Ul. Dworcowa 10.
Tel: (094) 352 8211 ext 150.
Fax: (094) 352 4478.

Open: 11am–1am.
Expensive restaurant located in the Skandia hotel. Wide range of meals. Specialities include wild boar roast; good selection of wines. **$$$**

Leba

Najlepsza Smalalnia
Ul. Nad Ujzciem 2.
Tel: (059) 662620.
Close to the marina, serving smoked and grilled fish. **$**

Wodnik
Ul. Nadmorska 10.
Tel: (059) 661366.
Fax: (059) 661542.
Open: 7am–10pm.
Basic Polish cuisine. **$**

Słupsk

Staromiejska
Ul. Jednozci Narodowej 4.
Tel: (059) 842 0336.
Open: 11am–11pm.
Polish and Hungarian cuisine. Specialities include cutlets cooked Hungarian style, and deer fillet. **$$**

Franciszkańska
Ul. Jednozci Narodowej 3.
Tel: (059) 842 5287.
Open: 7.30am–10pm.
Polish cuisine in the city centre. Specialities are *pierogi ruskie.* **$$**

THE NORTHEAST

Białystok

U Cezara
Ul. Sienkiewicza 26.
Tel: (085) 743 6083.
Open: 9am–11pm.
Traditional Polish cuisine. **$**

Oaza
Ul. Zwitojałska 4.
Tel: (085) 32 8020.
Open: 10am–10pm.
Arabic cuisine. **$$**

Cristal
Ul. Lipowa 3.
Tel: (085) 742 5061.
Open: 7am–11am; 1pm–3am.
In the Cristal Hotel (*see page 386*), serving French and Polish cuisine. The best place to eat in the city. **$$**

China Garden
Ul. Włókiennicza 2.
Tel: (085) 652 4117.
Chinese cuisine. **$$**

Elblag

Mandaryn
Ul. Zw. Ducha 8.
Tel: (055) 232 7786.
Open: noon–midnight.
Chinese restaurant in the Old Town. Good food at reasonable prices. **$**

Europejska
Pl. Słowiański 2.
Tel: (055) 234 8111.
Fax: (055) 232 4083.
Open: 6am–11am; 1pm–midnight.
European cuisine and elegant atmosphere. Specialities include pork croissant in a wine sauce. **$$**

Myzliwska
Ul. Marymoncka 5.
Tel: (055) 234 2861.
Open: 10am–8pm; 10pm–10pm (high season).
Traditional Polish cuisine, specialising in game. The place is designed in a hunters' style, with a huge fireplace in the centre and hunters' trophies on the walls. Discotheque and billiards. **$$**

Malbork

Nad Nogatem
Pl. Słowiański 5.
Tel/fax: (055) 272 3131.
Open: 1pm–2am.
Polish and Chinese cuisine. Beautiful waterfront location. **$**

Zamkowa
Ul. Starozcimska 14.
Tel/fax: (055) 272 2738.
Open: 7am–10pm.
Polish cuisine. Located close to the castle, in a hotel: Offers about 60 main courses, plus soups and starters. Specialities include castle pottage and vegetarians mushroom ragout. **$$$**

Olsztyn

Yu Grill Boro
Ul. Nowowiejskiego 11.
Tel: (089) 523 5301.
Open: 10am–11pm.
Yugoslavian cuisine, run by Serbs. Excellent food, delicious soups, grilled meat, and more. **$$**

U Piotra
Ul. Pana Tadeusza 6.
Tel: (089) 533 5077.
Open: 11am–11pm.
Chinese cuisine, with about 80 main courses, plus soups and

starters. Specialities are Peking duck and rice cakes. **$$**

Nowoczesna
Ul. Kozciuszki 49.
Tel/fax: (089) 533 4672.
Open: 8am–11pm (until 2am at weekends).
Polish cuisine in the Warmiński Hotel: Disco on Saturday nights. **$$**

THE NORTHWEST

Poznań
Avanti
Ul. Stary Rynek 95/96.
Tel: (061) 851 7868.
Good salad bar. **$**

Adria
Ul. Głogowska 14.
Tel: (061) 865 8485.
Open: 9am–10pm.
Polish and French cuisine. Next to the station. Speciality is pork knuckle Bavarian style. **$$**

U Garniewiczów
Ul. Wrocławska 18.
Tel: (061) 853 0382.
Open: noon–11pm.
Polish and Ukrainian cuisine. Specialities include pork ribs with apple, wheat pancakes. Reservations necessary. **$$**

Mysliwska
Ul. Libetta 37.
Tel/fax: (061) 852 9560.
Open: 1pm–last customer: Polish cuisine. Located in the centre of the city. Specialities include deer leg and roast piglet with stuffing. **$$**

Kresowa
Ul. Stary Rynek 3.
Tel: (061) 853 1291.
Fax: (061) 852 9501.
Open: noon–11pm.
Polish and Ukranian cuisine. Located on the Old Marketplace. Specialities include *kołduny* (boiled meatballs filled with mutton), and buckwheat pancakes. **$$$**

Meridian
Ul. Litewska 22.
Tel: (061) 847 1564.
Fax: (061) 847 3441.
Open: from 1pm.
European cuisine; one of the most expensive restaurants in the city. Seafood is a speciality. **$$$**

Szczecin
Szmaragd
Ul. Kopalniana 2.
Tel: (091) 460 8132.
Open: 9am–10pm.
Polish cuisine outside the city centre. Fish is a speciality. **$$**

Neptun
Ul. Matejki 18.
Tel: (091) 488 3883.
Fax: (091) 488 4117.
Open: 7am–midnight.
Polish and international cuisine in the Neptun Hotel in the centre of the city. Frog's legs are a speciality, as are *pierogi* with cabbage and mushroom filling. **$$**

Hotel Park
Ul. Plantowa 1.
Tel: (091) 488 1524.
Fashionable place. **$$**

Chief
Ul. Rayskiego 16.
Tel: (091) 434 326/488 1417.
Fax: (091) 434 3765.
Open: 10am–last customer
Polish cuisine, and reportedly the best fish restaurant in Poland. Perfect shark goulash, zander in three ways, salmon tartare. **$$$**

Radisson
Pl. Rod Ba 10.
Tel: (091) 359 5595.
Open: 7am–midnight.
Polish and Italian cuisine served in two elegant restaurants. Shrimp soup, rabbit Maltese style and *bigos og pierogi* are particularly good. **$$$**

THE SOUTHEAST

Lublin
Słupska Karczma
Al. Racławickie 22.
Tel: (081) 533 8813.
Open: 10am–10pm.
Traditional Polish cuisine with a choice of about 40 main courses. A speciality is grilled pork loin and ravioli with lentils. **$**

Unia
Al. Racławickie 12.
Tel: (081) 533 2061.
Open: 1pm–midnight.
European cuisine. Many Polish dishes. Speciality includes pork loin cooked the Hungarian way, meat

casserole in a pancake with asparagus, quails. **$$**

Jazz Pizzeria
Ul. Krakowskie Przedmiescie 55.
Tel: (081) 743 6149.
Italian cuisine. **$$**

THE SOUTHWEST

Jelenia Góra
Grodzka Karczma
Ul. Grodzka 5.
Polish and German cuisine, as well as pizzas. **$**

Joland
Ul. Krótka 23/24.
Tel: (075) 764 6304.
Open: noon–midnight.
Polish cuisine. Specialities include roast duck in gravy. Also a discotheque. **$$**

Mama
Pl. Piastowski 21b.
Tel: (075) 755 9112.
Open: 11am–11pm
Serving Polish and Italian cuisine, including a variety of pizzas, fondue, grilled meat; great selection of wines. **$$**

Nefryt
Ul. Sudecka 63.
Tel: (075) 764 6481.
European cuisine. Specialities include: fondue, rabbit roulade; for vegetarians, *pierogi ruskie* (a kind of ravioli filled with cottage cheese and potato paste). **$$$**

Wrocław
Pod Złotym Jeleniem
Rynek 44.
Tel: (071) 372 3951.
Open: 11am–2am.
Grilled meats are the speciality here, such as pork shoulder rissole with honey. **$$**

Karczma Piastów
Rynek 5.
Tel: (071) 344 1633.
Open: 11am–midnight.
Traditional Polish cuisine. The interior is arranged in a folk style. *Pierogi*, filled roulade, delicious *bigos* (sauerkraut stewed with sausages and mushrooms) and *faramuszka* (a beer soup with caraway seeds and cottage cheese) are recommended. **$$**

Academia Brasserie
Ul. Kuznicza 65/66.
Tel: (071) 343 4529.
Open: 11am–midnight.
European cuisine. The chef's
specialities include pancakes and
steak with camembert or banana.
Wide range of wines. **$$**

Dwór Polski
Ul. Kiełbaznicza 6.
Tel: (071) 372 4896/8.
Open: 11am–last customer.
Polish cuisine, including beef
roulade with buckwheat groats and
beetroot salad, *pierogi*, and *krupnik*
(barley soup). **$$**

Belle Epoque
Rynek 20–21.
Tel: (071) 343 5617.
Fax: (071) 342 0812.
Open: noon–11pm.
French cuisine in the heart of the
Old Town. Specialities include
fondue Burgundian style and sole
cooked with orange. Reservation
required. **$$$**

THE SOUTH

Kraków
Jak u Mamy
Ul. Zw. Tomasza 2.
Tel: (012) 429 2019.
Traditional Polish cuisine with
homemade dishes including pork
chops, dumplings and pancakes. **$**

Ariel
Ul. Szeroka 17.
Tel: (012) 411 1245.
Open: 9am–11pm.
Non-kosher Jewish cuisine.
Vegetarian dishes available. **$$**

A-Dong
Ul. Brodzińskiego 3.
Tel: (012) 656 4872.
Chinese and Vietnamese cuisine.
One of the best places in Kraków
for Oriental food. Walking distance
from the Old Town. **$$**

Chłopskie Jadło
Ul. Zw. Agnieszki 1.
Tel: (012) 42852.
Open: noon–midnight (later Sat–Sun).
Traditional Polish cuisine served in
a pleasant atmosphere. Always
crowded, so make a reservation
unless you are willing to wait for a
table. Reportedly the best *golabki*

(stuffed cabbage leaves) in the
country, as well as dumplings and
potato cakes. **$$**

Chimera
Ul. Zw. Anny 3.
Tel: (012) 423 2178.
Open: 7.45am–10pm (salad bar);
noon–last customer (restaurant).
Located in the Old Town;
The Salad Bar offers, as the name
suggests, a variety of salads, at a
budget price. The smart restaurant
is traditionally Polish; good food,
speciality is roast lamb in almonds,
and for vegetarians: cauliflower
purée with spinach. **$–$$**

Cyrano de Bergerac
Ul. Sławkowska 26.
Tel: (012) 411 7288.
Open: noon–last customer.
French cuisine, with an emphasis
on fish. Located in the heart of the
Old Town. The duck foie gras is
particularly recommended, as is the
lamb curry with apples. Expensive
wine. **$$$**

Floriańska
Ul. Floriańska 43.
Tel: (012) 421 1584.
Open: 7.30am–11pm.
Tasty Spanish cuisine, but
expensive. **$$**

Orient Express
Ul. Poselska 22.
Tel: (012) 422 6672.
Open: 1pm–last customer.
Delicious European cuisine, highly
recommended. The specialities
include veal escalopes in
Roquefort sauce and the
vegetarian tart. **$$**

U Szkota
Ul. Mikołajska 4.
Tel: (012) 422 1570.
Open: noon–midnight.
Scottish and Continental cuisine.
Probably the best British restaurant
in Poland. **$$**

Wierzynek
Rynek Główny 15.
Tel: (012) 422 1035.
Open: 8am–midnight.
Polish, French and vegetarian
cuisine. A historic restaurant where
kings, dukes and princes dined in
the 14th century. Nowadays
everybody can eat there, if their
wallet can bear it. **$$$**

Częstochowa
Chinska
Ul. Racławicka 3.
Tel: (034) 246235.
Open: noon–last customer.
Chinese cuisine. Delicious sweet
and sour chicken with fruit, sirloin
and mushrooms, or hot pork and
leeks. Excellent value food. **$$**

Viking
Ul. Nowowiejska 10.
Tel: (034) 324 5768.
Open: 10am–midnight.
Polish, Chinese and Swedish
cuisine! The speciality is Polish
"noblemen soup", and Viking beef
with asparagus spears. **$$**

Gia Long
Ul. Warszawska 9.
Tel: (034) 324 6735.
Open: noon–11pm.
Vietnamese. Specialities include
"burning" shrimps. **$$$**

Orbis
Al.wojska Polskiego 281/291.
Open: 7am–11pm.
Tel: (034) 361 0233.
Traditional Polish cuisine.
Specialities include broccoli cream,
Hetman sirloin and wild rice. **$$$**

Gliwice
Huzar
Ul. Zawiszy Czarnego 5.
Tel: (032) 319251.
Open: 7am–10pm.
Polish cuisine – the pork knuckle is
recommended. **$**

Kim Lan
Rynek 21.
Tel: (032) 310468.
Open: 10am–10pm
Chinese and Vietnamese. **$$$**

Katowice
Zielone Oczko
Ul. Kozciuszki 101.
Tel: (032) 205 3077.

Cafés in Poland

Białystock

Hortex
Ul. Curie-Skłodowskiej 15.
Tel: (085) 72369.
Open: 11am–10pm.
Cakes, ice cream and snacks. **$$**

Polegnanie z Zfryk
Ul. Czestochowska 6.
Tel: (085) 524684.
Open: 10am–10pm.
Small but pleasant place, with
excellent coffee. **$**

Bielsko Biała

Polegnanie z Zfryk
Rynek 16.
Tel: (033) 26896.
Open: 10am–10pm.
Coffee shop set in a historic
building. **$**

Papuga
Ul. A. Frycza-Modrzewskiego.
Viennese-style, with a good variety
of drinks and cakes. **$$**

Tex Mex (Indiana Steak)
Ul. Cechowa 8.
Tel: (033) 811 0255.
Set in an Old Town cellar, you can
taste wines here from all over the
world. **$$**

Shakespeare's Pub
Ul. Dbrowskiego.
English-style pub with excellent
atmosphere, located close to the
Longman Centre. Good music and
fireplace. **$**

Elblag

Zagłoba
Stary Rynek 11.
Open: noon–midnight.
Country style café. **$**

Carrilon
Stary Rynek.
Art Deco style café, offering coffee
and ice cream. **$**

Gdańsk

Polegnanie z Afryka
Ul. Kołodziejska 4.
Tel: (058) 305 7550.
Wide range of coffees. **$**

Capri
Ul. Długa 59/61.
Open: 10am–10pm.
Crowded café, serving excellent

ice cream and cakes. **$**

Irsih
Ul. Korzenna 33/35.
Tel: (058) 301 2482.
Stylish pub located in the historic
cellars of the old town hall. **$**

Kazimierz Dolny

U Dziwisza
Ul. Krakowska 6.
The only tea-shop in town. Good
cakes. **$**

Kolobrzeg

Polegnanie z Lfryk
Ul Giełdowa 8c/2.
Open: 10am–10pm.
Chain café, serving delicious
coffees. **$**

Kraków

Cafe Larousse
Ul. zw. Tomasza 22.
Open 10am–10pm.
Nice place for a coffee break. **$**

Jama Michalikowa
Ul. Floriańska 45.
Tel: (012) 422 1561.
In the heart of the Old Town, the
best known café in Poland. Always
crowded. **$**

Maska
Ul. Jagiellońska 1.
Tel: (012) 422 8020 ext 131.
Open: 9am–3am.
Close to the Old Theatre. **$**

Noworolski
Ul. Rynek Główny 1/3.
Tel: (012) 422 4771.
Open: 9am–last customer.
A tourists' favourite. **$**

Polegnanie z Afryka
Ul. Zw. Tomasza 21.
Open: 10am–10pm.
The Kraków firm has many
branches in numerous cities,
offering more than 40 types of
coffee of the best quality. **$**

Łódź

Cafeteria u Michała i Darka
Al. Kozciuszki 80/82.
Tel: (042) 636 5055 ext 308.
Open: 10am–10pm.
Delicious range of coffees. **$**

Olstyn

Polegnanie z Lfryk
Ul. Podwale 2.
Open: 10am–10pm.
Small café and coffee shop
offering over 40 varieties. **$**

Warsaw

Literacka
Krakowskie Przedmiecie 87/89.
Tel: (022) 635 8995.
Good coffee and delicious
desserts. **$**

Blikle
Nowy Zwiat 33.
Tel: (022) 826 6619.
Open: 10am–8pm.
Elegant café and popular meeting
place. Delicious doughnuts, ice
cream and snacks. **$**

Calypso
Ul. Chłodna 15.
Open: 10am–7pm.
The best ice cream café in
Warsaw; also has delicious cakes.
$

Café Bristol
Bristol Hotel, Ul. Krakowskie
Przedmiecie 42/44.
Tel: (022) 625 2525.
Open: 10am–1am.
Elegant Viennese-style café that
serves delicious desserts, coffee
and lunches. **$$**

Corso
Ul. Marszalkowska 41.
Open: 10am–9pm.
Delicious ice cream and cream
cakes. **$**

Batida
Ul. Nowogrodzka 1/3.
Tel: (022) 621 4534.
Open: 7am–8pm (Mon–Fri),
8am–4pm (Sat), closed Sun.
Suitable place for breakfast or
lunch. Variety of salads, freshly
baked croissants. Delicious cakes
and tarts with fruit. Excellent
coffee. **$**

Polegnanie z Alfryka
Ul. Freta 4/6.
Open: 11am–9pm.
Situated in the Old Town, serving
more than 40 types of coffee,
which is offered for sale as well.
Part of a national chain. **$**

Open: 11am–midnight.
Polish and Italian cuisine.
Pleasantly located in a park with a large, open-air café. The *lurek* (sour soup) with sausage is recommended, followed by fruit salad. **$$**
La France
Ul. Mariacka 6.
Tel: (032) 253 7737.
Open: noon–10pm.
French cuisine, with excellent seafood, including snails. The chef's lobster is a speciality. **$$**
Czerwona Oberla
Ul. Wita Stwosza 5.
Tel: (032) 516030.
Open: noon–last customer.
Fashionable and expensive. Located in cellars with a nice atmosphere, live music. The fixed menu changes daily. **$$$**

Łańcut
Zabytkowa
Ul. Dominikańska 1.
Tel: (017) 225 2923.
Open: 10am–midnight.
Polish cuisine in the Old Town.
Homely atmosphere. **$**
Zajazd Dymarka
Dbrówki.
Tel: (017) 225 1407.
Open: 8am–10pm.
Polish and Greek cuisine. Hunter's soup is a speciality. **$$**
Zamkowa
Ul. Zamkowa 1.
Tel: (017) 225 2805.
Traditional Polish cuisine, located in the castle. *Lurek* (sour soup) and Counts' roulade are specialities. **$$**

THE MOUNTAINS

Bielsko-Biała
Sao Mai
Ul. Wzgórze 22.
Open: 11am–10pm.
Chinese and Vietnamese food. **$**
Klimczok Zajazd
Ul. Bystrzałska 94.
Tel: (033) 814 1567.
Open: 9am–10pm.
Polish cuisine, homely atmosphere in a wooden house with fireplace. On the road to Szczyrk. **$$**
Patria
Ul. Wzgórze 19.

Tel: (033) 812 2408.
Open: 10am–2am.
Traditional Polish cuisine. Art Nouveau interior with pleasant atmosphere. **$$**
Prezydent
Ul. 3 Maja 12.
Tel: (033) 812 2563.
Open: 7am–midnight.
Polish, Italian and French cuisine served in a smart restaurant in a 19th-century hotel building. **$$$**

Price Guide

The following price categories are an indication only, based on a two-course meal for one, without alcohol.
$$$ = $15–$30
$$ = $8–$15
$ = $5–$8

Szczyrk
Sylica
Ul. Beskidzka 12.
Tel: (033) 817 8746.
Open: noon–3am.
Polish cuisine. Located in the city centre. Specialities include gypsy-style cutlets and *knedle* (fruit-filled dumplings). **$**
Impresja
Ul. Poziomkowa 20.
Tel: (033) 817 86783.
Fax: (033) 817 8907.
Open: noon–11pm.
Polish and European cuisine.
Specialities are hot smoked ribs, *zur* (sour soup). **$$**
Stara Karczma
Ul. Myzliws a 2.
Tel/fax: (033) 817 8653.
Open: 10am–last customer.
Polish cuisine in the city centre. **$$**
Klimczok
Ul. Poziomkowa
Tel: (033) 817 8906/8673.
Open: 10am–midnight.
Polish and European cuisine 2km (1 mile) from the city centre.
Elegant hotel restaurant serving veal with mushrooms, cream and cranberries among other dishes. **$$$**

Culture

Theatre

Theatre is very popular in Poland. In Warsaw alone there are 23 theatres to choose from. Theatre groups such as the Teatr Stary in Kraków are usually present at international theatre festivals.

Polish drama ranges from productions of classical works by both Polish and international dramatists to contemporary experimental plays. Kraków's Cricot 2 (Kanonicza 5) acquired its reputation from the avant garde playwright Tadeusz Kantor (1915–91) and the theatre specialises in the production of his works. In Warsaw, the Jewish Theatre (Teatr Sydowski) performs Jewish popular drama in Yiddish with the audience able to follow the action with the aid of a translation played on headphones. No words are necessary at the Warszawski Teatr Pantomimy and in Wrocław's Teatr Polski, where Henryk Tomaszewski's world-famous mime group once played. The repertoire of the Wybrzeźe-Theatre in Gdańsk often includes plays by Shakespeare. Children and adults are fascinated by the puppet theatres: the Miniatura in Gdańsk and Szczecin's Pleciuga.

Cabaret is often performed in Warsaw's Stodoła student club, in Gdańsk's Zak or in Kraków's famous Piwnica pod Baranami.

THEATRES & CONCERT HALLS

Kraków
Karol Szymanowski State Philharmonic
1 Zwierzyniecka.
Tel: (012) 422 4364.

Helena Modrzejewska Stary Theatre
4 Jagiellońska.
Tel: (012) 422 4040.
Juliusz Slowacki Theatre
1 Plac sw. Ducha.
Tel: (012) 422 4364.

Gdańsk
Wybrzeże Theatre
Targ Węglowy.
Tel: (058) 301 7028.
Baltic State Opera and Philharmonic
15 Aleja Zwycięstwa.
Tel: (058) 341 0563.
Miniature Puppet and Actor Theatre
16 Grunwaldzka.
Tel: (058) 345 1580.

Poznań
Stanislaw Moniuszko Grand Theatre
9 Aleksandra Fredry.
Tel: (061) 852 8291.
Music Theatre
1c Niezlomnch.
Tel: (061) 852 1786/2927.
Poznań State Philharmonic
81 Sw. Marcin.
Tel: (061) 853 6935.
Polish Dance Theatre
4 Kozia.
Tel: (061) 853 2370.

Warsaw
Grand Theatre of Opera and Ballet
1 Plac Teatralny.
Tel: (022) 692 0200/0753
Fax: (022) 826 0423.
Ateneum Theatre
2 Jaracza.
Tel: (022) 625 7330.
Dramatyczny Theatre, Palace of Science and Culture.
Tel: (022) 656 6865.
Polski Theatre
2 Karasia.
Tel: (022) 826 7992.
Jewish Theatre
12/16 Plac Grzybowski.
Tel: (022) 620 6281.
National Philharmonic
5 Jasna.
Tel: (022) 826 7281.
Roma Musical Theatre
49 Nowogrodzka.
Tel: (022) 628 0360.

Rampa Musical Theatre
20 Kołowa.
Tel: (022) 679 8976.

Cinema

In main cities in Poland you will find modern cinemas usually equipped with Dolby stereo sound system. Check in the local newspapers for titles and times. Small towns, however, still have simple, old-fashioned cinema halls.

Foreign films are shown in their language with Polish sub-titles.

Music

Classical music

Poland's concert halls do not just offer Chopin's piano concertos, which are most people's idea of Polish classical music. Other options include experimental works by Krzysztof Penderecki or Witold Lutosławski – composers whose reputation has admittedly not spread that far afield.

Opera and ballet are performed at The Grand Theatre in Warsaw (Teatr Wielki). If the Polish national opera is performing *Halka* during your stay, do try to get a ticket. Even if you cannot understand a word of Polish, you will still be able to follow this sad love story about a poor girl from the mountains.

The finest musicals in Warsaw can be enjoyed at the Roma and Rampa Musical Theatres.

Jazz

If live jazz is more to your liking, there are a number of clubs in the main cities, such as Zak in Gdańsk, on Waly Jagiellonshie, Akwarium in Warsaw at Emilii Plater 49 and Pod Jaszczurami in Kraków at Rynek Główny 8.

Urszula Dudziak, Zbigniew Namysłowski and Michał Urbaniak, the top names on the contemporary Polish jazz scene, are regular performers at these venues.

Rock and Pop

When international rock and pop stars such as Tina Turner and Michael Jackson perform in

Warsaw, they play to full houses, either in sports stadiums or at the site of Warsaw's old airport. If any top name is due in Warsaw while you are there, you will see fly posters around the city.

The dates and times of events can be found in daily newspapers, on posters and in information leaflets (available from kiosks).

Information & Tickets

Information about all cultural events can be found in local newspapers. In the *Gaezeta Wyborcza-Cojest grane*, in the Friday supplement, there is everything about the latest films, exhibitions and performances taking place in Warsaw. The *WIK-Warszawski Informator Kulturalny* (Warsaw's Cultural Guidebook), website: WIK: http//www.pol.pl/ witryna/wlk.htm. is also a good way to find out what's on. There is a cultural diary for a whole year which can be found on the website: www. kultura-polska.biz.pl or in hotels, kiosks or tour agents.

Tickets for theatres, concerts and all cultural events can be bought at major hotels, at theatre box offices or these locations:

ZASP Box Office
Ul. Aleje Jerozolimskie 25
Tel: (022) 621 9383/9454.
Open: Mon–Fri 11am–2pm; 2.30pm–6pm, Sat 11am–2pm.
Stołeczna Estrada
Ul. Flory 9
Tel: (022) 849 3293.
Open: Mon–Fri 8am–4pm.

Cultural Centres in Warsaw

The American Centre
American Embassy
Al. Ujazdowskie 29/31.
Tel: (022) 625 7750, 628 3041.
Austrian Institute of Culture
8 Próżna.
Tel: (022) 620 1134.
British Council
59 Jerozolimskie.
Tel: (022) 695 5900.
Goethe Institute
1 Defilad Square, Palace of Science and Culture.
Tel: (022) 656 6050.
French Institute
38 Senatorska.
Tel: (022) 826 6271.
Italian Institute of Culture
11 Foksal.
Tel: (022) 826 6288.
Russian Culture and Information Centre
25 Belwederska.
Tel: (022) 849 2730.
The Institute of Polish for Foreigners
22/28 Nowy Zwiat.
Tel: (022) 828 5267.

Tours

Since the political upheavals of 1989, a large number of small, privately owned travel companies have emerged that run coach excursions or organise tours. We recommended using well known and recognisable companies such as

Orbis, Mazurkas Travel, PTTK, Air Tours or Trakt (tours of Warsaw and surroundings). All of them provide a good service (*see page 381*).

Suggested tours
From Kraków to Wieliczka and the famous 13th-century **salt mine**.
Oświęcim, the World War II concentration camp, better known by its German name, Auschwitz.
Ojców National Park, by the Pradnik River. The PTTK (*see page 375*) organises hiking, canoeing, sailing and motorcycling tours within the park, as well as excursions on foot, on skis and in the mountains. Local tour guides are available.
From Gdańsk to Westerplatte and the **National Memorial** to 1 September 1939.
Oliwa and organ recitals in the old cathedral.
Malbork and the Castle of the Teutonic Knights.
Sztutowo, formerly Stutthof concentration camp.
Frombork, where Nicholas Copernicus (Mikołaj Kopernik) spent 28 years of his life.
From Warsaw to Zelazowa Woła, **Chopin's birthplace**.
Wilanów, the former residence of Jan III Sobieski.
Puszcza Kampinowska, with woods, marshland and dunes populated by elk, fox, boar and bird species.
Zalew Zegrzyński, a large reservoir offering leisure and watersports opportunities.

Museums

Most of the 600 or so museums in Poland are open every day, except Monday, from 10am to 4pm, with some open until 6pm on Thursday and Friday. Below is a list of the principal museums in Poland.

National Parks

No one should visit Poland without exploring at least one of the 23 national parks (*see page 129*). Some areas of the country were designated as nature reserves many years ago, but the authorities have taken steps in recent years to

widen protection of the natural environment. There is now a huge variety of preserved terrains: from the rocky, Alpine Tatras to the wooded Pieniny or Bieszczady ranges, from the ancient Białowieska Forest to the shifting dunes in the mini-desert on the shores of the Baltic, from the rivers and lakes hidden away among the forests of the Suwałski region to the Roztocze plateau.

All the parks are open to tourists, many accessible only on foot. The only exception is the Białowieski Park, where visitors must explore the forest in the company of a local guide. Overnight accommodation is available in – or near – all the national parks, but do not expect anything too luxurious.

Białowieski National Park
5 Park Palacowy,
17-230 Białowieża
Tel: (085) 681 2306/2323.
This is the oldest forested park in the country (founded 1921) and the most extensive wooded area in Europe, covering 5,348 hectares (13,200 acres). It has a breeding centre for European bison, tarpan (Polish horses), stag, roe deer and wild boar. There are several tourist trails through the park.
Babiogórski National Park
34-223 Zawoja
Tel: (033) 877 5110.
Park management:
34-223 Zawoja 1403
Tel: (033) 877 5110/5124.
Contains the highest portions of the Western Bieszczady Mountains, including Mount Tarnica, from 700–1,725 metres (2,300–5,560 ft).
Kampinoski National Park
38 Tetmajera Ulica, 05-080 Izabelin
Tel: (022) 722 6001/6559.
The largest national park in Poland covers the Vistula River Valley.
Bory Tucholskie
Park management:
89-606 Harzykowy, Ul. Długa 23
Tel: (0531) 88397.
Bieszczadzki
Park management:
38-714 Ustrzyki Górne
Tel: (090) 309156/(134) 610650.
In the Krośnienskie Province covers

27,064 hectares (66,848 acres) and rises 660– 1,346 metres (1,950–4,414 ft) over the West Bieszczady Mountains and part of the Carpathians. Traces of old charcoal burning kilns and ancient sacred sites; the Bieszczadzkie Museum is in Ustrzyki Dolne.

Drawieński
Park management:
73-220 Drawno, Ul. Leśnikow 2
Tel/fax: (095) 768 2051/2510.
In Gorzowskie Province, covering 9,068 hectares (22,397 acres): between the Drawa and Płociczna rivers; mud turtles, beavers, otters and many rare bird species.

Gorczański
Park management:
Po r ba Wie Ika, 34-735 Niedzwiedz
Tel: (018) 331 7207.
In Nowosadeckie Province, covering 6,763 hectares (16,700 acres): the central section of the Gorce massif (part of the West Beskid Mountains).

Góry Stołowe
Park management: 57-350 Kudowa-Zdrój, Ul. Słoneczna 31
Tel: (074) 866 2097/1436.
In the Wałbrzyskie Province, cover-ing 6,280 hectares (15,511 acres); a newly founded park that takes in part of the Kłodzka valley and the Stołowe mountains. Bizarre rock formations and table mountains.

Karkonoski
Park management: 58-570 Jelenia Góra, Ul. Chałubinskiego 23
Tel: (075) 755 3348/3726.
In Jeleniogórskie Province covering 5,562 hectares (13,738 acres): Alpine park with post-glacial features covering the highest areas of the Karkonosze Mountains.

Magurski
Park management: 38-232 Nowy Zmigród, Ul. Krampna 59
Tel: (090) 395197.
In the Krośnienskie Province, covering 19,962 hectares (49,306 acres): it takes in part of the Beskid Niski Mountains.

Ojcowski
Park management: 32-047 Ojców, Ojcow 5, Skała 39,
Tel: (012) 389 1039/2005
Fax. (012) 389 2006.
In Krakowskie Province, covering

1,890 hectares (4,668 acres) and part of the Kraków-Częstochowa Upland and the Pradnik valley; numerous underground springs, some accessible to tourists.

Pieniński
Park management: 34-450 Krościenko, Ul. Jagiellońska 107
Tel: (018) 262 5601/2
Fax: (018) 262 5603.
In Nowosadeckie Province covering 2,231 hectares (5,510 acres): takes in the middle section of the Pieniny mountains; very varied landscape – for a unique experience, try a raft ride through the Dunajec valley.

Park Information

For further details of national parks and nature reserves contact:
National Parks Association
00-922 Warsaw,
Ul. Wawelska 52/54
Tel: (022) 825 1493/5748.

Poleski
Park management:
22-234 Urszulin, Ul. Chełmska 7
Tel: (082) 571 3071/2
Fax: (082) 571 3003.
In Chełmskie Province covering 9,647 hectares (2,382 acres): countless lakes, flood area, peat bogs and marshland.

Roztoczanski
Park management:
22-470 Zwierzyniec, Ul. Płazowa 2
Tel: (084) 687 2286/2207
Fax: (084) 687 2066.
In Zamojskie Province covering 7,886 hectares (19,478 acres): the geologically varied region in the western part of the park with the Wieprz valley.

Słowiński National Park
Park management: Bohaterów Warszawy Ul, 76-214 Smoldzino.
Tel: (059) 811 7204/7339.
Beside the Baltic, with moving sand dunes over 50 m (160 ft) high and unique desert landscape which includes a 100-metre (328-ft) wide beach. The nearby tourist centre has two campsites. There is a Slovine open-air museum in the

village of Kluki.
Świętokrzyski
Park management: 26-010 Bodzentyn, Ul. Suchedniowska 4
Tel: (041) 311 5025
Fax. (041) 311 5106.
In Kieleckie Province, covering 6,054 hectares (14,953 acres): covers the oldest Polish mountain range, the Gory Świętorkrzyskie. The remains of an early smelting furnace were discovered near Nowa Słupia, a village that was once one of Europe's largest metal-working centres and is now home to the Museum of Ancient Metallurgy; Święty Krzyż abbey nearby.

Tatrzański
Park management: 34-500 Zakopane, Ul. Chałubińskiego 42 A
Tel: (018) 206 3203
Fax: (018) 206 3579.
In Nowosądeckie Province covering 21,164 hectares (52,275 acres): Alpine park containing Poland's highest mountain range, the Tatras, and Mount Rysy (2,499 metres/ 8,196 ft). Tytus Chałubiński Tatra Museum is at 34-500 Zakopane, Ul. Krupówki 10, tel: (018) 201 5205.

Wielkopolski
Park management:
Jeziory, 62-050 Mosina
Tel/fax: (061) 813 6299/2206.
In Poznańskie Province covering 5,337 hectares (13,182 acres); post-glacial landscape with typical geological formations; Puszczykowo Museum is at Ul. Wczasowa 1, tel: (061) 813 3246.

Wigierski
Park management:
16-400 Suwałki, Krzywe 82
Tel/fax: (087) 566 6322, 565 1433.
In Suwałskie Province covering 15,113 hectares (37,329 acres); surrounds one of the largest and deepest lakes in Poland, Lake Wigry; 45 other lakes and a section of the Augustówek Forest.

Wolinski
Park management: 72-510 Międzyzdroje, Ul. Niepodległości, ci 3
Tel: (091) 328 0737/27
Fax: (091) 328 0357.
In Szczecińskie Province covering 5,001 hectares (12,352 acres): Wolin Island and a part of Szczecin Lagoon.

Nightlife

Most luxury hotels have bars and nightclubs. Roulette and other games of chance are offered in hotel casinos, with credit cards always accepted. The two finest casinos in Poland are the Grand Hotel in Sopot and the Marriott in Warsaw.

If you prefer a carefree evening of dancing to a night of gambling, there are several alternatives. In Warsaw you might want to pay a visit to the nightclub Czarny Kot in the Victoria Hotel, Tango or, if you're in Kraków, try the Crazy Dragon at the Forum Hotel. If discos are more your style, shake a leg in Warsaw at the Park or the Remont; in Gdańsk at the Rudy Kot; or in numerous venues the resort town of Sopot.

Warsaw Nightlife

There are more and more places where you can spend a pleasant evening and stay out to the early hours in the capital.

Discos/nightclubs
Akwarium
Ul. Emilii Plater 49
Tel: (022) 620 5072.
Best jazz concerts in town.
Ground Zero
Ul. Wspólna 62
Tel: (022) 625 3976/4380.
Friendly, trendy club where everyone gets down.
Labirynt
Ul. Smolna 12
Tel: (022) 826 1234.
This is one of the best discos in town.
Barbados
Ul. Wierzbowa 9
Tel: (022) 827 7161.
Open 10pm–3am.

Next to Old Town. Popular with expats.
Trend
Al. Krakowska 171
Tel: (022) 846 0994.
Techo and house music.
Tango
Ul. Jerozolimskie 4
Tel: (022) 622 1919.
Two cabaret-style shows, with a disco on Saturdays.
Stodoła
Ul. Batorego 10
Tel: (022) 825 8625.
Polish pop music venue, popular with students.
Park
Al. Niepodległozci 196
Tel: (022) 825 7199.
Mainly live music gigs, relaxed atmosphere.

Pubs
Irish Pub
Ul. Miodowa 3
Tel: (022) 826 2533.
Open: daily, 11am–last customer.
Very popular live music pub.
John Bull Pub
Ul. Jezuicka 4
Tel: (022) 831 3762.
Open: daily, 11am–11pm.
English-style pub with pleasant outdoor terrace.

Casinos
Casinos Poland
Marriot Hotel,
Al. Jerozolimskie 65/79
Tel: (022) 830 0177/5528.
Open: daily 11am–7am.
Queen's Casino
Palace of Science and Culture,
Pl. Defilad 1
Tel: (022) 620 8812.
Open: 4pm–6am.

Around Poland

Bielsko-Biała
Number One
Ul. Wzgórze 7
Tel/fax: (033) 812 4812.
Open: 4pm–3am.
Restaurant-nightclub.
Highlander
Pl. Wojska Polskiego
Open: noon–last customer.
Scottish atmosphere and music.

Bydgoszcz
W gliszek
Ul. Batorego 1
Tel: (052) 226673.
Open: 11am–11pm, Tue–Sun.
Jazz concerts, coffee and cakes in the Old Town.

Elblag
Night Club
Pl. Słowoański 2
Open: 9pm–3am.
Disco in the Hotel Elzam.

Gdańsk
Cotton Club
Ul. Złotników 25/29
Tel: (058) 301 8813.
Open: 4pm–last customer.
One of the nicest discos in the city.

Kraków
Free Pub
Ul. Sławkowska 3
Tel: (012) 421 2843.
One of the city's best nightclubs which is why it is always crowded, popular with locals.
Rentgen
Pl. Szczepański 3
Acid jazz venue in atmospheric basement.
Piwnicait pod Ogórkiem
Ul. Jagiellońska 6
Tel: (012) 421 6029.
Open: 1pm–last customer.
Live music, good food and pleasant atmosphere.

Katowice
Jazz Club Restaurant
Pl. Sejmu Zl skiego 2
Tel: (032) 255 4369 ext 49.
Monthly jazz concerts at 6pm.

Łódz
Akademia
Ul. Zeromskiego 52
Tel: (042) 630 3181.
Open: 5pm–midnight.
Good music and atmosphere.

Malbork
Nad Nogatem
Pl. Słowiałski 5
Tel/fax: (055) 272 3131.
Open: 1pm–2am (until 4am Fri–Sat).
Mainstream disco, mixed crowd.

Shopping

Where to Shop

Poles love to shop and this is reflected in the innumerable shopping areas in the main cities. The amount of shops, particularly shopping centres, is rapidly increasing. Many European firms now have branches Poland, such as Auchan, Billa, Geant – even Marks & Spencer. Yet, amid the modern and elegant stores, you are also likely to find street traders nearby, selling anything from books to perfume. The main shopping centres, resembling American shopping malls, are located out of the city and here you might find cinemas and restaurants as well as a wide range of shops.

The price displayed is the price that is paid – it is not done to haggle or bargain in Poland. Most shops open at 8am (some food shops at 6am) and close at 7pm, on Saturday a little earlier. Department stores generally close at 6pm. Most shops are closed on Sunday.

What to Buy

Folk Art

Polish folk art, such as embroidered tablecloths, brightly painted wooden eggs, leather goods made by the people of the High Tatra region and Kashubian pottery, are sold in the Cepelia shops found throughout Poland.

Hand-carved figures have greatly appreciated in value in recent years. These are often Christian in origin, depicting angels or nativity figures, but may also show characters from Polish village life. Also very popular are folk artists' naïve and glass paintings.

Shopping Centres

Warsaw:
Auchan, Ul. Modlińska
Leclerc, Ul. Ciszewskiego 15
Hit, Ul. Górczewska 212/226/
Ul. Puławska 427
Klif, Ul. Okopowa 58/72
Carrefour, Ul. Głbocka 15/ A l.
Jerozolimskie 148
Kraków:
Allkauf, Ul. Witosa 7
Billa, Ul. Mackiewicza 17
Carrefour, Ul. Zakopiańska 62
Hit, Ul. Wielicka 259
Gdańsk:
Auchan, Ul. Szczliwa 3
Billa, Ul. Sikorskiego 8/10
Hit, Hutnicza 8
Klif, Ul. Zwyci stwa 256

Amber

Amber of varying quality is sold along the Baltic coast and throughout Poland *(see page 341)*. It is often arranged in necklaces, either polished or unpolished form, but rings, paperweights and lamp bases are also made from this semi-precious material. Potential buyers should, however, take care. Street sellers often sell reasonably good imitations made from plastic. The general rule is, the clearer the stone, the more expensive it will be. Particularly valuable are those pieces of amber that contain the tiny creatures and insects that were trapped within this hard, brown substance (not really a stone, but fossilised resin) many thousands of years ago.

Jewellery is also made with what is sometimes called black amber, but it is in fact not amber at all but jet, polished black lignite. Mounted in silver, jet rings and brooches make very attractive gifts.

Art and antiques

Antiques, prints, paintings, sculptures and *objets d'art* are sold in the Desa shops. Take care before handing over large amounts of money for anything resembling an antique, as customs regulations now restrict the export of anything made before 1945 *(see page 372)*.

The abundance of contemporary works of art more than makes up for these difficulties.

Books

Well-illustrated coffee table books are widely available in Poland and make good souvenirs. Many are published in German, English or in multi-language editions.

The following shops sell English-language books and guides in Warsaw:
Academic Bookshop
Ul. Grzybowska 37a
Tel: (022) 682 2233
Open: Mon–Fri 9am–6pm, Sat 10am–2pm.
HYPERLINK http://www.abe.com.pl
American Bookstore
Ul. Krakowskie Przedmiezcie 45
Tel: (022) 826 0161.
Open: Mon–Fri 11am–7pm, Sat 11am–8pm, Sun 11am–6pm.
Fiction, classic guidebooks and dictionaries.
Travellers' Shop
Ul. Kaliska 8/10
Tel: (022) 658 4626.
Open: Mon–Fri 11am–7pm, Sat 10am–4pm.
Guidebooks and maps.
Odeon
Ul. Hola 19
Tel: (022) 622 5173.
Open: Mon–Fri 11am–7pm, Sat 11am–8pm, Sun 11am–6pm.
Albums and biographies.
Empik
Ul. Marszalkowska 116/122
Tel: (022) 827 8296;
Ul. Nowy Zwiat
Tel: (022) 627 0650.
Open: Mon–Sat 9am–10pm, Sun 11am–5pm.
Foreign language newspapers and magazines.

Sport

Golf

There are some golf courses in Poland. The most expensive and élite is the Gdańsk Golf and Country Club. The Amber Baltic Golf Club is probably the best in the country. All courses have equipment available for hire.

Warsaw
First Warsaw Golf & Country Club
Rajszew/Jabłonna.
Tel: (022) 782 4952.
Email: mailto:golfclub@it.com.pl
Twenty minutes drive from the city centre.

Gdańsk
Gdańsk Golf & Country Club
Postołowo
Tel: (058) 682 8371
Fax: (058) 683 7200.
HYPERLINK http://www.golf.com.pl

Olsztyn
Naterki Golf Club
Tel: (089) 513 0540.
Ten minutes from the city centre.

Szczecin
Kołczewo/Midzyzdroje
Tel: (091) 326 5110.
Seventy km (45 miles) from the city – probably the finest golf course in Poland.

Horse Riding

Poland has many stud farms and riding centres for holiday-makers who wish to explore on horseback. In the tourist regions, particularly Mazuria, some of the large hotels even have their own stables.

For further information, contact the local travel agents (*see page 377*) or the **Polish Prestige** office,

tel: (022) 620 9817, fax: 624 3628, which organises auctions and transports horses in Poland.

Fishing

For angling enthusiasts Poland, with its crystal-clear lakes and clean rivers in idyllic rural settings, comes close to paradise. Visitors will need a licence to fish and this, plus a list of the closed season dates for the various species, can be obtained from the:

Polish Angling Association (PZW),
Ul. Twarda 42,
Warsaw
Tel/fax: (022) 620 5089.

Hunting

It is no accident that game specialities are a popular delicacy on Polish menus. The woodland and forests are ideal haunts for amateur hunters. A licence is required and costs can be quite steep. For further information, contact the following:

Lowez (Polish Hunting Association)
Ul. Nowy Zwiat 35,
Warsaw
Tel: (022) 826 7949
Fax: (022) 826 6242.
Elite Expeditions
Ul. Tarczyńska 1
(close to the Sobieski Hotel),
Warsaw
Tel: (022) 658 4919
Fax: (022) 658 4902.

Skiing

Zakopane and Szczyrk, to the south of Katowice, are Poland's main skiing regions. Unfortunately, during busy periods, skiers can expect long waits at the ski lifts at all the centres. In the Silesian Beskid Mountains, an alternative is a well-developed network of cross-country tracks. Nevertheless, the downhill runs are good and overall costs are much lower, when compared with the more expensive Alpine skiing regions of Europe, so it is often worth the wait.

Hiking

Buy a good map from one of the kiosks or bookshops and you can explore Poland along colour-marked footpaths. Walkers are well catered for in the magnificent national parks (*see page 401*). The routes through the High Tatras are quite demanding and hikers need to have a good head for heights and some climbing experience. The best months for a walking holiday are August and September. The PTTK (*see page 381*) run a number of hostels in walking country.

Watersports

Sailing and watersports enthusiasts adore the lakes and rivers of Poland, particularly in Mazuria. The lakes in this northern region are linked by rivers and canals with locks. These waterways are becoming increasingly popular with canoeists, rowers and amateur sailors, with many people making overnight stops in the waterside campsites. If all you want to do is swim, windsurf or paddle, then, wherever you are, you are sure to find an attractive lake close by.

It is possible to hire boats, canoes and other watersports equipment in the larger resorts. For information about the best routes and campsites, contact one of the following clubs:

Polish Sailing Association (Polski Zwiazek Zeglarski)
Ul. Chocimska 14,
00791 Warsaw.
Tel: (022) 849 5731/848 0483
Fax: (022) 848 0482.
Regional Sailing Association
Tel: (022) 379 223.
Polish Canoeing Association (Polski Zwiazek Kajakowy)
Ul. Ciołka 17,
01445 Warsaw.
Tel: (022) 374059
Fax: (022) 371470.

Cycling

Northern Poland attracts many cycling enthusiasts. The surfaced roads are not too busy, the countryside not too hilly and the scenery is quite varied. Country roads often follow ancient oak-lined tracks through picturesque villages. Keep well away from the main highways at all costs. As well as a tyre repair kit, make sure you have a heavy-duty bike lock. If you don't have your own bike, don't worry. In many hotels and boarding houses you can rent mountain bikes.

Tennis

Tennis is popular in Poland but it remains an élitist game. There are a few tennis courts in each of Poland's cities where everybody can book courts by the hour, but there area also many private clubs only open to members.

Language

Polish, along with Czech, Slovakian and Serbian, is one of the western Slavic languages and makes use of the Latin alphabet. As a general rule, the accent falls on the penultimate syllable.

Pronunciation

Polish vowels:
a = as the u in "cut"
ą = a nasal vowel, as in the French "Jean"
ę = as in the French "un"
i = as in feet
ó = as the English u ⌀○
u = as in book

Polish consonants:
Pronounced as in English except
ć is pronounced in a much softer way than the Polish c
ch = as in the Scottish loch
cz = ch as in church
dź = as in beds
dż = j as in jam
ł = w
ń = ny (as in canyon)
rz = zh as in pleasure
ś = like s but much softer
sz = sh as in show
szcz = shch as in pushchair
w = v

Useful Phrases

Yes *Tak (tack)*
No *Nie (nee-ar)*
Thank you *Dziękuje (gen-coo-yea)*
Please *Proszę (proshay)*
Good morning *Dzień dobry*
/afternoon *(jane dobray)*
Good evening *Dobry wieczór* *(dobray vieer-chew)*
Goodbye *Do widzenia (do-vitzania)*
Sorry/Excuse me *Przepraszam*

(puh-shay prusham)
How much is it? *Ile to kosztuje? (e-lay toe coshtu yea)*
I would like... *Chciałabym (chow bim)*
Where is...? *Gdzie jest? (jay yest)*
How far? *Jak daleko? (yak daleko)*
How long? *Jak długo?(yak dwugo)*
Good/OK *Dobry (dobray)*
Bad/no good *Zły (zuh-wee)*
Cheap *Tanio (tan-yo)*
Expensive *Drogo (drogo)*
Hot *Gor·co (gorronso)*
Cold *Zimno (zhim-no)*
Free *Wolny (volney)*
Occupied *Zajęty (zigh-yente)*
Open *Otwarty (ot farrty)*
Closed *Zamknięte (zam kuh ni-ente)*
I don't understand *Janie rozumiem (ya nie rozumee-em)*

Further Reading

General

Between East and West by Anne Applebaum. US journalist's account of her travels through Poland.
Old Polish Legends by F. C. Anstrutter. Enjoyable book of traditional Polish tales and legends.
Hiking Guide to Poland and Ukraine by Tim Burford. Best hiking guide to the region.
Poland's Jewish Heritage by Joram Kagan. Short history of Jews in Poland.
Colloquial Polish by B.W. Mazur.
Jewish Roots in Poland: Pages from the Past and Archival Inventories by Miriam Weiner. The most comprehensive guide to Polish Jewry.

History

The Jews in Poland by Chimen Abramsky, Maciej Jachimczyk and Anthony Polonsky. Comprehensive historical background to the Jewish community in Poland.
The Struggles for Poland by Neal Ascherson. Book to accompany the UK Channel 4 series. Good introduction to modern Polish history and politics.
Winter in the Morning by Janina Bauman. Moving account of life in the Warsaw Ghetto written by survivor.
God's Playground: A History of Poland by Norman Davies. Intelligent and entertaining history of pre-Solidarity Poland.
Heart of Europe: A Short History of Poland by Norman Davies. Balanced and entertaining history from World War II onwards.
The Holocaust by Martin Gilbert. Most-read account of the Polish role in the Holocaust.
Nice Promises by Tim Sebastian. Accessible account of Poland in the early 1980s by former BBC correspondent in Warsaw.

The Poles by Stewart Stevens. Personal journalistic account of Poland in the 1980s.
A Path of Hope by Lech Wałęsa. Autobiography of the Solidarity leader of his pre-presidential days.
The Polish Way by Adam Zamoyski. Accessible history of Poland going up to the 1989 elections.

Literature

The Burning Forest ed Adam Czerniawski. Anthology of modern Polish poetry from the 19th century to the present day.
Selected Poems by Zbigniew Herbert (1977). Probably the best Polish poet. Political contemporary observations. Herbert's death in 1998 was mourned throughout the nation.
Insatiability by Stanisław Ignacy Witkiewicz. In-depth twelfth century account of artistic lifestyle, not an easy read but worth it.
A Minor Apocalypse by Tadeusz Konwicki. Highly political novel narrating a day in the life of a political activist.
The History of Polish Literature by Czesław Miłosz. Written in the 1960s this is still the most comprehensive book on Polish literature.
The Issa Valley by Czesław Miłosz. Semi-autobiographical account of childhood in a Lithuanian rural community.

Culture, art and architecture

Atlas of Warsaw's Architecture by J.A. Chrościcki and A. Rottermund. Interesting and informative atlas of Warsaw's architectural treasures.
Kraków: City of Museums by Jerzy Banach (ed). Book detailing Kraków's many museums.
Book of Warsaw Palaces by T.S. Jaroszewski.
Warsaw: the Royal Way by Jerzy Lileyko. Details the sights and history of the Royal Way.
Double Vision: My Life in Film by Andrzej Wajda. Autobiography of Poland's greatest director.

Other Insight Guides

Europe is comprehensively covered by the over 400 books in Apa Publication's three series of guidebooks which embrace the world. *Insight Guides* provide a full cultural background and top-quality photography. *Insight Compact Guides* combine portability with encyclopedia-like attention to detail and are ideal for on-the spot reference and *Insight Pocket Guides* highlight recommendations from a local host and include a full-size fold-out map. Eastern European destinations covered by the series include Eastern Europe; Czech and Slovak Republics; Prague; the Baltic States; Hungary and Budapest. In addition, a new range of *Insight Maps* combine durability and elegance of design with accurate and up-to-date information. *Insight Maps* are available to Budapest and Prague.

ART & PHOTO CREDITS

Pictures Spreads

Pages 114–115
Top row, left to right: János Kalmár;
Jerry Dennis; Jerry Dennis; János
Kalmár. *Centre row*: Michael Jenner.
Bottom row: Jerry Dennis; János
Kalmár; Jerry Dennis; János
Kalmár.
Pages 176–177
Top row, left to right: János Kalmár;
Jerry Dennis; Jerry Dennis; Gregory
Wrona. *Centre row*: János Kalmár;
János Kalmár. *Bottom row*: János
Kalmár; Jerry Dennis; Jerry Dennis.
Pages 196–197
Top row, left to right: János Kalmár;
Michael Jenner; János Kalmár.
Centre row: János Kalmár. *Bottom
row*: Gregory Wrona; János Kalmár;
János Kalmár; Jerry Dennis.
Pages 264–265
Top row: all photography by Jerry
Dennis. *Centre row*: all photography
by Jerry Dennis. *Bottom row*: János
Kalmár; Gregory Wrona; Jerry
Dennis.

Map Production Colourmap
Scanning Ltd.
© 2000 Apa Publications GmbH & Co.
Verlag KG (Singapore branch)

INSIGHT GUIDE
POLAND

Cartographic Editor **Zoë Goodwin**
Production **Stuart A Everitt**
Design Consultants
Carlotta Junger, Graham Mitchener
Picture Research **Hilary Genin**

Index

✵ INSIGHT GUIDES

The world's largest collection of visual travel guides

Insight Guides – the Classic Series
that puts you in the picture

Alaska
Alsace
Amazon Wildlife
American Southwest
Amsterdam
Argentina
Asia, East
Asia, South
Asia, Southeast
Athens
Atlanta
Australia
Austria

Bahamas
Bali
Baltic States
Bangkok
Barbados
Bay of Naples
Beijing
Belgium
Belize
Berlin
Bermuda
Boston
Brazil
Brittany
Brussels
Budapest
Buenos Aires
Burgundy
Burma (Myanmar)

Cairo
Calcutta
California
California, Northern
California, Southern
Canada
Caribbean
Catalonia
Channel Islands
Chicago
Chile

China
Cologne
Continental Europe
Corsica
Costa Rica
Crete
Crossing America
Cuba
Cyprus
Czech & Slovak
   Republic

Delhi, Jaipur & Agra
Denmark
Dominican Republic
Dresden
Dublin
Düsseldorf

East African Wildlife
Eastern Europe
Ecuador
Edinburgh
Egypt
England

Finland
Florence
Florida
France
Frankfurt
French Riviera

Gambia & Senegal
Germany
Glasgow
Gran Canaria
Great Barrier Reef
Great Britain
Greece
Greek Islands
Guatemala, Belize &
   Yucatán

Hamburg
Hawaii

Hong Kong
Hungary

Iceland
India
India's Western
   Himalayas
India, South
Indian Wildlife
Indonesia
Ireland
Israel
Istanbul
Italy
Italy, Northern

Jamaica
Japan
Java
Jerusalem
Jordan

Kathmandu
Kenya
Korea

Laos & Cambodia
Lisbon
Loire Valley
London
Los Angeles

Madeira
Madrid
Malaysia
Mallorca & Ibiza
Malta
Marine Life of the
   South China Sea
Mauritius &
   Seychelles
Melbourne
Mexico City
Mexico
Miami
Montreal

Morocco
Moscow
Munich

Namibia
Native America
Nepal
Netherlands
New England
New Orleans
New York City
New York State
New Zealand
Nile
Normandy
Norway

Old South
Oman & The UAE
Oxford

Pacific Northwest
Pakistan
Paris
Peru
Philadelphia
Philippines
Poland
Portugal
Prague
Provence
Puerto Rico

Rajasthan
Rhine
Rio de Janeiro
Rockies
Rome
Russia

St. Petersburg
San Francisco
Sardinia
Scotland
Seattle
Sicily

Singapore
South Africa
South America
South Tyrol
Southeast Asia
   Wildlife
Spain
Spain, Northern
Spain, Southern
Sri Lanka
Sweden
Switzerland
Sydney
Syria & Lebanon

Taiwan
Tenerife
Texas
Thailand
Tokyo
Trinidad & Tobago
Tunisia
Turkey
Turkish Coast
Tuscany

Umbria
USA: Eastern States
USA: Western States
US National Parks:
   East
US National Parks:
   West

Vancouver
Venezuela
Venice
Vienna
Vietnam

Wales
Washington DC
Waterways of Europe
Wild West

Yemen

Complementing the above titles are 120 easy-to-carry Insight Compact Guides, 120 Insight Pocket Guides with full-size pull-out maps and more than 60 laminated easy-fold Insight Maps